PRESIDENTIAL
ANECDOTES

★★★★★★★★ ★★★★★★★★

PRESIDENTIAL ANECDOTES

REVISED EDITION

Paul F. Boller, Jr.

New York   Oxford
OXFORD UNIVERSITY PRESS
1996

Oxford University Press

Oxford   New York
Athens   Auckland   Bangkok   Bombay
Calcutta   Cape Town   Dar es Salaam   Delhi
Florence   Hong Kong   Istanbul   Karachi
Kuala Lumpur   Madras   Madrid   Melbourne
Mexico City   Nairobi   Paris   Singapore
Taipei   Tokyo   Toronto

and associated companies in
Berlin   Ibadan

Copyright © 1981, 1996 by Paul F. Boller, Jr.

First published as an Oxford University Press paperback, 1996, revised edition

Published by Oxford University Press, Inc.,
198 Madison Avenue, New York, New York 10016

Oxford is a registered trademark of Oxford University Press

Library of Congress Cataloging-in-Publication Data
Boller, Paul F.
Presidential anecdotes / Paul F. Boller, Jr. — Rev. ed.
p. cm.   Includes bibliographical references (p.)
ISBN 978-0-19-509731-3
1. Presidents—United States—Anecdotes.   I. Title.
E176.1.B68   1996
973'.099—dc20   [B]   95-47919

9

Printed in the United States of America

Grateful acknowledgment is made to the following for permission to quote material in copyright:

Atheneum Publishers, Inc.: *John F. Kennedy: President*, by Hugh Sidey, pp. 98, 167, 188, 223. Copyright © 1963, 1964 by Hugh Sidey. Reprinted by permission of Atheneum Publishers.

Julian Bach Literary Agency, Inc.: Eugene Lyons, *Herbert Hoover: A Biography* (Doubleday, 1964), pp. 120, 167, 189–90, 210, 328, 337.

The Bobbs-Merrill Company, Inc.: *Patriots off their Pedestals* by Paul Wilstach, pp. 32–33. Copyright 1927 by the Bobbs-Merrill Company. *Presidents I've Known and Two Near Presidents* by Charles W. Thompson, pp. 291, 356. Copyright 1929 by Charles W. Thompson. *The Life of Andrew Jackson* by Marquis James, pp. 262–64. Copyright 1938 by Marquis James. *My Memoir* by Edith Bolling Wilson, p. 315. Copyright 1939 by Edith Bolling Wilson.

Brandt & Brandt Literary Agents, Inc.: Ishbel Ross, *Grace Coolidge* (Dodd, Mead & Co., 1962), p. 281.

Broadman Press: *Why Not the Best?* by Jimmy Carter (Nashville: Broadman Press, 1975), pp. 36–37. Used by permission.

James F. Byrnes Foundation: *Speaking Frankly* by James F. Byrnes. Copyright 1947 by James F. Byrnes.

Citadel Press: *The Complete Kennedy Wit*, edited by Bill Adler, p. 12. Copyright © 1967. Published by arrangement with Lyle Stuart. *The Quotable Kennedy*, edited by Alex J. Goldman, p. 140. Copyright © 1965. Published by arrangement with Lyle Stuart.

Frank Cormier: *LBJ: The Way He Was* (Doubleday, 1977) by Frank Cormier, pp. 76, 77, 78, 160, 240.

Dodd, Mead & Company: Philip Jessup, *Elihu Root* (2 vols., 1938), I, pp. 404–5.

Doubleday & Company, Inc.: Excerpts from *Ruffles and Flourishes* by Liz Carpenter, pp. 32, 35. Copyright © 1968, 1970 by Liz Carpenter. Reprinted by permission of Doubleday & Company, Inc. Excerpts from *At Ease: Stories I Tell to Friends* by Dwight D. Eisenhower, pp. 285, 357. Copyright © 1967 by Dwight D. Eisenhower. Reprinted by permission of Doubleday & Company, Inc. *Hoover off the Record* by Theodore G. Joslin, pp. 9–11. Copyright 1934. *Woodrow Wilson as I Knew Him* by Joseph P. Tumulty, p. 463. Copyright © 1921.

E. P. Dutton: *Favorite Jokes of Famous People* by Frank Ernest Nicholson (1927), pp. 59–60. *The Proper Bostonians* by Cleveland Amory (1947), p. 27.

James Thomas Flexner: *Gilbert Stuart: A Great Life in Brief* (Random House, 1955) by James Thomas Flexner, p. 124.

Bernard Geis Associates, Inc.: Episodes summarized from *Mr. Citizen* by Harry S. Truman, pp. 63, 86–87, with permission of the publishers, Bernard Geis Associates, Inc. Copyright © 1960 by Harry S. Truman.

The Stephen Greene Press: Edward Connery Lathem, ed., *Meet Calvin Coolidge* (1960), pp. 85, 148, 150.

Harcourt Brace Jovanovich, Inc.: Henry Pringle, *Theodore Roosevelt* (1931), pp. 186–87. *The Autobiography of Lincoln Steffens* (1931), pp. 843–44. *Always the Young Strangers* by Carl Sandburg, p. 33. Copyright 1952 by Carl Sandburg; renewed 1980 by Margaret Sandburg, Helga Sandburg Crile, and Janet Sandburg. By permission of Harcourt Brace Jovanovich, Inc.

Harper & Row, Publishers, Inc.: *The True Ulysses S. Grant* by Charles King (1914). *As I Knew Them: Presidents and Politics from Grant to Coolidge* by Henry L. Stoddard (1927). *This Is My Story* by Eleanor Roosevelt. Copyright 1937 by Anna

For Margaret and Vickie

Preface

One evening Calvin Coolidge took a short walk around the White House grounds with Senator Selden P. Spencer of Missouri. As they were returning, Spencer pointed to the Executive Mansion and said facetiously: "I wonder who lives there." "Nobody," said "Silent Cal" glumly. "They just come and go."[1]

Coolidge exaggerated. There were never any real "nobodies" in the White House, though some of its occupants displayed modest abilities indeed. Many of the White House tenants, however, possessed talents and skills worthy of respect in any time and place; and some were unusually gifted. Even the most undistinguished are not without interest. Coolidge himself came and went without leaving much of an imprint on American history. But some of the remarks he made and many of the anecdotes told about him have amused and delighted Americans for decades.

This is a book of anecdotes about the forty-one Presidents of the United States, commencing with that aristocratic Virginian, George Washington, and ending with that amiable Arkansan, Bill Clinton. Some of the anecdotes are dramatic in nature and a few are rather poignant. Most, however, are on the light side. Though our Presidents (except for Abraham Lincoln) were not noted especially for their wit and humor, many of the things they said and did were amusing to their contemporaries and still seem funny today. Some of the incidents recounted here tell us a great deal, I think, about our

Chief Executives—their characters, personalities, and central visions—as well as about the nature and quality of the culture in which they lived and worked. Lincoln biographer and diplomat John Hay overdid it when he said that "real history" was to be found "in the personal anecdotes and private letters of those who make history."[2] Still, anecdotal evidence surely reveals a lot about America.

The Founding Fathers evidently expected Congress to be the leading branch of government; fearing executive tyranny, they placed the section on Congress first in the U.S. Constitution. But from the outset the President, beginning with Washington, was extremely influential; and in the twentieth century the executive has become the dominant branch. Our thirty-nine Presidents have been a varied lot. Some were born to wealth; others worked their way up from poverty. Several were highly educated; but a few had very little formal schooling. Most were lawyers when they entered politics; but among them are two West Pointers, an Annapolis man, a college professor, and an actor. Virginia, New York, Massachusetts, and Ohio have furnished most of the nation's Chief Executives; but such widely scattered states as New Hampshire, Tennessee, Missouri, Michigan, Georgia, and California have also sent native sons to the White House. Jefferson thought being President was "a splendid misery," but most Presidents enjoyed the job and worked hard to get it. The majority were conscientious about their responsibilities, but a few took it fairly easy in the White House.

The American people have enjoyed giving their Presidents nicknames. Some of these stress achievement: Father of His Country (Washington), Sage of Monticello (Jefferson), Father of the Constitution (Madison), Hero of Appomattox (Grant), Great Emancipator (Lincoln). Others call attention to outstanding personal traits: Old Hickory (Jackson), Old Rough and Ready (Taylor), Honest Abe (Lincoln), Silent Cal (Coolidge), Mr. Nice Guy (Ford). A few are uncomplimentary: the Plodder (Polk), the Little Magician (Van Buren), White House Iceberg (Benjamin Harrison), His Obstinacy (Cleveland). Theodore Roosevelt had at least two nicknames, Rough Rider and Teddy, but he disliked the latter. Woodrow Wilson had none. Once Wilson overheard some people calling him "Woody" and was delighted; but it was a rare occurrence. Theodore Roosevelt was the first to be referred to by his initials; but presidential initials did not become customary until Franklin Roosevelt. James Earle wit and wisdom of the Civil War President. On the other hand it

was not possible to do much with men like John Tyler, Millard
Fillmore, Rutherford B. Hayes, and James A. Garfield. The most
important Presidents, not surprisingly, turned out to be the most
anecdotable. There was one exception: Silent Cal. An undoubted
mediocrity, Coolidge was at times as funny in his own way as the
film comedian Buster Keaton, another Great Stone Face of the
1920's. As a consequence Collidge ended up receiving far more
attention here than William Howard Taft, who was surely a much
bigger man, intellectually as well as physically, than Cal. An exception is sometimes more interesting than the rule.

Fort Worth, Texas   Paul F. Boller, Jr.
January 1996

★★★★★★★★   ★★★★★★★★

Contents

PRESIDENTIAL
ANECDOTES

ONE

George Washington
1789–97

Nineteenth-century Americans apotheosized George Washington (1732–99); many people regarded him as little short of divine. Mason Locke ("Parson") Weems, Washington's first biographer, called him a demigod and insisted that he possessed all the virtues. "It is hardly an exaggeration," wrote Weems in 1800, "to say that Washington was pious as Numa; just as Aristides; temperate as Epictetus; patriotic as Regulus; in giving public trusts, impartial as Severus; in victory, modest as Scipio; prudent as Fabius; rapid as Marcellus; undaunted as Hannibal; as Cincinnatus disinterested; to liberty firm as Cato; as respectful of the laws as Socrates."[1] In February 1832, during the centennial celebration of Washington's birthday, John Quincy Adams heard a sermon which, he thought, "exalted the character of Washington perhaps too much. There were close approaches to the expression of the belief that there was something supernatural in his existence. There seemed little wanting to bring out a theory that he was a second Savior of mankind. That he had a charmed life, and was protected by a special Providence, was explicitly avowed as a belief."[2]

When William Thackeray used Washington as a character in *The Virginians* (1857–59), many Americans were horrified. "Mr. Thackeray," said one critic, "should never have ventured upon bringing Washington into his story further than to permit him to cross the stage and be seen no more."[3] Another critic was appalled that Thackeray had portrayed Washington "like other men" in his novel. "Why, this is the essence of falsehood," he exclaimed. "Washington was not like other men; and to bring his lofty character down to the level of the vulgar passions of common life, is to give the lie to the grandest chapter in the uninspired annals of the human race."[4] Horatio Greenough's huge marble statue of Washington, presenting him as an old Roman, stripped to his waist, with a toga draped over his knees, balancing a sword, and sitting on a Roman chair, raised an even greater storm than Thackeray's novel when it was unveiled in the Capitol Rotunda in 1841. "Our people," said architect Charles Bulfinch, "will hardly be satisfied with looking on well-developed muscles when they wish to see the great man as their imagination has painted him. I fear that this [statue] will only give the idea of entering or leaving a bath. If I should give my advice, it would be to send the statue to Athens, to be placed in the Parthenon with other naked great men." The statue was not sent to Athens; but eventually it was put away in the basement of the Smithsonian Institution, where it could embarrass the nation no longer.[5] Nathaniel Hawthorne was amused by all the commotion. "Did anybody ever see Washington nude?" he asked playfully. "It is inconceivable. He had no nakedness, but I imagine he was born with his clothes on, and his hair powdered, and made a stately bow on his first appearance in the world."[6]

Even Americans who did not deify Washington were awed by his presence. In 1787, when the Constitutional Convention was meeting in Philadelphia, Pennsylvania's Gouverneur Morris boasted to Alexander Hamilton that "he could be as familiar with Washington as with any of his other friends." Hamilton replied, "If you will, at the next reception evening, gently slap him on the shoulder, and say, 'My dear General, how happy I am to see you look so well,' a supper and wine shall be provided for you and a dozen of your friends." Morris accepted the challenge. On the evening agreed upon a large number of people were present when Morris entered the room, bowed, shook hands with Washington, laid his left hand on the latter's shoulder, and said, "My dear General, I am very happy to see you look so well!" Washington, according to one report, "withdrew his hand, stepped suddenly back, fixed his eye on Morris for several minutes with an angry frown, until the latter retreated, abashed, and sought refuge in the crowd. The company looked on in silence." At the supper to which Hamilton treated him afterward,

Morris said ruefully: "I have won the bet, but paid dearly for it, and nothing could induce me to repeat it!"[7] It is not surprising that when Chief Justice John Marshall, no sentimental filiopietist like Parson Weems, came to write a serious biography of the Father of His Country, it turned out to be "a Mausoleum," as John Adams put it, "100 feet square at the base, and 200 feet high." No wonder Gertrude Stein said: "She is very sleepy. George Washington."[8]

Washington was dignified enough, and certainly worthy of the highest respect. As Commander-in-Chief of the Continental Army during the American Revolution, he performed heroically to overcome heartbreaking difficulties in furtherance of the American cause; he was probably indispensable to the winning of American independence from Britain in 1783. His stern refusal to seize power in the chaotic period toward the end of the war, despite suggestions that he do so, was important to the triumph of civilian government in America. His presence at the Constitutional Convention of 1787 and his firm support of the Constitution that emerged from it were crucial to the experiment in republican government that was launched in 1789. And as first President of the United States, he showed a great deal of common sense, pursuing policies that enabled the new republic to get off to a good start. He made mistakes, of course, both as Continental Commander and as President. But most of the time he showed sound judgment; and his devotion to the public good in all exigencies was unwavering. Even Thomas Jefferson (who disagreed with him politically) and John Adams (who was irked by his fame and popularity) could not help being impressed by him.

Washington was impressive all right; but he was never as stiff, formal, cold, aloof, and impersonal as legend has pictured him. As a young man, he engaged in derring-do like any romantic hero; he was eager to prove himself as a fighter and so was careless of his own safety in the midst of battle. All his life, moreover, he had an eye for good-looking women, with whom he liked to flirt. He had an earthy sense of humor, growing out of his experiences as a Virginia farmer-planter, and was not put off by the subject of sex. He also liked good food and wine, enjoyed card-playing, horse-racing, and fox-hunting, and had a great passion for the theater. At his wife Martha's tea parties, he circulated with obvious pleasure among the ladies and impressed John Adams's wife Abigail as being "polite with dignity, affable without familiarity, distant without haughtiness, grave without austerity, modest, wise, and good."[9]

But Washington's teeth eventually did him in. Later in life he suffered frequently from toothaches; finally he had his teeth pulled and a plate made for him by a silversmith. But his first dentures were so ill-fitting that he could barely close his lips when wearing them, and it was extremely difficult for him to smile. When portraitist Gilbert Stuart came to paint him, he emphasized the severe lines on Washington's mouth produced by his false teeth—perhaps deliberately. Washington did not enjoy sitting for portraits, with the result that he and Stuart seemed not to hit it off very well. At one point, in an effort to put Washington at ease, Stuart remarked, "Now, sir, you must let me forget that you are General Washington and I am Stuart the painter." But Washington's mild and apparently well-intentioned reply—"Mr. Stuart need never feel the need for forgetting who he is and who General Washington is"—irritated him. As a result, Stuart, possibly out of sheer pique (according to biographer James Thomas Flexner), accentuated the distortions of Washington's mouth in his famous portrait, thereby distorting Washington the man in the eyes of future generations of Americans.[10] For Washington was far from being the stiff, awkward, glum, square-jawed stuffed shirt who peers at us from Stuart's portrait. The anecdotes which follow (except for Parson Weems's goody-goody fabrications) show him to be a many-sided individual possessing kindliness as well as reserve, playfulness as well as dignity, and passionate feeling as well as prudent restraint.

★ ★ ★

George's Apple

One morning in the fall of 1737, according to Parson Weems, Mr. Washington took little George by the hand and led him and his cousin to a nearby orchard whose trees were laden with apples. "Now, George," said his father, "look here, my son! don't you remember when this good cousin of yours brought you that fine large apple last spring, how hardly I could prevail on you to divide with your brothers and sisters; though I promised you that if you would but do it, God Almighty would give you plenty of apples this fall." Poor George, says Weems, could not say a word; but "hanging down his head, looked quite confused, while with his little naked toes he scratched in the soft ground." Then, lifting his eyes, "filled with shining moisture," to his father, he softly said, "Well, Pa, only forgive me this time; see if I ever be so stingy any more."[11]

The Cherry Tree Story

When George was about six years old, Parson Weems tells us, he was made "the wealthy master of a *hatchet!*" of which, like most boys, he was immoderately fond; he was constantly going about chopping everything that came his way. One day, he unluckily tried the edge of his hatchet on the body of a beautiful young English cherry tree, which he "barked so terribly" that he ruined it. The next morning, George's father discovered what had happened to his tree and was filled with sorrow and anger. Presently George and his hatchet made their appearance. "George," said Mr. Washington sternly, "do you know who killed that beautiful little cherry-tree yonder in the garden?" This, says Weems, was a *tough question,* and George staggered under it for a moment; but quickly recovered himself, and, looking at his father "with the sweet face of youth brightened with the inexpressible charm of all-conquering truth," he bravely cried out: "I can't tell a lie, Pa; you know I can't tell a lie. I did cut it with my hatchet." "Run to my arms, you dearest boy," cried his father in transports, "run to my arms; glad am I, George, that you killed my tree, for you have paid me for it a thousand fold. Such an act of heroism in my son, is worth more than a thousand trees, though blossomed with silver, and their fruits of purest gold."[12]

The Coonskin

The story of George and the coonskin is no more probable than the apple and cherry-tree stories, but it provides a welcome relief from Parson Weems's fables. One day, the story goes, Washington, a young surveyor in the employ of Lord Fairfax, walked into a tavern and demanded a dram of whiskey. The liquor was placed before him, but when he went to pay for it, he found he had no money. Undismayed, he drew a coonskin from his bag; the innkeeper accepted this in payment for the drink and returned 158 rabbit skins in change. George was so pleased—by both the drink and the change the inn-keeper gave him—that he proceeded to treat everybody in the tavern and kept on treating them until the last rabbit skin had been returned over the bar.[13]

The Charm of Bullets

In August 1754, the *London Magazine* quoted young Washington's remark after a skirmish with the French and Indians at Great Meadows: "I heard the bullets whistle, and, believe me, there is something charming in the sound." Commented King George II dryly: "He would not say so, had he been used to hear many." Years later, when someone asked Washington whether he had said he found charm in the whistling of bullets, he is supposed to have replied: "If I said so, it was when I was young."[14]

Apology

In 1754, when Washington was a colonel stationed with his men in Alexandria, there was an election for members of the Virginia Assembly, and a man named William Payne opposed the candidate supported by Washington. At one point, according to a popular story, Washington got into a heated argument with Payne about the election and said something extremely offensive to him. In a fury, Payne knocked Washington to the ground. But when Washington's men came running up, determined to avenge their commander, Washington intervened and persuaded them to return peacefully to the barracks. Early the next morning he sent Payne a note requesting his presence at the local tavern as soon as possible. Payne went to the tavern expecting a duel. To his surprise, he saw wine and glasses instead of pistols. Washington rose to meet him and, smiling, offered his hand. "Mr. Payne," he said, "to err is nature; to rectify error is glory. I believe I was wrong yesterday; you have already had some satisfaction, and if you deem that sufficient, here is my hand— let us be friends." From then on, ends the story, happily enough, Payne was an enthusiastic admirer of Washington.[15]

The Sorrel Story

When Washington was a boy, according to Martha's grandson, G. W. P. Custis, his mother owned a blooded brood stallion with a fierce and ungovernable nature. Several people had tried without success to ride him. Washington determined to master the horse. Aided by some friends, he bridled him and leaped astride him. The furious horse tried to unseat the young rider, but Washington clung tightly to his seat. A long and stormy struggle ensued. Finally, says Custis, "the gallant horse, summoning all his powers to one mighty effort, reared, and plunged with tremendous violence, burst his noble heart, and died in an instant." A little later, at breakfast, Mrs. Washington asked about the horse. "Your favorite, the sorrel, is dead," Washington told her regretfully. "Dead!" she exclaimed, "Why, what has happened?" Washington then told her what had taken place. His mother was silent for a moment, then said: "It is well; but while I regret the loss of my favorite, *I rejoice in my son, who always speaks the truth.*"[16]

Continental Commander

In June 1775, a few weeks after the skirmish at Lexington and Concord, John Adams got up in the Continental Congress, meeting in Philadelphia, to nominate a Commander-in-Chief for the Continental forces. John Hancock, who as president of Congress was in the chair, thought that Adams intended to name him, so he listened with mounting satisfaction as Adams outlined the superior qualifications needed by the new commander. "Gentlemen," exclaimed Adams finally, "I know these qualifications are high, but we all know they are needful in this crisis in this chief. Does any one say they are not to be obtained in this country? In reply, I have to say they are; they reside in one of our own body—" At this point, Hancock could scarcely conceal a smile. But when Adams went on to say, "—and he is the man whom I now nominate—George Washington," Hancock's face fell with a sudden thud. Adams said afterward that he had never seen anyone's expression change as quickly as Hancock's did that day. Washington himself was apparently startled at Adams's choice, for he jumped up and left the room in a hurry. Later on, after Congress voted unanimously to accept Adams's nomination, Washington, "with a tear glistening in his eye," told Patrick Henry: "This will be the commencement of the decline of my reputation."[17]

Out of His Depth

While Washington was out riding one day with his aide-de-camp, Colonel David Humphreys, the latter, knowing how proud the General was of his riding, offered him a bet that he would not follow him over a tall hedge. Washington accepted the challenge. Humphreys led the way and took the leap boldly, but, to his consternation, discovered that he had mistaken the spot and was deposited on the other side, up to his horse's girth, in a quagmire of mud. Washington either knew the ground better or had suspected something, for, following at an easy pace, he reined up at the hedge and, looking over at his engulfed aide, exclaimed: "No, no, Colonel, you are too *deep* for me!"[18]

Receiving Fire

One evening, as Washington sat at the table after dinner, the fire behind him flared up, leading him to say that it was too hot and he'd better move. When someone said it behooved a general to stand fire, Washington retorted that it didn't look good for a general to receive it from behind.[19]

The Valley Forge Prayer

One of the most delightful of all the fanciful anecdotes narrated by Parson Weems has to do with the Quaker who abandoned his pacifism after hearing Washington pray. In the winter of 1777, Weems tells us, while Washington, with the American army, lay encamped at Valley Forge, "a certain good old FRIEND, of the respectable family and name of Potts, if I mistake not, had occasion to pass through the woods near headquarters. Treading his way along the venerable grove, suddenly he heard the sound of a human voice, which, as he advanced, increased on his ear; and at length became like the voice of one speaking much in earnest. As he approached the spot with a cautious step, whom should he behold, in a dark natural bower of ancient oaks, but the commander in chief of the American armies on his knees in prayer! Motionless with surprise, friend Potts continued on the place till the general, having ended his devotions, arose, and, with a countenance of angelic serenity, retired to headquarters. Friend Potts then went home, and on entering his parlour called out to his wife, 'Sarah! my dear Sarah! all's well! all's well! George Washington will yet prevail!' 'What's the matter, Isaac?' replied she, 'thee seems moved.' 'Well, if I seem moved, 'tis no more than what I really am. I have this day seen what I never expected. Thee knows that I always thought that the sword and the gospel were utterly inconsistent; and that no man could be a soldier and a Christian at the same time. But George Washington has this day convinced me of my mistake.' Friend Potts then related what he had seen, and concluded with this prophetical remark: 'If George Washington be not a man of God, I am greatly deceived—and still more shall I be deceived, if God do not, through him, work out a great salvation for America.' "[20]

Washington at Monmouth

In July 1778, British forces left Philadelphia and started northward through New Jersey toward New York. Washington followed and, on the twenty-eighth, forced them to fight at Monmouth. The Americans might have won except for the blundering of General Charles Lee. Instead of attacking, as Washington had ordered, Lee gave several confusing commands and then retreated. Washington was furious when he saw his men retreating; riding up to Lee, he cried, "What is the meaning of this, sir?" Lee did not reply, and Washington again exclaimed, "I desire to know the meaning of this disorder and confusion!" Lee then angrily said that "the American troops would not stand the British bayonets," and Washington snapped back, "You damned poltroon, you have never tried them!" In the end, Washington managed to halt the retreat and save the day for his army, but the opportunity to destroy a large part of the British force was lost. After the battle, Lee was suspended from his command for a year. Lafayette, who witnessed the exchange between Washington and Lee, said later that it "was the only time I ever heard General Washington swear" and that his fury at Lee's behavior was terrible to behold.[21]

Quarrel with Hamilton

In February 1781, Alexander Hamilton, one of Washington's aides since 1777, had a quarrel with the Commander-in-Chief that led to his resignation. "The General and I passed each other on the stairs," Hamilton recalled; "he told me he wanted to speak to me. I answered that I would wait on him immediately. . . ." He then went downstairs to give Tench Tilghman, a fellow aide, a letter he was waiting for; as he was about to go up to Washington, he was stopped on the stairs by Lafayette, and they "conversed together a minute." When he finally came into Washington's room, Washington exclaimed angrily, "Colonel Hamilton, you have kept me waiting at the head of the stairs these ten minutes. I must tell you, sir, you treat me with disrespect!" "I am not conscious of it, sir," replied Hamilton, "but since you have thought it necessary to tell me so, we part." "Very well, sir," returned Washington, "if it be your choice."

An hour later Washington sent Tilghman to Hamilton to tell him he was sorry the outburst had occurred and that he was willing to forget it. But Hamilton refused to reconsider his resignation; the most he would do was agree to stay on until Washington found a replacement for him. Hamilton was too ambitious to be satisfied as a mere aide-de-camp; he was also anxious for active duty. In the end, Washington, who had great affection for Hamilton, overlooked his young aide's rudeness and gave him an active command. Hamilton served at Yorktown.[22]

Yorktown

When General Charles Cornwallis surrendered at Yorktown in October 1781, Washington insisted that "the same honors shall be granted to the surrendering army as were granted to the garrison of Charleston." He was thinking of the humiliation General Henry Clinton had inflicted on American forces when General Benjamin Lincoln surrendered Charleston, South Carolina, to the British in 1780 and his refusal to accord them "the honors of war" at the surrender ceremony. The minute Cornwallis heard of Washington's decision, he announced that he was ill and would send Brigadier General Charles O'Hara in his place. At the ceremony, O'Hara tried to hand his sword over to the French rather than to the Americans, but Washington thereupon refused to accept it. He also forced O'Hara to surrender to General Lincoln, the officer whom Clinton had insulted at Charleston. After all, if Cornwallis was to be represented at the surrender by a deputy, the American commander would be too![23]

Yorktown Toasts

After the British surrender at Yorktown, Washington invited Cornwallis and his officers to dinner. "The United States!" toasted French commander Rochambeau. "The King of France!" toasted Washington. "The King!" toasted Cornwallis. To which Washington is said to have added: "Of England! Confine him there and I'll drink him a full bumper!"[24]

Franklin's Toast

Benjamin Franklin, as American minister to France, attended a diplomatic dinner in Paris shortly after Yorktown. The French foreign minister, Vergennes, opened the dinner by toasting his King in champagne: "His Majesty, Louis the Sixteenth, who, like the moon, fills the earth with a soft, benevolent glow." The British ambassador then rose to give his toast: "George the Third, who, like the sun at noonday, spreads his light and illumines the world." Then the aging Franklin rose and exclaimed: "I cannot give you the sun nor the moon, but I give you George Washington, General of the armies of the United States, who, like Joshua of old, commanded both the sun and the moon to stand still, and both obeyed."[25]

Refuses a Crown

Conditions in America after the victory at Yorktown were far from reassuring. Inflation was rampant, and the expression "not worth a Continental," referring to paper money issued by the Continental Congress, began circulating. Army pay was months in arrears and, since Congress seemed incapable of meeting its financial obligations, many soldiers faced the prospect of returning to civilian life, upon the disbanding of the army, without money or jobs. Overcome by the apparent hopelessness of the situation, Colonel Lewis Nicola of Pennsylvania wrote Washington a letter on May 22, 1782, in which he proposed that the Commander-in-Chief seize power with the help of the army, make himself king or dictator, and establish a strong, stable government able to meet its financial obligations. "Republican bigots," said Nicola, would undoubtedly consider his plan as "meriting fire and fagots" if they got wind of it, but he trusted Washington to keep it in strict confidence until the time came to act.

Washington did keep Nicola's scheme in strict confidence; but he also rejected it at once with scorn and contempt. "With a mixture of great surprise and astonishment," he told Nicola, "I read with attention the sentiments you have submitted to my perusal. Be assured, Sir, no occurrence in the course of the War, has given me more painful sensations than your information of there being such ideas existing in the Army as you have expressed, and I must view [them] with abhorrence and reprehend with severity. . . . I am much at a loss to conceive what part of my conduct could have given encouragement to an address which to me seems big with the greatest mischiefs that can befall my Country. If I am not deceived in myself, you could not have found a person to whom your schemes were more disagreeable. . . . Let me conjure you then, if you have any regard for your Country, for yourself or posterity, or respect for me, to banish these thoughts from your Mind, and never communicate, as from yourself, or any one else, a sentiment of like nature."

That was the end of Nicola's scheme. In a state of extreme agitation, Nicola dashed off a letter of apology to Washington for having made such proposals. Then, worried lest this letter had been too confused, he sent off another imploring Washington to clear him of "every suspicion of harbouring sinister designs." Still reeling from the impact of Washington's reply, he wrote again to disavow the ideas he had advanced in his first letter. He took no part in the Newburgh crisis which developed a few months later.[26]

The Newburgh Crisis

During the winter of 1782–83, as the American people awaited the final conclusion of peace with Great Britain, the officers at Washington's headquarters in Newburgh, N.Y., became increasingly restless. Despite considerable pressure, Congress still had not raised money to pay their salaries; it also showed signs of going back on its promise to give them pensions when they left the service after the peace treaty was signed. The situation at Newburgh was potentially explosive and Washington knew it. Instead of going to Mount Vernon for a few weeks, as he had originally planned, he decided to remain in Newburgh that winter.

Washington's fears turned out to be well-founded. On March 10, 1783, anonymous papers began circulating in the Newburgh camp, calling for a mass meeting of the officers to discuss their grievances and plan strong action of some kind. Washington denounced the proceedings as "irregular and disorderly" and called a meeting of his own for Saturday, March 15, at noon. When he met with his officers on that day, he faced, for the first time in his career, a

sullen and hostile audience. In his address, he did his best to bring
his men to their senses. He promised to do everything humanly
possible to see that they received their just dues from their civilian
superiors in Congress. He also urged continued patience with Congress which, he explained, moved slowly, like all deliberative bodies.
"By thus determining and thus acting," he said in conclusion, the
officers would "afford occasion for posterity to say, when speaking
of the glorious example you have exhibited to mankind, 'had this
day been wanting, the world had never seen the last stage of perfection
to which human nature is capable of attaining.' "

But the officers were unmoved by Washington's plea. The chill
in the room was unmistakable. Then, remembering that he had
brought with him a letter from a Congressman promising speedy
action on the officers' grievances, Washington took it out of his
pocket to read. At this point, he seemed bewildered, paused for a
moment as though he were having difficulty with the letter, and
then reached into his pocket again and took out a pair of eyeglasses.
Apologizing for the interruption, he remarked quietly: "I have already grown gray in the service of my country. I am now going
blind." His remark stunned the officers. "Never, through all the
war, did his Excellency achieve a greater victory than on this occasion," said General Philip Schuyler afterward. "The whole assembly
were in tears at the conclusion of his address." According to David
Humphreys, it was "a proud day" for the army; Washington appeared
"unspeakably greater" on this occasion "than ever he did before."
After Washington left, the officers voted unanimously to follow his
advice. "I have ever considered," wrote David Cobb, one of Washington's aides, many years later, "that the United States are indebted
for their republican form of government solely to the firm and determined republicanism of General Washington at this time."[27]

Resigns Commission

After the signing of the peace treaty with Britain, Washington had
a farewell meeting with his officers in New York and then went to
Annapolis to surrender the commission he had accepted from Congress eight years before. At noon on December 23, 1783, he entered
the Hall of Congress, crowded with spectators, civilian and military,
and took the place assigned him. After a brief pause, Thomas Mifflin,
President of Congress, announced that Congress was ready to receive

his communication. Washington thereupon rose and began reading his prepared address: "The great events on which my resignation depended, having at length taken place, I now have the honor of offering my sincere congratulations to Congress, and of presenting myself before them, to surrender into their hands the trust committed to me, and to claim the indulgence of retiring from the service of my country." With increasing emotion, he continued for a few brief paragraphs, paused for a moment to regain his composure, then concluded simply: "Having now finished the work assigned me, I retire from the great theatre of action; and, bidding an affectionate farewell to this august body, under whose orders I have long acted, I here offer my commission, and take my leave of all the employments of public life." Delivering his commission to the President, he returned to his place and received, standing, the response of Congress, delivered by Mifflin. After listening quietly to some words of praise, he left. The next morning he hastened down to Mount Vernon. "The scene is at last closed," he wrote Governor Clinton of New York. "I feel myself eased of a load of public care. I hope to spend the remainder of my days in cultivating the affections of good men, and in the practice of the domestic virtues."[28]

The Ragged Boys

Once, after the Revolution, it is said, Washington was staying in an inn in Boston where General Howe had once lodged. He supposedly got into a conversation with a little girl there. "You have seen the soldiers on both sides," he said; "which do you like best?" The little girl said she liked the redcoats best. Washington laughed and said: "Yes, my dear, the redcoats do look the best, but it takes the ragged boys to do the fighting."[29]

Washington Makes Up His Mind

Shortly after the Revolution, young Albert Gallatin (later Jefferson's Secretary of the Treasury) went to Virginia to buy some land in the western part of the state. While there he attended a meeting to select a pass for a road through the Allegheny Mountains, presided over by Washington. Gallatin was impressed by the care with which the former Revolutionary commander interrogated the settlers and hunters in the region, but he was put off by Washington's delay in settling on what was clearly the best route to follow. Suddenly he pointed impatiently to the only pass on the map that seemed practicable and cried: "Oh, it is plain enough!" The room became silent. Washington himself paused, laid down his pen, and, obviously offended, looked up sternly at the young Frenchman for a moment. Then he resumed his inquiries. But after a few minutes he stopped abruptly, threw down his pen, and, looking at Gallatin, announced: "You are right, sir!" Reflected Gallatin later: "It was so on all occasions with General Washington. He was slow in forming an opinion, and never decided until he knew he was right."[30]

Royal Gift

In 1786, the King of Spain presented Washington with two highborn jackasses. One died en route to America, but the other, an enormous creature of pure Andalusian breed which Washington named Royal Gift, was taken to Mount Vernon, where a large harem of mares awaited him for breeding mules. But when a mare was placed in Royal Gift's paddock, he sniffed at her gingerly and then turned away. After exposing him to a long succession of mares without rousing his passions, Washington began wondering whether the jackass was impotent, too "full of Royalty to have anything to do with a plebeian race" of Americans, or, like the Spanish King himself, too old to react speedily to "female allurements." But at length he discovered a way of tricking Royal Gift into performing. He introduced him to "the excitements of a female ass"; then, when the royal beast began to "evidence desires to which he [had] seemed almost a stranger" before, he quickly removed the donkey and substituted a mare.[31]

National Defense

When the Constitutional Convention got around to discussing the power of Congress to raise an army, one of the delegates moved "that the standing army be restricted to five thousand men at any time." Washington was amused by the motion, but as chairman could not offer a motion himself. Instead, he whispered to one of the delegates sitting near him that they had better amend the motion so as to provide that "no foreign army should invade the United States at any time with more than three thousand troops."[32]

Cooling Things

After his return from France, Thomas Jefferson asked Washington at breakfast one morning why the Constitution-framers had agreed to a second chamber in Congress at the 1787 convention. "Why did you pour that coffee into your saucer?" Washington asked him. "To cool it," said Jefferson. "Even so," said Washington, "we pour legislation into the senatorial saucer to cool it."[33]

The First Inauguration

At sunrise on April 30, 1789, thirteen guns sounded at the southern end of Manhattan; a little later Washington rose and began preparing for the day's festivities. He had his hair powdered, donned a brown suit with buttons decorated with spread eagles, and put on white silk stockings and shoes with silver buckles. He also got out his dress sword. By the time he had eaten breakfast, church bells were ringing and people were gathering before his house.

A few minutes after noon, a delegation from Congress arrived to escort the President-elect to Federal Hall. Washington bowed, shook hands, entered a grand coach drawn by four fine horses, and, at twelve-thirty, started off amid cheering crowds. At Federal Hall he got out of the carriage, walked through the ranks of militiamen lined up outside, entered the building, and was escorted to the Senate Chamber, where the Senators, members of the House of Representatives, foreign diplomats, and other dignitaries awaited him. Vice-President–elect John Adams formally welcomed him, then announced: "Sir, the Senate and the House of Representatives are ready to attend you to take the oath required by the Constitution. It will be administered by the Chancellor of the State of New York." "I am ready to proceed," replied Washington. Adams bowed and led him into a small half-enclosed portico overlooking Wall and Broad streets. In front of him was a small table draped in red on which lay a large Bible on a crimson velvet cushion. The streets below were crowded with people; so were the windows and rooftops of all the adjoining buildings.

As Washington appeared on the portico, a great shout went up. Washington bowed three or four times, put his hand on his heart, and finally sat down in an armchair next to the table. A moment later he arose, moved to the railing where he could be seen by as many people as possible, and prepared to take the oath of office. The crowd became suddenly still. The Secretary of the Senate raised the Bible, and Chancellor Robert R. Livingston came forward to administer the oath. Washington put his hand on the Bible, and Livingston asked: "Do you solemnly swear that you will faithfully execute the office of President of the United States and will, to the best of your ability, preserve, protect, and defend the Constitution of the United States?" "I solemnly swear," replied Washington, repeating the oath and adding "So help me God," then bent forward to kiss the Bible. "It is done," announced Livingston; turning to the crowd below, he shouted: "Long live George Washington, President of the United States!" The crowd echoed his cry, the flag was raised on the cupola of Federal Hall, thirteen guns sounded on the Battery, and church bells began tolling. After bowing several times to acknowledge the congratulations of the spectators, Washington re-entered the Senate Chamber, took his seat on the dais there, and waited for people to resume their places. As he rose to read his inaugural address, all the spectators rose with him; and after he bowed, they sat down again.

In his inaugural address, which he delivered in a deep, low, tremulous voice, Washington called on "that Almighty God who rules over the universe" to help the American people find "liberties and happiness" under "a government instituted by themselves" and urged a spirit of moderation in the years ahead. "This great man," observed Pennsylvania Senator William Maclay, "was agitated and embarrassed more than ever he was by the leveled cannon or pointed musket. He trembled, and several times could scarce make out to read. . . ." His face, according to another observer, was "grave almost to sadness" throughout. While Washington was speaking, he moved his manuscript nervously from his left to his right hand, put several fingers of his left hand in the pocket of his breeches, and, at one point, made a flourish with his right hand which "left a rather ungainly impression." Maclay, disappointed at Washington's delivery, "felt hurt that he was not first in everything." But most people were deeply moved by the address. "It seemed to me," said the famous orator Fisher Ames afterward, "an allegory in which virtue was personified, and addressing those whom she would make her votaries. Her power over the heart was never greater."

After his inaugural, Washington walked with other public officials to St. Paul's Chapel to hear services performed by the Chaplain of

Congress. After church he dined at home and in the evening joined friends in observing the illumination of the city and the display of fireworks. After it was all over he wrote his friends: "I greatly fear that my countrymen will expect too much from me."[34]

First Reception

After he became President, Washington began holding three kinds of official receptions: "levees" on Tuesdays for men only; Martha's tea parties for both men and women on Fridays; and official dinners on Thursdays. At the first levee, David Humphreys, Washington's aide, arranged for the guests to assemble in what he called the "presence chamber," and then he took Washington to the door, threw it open, and shouted: "The President of the United States!" According to Jefferson, Washington was so unnerved by Humphreys's ceremonial arrangements that he felt ill at ease throughout the reception. When it was over he told his aide angrily: "Well, you have taken me in once, but by God, you will never take me in a second time!" After that, the receptions were not so ceremonious, though they never became informal.[35]

On Time

When Washington invited people to his official dinners, he expected them to be on time. Once a Congressman arrived late and found everyone at the table. "We are obliged to be punctual here," Washington told him. "My cook never asks whether the company has arrived, but whether the hour has."[36]

Advice and Consent

On Saturday, August 22, 1789, Washington went to the Senate Chamber with Secretary of War Henry Knox and announced that he had called to receive "advice and consent" on some provisions in a treaty with the Creek Indians. He handed Vice-President Adams some papers, and Adams read from them to the Senators. Unfortunately, carriages driving by outside made him almost inaudible; and when he had finished, Robert Morris asked that the papers be read again. Adams at once obliged, then asked: "Do you advise and consent?" There was a moment of silence. Then William Maclay said that the Senate needed more information and asked for additional documents. Washington "wore an aspect of stern displeasure" while Maclay was speaking. The Senate decided to postpone the first article of the treaty and move on to the others. After more debate Morris moved that the treaty be referred to a committee. Washington "started up in a violent fret" at this and cried: "This defeats every purpose of my coming here!" But he finally agreed to postponing the discussion until Monday and withdrew "with a discontented air."

On Monday Washington returned to the Senate Chamber. He was now "placid and serene, and manifested a spirit of accommodation." But a long, tedious debate on two of the treaty's provisions left him completely frustrated. Leaving the chamber, he reportedly exclaimed that "he would be damned if he ever went there again!" He never did. Though the Senate eventually approved the treaty with only minor revisions, Washington stopped trying to consult personally with the Senators about treaties. Instead, he sent the Senate written messages. Subsequent Presidents have followed his precedent.[37]

Pacifism

When Philadelphia Quaker Warner Mifflin visited the President to discuss slavery with him, he was treated with "kindness and respect" and reported afterward that Washington showed some understanding of the Friends' pacifist policy during the Revolution. "Mr. Mifflin," Washington asked at one point, "will you please to inform me on what principle you were opposed to the revolution?" "Yes, friend Washington," replied Mifflin, "upon the same principles that I should be opposed to a change in this government—all that ever was gained by revolutions are not an adequate compensation to the poor mangled soldier for the loss of life or limb." After a moment's pause, Washington declared: "Mr. Mifflin, I honor your sentiments; there is more in that than mankind have generally considered."[38]

Poses for Life Mask

Once Washington posed for a life mask by the young American artist Joseph Wright. "He oiled my features over," Washington recalled, "and, placing me flat upon my back upon a cot, proceeded to daub my face with the plaster. Whilst in this ludicrous attitude, Mrs. Washington entered the room, and seeing my face thus overspread with the plaster, involuntarily exclaimed. Her cry excited in me a disposition to smile, which gave my mouth a slight twist or compression of the lips that is now observable in the busts which Wright afterwards made."[39]

Loses His Temper

In November 1791, an American army under General Arthur St. Clair operating in the west was ambushed by Indians and cut to pieces. Washington had warned St. Clair against surprise, and the news came as a terrible blow. He was entertaining guests at dinner when a messenger arrived with a dispatch. He left the table, read it and then returned without any signs of agitation. When the guests moved to the drawing room, he "spoke courteously to every lady in the room, as was his custom"; afterward, alone with his secretary, Tobias Lear, he still struggled for self-control. He "walked backward and forward for some minutes" without speaking; then he "broke out suddenly in bitter lamentations." In a renewed effort at self-control, he "walked about the room several times, agitated but saying nothing," then "stopped short and stood still a few seconds, when his wrath became terrible." In a paroxysm of anguish, he struck his fists against his forehead and "hurled imprecations upon St. Clair." He then sat down, remaining still for a few moments; and finally, having gained control of his emotions, said quietly: "This must not go beyond this room." After another pause, he said: "General St. Clair shall have full justice." Later on, he expressed sympathy for St. Clair in his terrible "misfortune."[40]

Controls Temper

Washington's "features," said painter Gilbert Stuart, "were indicative of the strongest and most ungovernable passions. Had he been born in the forests, he would have been the fiercest man among the savages." Talking one day to General "Light Horse Harry" Lee, Stuart happened to remark that Washington had a terrible temper but held it under wonderful control. General Lee reported the remark to the Washingtons at breakfast a few days later. "I saw your portrait the other day, a capital likeness," said Lee, "but Stuart says you have a tremendous temper." "Upon my word," said Mrs. Washington, coloring, "Mr. Stuart takes a great deal on himself, to make such a remark." "But stay, my dear lady," said General Lee, "he added that the President had it under wonderful control." With something like a smile, Washington remarked, "He's right."[41]

Recommendation

In the summer of 1797, the French revolutionist Constantin Volney visited Mount Vernon at the beginning of a tour of the United States; before leaving he asked Washington for a general letter of recommendation to the American people. Anxious to avoid any controversy over the Frenchman, who was a freethinker, Washington simply wrote on a sheet of paper: "C. Volney needs no recommendation from Geo. Washington."[42]

Fireman

Washington, it is said, was an enthusiastic fireman. He began running to fires when he was a boy and was still running to them in his old age. Only a few months before his death, he was riding down King Street in Alexandria when a fire was discovered near the market. He stopped his horse at once and yelled to some men who stood idly by: "It is your duty to lead in such matters! Follow me!" Throwing his reins to his servants, he leaped to the ground and began pumping the engine, into which a few boys were languidly dumping buckets of water. Cheering citizens rushed to aid him, and within a few minutes the old engine was throwing the highest stream that had ever gushed from its pipe.[43]

TWO

John Adams
1797–1801

It was not easy being the second President of the United States; George Washington was a hard act to follow. At his inauguration in March 1797, John Adams (1735–1826) could not help noticing that people were looking at his predecessor, who was sitting quietly on one side of the dais, with tears in their eyes, rather than at him. Washington, moreover, seemed "to enjoy a triumph over me," Adams told his wife Abigail afterward. "Me-thought I heard him say, 'Ay, I am fairly out and you fairly in! See which of us will be happiest!' "[1]

Adams's Presidency was not a happy one, and it lasted only one term. A Federalist, Adams not only clashed with the Jeffersonian Republicans but was also at odds with members of his own party a great deal of the time. He did show wisdom and courage in keeping an undeclared war with France from escalating into a full-fledged shooting war, but he also signed the notorious Alien and Sedition Acts of 1798 which the Federalists pushed through Congress in order to stifle all criticism of Federalist policies. His Presidency did him an injustice; for if he was not a great President, he was undoubtedly a great patriot. During the American Revolution he served on ninety committees in the Continental Congress, pushed incessantly for bold measures, and came to be called the "Atlas of Independence."[2] "In Congress," he once complained impatiently, "nibbling and quibbling—as usual. There is no greater Mortification than to sit with half a dozen Witts, deliberating upon a Petition, Address or Memorial. These great Witts, these subtle Criticks, these refined Geniuses, these learned Lawyers, these wise Statesmen, are so fond of showing their Parts and Powers, as to make their Consultations very tedious."[3]

In February 1778, Adams boarded a frigate commanded by Captain Samuel Tucker and headed for France to represent the United States in Paris. A popular story grew out of the voyage. Tucker, it was said, instructed Adams to stay below and out of the way if there was any fighting en route. But no sooner had he sighted an enemy ship and engaged it in battle than Adams rushed up to the deck with a musket in his hand, ready to do his part. Tucker peremptorily ordered him below and then left to direct the engagement. An hour or so later he discovered Adams still at his post, diligently firing away at the enemy. "Why are you here, sir?" he cried angrily. "I am commanded by the Continental Congress to carry you safely to Europe, and I will do it!" With that, he seized Adams in his arms and forcibly carried him off from the scene of danger. Years later, when asked about the story, Tucker insisted that it was highly exaggerated. But he admitted there was a germ of truth in it: Adams did join the marines during one encounter with a British ship and impressed everyone with his patriotic determination to risk his life for his country.[4]

With the achievement of independence, Adams became minister to England. Just before leaving Paris in 1785 he got into a conversation with one of the foreign diplomats there. "You have been often in England?" the ambassador asked him. "Never but once in November and December 1783," Adams told him. "You have relations in England no doubt," said the ambassador. "None at all," said Adams. "None!" exclaimed the ambassador, "how can that be? You are of English extraction?" Said Adams stoutly: "Neither my father or mother, grandfather or grandmother, great grandfather or great grandmother nor any other relation that I know or care a farthing for have been in England these 150 years. So that you see, I have not one drop of blood in my veins, but what is American." "Ay," nodded the ambassador, "we have seen proofs enough of that!"[5]

Adams was one of the most intelligent, learned, industrious, public-spirited, and far-seeing of all the Patriot Fathers. He was also one of the vainest, most outspoken, testiest, and most abrasive. Benjamin Franklin once said that Adams was "always an honest man, often a wise one, but sometimes, and in some things, absolutely out of his senses."[6] Throughout his entire public career, Adams felt that his own enormous contributions to the cause of American liberty were unfairly overshadowed by those of Franklin and Washington. "The history of our Revolution," he once told Dr. Benjamin Rush sarcastically, "will be one continued Lye from one end to the other. The essence of the whole will be that *Dr. Franklin's electrical rod, smote the Earth and out sprung General Washington. That Franklin electrified him with his rod—and thence forward these two conducted all the Policy, Negotiations, Legislatures, and War.*"[7] Adams could express himself forcefully when he wanted to. Alexander Hamilton he called "the bastard brat of a Scotch peddler," Thomas Paine's *Common Sense* he described as "a poor, ignorant, malicious, short-sighted, crapulous mass," and the eighteenth century itself he once characterized as "the Age of Folly, Vice, Frenzy, Brutality, Daemons, Buonaparte, Tom Paine, or the Age of the Burning Brand from the Bottomless Pit, or anything but the Age of Reason."[8] But Adams probably didn't mind it all as much as this sounds. "For my own part," he once confessed, "I should not like to live in the Millenium. It would be the most sickish life imaginable."[9]

In his old age, Adams mellowed somewhat. Through the intercession of Benjamin Rush, he and Thomas Jefferson (who had been estranged since Adams's Presidency) became friends again and spent their final years conducting a lively correspondence about every subject under (and beyond) the sun. When Jefferson, in answer to a query from Adams, said he was willing to live his life over again, Adams had this to say about his own life: "I have had a Father and lost him. I have had a Mother and lost her. I have had a Wife and lost her. I have had Children and lost them. I have had honourable and worthy Friends and lost them—and instead of suffering these Griefs again, I had rather go forward and meet my destiny."[10] On June 17, 1826, Daniel Webster visited the ninety-year-old man in Quincy, Massachusetts. It was a hot day, and he found the former President lying on the sofa, being fanned by one of his relatives. "I hope the President is well today," ventured Webster. "No, I don't know, Mr. Webster," returned Adams; "I have lived in this old and frail tenement a great many years; it is very much dilapidated; and, from all that I can learn, my landlord doesn't intend to repair it."[11]

About the time of Webster's visit the inhabitants of Quincy asked Adams to make a speech to commemorate the fiftieth anniversary of the signing of the Declaration of Independence. Adams flatly refused. But after they pressed him to reconsider, he finally agreed to propose a toast: "Independence forever." When asked if he would add anything to it, he said firmly: "Not a word."[12] By Independence Day Adams was confined to his bed. At dawn he awakened and a servant asked him, "Do you know, sir, what day this is?" "Oh yes," responded Adams, "it is the glorious Fourth of July. God bless it. God bless you all." Then he lapsed into a coma. Early that afternoon, unknown to Adams, Thomas Jefferson died in his home in Monticello. About one o'clock, Adams awakened and exclaimed feebly, "Thomas Jefferson survives!" They were his last words. He ceased to breathe about sunset.[13]

★ ★ ★

Ditching

"When I was a boy," John Adams told his friends, "I had to study Latin grammar, but it was dull and I hated it. I told my father I did not like Latin, and asked for some other employment." "Well, John," said his father, "you may try ditching. My meadow yonder needs a ditch." So young Adams went to work in the meadow, soon found that "ditching" was arduous work, and by midnight was ready to resume his studies. Too proud to admit it, however, he spent another day digging. But by nightfall, he said, "toil conquered my pride," and he went back to his Latin. To the end of his life Adams always insisted that "ditching" played an important part in building his character.[14]

Leggs of a Lady

In May 1764, while courting Abigail Smith, Adams sent her "a Catalogue" of her "Faults, Imperfections, Defects, or whatever you please to call them." She wasn't a good card-player, for one thing, he said, and held the cards awkwardly in her hands. She was a bit too prudish, for another, and blushed when she heard people speaking frankly. She also hadn't learned to sing; she hadn't developed a "stately strutt" but walked with "toes bending inward"; and she often sat with her head hanging "like a Bulfish" and her "Leggs across." Abigail responded good-naturedly to John's bill of particulars. "I must confess," she told him, "I was so hardened as to read over most of my Faults with as much pleasure, as another person

would have read their perfections." But, she added, "Lysander must
excuse me if I still persist in some of them, at least till I am convinced
that an alteration would contribute to his happiness." And she concluded: "You know I think that a gentleman has no business to
concern himself about the Leggs of a Lady."[15]

Hath a Devil

Abigail's father was Rev. William Smith, a Congregational minister
who was extremely unenthusiastic about his daughter's marriage to
Adams. Adams was a lawyer, and Smith shared the contemporary
New England prejudice against lawyers. Adams was also the son
of a small farmer, and thus not considered good enough to marry
the daughter of a minister who was descended from a long line of
Massachusetts clergymen. Smith therefore opposed the match and
treated Adams with scant courtesy. But when John and Abigail
went ahead and married anyway on October 25, 1764, Smith preached
a sermon for the occasion based on the text, "For John came neither
eating bread nor drinking wine and ye say, he hath a devil." Abigail
was highly amused by the choice of text; Adams kept his peace
about it.[16]

No Tea

When Adams was in Falmouth on legal business in July 1774, he
stopped at Mrs. Huston's tavern. "Madam," he asked, "is it lawful
for a weary traveler to refresh himself with a dish of tea, provided
it has been honestly smuggled or paid no duties?" "No, sir," said
Mrs. Huston sternly, "we have renounced all tea in this place, but
I'll make you coffee." Adams, who loved tea, reluctantly drank coffee
instead. "Tea must be universally renounced," he told his wife, "and
I must be weaned, and the sooner the better." He added: "I have
drank coffee every afternoon since, and have borne it very well."[17]

Comes the Revolution

Revolutions are never genteel affairs. The American Revolution had
its share of riots, vandalism, tarring and feathering, and property
confiscations. John Adams was a stout supporter of American resis-

tance to British policies, but he insisted on law and order. He opposed mob rule, denounced patriots who used the crisis as an excuse for cancelling debts owed to people loyal to Britain, and was anxious for the courts to continue enforcing the obligations of contract. In August 1775, to his dismay, "a common horse jockey," once a client of his, came up to him in court and said jovially: "Oh! Mr. Adams, what great things have you and your colleagues done for us! We can never be grateful enough to you. There are no courts of justice now in this Province, and I hope there never will be another!" Adams was shocked. "Is this the object for which I have been contending?" he asked himself as he left without answering the jockey. "Are these the sentiments of such people? And how many of them are there in the country? Half the nation for what I know: for half the nation are debtors if not more, and these have been in all countries, the sentiments of debtors. If the power of the country should get into such hands, and there is great danger that it will, to what purpose have we sacrificed our time, health, and everything else? Surely we must guard against this spirit and these principles or we shall repent of all our conduct."[18]

The Ladies

"I long to hear that you have declared an independency," Abigail wrote her husband in March 1776. "And, by the way," she added, "in the new code of laws which I suppose it will be necessary for you to make, I desire you would remember the ladies and be more generous and favorable to them than your ancestors. Do not put unlimited power into the hands of the husbands. Remember, all men would be tyrants if they could. If particular care and attention is not paid to the ladies, we are determined to foment a rebellion, and will not hold ourselves bound by any laws in which we have no voice or representation. That your sex are naturally tyrannical is a truth so thoroughly established as to admit of no dispute."

Adams, who favored education for women and appreciated their role in civic affairs, replied humorously to his wife's comments. "We are obliged to go fair and softly," he told her, "and, in practice, you know we are the subjects. We have only the name of masters, and rather than give up this, which would completely subject us to the despotism of the petticoat, I hope General Washington and all our brave heroes would fight."[19]

Second of July

On June 7, 1776, Richard Henry Lee, delegate to the Second Continental Congress from Virginia, submitted a resolution calling for independence from Britain. On July 2, Congress voted to accept it. The following day Adams wrote his wife from Philadelphia with great excitement about the momentous vote. "The second day of July 1776," he said, "will be the most memorable epocha [sic] in the history of America. I am apt to believe that it will be celebrated by succeeding generations as the great anniversary festival. It ought to be solemnized with pomp, and parade, with shows, games, sports, bells, bonfires, and illuminations, from one end of this continent to the other, from this time forward forevermore." There were celebrations, indeed, as Adams predicted. But he got his date wrong. For beginning in 1777, they were held on the fourth, when Congress adopted the Declaration of Independence, not on the second, when it voted for independence.[20]

Theory of Colds

In September 1776, Adams and Franklin traveled from Philadelphia to Staten Island to confer with Lord Richard Howe, the British admiral, and Sir William Howe, the general, about a British peace offer. En route they stopped for the night at New Brunswick. But the inn there was so crowded that the two men had to share a bed in a tiny room with only one small window. The window was open, but Adams at once closed it. "Oh!" said Franklin, "don't shut the window; we shall be suffocated." Adams said he was afraid of catching cold, but Franklin said the air in the room was worse than that outdoors. "Come," he said, "open the window and come to bed, and I will convince you. I believe you are not acquainted with my theory of colds." Adams was so curious about Franklin's theory that he decided to take a chance and let the window stay open. "The Doctor," he recalled, "then began a harangue upon air and cold, and respiration and perspiration, with which I was so amused that I soon fell asleep, and left him and his philosophy together, but I believe they were equally sound and insensible, within a few minutes after me, for the last Words I heard were pronounced as if he was more than half asleep. . . ."[21]

Learning French

While in France as U.S. minister, Adams did everything he could to master the French language: studied grammars and dictionaries, read French literature, visited French law courts, attended church services in French, and saw plays at the Comédie Française. One evening, when he was dining with John Paul Jones on the *Bon Homme Richard,* the conversation turned to language study. One of the diners said there were two ways to learn French: take a mistress or go to the Comédie Française. The ship's surgeon looked over at Adams and said impishly: "Pray, sir, which, in your opinion, is the best?" Replied Adams lightly: "Perhaps both would teach it soonest; to be sure, sooner than either." Then, turning serious, he added: "But the language is nowhere better spoken than at the Comédie. The pulpit, the bar, the Academy of Sciences and the faculty of medicine—none of them speak so accurately as the French Comédie."[22]

Adams and Eve

At a dinner in Paris, one of the most elegant ladies at the table suddenly turned to Adams and said: "Mr. Adams, by your name I conclude you are descended from the first man and woman, and probably in your family may be preserved the tradition which may resolve a difficulty which I could never explain. I never could understand how the first couple found out the art of lying together." Surprised and shocked by her question, Adams blushed; then, speaking through a translator, he told her: "There is a physical quality in us resembling the power of electricity or of the magnet, by which when a pair approached within a striking distance they flew together like the needle to the pole or like to objects in electric experiments." "Well," said the French lady, "I know not how it was, but this I know: it is a very happy shock."[23]

Franklin and Voltaire

In April 1778, Adams attended a meeting of the Academy of Sciences in Paris and heard D'Alembert, editor with Diderot of the great *Encyclopédie,* speak. Both Voltaire and Franklin were present and, to Adams's wry amusement (for Franklin's popularity in France rather irked him), "there presently arose a general Cry that Monsieur Voltaire and Monsieur Franklin should be introduced to each other. This was done and they bowed and spoke to each other. This was no Satisfaction. There must be something more. Neither of our Philosophers seemed to divine what was wished or expected. They however took each other by the hand. . . . But this was not enough. The Clamour continued, untill the explanation came out, 'Il faut s'embrasser a la francoise.' The two Aged Actors upon this great Theatre of Philosophy and frivolity then embraced each other by hugging one another in their Arms and kissing each others cheeks, and then the tumult subsided. And the Cry immediately spread through the whole Kingdom and I suppose over all Europe, 'Qu'il etoit charmant. Oh! il etoit enchantment, de voir Solon et Sophocle embrassans. How charming it was! Oh! it was enchanting to see Solon and Sophocles embracing!' "[24]

John and Abigail

Adams's long stays in Europe were hard on both him and Abigail. "No man," Abigail told him, "even if he is sixty years of age ought to live more than three months at a time from his family." "Oh, that I had a bosom to lean my head upon!" Adams wrote back. "But how dare you hint or lisp a word about 'sixty years of age.' If I were near I would soon convince you that I am not above forty."[25]

Adams Dynasty

When Adams was President, many people considered him too high-toned and charged he was partial to royalty. A story began making the rounds to the effect that Adams planned to marry one of his sons to a daughter of George III and start an American dynasty which would reunite the United States and Britain. Before his death, Washington, the story went, heard of Adams's plan and, dressed in a white uniform, sought Adams out to plead with him. But Adams was adamant. Washington went to him a second time dressed in black and renewed his arguments. But Adams still refused to abandon his scheme. Washington then visited him a third time dressed in his Revolutionary uniform and threatened to run him through with his sword if he did not give up his plan. Only then, according to this fanciful story, did Adams give up his ambition to become King.

Another widely circulated story stated that Adams had sent General Charles Cotesworth Pinckney to England in a U.S. frigate to procure four pretty girls as mistresses, two for the General and two for himself. Adams was amused by this story. "I do declare upon my honor," he wrote his friend William Tudor, "if this be true, General Pinckney has kept them all for himself and cheated me out of my two!"[26]

THREE

Thomas Jefferson
1801–1809

On March 4, 1801, Thomas Jefferson (1743–1826) walked to his inauguration in the new capital, Washington, D.C., and then headed back to his boarding house when the ceremony was over. A few months later, when Congress met, he sent a written message to the two houses instead of appearing in person amid much fanfare (as had been the custom). He was just as informal about diplomatic receptions. When Andrew Merry, the British minister to the United States, presented himself at the Executive Mansion, Jefferson received him in dressing gown and slippers. Merry was infuriated. "I, in my official costume," he raged afterward, "found myself at the hour of reception he had himself appointed, introduced to a man as president of the United States, not merely in an undress, but ACTUALLY STANDING IN SLIPPERS DOWN AT THE HEELS, and both pantaloons, coat, and under-clothes indicative of utter slovenliness and indifference to appearances, and in a state of negligence actually studied. I could not doubt that the whole scene was prepared and intended as an insult, not to me personally, but to the sovereign I represented."[1]

Jefferson probably did not mind needling the pompous and humorless Merry. But he was more interested in introducing what he called "Republican simplicity" into the American system. He thought the federal government had become too high-toned under his Federalist predecessors, so he called his victory as a Republican in the recent presidential election the "revolution of 1800." It was not a real revolu-

tion, of course, but the campaign of 1800 had been a stormy one.
Because of Jefferson's sympathy for the French Revolution and his
liberal views on religion, Federalist conservatives called him a radical
and predicted that if he became President all Bibles would be burned,
property rights destroyed, and the marriage institution abolished.
"Oh Lord!" prayed a Federalist minister in Connecticut, "wilt Thou
bestow upon [Jefferson] a double portion of Thy grace, *for Thou
knowest he needs it.*"[2]

Jefferson's foes did more than pray for his soul. They also spread
stories about his lack of faith. The most famous portrayed him as
revealing contempt for Jesus while showing his Italian friend Philip
Mazzei around Monticello. Mazzei, it was said, expressed surprise
that Americans did not take better care of their public buildings.
"What buildings?" Jefferson wanted to know. "Is not that a church?"
asked Mazzei, pointing to some ruins. "Yes," answered Jefferson.
"I am astonished," Mazzei told him, "that they permit it to be in
so ruinous a condition." "It is good enough," Jefferson is supposed
to have remarked scornfully, "for him that was born in a manger."
When the story appeared in print during the campaign of 1800,
Jefferson's friends rushed to his defense; what he meant, they insisted,
was that expensive churches were no evidence of Christian piety.
Actually, the story was pure fabrication, though Jefferson refused
to say so publicly. He was willing, he told a friend, to leave "slander
and slanderers" to the "scourge of public opinion."[3] But the New
England Federalists continued to hammer away at him after he became President. In 1801, when he invited Thomas Paine to return
to the United States from France on a government vessel, they exploded in wrath. "What!" cried the *New England Palladium,* "invite
to the United States that lying, drunken, brutal infidel, who rejoiced
in the opportunity of basking and wallowing in the confusion, devas-
tation, bloodshed, rapine, and murder, in which his soul delights!"[4]

Jefferson had devout disciples as well as implacable enemies. When
he became President some of his admirers wanted to celebrate his
birthday publicly. "The only birthday I ever commemorate," he told
them, "is that of our Independence, the Fourth of July."[5] But John
Leland, Baptist minister in Cheshire, Massachusetts, decided to do
something special to honor the new President. Shortly after Jefferson's
inauguration, he asked his congregation to make the biggest cheese
in the world to give the new Chief Executive. "Every man and woman
who owned a cow," according to one observer, "was to give for

this cheese all the milk yielded on a certain day—only no *Federal
cow* must contribute a drop. A huge cider-press was fitted up to
make it in, and on the appointed day the whole country turned
out with pails and tubs of curd, the girls and women in their best
gowns and ribbons, and the men in their Sunday coats and clean
shirt-collars. The cheese was put to press with prayer and hymn
singing and great solemnity. When it was well dried it weighed 1600
pounds. It was placed on a sleigh, and Elder Leland drove with it
all the way to Washington. It was a journey of three weeks. All
the country had heard of the big cheese, and came out to look at
it as the Elder drove along." When Leland got to Washington, he
preached a pro-Jefferson sermon, based on the text "And behold,
a greater Solomon is here," and formally presented the cheese to
the President. Jefferson expressed his gratitude and then cut a great
wedge from it to send back to the donors. After that, he invited
everyone present to help themselves. As late as 1805 the cheese
was still being served to White House guests along with cake and
hot punch.[6]

Jefferson did not regard the Presidency as the major happening
of his long life. To him the biggest event was drafting the Declaration
of Independence. Jefferson's "peculiar felicity of expression," according to John Adams, made him the logical choice for writing the
Great Declaration.[7] In June 1776, the Continental Congress appointed a committee of five to draft a statement of reasons for American independence; it included Jefferson, Adams, Franklin, and two
other Congressmen. "The committee met," according to Adams,
"discussed the subject, and then appointed Jefferson and me to make
the draught, I suppose because we were the two first on the list."
When the subcommittee met, Jefferson suggested that Adams prepare
a draft. "I will not," said Adams. "You should do it," said Jefferson.
"Oh! no," exclaimed Adams. "Why will you not?" asked Jefferson.
"You ought to do it." "I will not," said Adams stubbornly. "Why?"
asked Jefferson. "Reasons enough," said Adams. "What can be your
reasons?" Jefferson wanted to know. "Reason first—you are a Virginian, and a Virginian ought to appear at the head of this business,"
explained Adams. "Reason second—I am obnoxious, suspected, and
unpopular. You are very much otherwise. Reason third—you can
write ten times better than I can." "Well," said Jefferson, "if you
are decided, I will do as well as I can." "Very well," said Adams,
"when you have drawn it up, we will have a meeting."[8]

Justly proud of his Declaration, Jefferson was extremely upset when Congress began hacking away at it after the committee made its report. Seeing his younger colleague's chagrin over the revisions being made in the document, Benjamin Franklin tried to comfort him with a little story. "When I was a journeyman printer," he told Jefferson, "one of my companions, an apprentice hatter, having served out his time, was about to open a shop for himself. His first concern was to have a handsome sign-board, with a proper inscription. He composed it in these words, *'John Thompson, Hatter, makes and sells hats for ready money,'* with the figure of a hat subjoined; but he thought he would submit it to his friends for their amendments. The first he showed it to thought the word 'Hatter' tautologous, because followed by the words 'makes hats,' which showed he was a hatter. It was struck out. The next observed that the word 'makes' might as well be omitted, because his customers would not care who made the hats. If good and to their mind, they would buy, by whomsoever made. He struck it out. A third said he thought the words *'for ready money'* were useless, as it was not the custom of the place to sell on credit. . . . They were parted with, and the inscription now stood, 'John Thompson sells hats.' *'Sells* hats!' says the next friend. 'Why nobody will expect you to give them away; what then is the use of that word?' It was stricken out, and 'hats' followed it the rather as there was one painted on the board. So the inscription was reduced ultimately to 'John Thompson' with the figure of a hat subjoined." Franklin's story made Jefferson feel a little better; and in the end Congress accepted most of what he had written, and the revisions it made probably improved the Declaration.[9]

Jefferson had an abundance of talents and interests. Once, while traveling in Virginia, it was said, he stopped at a country inn and got into conversation with a stranger. The stranger mentioned some mechanical operations he had seen recently, and Jefferson's knowledge of the subject convinced him that Jefferson was an engineer. Then they got to talking about agriculture, and the stranger decided that Jefferson was a farmer. More talk led the stranger to believe that Jefferson was a lawyer; then a physician. Finally the topic of religion was broached, and the stranger concluded that Jefferson was a clergyman, though he wasn't sure of what denomination. The following day he asked the landlord the name of the tall man he had engaged in conversation the night before. "What," said the landlord, "don't you know the Squire?—that was Mr. Jefferson." "Not President Jefferson?" exclaimed the stranger. "Yes," nodded the landlord, "President Jefferson!"[10]

The story of Jefferson and the stranger is improbable (why didn't they introduce themselves?), but not misleading. Jefferson was in fact a skillful architect, an accomplished violinist, an ingenious inventor, a competent scientist, a serious student of religion, and an expert on agricultural methods. When President John Kennedy entertained a group of Nobel Prize winners in the White House in December 1962, he welcomed them as the most distinguished gathering of talents ever assembled in the Executive Mansion except for when Jefferson dined there alone.

Personally, Jefferson was thin-skinned and somewhat shy, and hated head-on collisions with his adversaries. This meant that he sometimes expressed his opinions more frankly in private than in public and that he wasn't always candid with his associates. But his enemies not only called him a dangerous radical and a hypocrite; they also charged that he had fathered several children by Sally Hemings, a young slave woman. Jefferson (whose wife Martha died in 1782) never said anything, publicly or privately, about the charge; and there is no conclusive proof that there was any truth to the accusation. But he became so disgusted by the slanderous attacks on him in the Federalist press that he once suggested that editors divide their newspapers into four sections and plainly label each of them: (1) Truth; (2) Probability; (3) Possibility; and (4) Lies. "The third and fourth," he said, "should be professedly for those readers who would rather have lies for their money than the blank paper they would occupy."[11]

Jefferson was upset by the viciousness of party strife in the new republic and tremendously bothered by the existence of slavery in a nation dedicated to freedom. "I tremble for my country," he once exclaimed, "when I reflect that God is just."[12] But he never lost hope for the future. "I shall not die," he told Adams, "without a hope that light and liberty are on a steady advance." The "flames kindled on the 4th of July 1776," he said, "have spread over too much of the globe to be extinguished by the feeble engines of despotism."[13] A few days before he died, he told the people who had invited him to Washington to take part in celebrating the fiftieth anniversary of the Great Declaration: "All eyes are opened, or opening, to the rights of man. The general spread of the light of science has already laid open to every view the palpable truth, that the mass of mankind has not been born with saddles on their backs, nor a favored few booted and spurred, ready to ride them legitimately, by the grace of God."[14]

On July 3, 1826, Jefferson was confined to his bed and sinking rapidly. At eleven that evening he whispered, "This is the Fourth?" Nicholas P. Trist, his young lawyer-friend who was at the bedside, couldn't bring himself to say "not yet," and remained silent. "This is the Fourth?" Jefferson asked again. This time Trist nodded his assent. "Ah!" breathed Jefferson with a look of satisfaction on his face, then sank into a deep sleep. The next day, a little before 1:00 P.M., he ceased to breathe.[15]

The coincidence of Jefferson's and Adams's deaths on the fiftieth anniversary of the Declaration of Independence produced much commentary. "Great God!" exclaimed a New York editor. "Thy ways are inscrutable!" But one Virginian, who still nourished a grudge against the New England Federalists, greeted the news of Adams's death on the same day as Jefferson's with the exclamation: "It's a damned Yankee trick!"[16]

*　　*　　*

Fiddle Saved

In February 1770, when Jefferson and his mother were visiting a neighbor, one of their slaves rushed up in great excitement to report that their house at Shadwell had caught fire and that everything in it had been destroyed. "But were none of my books saved?" cried Jefferson in great distress. "No, master," said the man; then he added with a smile, "But we saved the fiddle!"[17]

The Food of Love

Martha Skelton, the attractive young widow whom Jefferson married in 1772, had many suitors before she settled on Jefferson. One day, according to a popular story, two gentlemen happened to call on her at the same time. They were friends and decided to go in together. But as they were about to pass from the hall into the drawing-room, they heard some music. Someone was playing the violin, accompanied by the harpsichord, and a lady and a gentleman were singing. The two gentlemen knew at once who it was: Jefferson was the only violinist in the neighborhood. They looked resignedly at each other. "We are wasting our time," said one of them. "We may as well go home." So they donned their hats and left.[18]

The Influence of Flies

When Congress was discussing independence, according to a story Jefferson told a friend in his old age, meetings were held near a livery-stable, and the meeting hall was besieged by flies. The delegates wore short breeches and silk stockings; while they talked they also busily lashed the flies from their legs with their handkerchiefs. The flies were so vexatious, Jefferson said, that the delegates finally decided to sign the Declaration of Independence at once and get away from the place as quickly as possible. Jefferson told the story "with much glee," said the friend; he was amused by "the influence of the flies" on so momentous an event.[19]

Succession

When Jefferson arrived in Paris as U.S. minister to France and presented himself to the French Minister of Foreign Affairs, the latter said, "You replace Monsieur Franklin?" "I *succeed* him," replied Jefferson. "No one can replace him."[20]

Dirty Farmer

It is said that Jefferson, unattended by servants, once stopped at the main hotel in Baltimore, dismounted, and, with whip in hand, entered the barroom and sought accommodations for the night. The landlord surveyed him critically, concluded he was a farmer of not much account, and told him curtly, "We have no room for you, sir." Jefferson, appearing not to have heard the remark, repeated his request, and got the same answer. He then turned around, called for his horse, and departed. Soon afterwards a wealthy gentleman entered the hotel and told the landlord that the man who had just left was Thomas Jefferson, Vice-President of the United States. "Vice-President of the United States!" exlcaimed the landlord. "Yes, and the greatest man alive," said his informant. "Murder and death, what have I done?" wailed the landlord; and he ordered his servants to overtake Jefferson and tell him he could have the best of everything in the hotel. The servants finally located Jefferson in a hotel in another part of town and gave him the landlord's message. "Tell him I have engaged a room here," said Jefferson. "Tell him that I value his good intentions highly, but if he has no room for a dirty farmer he shall have none for the Vice-President."[21]

Midnight Judges

Just before the Adams administration came to a close, the Federalists rushed a law through Congress increasing the number of U.S. courts throughout the country. Adams selected Federalists for the judgeships, and John Marshall, his Secretary of State, went to work filling out their commissions as rapidly as he could in order to beat the midnight deadline, March 3, when Adams's administration expired. Jefferson got wind of the matter, gave Levi Lincoln (his Attorney General designate) his watch, and ordered him to go to the State Department at midnight, take over the place, and see to it that no papers were removed from it after that hour. Lincoln accordingly entered Marshall's office at the appointed time. "I have been ordered by Mr. Jefferson," he told Marshall, "to take possession of this office and its papers." "Why," exclaimed Marshall, "Mr. Jefferson has not yet qualified." "Mr. Jefferson considers himself in the light of an executor," said Lincoln, "bound to take charge of the papers of the Government until he is duly qualified." "But it is not yet twelve o'clock," said Marshall, taking out his watch. Lincoln took out the watch Jefferson had given him and, holding it up, said, "This is the President's watch, and rules the hour." Marshall yielded at this point and, casting a farewell look at the commissions on the table, left the room. In after years he used to laugh and say he had been allowed to pick up nothing but his hat. But he did have one or two commissions in his pocket when he left, so the judges who received them came to be known as "John Adams's midnight judges."[22]

Freedom of the Press

During a visit to Jefferson, the German scientist Baron Alexander von Humboldt saw a newspaper in the President's study filled with scurrilous abuse of him. "Why are these libels allowed?" exclaimed the Baron, picking up the paper. "Why is not this libelous journal suppressed, or its Editor, at least, fined and imprisoned?" "Put that paper in your pocket, Baron," said Jefferson, smiling, "and should you hear the reality of our liberty, the freedom of the press questioned, show them this paper, and tell them where you found it."[23]

Jefferson's Yes

On a visit home once, according to a popular story, Jefferson was out riding with some young men. They came across a rough-looking Kentuckian seated on the bank of a swollen stream waiting for someone to give him a ride. The Kentuckian waited until everyone but Jefferson had entered the stream, then asked the latter to take him across. Jefferson gave him the ride. When he had safely deposited him on the opposite bank, one of the young men cried: "I say! what made you let the young men pass and ask that gentleman to carry you over the creek?" "Wall," said the Kentuckian, "if you want to know, I'll tell you: I reckon a man carries yes or no in his face— the young chaps' faces said no—the old 'un's said yes." "It isn't every man that would have asked the President of the United States for a ride behind him," said the young man severely. The Kentuckian was astonished. "You don't say that was Tom Jefferson, do you?" he exclaimed. Then he added: "He's a . . . fine old fellow, anyway." "That was the President," emphasized the young man. The Kentuckian thought for a minute, then burst out with a laugh: "What do you suppose my wife, Polly, will say when I get back to Boone County, and tell her I've rid behind Jefferson? She'll say I voted for the *right man!*"[24]

Quarreling with God

One afternoon when Jefferson was visiting his friend William Fitzhugh of Ravensworth, a servant ran up to report that a black man had cut himself severely with an axe. Fitzhugh immediately ordered the servant to go for a doctor. But Jefferson said the man might bleed to death before the doctor arrived and, pointing out that he himself had some experience with surgery, suggested they go and see what could be done at once for the poor fellow. Fitzhugh agreed; and when they reached the wounded man they found he had a severe cut in his calf. Jefferson quickly procured a needle and silk and in a little while had sewed up the wound and carefully bandaged the leg.

As they walked back from the black man's cabin, Jefferson remarked to his friend that, although the ways of Divine Providence were wise and beneficent, he had always thought it strange that the thick, fleshy coverings and defenses of the bones in the limbs of the human frame were placed in the rear when the danger of their injury usually came from the front. Fitzhugh was struck by Jefferson's observation.

Not long after Jefferson left, Fitzhugh's friend Dr. Stuart, a Federalist with an abiding hatred of Jefferson, came by for a visit. Hearing that the President had been there, he cried: "What news did your friend give you, and what new heresy did he attempt to instill into your mind?" "Ah! Stuart," said Fitzhugh, "you do Mr. Jefferson an injustice; he is a great man, a very great man." Then he told about the accident that had befallen the black man, Jefferson's skill in dressing the wound, and the remark he had made afterward about the human anatomy. "Well," said Dr. Stuart, raising his hands in horror, "what is this world coming to? Here this fellow, Jefferson, after turning upside down everything on this earth, is now quarreling with God Almighty himself!"[25]

Gentleman

Jefferson and his grandson were out riding in a carriage one day near Monticello when they passed a slave who was a stranger to them. The slave, according to Jeffersonian folklore, took off his hat and bowed to them. Jefferson raised his hat and bowed, as was the custom, but his grandson, who was busily talking, ignored the man. "Thomas," said Jefferson severely, turning to the lad, "do you permit a slave to be more of a gentleman than you are?"[26]

Animal House

In March 1825, the University of Virginia, which had been lovingly planned by Jefferson down to its last detail, opened its doors to forty students, with several distinguished professors from Europe on the faculty. By the fall there were more than a hundred students in attendance, governed by a loose code of discipline. Jefferson hoped the university would attract serious students; instead, most of them turned out to be hell-raisers. They walked out of classes, turned their dormitories into gambling dens, got roaring drunk in the local taverns, and threw stink bombs into the professors' rooms. One night a group of students marched around the campus shouting, "Down with the European professors!" When some of the professors tried to restore order, the students attacked them with canes and bricks. Two of the professors threatened to resign.

The day after the riot the Board of Visitors, which governed the University, had an emergency meeting with the students in the University Rotunda. There were three ex-Presidents present as members of the Board: Jefferson, Madison, and Monroe. Jefferson was the first to speak. He began by declaring that "it was one of the most painful events of his life." But he was so overcome by emotion that he could not go on. "His lips moved," according to Margaret Bayard Smith, "he essayed to speak—burst into tears and sank back into his seat. The shock was electric." The students were so moved by Jefferson's grief that when Chapman Johnson, another Visitor, took over and asked the rioters to come forward and give their names, nearly all of them did so. "It was not his words," said one of the students afterward, "but Mr. Jefferson's tears that melted their stubborn purpose." Following the meeting, the Board established a stricter code of discipline. As Jefferson put it, rather regretfully: "Coercion must be resorted to where confidence has been disappointed."[27]

James Madison
(1809–17)

James Madison (1751–1836) was not a great President, but he was one of America's greatest statesmen. Even in his own day he was known as the "Sage of his time," "the great little Madison," and as the "Father of the Constitution." With his customary modesty, Madison disclaimed the last title. "You give me credit to which I have no claim, in calling me 'the writer of the Constitution of the U.S.,'" he protested to a correspondent in his old age. "This was not, like the fabled Goddess of Wisdom, the offspring of a single brain. It ought to be regarded as the work of many heads & many hands."[1]

But Madison's was the busiest of all the heads and hands when it came to Constitution-making. He made an exhaustive study of confederacies, ancient and modern, went to the Constitutional Convention full of ideas on government, and played a leading role in the great debate there, speaking on seventy-one out of eighty-six days. He got so excited at times that he finally asked a friend to tug at his coattails if he became too wrought up. Once, after talking himself to the point of exhaustion, he reproved his friend: "Why didn't you pull me when you heard me going on like that?" Said the friend: "I would rather have laid a finger on the lightening."[2] Madison, said Daniel Webster, "had as much to do as any man in framing the Constitution, and as much to do as any man in administering it."[3]

As President, though, Madison was far less impressive. His Presidency was marked by a series of disasters: the outbreak of an unnecessary war with Britain in 1812; humiliating early defeats for American forces; vociferous opposition to the war ("Mr. Madison's War") by many citizens; the invasion of Washington by the British and the burning of the President's house, the Capitol, and other public buildings; the refusal of the New England states to support the war effort and serious talk of secession on their part. Madison did his best through it all. According to Attorney General Richard Rush, "he visited in person—a thing never known before—all the offices of the departments of war and navy, stimulating everything in a manner worthy of a little commander-in-chief, with his little round hat and huge cockade."[4] He even reviewed American troops in the field shortly before the British moved in on the nation's capital. By October 1814, however, he looked "miserably shattered and woe-begone."[5] Fortunately a series of victories in the closing months of the war— especially Andrew Jackson's victory over the British at New Orleans after the peace treaty was signed—lifted American spirits and reunited the American people. And the economic prosperity that followed the war permitted Madison to leave the White House in 1817 in an atmosphere of friendliness and good will.

Madison was one of the most conscientious, fair-minded, and even-tempered of all our Presidents. John Quincy Adams spoke of his "imperturbable patience." He appeared unruffled by slanderous attacks on him at election time and during the War of 1812. When he returned to Washington a few days after the British left, according to one observer, he was "tranquil as usual, and tho' much distressed by the dreadful event, which had taken place, not dispirited."[6] But to some people he seemed a bit stuffy. He always wore black and was considered old-fashioned in his garb, reminding an English visitor of a schoolmaster dressed up for a funeral. "What Presidents we might have had, sir!" a Washington barber who was shaving a Senator suddenly burst out one day. "Look at Daggett, of Connecticut, and Stockton, of New Jersey, with queues as big as your wrist, and powdered every day, like real gentlemen they are! But this little Jim Madison with a queue no bigger than a pipe-stem! Sir, it is enough to make a man forswear his country!"[7] Madison's wife Dolley delighted people with her vivacity and good humor; but Madison himself seemed ill at ease at public functions. "As to Jemmy Madison," exclaimed Washington Irving, after attending the inaugural ball in

March 1809, "ah! poor Jemmy! he is but a withered little Apple-John."[8] Madison himself told a friend: "I would much rather be in bed."[9]

But Madison was not really a solemn man. When relaxing with friends he was full of fun. He had a fund of amusing anecdotes, some of them on the earthy side, with which he regaled people he liked, and he didn't mind laughing at himself. One of his favorite stories was about his "Scotch French." When he was a student at the College of New Jersey, according to this tale, he was called on to act as interpreter for President Witherspoon and a visiting Frenchman. By listening with all his might, he was able to catch a few of the Frenchman's words, but when he launched into French himself, the visitor was dumbfounded. "I might as well have been talking kickapoo at him," Madison recalled. "I had learnt French of my Scotch tutor, reading it with him as we did Greek and Latin; that is, as a dead language"; and his "Scotch accent" (which he claimed he never lost) made his French unrecognizable.[10] Another story he enjoyed telling had to do with the "scar" he received in defense of his country. When campaigning in 1788 for election to the lower house of the First Congress, he said, he met his opponent, James Monroe, at a church for a debate. After the service the two of them "addressed the people, and kept them standing in the snow listening to the discussion of constitutional subjects. They stood it out very patiently—seemed to consider it a sort of fight of which they were required to be the spectators. I then had to ride in the night, twelve miles to quarters, and got my nose frost-bitten, of which I bear the mark now." Then, pointing to a scar on the left side of his nose, Madison would laugh and claim it as "his scar of a wound received in defense of his country."[11]

In retirement, Madison busied himself managing his plantation in Montpelier, reading widely, visiting friends, and doing entertaining of his own. When Margaret Bayard Smith called on him in 1828, she found him utterly charming. His conversation, she reported, was "a stream of history . . . so rich in sentiments and facts, so enlivened by anecdotes and epigrammatic remarks, so frank and confidential as to opinions on men and measures, that it had an interest and charm, which the conversation of few men now living, could have. . . . His little blue eyes sparkled like stars from under his bushy grey eye-brows and amidst the deep wrinkles of his poor thin face."[12] Once when the Madisons were entertaining, James was ill and confined to bed. But when the party sat down to dinner, he insisted that the door of his room be left open so he could hear what was going on. Every few moments he would call out to a friend in his feeble voice: "Doctor, are you pushing about the bottle? Do your duty, Doctor, or I must cashier you."[13]

By 1831, Madison was the last of the Founding Fathers still alive. Not only was he the last living signer of the Constitution; he was also the sole survivor of the Continental Congress and of the Virginia Constitutional Convention of 1776. "Having outlived so many of my contemporaries," he mused, "I ought not to forget that I may be thought to have outlived myself."[14] In his last illness, a friend begged him not to try to talk while lying in bed. "Oh," said Madison playfully, "I always talk most easily when I lie."[15] As he neared the end in the summer of 1836, he refused his friends' request that he take stimulants to prolong his life until the sixtieth anniversary of the Declaration of Independence and died a few days before July fourth. Afterward, among his papers was found one entitled "Advice to My Country." What did he advise? "The advice nearest to my heart and deepest in my convictions," he had written, "is that the Union of the States be cherished and perpetuated. Let the open enemy to it be regarded as a Pandora with her box opened; and the disguised one, as the Serpent creeping with his deadly wiles into Paradise."[16]

★ ★ ★

Office-Seeker

When Madison was Secretary of State under Jefferson, a loyal Republican dropped into his office one day and asked to be governor of a western territory. Madison told him that other applicants had stronger claims. The man then asked for a collectorship. Unfortunately, Madison told him, they were all taken. How about a post-office? Out of the question. Well, said the man, did the Secretary have any old clothes he could spare?[17]

Treacherous Wine

Isaac Briggs of Maryland, dining with the Madisons one afternoon in the White House, found the President polite, affable, and expansive. "Dolly attempted to open a bottle of Champagne wine," he reported afterwards, and "the cork flew to the most distant corner of the room with an explosion as loud as—the sound of a popgun. She looked scared, and the wine seemed to be in haste to follow the cork. She however dextrously filled 3 large glasses, one for me, one for her sister Lucy, . . . and one for herself. She handed the bottle to her husband, but he would not take more than half-a-glass; I remarked, after tasting it, that it was very treacherous wine—yes, said the President addressing himself to Lucy, if you drink much of it, it will make you hop like the cork."[18]

Hair

One day during the War of 1812 the wife of a Federalist drove to the house of Dolley Madison's sister, loosened her long hair, and prayed loudly for the privilege of cutting it off so it could be used to make a rope with which to hang the President.[19]

Saving Washington

On August 23, 1814, Madison was in Maryland with American forces and Dolley was in the White House, with dinner on the table, awaiting his return. Suddenly a messenger arrived with the news that British troops were advancing on Washington and that Dolley must leave at once. With the help of the servants Dolley assembled four boxes of her husband's papers; she also insisted on taking Gilbert Stuart's portrait of George Washington with her. She did not, as legend has it, take down the painting herself. It was too high for her to reach and tightly screwed to the wall. Instead the gardener climbed a rickety ladder, broke the frame with an axe, and handed her the famous canvas. "It is done," she wrote her sister afterward, "and the precious portrait placed in the hands of two gentlemen from New York for safe keeping."

After leaving the President's house, Dolley hurried across the Potomac in a carriage looking for her husband. At one point she sought refuge in the house of an acquaintance. But she had just gone upstairs when the mistress of the house screamed out, "Miz Madison! Your husband's got mine out fighting and, damn you, you shan't stay in my house; *so get out!*" Dolley eventually ended up in Wiley's Tavern in Virginia. There the President, who had been frantically looking for her, finally joined his wife after thirty-six hours' separation.[20]

FIVE

James Monroe
1817–25

James Monroe (1758–1831) was the last of the Virginians to be President. He was also the last of the Revolutionary Fathers; he had served in the Continental Army under Washington and been wounded at Trenton. He was the last President, too, to wear a cocked hat. With his ancient knee breeches, silk stockings, cockade, and sword, he was a hangover from the age of the Revolution who, like his friend Jefferson, insisted on "friendly, republican, and unassuming manners."[1] When a European diplomat visited the White House for the first time and came across a bald-headed, watery-eyed man in a striped seersucker coat, a dirty waistcoat spotted with ink, and slippers down at the heels, writing at a desk, he was surprised that the President of the United States should employ such a slovenly clerk. He was even more surprised when the man turned out to be the President himself.[2]

Like Jefferson, Monroe preferred republican France to monarchical England. When President Washington sent him as minister to the new French republic in 1794, he compromised Washington's policy of careful neutrality in the conflict between France and England by appearing in person, at his own request, at the French National Convention. There he received the French President's warm *accolade* (fraternal embrace), made a speech filled with enthusiasm for France, and presented an American flag to the Convention to fly beside the tricolor. Washington recalled him from his post soon after; he wanted an envoy who would "promote, not thwart, the neutral policy of the government." When Monroe returned to the United States in the spring of 1797, he was so displeased with Washington that he passed Mount Vernon on his way home without bothering to pay his respects to his former Commander-in-Chief.[3]

In 1803 Monroe became President Jefferson's minister to England. British officials received him courteously enough; but London society was cool to the representative of the upstart new republic. At the first state dinner to which he was invited, Monroe found himself seated at the foot of the table between two representatives of German principalities. "James Monroe doesn't care where he eats his dinner," he said some years later, "but to find the American minister put at the bottom of the table between two little principalities no bigger than my farm in Albemarle made me mad." He was so mad, in fact, that when the first toast, "the King," was given and everyone rose to drink it, he purposely put his wine glass down in the finger-bowl when he sat down and splashed water all over the table. When Monroe's German neighbors exchanged sarcastic smiles at this, Monroe became even angrier. Then, suddenly, the Russian minister, who was at the right hand of the presiding Minister of State, rose and offered his toast: "A health and welcome to our latest-comer, the President of the United States." "Then I saw clear again," said Monroe afterward, "and when my country and General Washington had been honored, I rose and thanked the Russian minister, as I offered mine: 'The health and prosperity of our friend, the Emperor of Russia.' "[4] To the British diplomat Lord Henry Holland Monroe later admitted: "I find your monarchy more republican than monarchical and the French republic more monarchical than your monarchy."[5]

When Monroe succeeded Madison as President, the bitterness over the War of 1812 had long since subsided and the nation was entering an "Era of Good Feelings." Shortly after his inauguration in March 1817, Monroe toured New England, receiving a warm reception everywhere he went. Even Harvard was friendly. When it was announced at a faculty meeting that the student who commanded the Harvard Washington Corps was being suspended for misbehavior, President Kirkland exclaimed: "Send him away when Mr. Monroe is coming? Who will command my Harvard Washington Corps when the President visits the College?" The faculty at once dropped the charges against the student so that the lad was on hand to present arms for the visit.[6]

There was a circus in Haverhill, Massachusetts, the day Monroe made his visit, but little John Greenleaf Whittier preferred seeing the President to the exhibit of wild beasts. His Quaker parents, however, forbid him to see either. But the next day, the nine-year-old boy trudged all the way to town, bent on seeing at least some footsteps in the street that the President had left behind. After looking around for a while he found the impression of an elephant's foot in the road, and assuming that this was Monroe's track, he followed it as far as he could make it out. Then he returned home, happy in the knowledge that he had seen the footsteps of the greatest man in the United States.[7]

During Monroe's eight years in office, "tranquility," according to one observer, "pervaded the country like the placid calm of an Indian summer."[8] But Monroe's Presidency was not entirely marked by peace and harmony. One day Secretary of the Treasury William H. Crawford stormed into the White House with a list of the men he had recommended for office which Monroe had not acted on. When Monroe refused to approve any of them, Crawford lost his temper, brandished his cane, and rushed at the President, shouting, "You damned infernal old scoundrel!" Monroe quickly grabbed a pair of tongs and repulsed his angry Secretary. Then he ordered him off the premises, and, ringing for the servants, threatened to have him thrown out. Crawford then meekly offered his apologies, which Monroe somewhat grudgingly accepted, and departed.[9] On another occasion, at a White House dinner for diplomats, Sir Charles Vaughan, the British minister, seated opposite Count de Sérurier, the French minister, noticed with increasing irritation that whenever he made a remark the Frenchman bit his thumb. Finally he could contain himself no longer and exploded, "Do you bite your thumb at me, Sir?" "I do," replied the Count. The two men then drew their swords and ran at each other. But as they were about to clash, Monroe drew his own sword between them and stopped the fight.[10]

Brandishing canes and swords in the White House was one thing; the crisis over slavery in the nation at large was another. When Missouri requested admission into the Union as a slave state, the nation was thrown into turmoil. The Missouri crisis, said Monroe's friend, Jefferson, with deep forebodings for the future, was "like a firebell in the night.''[11] It was, mourned John Quincy Adams, "a mere preamble—a title page to a great tragic volume. . . ."[12] Monroe favored admitting Missouri as a slave state, but he accepted the Missouri Compromise proposed by Henry Clay: dividing freedom from slavery at the 36°30' line. Monroe's opinions about slavery were thoroughly conventional. He cherished a vague hope that it would disappear one day, but favored colonizing free blacks in Africa. The capital of Liberia, established as a homeland for blacks by American whites in the 1830's, was named Monrovia. But Monroe got more fame from a doctrinaire pronouncement he made in 1823 staking out the Western hemisphere as an American sphere of influence.

Monroe was highly regarded by his friends and associates. Jefferson said he was "a man whose soul might be turned wrong side outward, without discovering a blemish to the world."[13] Thomas Paine, whom Monroe rescued from a French prison in 1794 and took into his own household, also spoke of him with respect and gratitude. And his Secretary of State, John Quincy Adams, a man not given to promiscuous praise, said that future generations might regard the Monroe administration as the "golden age" of the Republic.[14] For all his popularity, though, Monroe was a bit slow, dull, unimaginative, and commonplace. There are, acknowledged one of his biographers, "but few humorous anecdotes or incidents that relate to Monroe."[15]

Monroe retained his Revolutionary patriotism to the end. Even when he joined Jefferson in applauding Revolutionary France he did not think it could compare with Revolutionary America. One day, walking in Paris with his daughter Eliza (who was studying in a French school), he remarked that the United States, though a young nation, was really a much finer country than France. "Yes, papa," said the little girl, "but we haven't any roads like this." "That's true," acknowledged her father. "Our country may be likened to a new house. We lack many things, but we possess the most precious of all—liberty!"[16]

* * *

Monroe and Hamilton

In 1792, Monroe was a member of a Senate committee investigating the finances of Secretary of the Treasury Alexander Hamilton. To clear his name of the charge that he was misusing public funds, Hamilton was forced to reveal his involvement with a Philadelphia woman, Mrs. Reynolds, whose husband was blackmailing him. The committee cleared Hamilton of any suspicion of corruption and agreed to keep the records of their inquiry confidential. But in 1797, someone (apparently not Monroe) leaked the records to the press, and Hamilton was forced to admit his clandestine love affair publicly.

Hamilton filled his confession with apologies to his wife, and she remained loyal to him. But he was bitter about Monroe. Holding him responsible for the leak, Hamilton, accompanied by John Barker Church, his brother-in-law, sought him out in New York City and gave him a tongue-lashing. Monroe, who was with a friend at the time, tried to explain his innocence in the matter, but Hamilton snapped: "This, as your representation, is totally false!" Monroe jumped up at that and cried, "Do you say I represent falsely? You are a scoundrel!" Hamilton too was on his feet by now. "I will meet you like a gentleman," he cried. "I am ready," said Monroe. "Get your pistols." "Gentlemen, gentlemen, be moderate," interposed Church as he and Monroe's friend separated the two. The confrontation ended with Church's suggestion that "any warmth or unguarded expression that has happened during the interview should be buried and considered as though it never had happened." "In that respect," said Monroe, "I shall be governed by Col. Hamilton's consent." Hamilton then agreed that "any intemperate expression should be forgotten" and took his leave. The two men continued their quarrel by an exchange of letters; but neither was willing to be the aggressor in challenging the other to a duel.[17]

Monroe and Napoleon

Monroe went to France with Robert Livingston to negotiate the Louisiana Purchase and first met with Napoleon in the Louvre palace on Sunday, May 1, 1803. "I am so happy to see him," said the Consul upon being introduced to Monroe. "You have been here fifteen days?" Monroe told him that he had. "You speak French?" asked Napoleon. "A little," replied Monroe. "You had a good voyage?" asked Napoleon. "Yes." "You came in a frigate?" "No," said Monroe, "in a merchant vessel charged for the purpose."

After dinner, Napoleon began quizzing Monroe about Washington, D.C. "How many inhabitants has it?" "It is just commencing," Monroe told him; "there are two cities near it . . . which if counted with the Federal City would make a respectable town; in itself it contains only two or three thousand inhabitants." "Well," Napoleon continued, "Mr. Jefferson, how old is he?" "About sixty." "Is he married or single?" "He is not married." "Then he is a garçon." "No, he is a widower." "Has he children?" "Yes, two daughters, who are married." "Does he reside at the Federal City?" "Generally." "Are the public buildings there commodious, those for Congress and President especially?" "They are." "You, the Americans, did brilliant things in your war with England; you will do the same again." "We shall, I am persuaded," said Monroe, "always do well when it shall be our lot to be in war." "You may probably be in war with them again," Napoleon predicted.[18]

A Little Flattery

"Are you not completely worn out?" a friend asked Monroe at a reception in the Executive Mansion. "Oh, no," said Monroe quickly. "A little flattery will support a man through great fatigue."[19]

Unwelcome Visit

Elizabeth Hamilton's loyalty to her husband was unwavering, and she shared his contempt for Monroe after the Treasury Department investigation in 1792 and the release of confidential material to the press in 1797. Many years afterward, when she was in her nineties, Monroe happened to be in the vicinity of her home and decided to pay his respects. "What has that man come to see me for?" she cried when she saw his calling card. "Why, Aunt," said her young nephew, "don't you know, it's Mr. Monroe and he's been President, and he is visiting here now in the neighborhood, and has been very much made of, and invited everywhere, and so—I suppose he has come to call and pay his respects to you." After thinking it over, Mrs. Hamilton said, "I will see him." When she entered the parlor, Monroe rose, bowed, and made a few polite remarks. "Mr. Monroe," she said coldly, "If you have come to tell me that you repent, that you are sorry, very sorry, for the misrepresentations and the slanders and the stories you circulated against my dear husband, if you have come to say this, I understand it. But, otherwise, no lapse of time, no nearness of the grave, makes any difference." When she stopped speaking, Monroe turned, picked up his hat, and left.[20]

SIX

John Quincy Adams
1825–29

John Quincy Adams (1767–1848), son of John Adams, became President by a fluke. In 1824, since none of the candidates—Adams, Henry Clay, Andrew Jackson, or William H. Crawford—had received an electoral majority, the presidential contest was taken to the House of Representatives. When the House voted on February 9, 1825, the deciding vote was cast by New York. But the New York delegation was divided; General Stephen Van Rensselaer, "the last of the Patroons," became the key figure. Van Rensselaer had originally been committed to Crawford; and Martin Van Buren, who was anxious to block Adams's election, urged him to hold firm. But Clay (who was releasing his votes to Adams) and Daniel Webster put great pressure on him to vote for Adams in order to keep Jackson from winning. When it came time to vote, Van Rensselaer was thoroughly perplexed; he simply didn't know what to do. But being a pious man, he dropped his head on the desk just before the ballot box reached him and prayed to the Lord for guidance. When he lifted his head and opened his eyes, he saw a ballot on the floor by his seat with Adams's name on it. Interpreting this as an expression of God's will, he cast his vote for Adams, and as a result Adams won New York and with it the Presidency.[1]

Adams experienced no great joy at his election. "Less possessed of your confidence in advance than any of my predecessors," he observed glumly in his inaugural address, "I am deeply conscious of the prospect that I shall stand more and oftener in need of your indulgence."[2] Despite misgivings about his status as a minority President, he formulated an ambitious set of plans for bettering the country which he loved with such deep-seated passion: federally sponsored scientific expeditions, astronomical observatories, roads and canals, and a national university. But Congress accepted none of his proposals. The American people, too, were lukewarm to one of the most intelligent, courageous, experienced, and public-spirited of all our Presidents.

Adams admitted it: "I am a man of reserved, cold, austere, and forbidding manners."[3] Though he could be charming and witty with intimates, he seemed to most people, including his admirers, "hard as a piece of granite and cold as a lump of ice."[4] Once, when he was a student at Harvard, his fellow students held a barbecue on Bunker Hill to celebrate the building of a new bridge; but young Adams stayed at home because he thought that the place where men had fought and died for liberty should not be profaned by gaiety.[5] In Europe, where he held a series of diplomatic posts between 1794 and 1801, he was disgusted by the eagerness of some Americans to move in high society and contemptuous of the wrangling about precedence and court etiquette that absorbed the energies of his fellow diplomats. "In all these controversies," he wrote, "I have endeavored to consider it as an affair in which I, as an *American* minister, had no concern; and that my only principle is to dispute upon precedence with nobody."[6] He did, though, insist on respect for himself as the proud representative of a new nation; and when he went to Berlin as minister in November 1797, he was not at all amused at being "questioned at the gates by a dapper lieutenant who did not know, until one of his private soldiers explained to him, who the United States of America were."[7]

Adams's candor and independence of mind gradually won him respect in Europe, and Czar Alexander I of Russia took a real liking to him. But his relations with Henry Clay, his fellow diplomat for a time, were not so good. When the two served together on the peace delegation at Ghent at the close of the War of 1812, their personalities and preferences clashed forcefully. Adams rose each morning at five to light a fire and begin his day's work by candlelight; but he always heard, with ill-concealed disapproval, the all-night card parties in Clay's room breaking up about that time. Nothing was harder for Adams to bear than the charge that he had made a "corrupt bargain" with Clay when he appointed the latter Secretary of State shortly after receiving his support in Congress for the Presidency. John Quincy Adams simply did not make corrupt bargains with anyone.

Adams was, everyone agreed, "unmanageable."[8] He put the good of the nation, as he conceived it, above the good of the party. After the Massachusetts Federalists elected him to the U.S. Senate in 1803, he felt duty-bound to support the Jefferson administration from time to time and became an outcast in Boston. "Curse on the stripling," groused one critic, "how he apes his sire!"[9] Adams, said one senatorial colleague, regarded every public measure which came up as he would a proposition in Euclid, abstracted from party considerations.[10] When Adams became Secretary of State under Monroe, he firmly upheld the prestige of the United States in its relations with other nations and he forced the arrogant British minister, Stratford Canning, after hours of stormy confrontation, to treat him as an equal and the United States with respect.

One day Canning stormed into Adams's office to protest some remarks made in the House of Representatives about plans for American settlements at the mouth of the Columbia River. Adams was annoyed. Not only did he believe that America's claim to the territory in question was as good as Britain's; he also resented being questioned by a foreign diplomat about remarks made during a debate in Congress. It was, he told Canning, just as if the U.S. minister to England, hearing about something said in the House of Commons about sending troops to the Shetland Islands, should proceed to question the British foreign minister about it. "Have you any claim to the Shetland Islands?" cried Canning in a great rage. "Have you any *claim* to the mouth of the Columbia River?" retorted Adams. "Why," exclaimed Canning, "do you not *know* that we have a claim?" "I do not *know* what you claim nor what you do not claim," returned Adams. "You claim India; you claim Africa; you claim . . ." "Perhaps a piece of the moon," interrupted Canning sarcastically. "No," said Adams calmly, "I have not heard that you claim exclusively any part of the moon; but there is not a spot on *this* inhabitable globe that I could affirm you do not claim." After more interruptions by Canning and more retorts from Adams, the British minister finally backed down, expressed a wish "to cultivate harmony . . . between the two countries," and promised he would "never forget the respect due from him *to the American government.*" Adams bowed, and

the interview ended. But a day or so later when the two met by
accident they barely spoke.[11]

Adams's haughty reserve served him well in the diplomatic game.
But he was doubtless too austere for democratic politics. During
the 1824 campaign an old farmer came up to shake his hand at a
cattle show which Adams's friends had persuaded him to attend.
"Mr. Adams," he cried with some warmth, "I am very glad to see
you. My wife, when she was a gal, lived in your father's family;
you were then a little boy; and she has often combed your head."
"Well," said Adams awkwardly, "I suppose she combs yours now."
Crestfallen, the farmer fell back into the crowd.[12]

The campaign of 1828, when Adams ran for re-election, was sheer
torture for the high-minded New Englander. The Jacksonians, convinced that their hero had been cheated out of the election in 1824,
not only harped on the "corrupt bargain" theme; they also said
that Adams was a snobbish aristocrat ("King John the Second")
who despised the people, a hypocrite who got drunk in private and
stole public funds, a Sabbath-breaker who rode horseback "like mad"
on Sundays, and a spendthrift who squandered the people's money
by filling the White House with costly furnishings and installing a
billiard table for gambling purposes. Worst of all, they said, when
Adams was in Russia he sold a lovely American girl to the Czar
and kept a bevy of concubines for his own use.[13] The charges were
all preposterous, of course; and Adams's supporters retaliated by
charging Jackson with a long list of high crimes and misdemeanors.
In the end, though, Adams went down to inglorious defeat. He was
deeply hurt by the outcome of the election; he thought it left his
"character and reputation a wreck." "The sun of my political life
sets in the deepest gloom," he mourned.[14] Like his father before
him, he left Washington without attending the inauguration of his
successor. He expected "to go into the deepest retirement and with-
draw from all connections with public affairs."[15] He did not realize
that he had many fruitful years of public service ahead of him.

In September 1830, Adams's neighbors asked him whether he
would be willing to run for Congress from Plymouth district, even
though he had once held the highest office in the land. "No person,"
he told them, "could be degraded by serving the people as a Representative to Congress. Nor in my opinion would an ex-President of
the United States be degraded by serving as a selectman of his town,
if elected thereto by the people."[16] A few weeks later he won the

election. "No election or appointment conferred upon me," he said, "ever gave me so much pleasure."[17] When Clay asked him how he felt at "turning boy again" and warned him that he would find his situation extremely laborious, Adams responded: "I well know this; but labor I shall not refuse, so long as my hands, my eyes, and my brain, do not desert me."[18] He was as good as his word. He worked harder than just about any other Congressman during his more than seventeen years in the House and claimed no special privileges by virtue of once having been Chief Executive.

On May 18, 1836, the House of Representatives took up a resolution stipulating that *"all petitions . . . relating in any way . . . to the subject of slavery, or the abolition of slavery, shall, without being either printed or referred, be laid upon the table, and that no further action whatever shall be had thereon."* When the roll was called and Adams's name came up, he rose and shouted (above the calls to order throughout the House): "I hold the resolution to be a direct violation of the Constitution of the United States, the rules of the House, and the rights of my constituents."[19] But the resolution passed by a vote of 117 to 68; and for the next eight years Adams fought pertinaciously, with every parliamentary weapon at his disposal, to have the "gag rule," as it was called, repealed.

Adams's fight for the right of petition soon attracted wide attention. Abolitionists flooded him with anti-slavery petitions, all of which he dutifully presented to the House and all of which were "laid on the table." Slaveholders also sent him petitions, testing his consistency, but he faithfully presented them all: petitions to deport free blacks, dissolve the Union, demote him from Chairmanship of the Foreign Affairs Committee because he was crazy, and expel him from the House as a public enemy. Day after day he made the same point: that the Constitutional right of petition obligated the House to refer these petitions to the appropriate Committees for consideration. Supporters of the "gag rule" were infuriated by his persistence; the shout, "Expel him!" regularly punctuated his presentations.

Early in 1837 Adams received a petition from some slaves upholding slavery. He thought it was a hoax, but decided to make the most of it. On February 6 he got up in the House, said he held in his hand a petition purporting to come from slaves, and wondered whether it came under the gag rule. The Speaker, momentarily confused, said he couldn't answer Adams's question until he knew the contents of the document. But there were cries of "Expel him! Expel him!" throughout the House at this point and motions to burn the petition and censure Adams for presenting a petition from slaves. Finally a Virginia Congressman suggested ascertaining whether Adams had in fact "attempted to offer" this petition in violation of the gag rule and also whether the petition did indeed call for the abolition of slavery. Adams thereupon rose and said, "I did not present the petition and I appeal to the Speaker to say that I did not. . . . I intended to take the decision of the Speaker before I went one step toward presenting or offering to present that petition." Then he went on to reveal that the petition in question called for the retention, not the abolition, of slavery. This touched off a new set of motions of censure, and a Georgia Congressman suggested burning the petition and Adams with it. But the only resolution that passed was one condemning petitions from slaves. In the South, though, Adams came to be called "the Madman from Massachusetts."[20]

For eight long years Adams carried on his battle. At the opening session of each new Congress he promptly offered a motion to rescind the gag rule and was promptly voted down. But each time he gained a few more votes. On December 3, 1844, at long last, his motion to rescind carried, 105 to 80. That night he wrote in his diary: "Blessed, forever blessed be the name of God!"[21] By this time he was known as "Old Man Eloquent." Even his enemies could not help admiring his courage and integrity. In 1846, he suffered a paralytic stroke, but recovered the full use of his body and returned to Congress the following year. When he walked into the House, slightly tottering, on the morning of February 13, everyone rose spontaneously and applauded, and two Congressmen conducted him to his seat. A year later he collapsed at his desk in the House and was carried to the Speaker's room, where he died two days later. Exclaimed Thomas Hart Benton: "Where could death have found him but at the post of duty?"[22]

★ ★ ★

Father and Son

Early in 1796, President Washington commissioned John Quincy Adams minister to Portugal, but instructed him to stay at The Hague, where he was serving as American minister to the Netherlands, until his successor there was named. In June 1797, Adams left The Hague for London; he planned to get married there and then to proceed to Lisbon on his new mission.

When Adams reached London, he learned that his father, now President, had changed the assignment and made him our first minister to Prussia. The young diplomat was upset by the news; he thought it was improper to accept an appointment from his own father. He wrote his father an anecdote he had heard in London. Louis XIV, the story went, expressing surprise at the stupidity of one of the ambassadors at his court, said: "He must be the relative of some Minister!" Said young Adams: "I have no desire to be the application for a similar reflection."

President Adams exploded when he read the anecdote. "Minister's relative!" he exclaimed. "I hope the puppies don't call the President of the United States a 'Minister.' " Then he went on to chide his son for his reluctance to accept the new assignment. He, too, had had scruples about the appointment, he said, but Washington himself had said that J. Q. Adams was "the most valuable public character we have abroad" and insisted that the new President should "not withhold merited promotion from [him] because he is your son." Adams went on to point out that his son's rank, salary, and qualifications were exactly the same for the Prussian post as for Lisbon. "Your disapprobation of a nomination by the President of his own son," he went on to say, "is founded on a principle which will not bear the test. It is a false principle. It is an unjust principle. The sons of Presidents have the same claim to liberty, equality, and the benefit of the laws with all other citizens." Neither the Constitution nor federal law prohibited such appointments, he added, and disqualifying a man from holding office was ordinarily considered a severe punishment for high crimes and misdemeanors. "Upon my honor," he told his son, "if such a law existed, I would not have accepted [this] office at my time of life. . . ." J. Q. Adams gave in at this point. After getting married, he proceeded with his bride to the capital of Prussia and served there with distinction.[23]

Stickler for Detail

In New York once, Adams visited John Trumbull to look over the latter's painting of the signing of the Declaration of Independence. He didn't think much of the painting and was especially annoyed by the fact that Trumbull had put books by Locke and Sidney on the table of the president of Congress. These books, he told Trumbull, would have been read at home but not brought to the meetings. He advised Trumbull to replace them with journals.[24]

Nude Bathing

When he was President, Adams was in the habit of rising an hour or two before dawn and taking long walks or rides or going down to the Potomac for a swim in the buff. When the New York political leader Thurlow Weed first visited Washington, he determined to see the President swimming. On the morning after his arrival he rose before daylight and went to the river bank. There, he said, he saw "a gentleman, in nankeen pantaloons and a blue pea jacket, walking rapidly from the White House toward the river. . . . I moved off to a respectful distance. The President began to disrobe before he reached a tree on the brink of the river, where he deposited his clothes, and then plunged in head first and struck out fifteen or twenty rods, swimming rapidly and turning occasionally upon his back, seeming as much at ease in that element as upon terra firma. Coming out, he rubbed himself thoroughly with napkins, which he had brought for the purpose in hand. The sun had not yet risen when he had dressed himself and was returning to the presidential mansion."

Adams was an excellent swimmer, but once in a while he ran into trouble. One morning someone stole his clothes while he was swimming so he had to ask a passing boy to run to the White House and get him some others. Another time, he planned to paddle across the river in a canoe and swim back, but everything went wrong: the canoe filled with water in midstream and sank; Adams's loose sleeves filled with water and "hung like fifty-two pound weights upon my arms," making it hard for him to reach shore; and, since he lost half of his clothes in the water, he had to return to the White House only "half dressed." He did, though, have "ample leisure" while swimming, he said afterward, "to reflect upon my own indiscretion" in planning such an outing.[25]

The most famous JQA swimming story (probably spurious) involved journalist Anne Royall. She followed him to the river one day, the story goes, bent on getting an interview, and parked herself on his clothes after he entered the water. "Come here!" she cried. Surprised, Adams swam back to shore and asked, "What do you want?" "I'm Anne Royall," she snapped. "I've been trying to see you to get an interview out of you for months on the State Bank question. I have hammered at the White House and they wouldn't let me in, so I watched your movements, and this morning I stalked you from the Mansion down here. I'm sitting on your clothes and you don't get them till I get the interview. Will you give it to me or do you want to stay in there the rest of your life?" "Let me get out and dress," pleaded Adams, "and I'll promise to give you the interview. Please go behind those bushes while I make my toilet." "No, you don't," replied Royall. "You are President of the United States and there are a good many millions of people who want to know and ought to know your opinion on this Bank question. I'm going to get it. If you try to get out and get your clothes I'll scream and I just saw three fishermen around the bend. You don't get out ahead of that interview!" She got her interview while Adams was chin-deep in the water.[26]

The Ivory Cane

One evening a delegation of Adams's supporters presented him with an ivory cane, tipped with silver, with a gold-inlaid eagle for a handle. Adams's name was inscribed on the cane, and under his name were the words "Right of Petition Triumphant," with a space beneath for the date to be added when the "gag rule" against receiving anti-slavery petitions in Congress was abolished. Adams was deeply moved by the gift, but he had a firm policy of not accepting gifts as a public official. So he took the cane to the Patent Office and entrusted it to the Commissioner of Patents. And when the gag rule was finally repealed, he had the date "December 3, 1844" engraved on the cane and bequeathed it to "the people of the United States."[27]

Sibylline Leaves

During the Marquis de Lafayette's visit to the United States in 1824–25, Adams attended a dinner in his honor and proposed a toast to the "Patriots of the Revolution—like the Sibylline leaves, the fewer they become, the more precious they are!" Afterwards he was asked how he happened to conceive of such a striking toast. Adams said the toast was inspired that morning by the sight of a picture of the Sibyl that hung in the banquet hall. "How strange!" mused one man. "I have been looking at that picture for years, and that thought never *occurred to me.*"[28]

Melancholy Example

Both Josiah Quincy, President of Harvard, and John Quincy Adams rose very early in the morning; thus when they sat down for a minute or two later in the day they sometimes dozed off. One day the two of them went into Justice Joseph Story's classroom at Harvard to hear him lecture to his law students. The judge received them politely, placed them on the platform by his side, and began delivering his lecture. In a few minutes both of his visitors were sound asleep. Story stopped speaking and, pointing to Adams and Quincy, announced: "Gentlemen, you see before you a melancholy example of the evil effects of early rising!" The students' roars of laughter roused the slumberers, and Story then resumed his lecture.[29]

SEVEN

Andrew Jackson
1829–37

The Presidency of Andrew Jackson (1767–1845) got off to a raucous start. Thousands of Jacksonian enthusiasts—small farmers, rough backwoodsmen, old soldiers, Irish immigrants, city workers, small-town editors—poured into the nation's capital to see their hero inaugurated on March 4, 1829. "I never saw such a crowd here before," exclaimed Daniel Webster. "Persons have come five hundred miles to see General Jackson, and they really seem to think that the country is rescued from some awful danger!"[1] "It was like the inundation of the northern barbarians into Rome," wrote one eyewitness, "save that the tumultuous tide came in from a different point of the compass. The West and the South seemed to have precipitated themselves upon the North and overwhelmed it. . . . Strange faces filled every public place, and every face seemed to bear defiance on its brow."[2]

Jackson's inaugural address was mild enough; but when he was finished, the crowd went crazy. People swarmed past the police up the Capitol steps to reach the new President and shake his hand; and it was only with difficulty that he managed to reach his horse and set out for the White House, followed by a long line of admirers. The inaugural reception, from the beginning, was a brawl. People poured into the White House through windows as well as doors, upset waiters carrying trays of food, broke china and glassware, overturned tables, brushed bric-a-brac from mantles and walls, spilled whiskey and chicken and squirted tobacco juice on the carpets, and stood with muddy boots on the damask-covered chairs in order to get a good look at "Old Hickory." Jackson finally escaped through the back door and returned to his hotel, while waiters succeeded in restoring order only by placing big tubs of punch on the White House lawn, luring people outside, and locking the doors behind them. Genteel Washingtonians were horrified. It was a "regular Saturnalia," according to one Congressman.[3] "I never saw such a mixture," exclaimed Justice Joseph Story; "the reign of KING MOB seemed triumphant."[4] But Amos Kendall, a Jacksonian editor from Kentucky, saw it differently. "It was a proud day for the people," he insisted. "General Jackson is *their own* president."[5] And Francis Scott Key, watching Jackson take the oath of office, exclaimed, "It is beautiful, it is sublime!"[6]

Jackson was by no means one of the masses himself when he became President. He was a well-to-do Tennessee planter owning hundreds of acres of land and a host of slaves. He had been born, it is true, to poverty in a log cabin on the Carolina frontier and orphaned at an early age. But during his long and colorful career as frontier lawyer, storekeeper, Indian fighter, and military commander, he had risen gradually to affluence; indeed, many of his habits and manners were those of an aristocrat. Nevertheless, he still displayed some of the rough-and-ready ways of his early frontier life; and it was not difficult for the Democrats who enticed him into presidential politics in the 1820's to present him to voters as a down-to-earth man of the people ("the Farmer of Tennessee") as well as the hero of the Battle of New Orleans ("Old Hickory"). Upper-class Americans, particularly in the Northeast, saw only the frontiersman; they regarded him as a crude, ignorant, and bellicose brawler who would probably shoot down White House visitors in cold blood if they said something he didn't like. During the 1828 campaign, the Whigs circulated a thick pamphlet entitled *Reminiscences; or an Extract from the Catalogue of General Jackson's Youthful Indiscretions, between the Age of Twenty-Three and Sixty,* which listed fourteen fights, duels, brawls, and shooting and cutting affairs in which Jackson "killed, slashed, and clawed various American citizens."[7] There was some truth in the charges. As a young man Jackson had been involved in a series of shooting matches. He seems to have taken seriously the advice his mother was said to have given him: "Never sue for assault or slander; settle them cases yourself."[8]

Jackson's fights usually involved his beloved wife Rachel. Rachel was unhappily married when Jackson first met her in a Nashville boarding house; and when her first husband left her to seek a divorce, she and Jackson married. Two years later they learned that there had been no divorce after all and that Rachel's former husband was now suing for divorce on the ground that his wife had been living in sin for two years. As soon as the divorce came through, the Jacksons were promptly re-married; but there was much malicious talk around town about Rachel's "adultery." Jackson made it clear that he would defend his wife's honor to the death. "For the man who dared breathe her name except in honor," said James Parton, "he kept pistols in perfect condition for thirty-seven years."[9]

Jackson's first big fight, with John Sevier, Governor of Tennessee, came in 1803. Jackson and Sevier met one day on the street in Nashville, got into an argument, and when Jackson mentioned his services to the country, Sevier sneered: "Services? I know of no great services you have rendered the country, except taking a trip to Natchez with another man's wife." "Great God!" shouted Jackson, "do you mention *her* sacred name?" and the shooting began at once. Fortunately, no one was hurt; and a later Jackson-Sevier confrontation also ended bloodlessly.[10] But the Dickinson affair, which came three years later, had a tragic outcome. Charles Dickinson, a wealthy young Nashville dandy, was the best pistol shot in Tennessee, and when Jackson took him on he considered himself practically a dead man. But he did not flinch from what he considered his duty. When Dickinson, during a quarrel over a horse-race wager, profaned the "sacred name" of Rachel, Jackson challenged him to a duel. The two men met across the Kentucky line, and eight paces (twenty-four feet) were measured off. "Are you ready?" asked John Overton, the second. "I am ready," said Dickinson. "Fere!" called Overton, in his country accent. Dickinson raised his pistol quickly and fired; but because of the loose coat Jackson was wearing the bullet fractured a rib instead of piercing the heart. "My God!" exclaimed Dickinson, "have I missed him?" Jackson then raised his pistol slowly and squeezed the trigger; but the hammer stopped at half-cock. He drew it back, aimed again, and this time killed Dickinson. "I intended to kill him," he said afterward. "I would have stood up long enough to kill him if he had put a bullet in my brain."[11]

In 1813, in a fight with Thomas Hart Benton and his brother Jesse, Jackson received a bullet which remained in his left arm for years. When in 1832 he finally had a surgeon remove the bullet, someone suggested giving it back to Benton, now a Senator from Missouri and a warm supporter of Jackson. Benton declined the offer, however, pointing out that twenty years' possession made the bullet Jackson's property. Told that it was only nineteen years, Benton said, "Oh, well, in consideration of the extra care he has taken of it—keeping it constantly about his person, and so on—I'll waive the odd year." Benton used to tell people: "General Jackson was a very great man. I shot him, sir."[12] "Yes," he liked to say, "I had a fight with Jackson. A fellow was hardly in the fashion who didn't."[13]

There were no shoot-outs after Jackson entered the White House, but his eight years as President were stormy. He took on the Second Bank of the United States, which he regarded as a dangerous monopoly inimical to the interests of the majority of Americans, vetoed a B.U.S. recharter bill in 1832, and, by withholding government deposits from the bank, succeeded in ruining it. He also took on South Carolina when it threatened to nullify a tariff law passed by Congress, and, by announcing he would use military force to secure compliance with the law, forced the nullificationists to back down. His confrontation with John C. Calhoun, his Vice-President but a leading nullificationist, was dramatic. Learning that the South Carolinian and other "nullies" were planning to use a Jefferson birthday dinner in Washington on April 13, 1830, as an occasion for promoting states'-rights sentiments, Jackson went to the banquet with feelings, it was said, more suitable "to the field of battle than to a festive board."[14] When he was called on to propose a toast, Jackson got up, lifted his wine glass, and, looking Calhoun straight in the eye, exclaimed: "OUR FEDERAL UNION: IT MUST BE PRESERVED!" Calhoun then raised his glass, his hand shaking, with some of the wine trickling down the side of the glass, and responded: "The Union: Next to our Liberty the most dear!"[15] Having taken on Calhoun, South Carolina, and the B.U.S., Jackson also defied the Supreme Court. When Chief Justice John Marshall rendered a decision favorable to the Cherokee Indians in Georgia, Jackson, an old Indian fighter, is said (with some exaggeration) to have cried: "John Marshall has made his decision. Now let him enforce it!"[16] And he refused to carry it out. Jackson may have been a man of the people; but his democratic sentiments included neither Indians nor blacks.

In foreign affairs as well Jackson was at times bellicose. In 1835 he took on the French. When France delayed paying some money it had agreed by treaty to pay the United States, Jackson ordered

the U.S. Navy to prepare for action and, in a belligerent message
to Congress, urged the seizing of French property in the United
States. The French were furious, and for a time the two nations
seemed on the brink of war. But Britain offered to mediate the dispute,
and in the end a peaceful settlement was reached. During the negotiations, Jackson refused to apologize to France, but he did say he
hadn't meant to insult it, and, somewhat mollified, the French began
making their payments. A cartoon of the time shows Jackson shaking
his cane at the French King and saying, " 'Tis well you have paid
me, or by the Eternal!" and the French King exclaiming, "Not another word of apology, dear General!"[17]

In 1833, Jackson toured New England. He made such a good
impression in Boston that President Josiah Quincy of Harvard called
a special meeting of the Board of Overseers to authorize the granting
of an honorary degree of Doctor of Laws to the President. John
Quincy Adams, one of the Overseers, objected strongly and asked
Quincy if there was not some way Harvard could avoid giving the
President this honor. "As the people have twice decided this man
knows enough law to be their ruler," said Quincy, "it is not for
Harvard College to maintain that they are mistaken."[18] The Overseers
voted the degree, but Adams refused to attend the ceremony honoring
Jackson. "I would not be present," he said, "to see my darling Har-
vard disgrace herself by conferring a Doctor's degree upon a barba-
rian who could scarcely spell his own name."[19]

The Harvard ceremony went swimmingly despite Adams's dissent,
and Old Hickory was a great success with the students. Francis
Bowen, leader of the Class of 1833, delivered a salutatory in Latin,
on behalf of the students, which ended with the words "Harvard
welcomes Jackson the President. She embraces Jackson the Patriot,"
which produced wild applause in the audience. Jackson turned to
Levy Woodbury, his Secretary of the Navy, and asked for a transla-
tion. "You're a college man, Woodbury," he said. "My Latin is a
little rusty. All I can make out is something about patriots." Woodbury quickly translated, and Jackson exclaimed: "A splendid compliment, sir, a splendid compliment; but why talk about so live a thing
as patriotism in a dead language?" When the exercises were over,
the students filed past the President to shake his hand and, "to
the infinite edification and amusement of the grizzly old warrior,"
greeted him with his new title, "Doctor Jackson." Just before leaving,

Jackson told the students: "I shall have to speak in English, not being able to return your compliment in what appears to be the language of Harvard. All the Latin I know is *E pluribus unum.*" At this, Woodbury reported, "There was even louder and longer applause than that which greeted Mr. Bowen's happy phrase; but this was probably because the people could understand General Jackson's Latin better than they could Mr. Bowen's."[20] Not long afterward, someone made up a story of how a man in the audience interrupted a speech the President was making a few days later: "You must give 'em a little Latin, Doctor!" "*E pluribus unum,*" Jackson is supposed to have shouted back, "my friends, *sine qua non!*"[21]

Jackson's supporters applauded his forthrightness, fearlessness, generosity, decisiveness, and championship of the people. His enemies thought he was reckless, intolerant, wrong-headed, and dictatorial; and they blamed the Panic of 1837 on his financial policies. But everyone—friend and foe alike—agreed on one thing: when Jackson made up his mind to do something, he did it regardless of opposition. Before he died, according to a story that may or may not be true, someone asked Alfred, one of Jackson's slaves, whether he thought his master would get into heaven on Judgment Day. "If General Jackson takes it into his head to git to heaven," he exclaimed, "who's gwine to keep him out?"[22]

★ ★ ★

Spartan Mother

Jackson, it was said, had a "Spartan mother." When he was about five years old, she saw him crying one day. "Stop that, Andrew," she ordered. "Don't let me see you cry again! Girls were made to cry; not boys!" "Well, then, mother, what are boys made for?" asked Andy. "To fight!" she told him. After that, Andy never cried again.

When Andy was about twelve and going to school one day, a fellow about eighteen or nineteen stopped him and gave him a severe thrashing. Andy's uncle wanted to have the young man arrested and prosecuted for assault and battery. "No, sir!" exclaimed Jackson's mother. "No son of mine shall ever appear as complaining witness in a case of assault and battery! If he gets hold of a fellow too big for him, let him wait till he grows some and then try it again!"[23]

Unconquerable

As a boy, Andy was good at running and riding, but he was too light to be a good wrestler. He remained unconquerable all the same. "I could throw him three times out of four," recalled one of his classmates, "but he would never *stay throwed.* He was dead game and never *would* give up." One day some of his friends gave him a gun to fire that was loaded to the muzzle. The recoil sent him sprawling to the ground. Instantly he jumped to his feet and blazed: "By God, if one of you laughs, I'll kill him!"[24]

Devil-ope-ment

Jackson always pronounced the word "development" as though it were written "devil-*ope*-ment," with the accent on *ope.* He may have learned this when he was a boy from a teacher named Waddell. Once when he was President he pronounced the word this way in conversing with a foreign minister who, though not English, had been educated in England and prided himself on his correct use of the English language. The ambassador lifted his eyebrows slightly and went out of his way to pronounce the word correctly in the conversation that followed. Jackson appeared not to notice the rebuke and a little later said "devil-*ope*-ment" again, whereupon the fastidious minister ventured once more to give the word its proper accent. "I repeat," continued Jackson, "this measure is essential to the devil-*ope*-ment of our resources." "Really, sir," replied the ambassador, "I consider the de-*vel*-opment of your country"—with a marked accent on the *vel.* Upon this, Jackson exclaimed: "Excuse me, sir. You may call it de-*vel*-opment, if you please; but *I* say devil-*ope*-ment, and will say devil-*ope*-ment as long as I revere the memory of good old Dr. Waddell!"[25]

Christmas Prank

When Jackson was living in Salisbury, North Carolina, he attended a dancing school, where he learned many of the social graces which he later displayed as President. But he also was something of a prankster. When the dancing school appointed him one of the managers of the Christmas ball, he sent invitations to two of the town's prostitutes, "to see what would come of it." On the evening of the ball, the two women appeared on the dance floor in gaudy clothing, bringing the festivities to a startled halt. While all the ladies withdrew, giggling, to one side of the room, the two prostitutes were quickly ushered out. Taken to task for what had happened, Jackson apologized meekly and said he had never dreamed that the women would actually show up at the party.[26]

Celebration

"Andrew Jackson," said an old Salisbury resident, "was the most roaring, rollicking, game-cocking, horse-racing, card-playing, mischievous fellow, that ever lived in Salisbury." One evening young Andy and some of his buddies decided to celebrate in the local tavern. It was a hilarious evening. Toward midnight they decided to smash the glasses and decanters they had been using. Then they decided to destroy the table. Next they destroyed the chairs and other furniture in the room. Finally they ripped up the curtains and the clothes they were wearing, piled them up, and set fire to them. The room was a shambles when they staggered away in the wee hours of the morning. Many years later, when Jackson began to be mentioned for the Presidency, a Salisbury lady was shocked. "What! Jackson for President!" she cried. "*Jackson? Andrew* Jackson? The Jackson that used to live in Salisbury? Why, when he was here, he was such a rake that my husband would not bring him into the house! It is true, he *might* have taken him out to the stable to weigh horses for a race, and might drink a glass of whiskey with him *there.* Well, if Andrew Jackson can be President, anybody can!" Years later, Jackson admitted, "Yes, I lived at old Salisbury. I was but a raw lad then, but I did my best."[27]

The Dancing Wagoners

One day in 1809 when Jackson was riding along the lonely wilderness road between Nashville and Knoxville, he was stopped by two burly wagoners, who ordered him to get out of his carriage and dance for them. Pretending to be frightened, Jackson told them he couldn't dance without his slippers and that his slippers were in a trunk strapped behind his carriage. The wagoners told him to get the slippers. Jackson opened his trunk, took out a pair of pistols, and confronting the wagoners, shouted: "Now, you infernal villains, you shall dance for me. Dance. . . . DANCE!" And a lively dance they did for him.[28]

To the Rescue

When Jackson's friend Patten Anderson got into trouble, which was often, Old Hickory always helped him out. On an afternoon in 1809, when Jackson was attending the races in Clover Bottom, Tennessee, Anderson got into a fight with a group of people at the end of a long table where dinner was being served. When someone remarked, "They'll finish Patten Anderson this time, I *do* expect," Jackson sprang to his feet, jumped atop the table, and started wading through the dishes to rescue his friend. As he neared the other end of the table, where the fighting was going on, he suddenly opened his tobacco box and then shut it with a loud click. "I'm coming, Patten," he roared. At this, some of the spectators began yelling, "Don't fire! Don't fire!" The sound of the tobacco box and the yells of "Don't fire" caught the ears of Anderson's enemies, who scattered at once, leaving Jackson's friend alone and unharmed.[29]

Jackson's Bacon

In August 1788, Colonel Waightstill Avery, an experienced older lawyer, opposed young Jackson in a suit before the Superior Court at Jonesborough, Tennessee. In an address to the court he teased Jackson for having quoted so much from Matthew Bacon's *Abridgement of the Law.* When he finished, Jackson cried angrily, "I may not know as much law as there is in Bacon but I know enough not to take illegal fees!" The courtroom became deadly still. Avery demanded to know whether Jackson was implying that he took illegal fees. "I do, sir," said Jackson. "It's false as hell!" shouted Avery. Jackson at once wrote out a challenge on the margin of a page in Bacon's *Abridgement,* tore it out, and handed it to the Colonel with a bow.

Avery didn't want to fight Jackson; in fact, he rather liked the short-tempered young lawyer. He had taken an unwarranted fee on one occasion, it is true; but he had returned it at once when he discovered his error. His reputation for probity was unquestioned in Jonesborough, so he saw no need to defend his honor. But Jackson was adamant. He was not accusing Avery of dishonesty, he told people who tried to mediate the dispute; he was simply charging him with ignorance of the statute governing fees. But he had no alternative except to fight, he insisted, after what Avery had said to him in court.

The next morning Avery entered the courtroom without taking any notice of Jackson's challenge. Jackson then wrote out another challenge and sent it over to him. "My character you have injured," he wrote; "and further you have insulted me in the presence of a court and a large audience I therefore call upon you as a gentleman to give me satisfaction. . . ." Avery accepted Jackson's challenge this time, and the two met on a hill near the town at sunset. But by this time the peacemakers had succeeded in patching things up; Jackson and Avery both fired in the air, then shook hands. "Mr. Jackson," said Avery afterward, producing a package, "I feared that in the event of my wounding you mortally you would be inconsolable in your last moments without your beloved Bacon." Jackson unwrapped the package and found it contained smoked pork. Everyone laughed; though for a moment or two it looked as though Jackson was going to lose his temper again. He didn't; but it was a long time before he saw the humor in Avery's gesture.[30]

Judge Jackson

One of the most popular Jackson stories is about his encounter with a bully named Russell Bean when he was presiding judge in a little Tennessee village in 1798. Bean, according to this story, started parading before the courthouse one day, armed with pistol and bowie knife, cursing the judge, the jury, and everyone else assembled there in a loud voice. "Sheriff," cried Jackson, "arrest that man for contempt of court, and confine him." Out went the sheriff; but he soon returned with the news that he found it impossible to make the arrest. "Summon a posse, then," said Jackson, "and bring him before me." The sheriff went out again, but he was unable to assemble a posse, since Bean threatened "to shoot the first skunk that comes within ten feet of him." Jackson exploded. "Mr. Sheriff," he cried, "since you cannot obey my orders, summon me; yes, sir, summon me." "Well, Judge," said the sheriff, "if you say so, though I don't like to do it; but if you will try, why I suppose I must summon you." "Very well," said Jackson, getting up and walking toward the door, "I adjourn this court ten minutes." When Jackson got outside, Bean was standing in the middle of a crowd of people, blaspheming at a terrible rate, flourishing his weapons, and vowing death and destruction to anybody who molested him. But Jackson walked calmly up to him, pistols in hand, and, eyes blazing, confronted him angrily. "Now," he roared, "surrender, you infernal villain, this very instant, or I'll blow you through!" Bean eyed Jackson a moment, then meekly surrendered. "There, judge," he said, "it's no use, I give in." He was led away to jail. A few days later someone asked Bean why he had knuckled under to Jackson. "Why," he said, "when he came up, I looked him in the eye, and I saw shoot, and there wasn't any shoot in nary other eye in the crowd; and so I says to myself, says I, hoss, it's about time to sing small, and so I did."

In his old age, Jackson wrote out an account of what had happened, correcting the story in one important detail. He did not ask the sheriff to summon him, he declared; it was the sheriff who, unable to cope with Bean, summoned Jackson and two other judges as a posse, but only Jackson agreed to act.[31]

Christmas Dinner

Just before the Battle of New Orleans, British Admiral Cochrane declared, "I shall eat my Christmas dinner in New Orleans." Told of this, Jackson remarked, "Perhaps so; but I shall have the honor of presiding at that dinner."[32]

Elevation

During the Battle of New Orleans, it was said, Jackson strode through the powder smoke to see the effect of his artillery fire and gave the order: "Boys, elevate them guns a little lower!"[33]

Contempt Citation

At the time of the Battle of New Orleans, a local editor attacked Jackson in his newspaper. When the battle was over Jackson put him in jail. The editor appealed to federal judge Dominick A. Hall and obtained a writ of habeas corpus. Jackson then had the judge jailed, too. But as soon as Jackson lifted martial law, Hall returned to his bench and summoned Jackson before him on a contempt cita-

tion. Jackson appeared and paid a $1000 fine. As he left the court-
room, he was surrounded by an angry mob of people who were
eager to avenge him. But Jackson stood up in his carriage and silenced
them. "I have," he cried, "during the invasion, exerted every one
of my faculties for the defense and preservation of the Constitution
and the laws. . . . Considering obedience to the laws, even when
we think them unjustly applied, as the first duty of a citizen, I did
not hesitate to comply with the sentence you have heard, and I
entreat you to remember the example."[34]

Jackson and Cartwright

One Sunday in October 1816, when Methodist evangelist Peter Cartwright was preaching in Nashville, General Jackson entered the
church, walked slowly up the aisle, and then, since all the seats
were taken, leaned against a pillar to listen. At Jackson's appearance,
one of the other preachers, Brother Mac, tugged at Cartwright's
coat and whispered, "General Jackson has come in—General Jackson
has come in!" Indignantly, Cartwright cried aloud, "Who is General
Jackson? If he don't get his soul converted, God will damn him as
quick as he would a Guinea negro!" The congregation laughed at
this, and so did Jackson. But after the service, Brother Mac rushed
over to Jackson's hotel to apologize for Cartwright's remarks. An
hour or two later Jackson ran into Cartwright on the street in front
of the hotel and with a big smile held out his hand and cried: "Mr.
Cartwright, you are a man after my own heart. I am very much
surprised at Mr. Mac, to think he would suppose that I would be
offended at you. No, sir; I told him that I highly approved of your
independence; that a minister of Jesus Christ ought to love everybody
and fear no mortal man. I told Mr. Mac that if I had a few thousand
such independent, fearless officers as you were, and a well drilled
army, I could take old England!"[35]

Jackson's Blessing

After Rachel joined the Presbyterian church, Jackson, in deference
to her wishes, asked a blessing before each meal. One day the Jacksons
were entertaining guests at the Hermitage, their plantation in Tennessee, and Jackson began telling a battle story with great animation,
interlarding it with a profusion of expletives. Rachel interrupted to

say, "Mr. Jackson, will you ask a blessing?" Jackson stopped at
once, pronounced a reverential blessing, and then resumed his story
in the same tone and language as before.[36]

Sailing with Jackson

In the summer of 1833, when President Jackson was sailing down
Chesapeake Bay in an old steamboat and the waves were high, an
elderly gentleman began expressing fears for their safety. "You are
uneasy," noted Jackson; "you never sailed with *me* before, I see."[37]

Vote Enough

A man called on President Jackson to plead the case of a soldier
who had lost his leg on a battlefield and needed to retain a small
postmastership in order to support his family. "But I must tell you,"
he said frankly, "that he voted against you." "If he lost a leg fighting
for his country," said Jackson, "that is vote enough for me."[38]

Better Office

A clergyman called on President Jackson several times seeking a
federal appointment. "Are you not a Christian minister?" Jackson
finally asked him. "I am." "Well," said Jackson, "if you discharge
the duties of that office, which is better than any I can confer, you
will have no time for any other."[39]

The General's Pipe

A Congressman whose heart was set on a foreign mission had tried
for some time without success to get the appointment. At length
he decided to use more indirect tactics. One day he called on the
President, who, as usual, was smoking his pipe. "General Jackson,"
he said, "I am about to ask you a favor—a favor, sir, that will
cost you nothing, and the government nothing, but will gratify me
exceedingly." "It's granted, sir," said Jackson. "What is it?" "Well,
General," said the Congressman, "I have an old father at home
who has as great an esteem for your character as one man can
have for another. Before I left home, he charged me to get for him,
if possible, one of General Jackson's pipes, and that is the favor I

now ask of you." "Oh, certainly," said Jackson, laughing and ringing the bell. When the servant came, he told him to bring two or three clean pipes. "Excuse me," said the Congressman, "but may I ask you for that very pipe you have just been smoking?" "This one?" said Jackson. "By all means, if you prefer it." He began to empty it of ashes, but the Congressman interrupted him again. "No, General," he said, "don't empty out the tobacco. I want that pipe, just as it is, just as it left your lips." When Jackson obligingly handed it to him, he put it carefully in a piece of paper, thanked Jackson for the precious gift, and left the room with the air of a man who had just achieved his highest ambition. Three weeks later he got his appointment and departed on a mission to one of the South American countries.[40]

Furriner

When the new minister from Lisbon arrived in Washington, Secretary of State Louis McLane made an appointment for him to be presented to the President. The hour was set, and McLane expected the man to call at the State Department. But the Portuguese diplomat misunderstood McLane's French and proceeded to the White House instead. When he rang the bell, the door was opened by the Irish porter, Jimmy O'Neill. "Je suis venu voir Monsieur le President," said the minister. "What the deuce does he mean?" muttered Jimmy to himself. "He says President, though, and I suppose he wants to see the General." Jimmy ushered him into the green room where Jackson was smoking his corncob pipe with great composure. The minister made his bow to the President and addressed him in French. "What does the fellow say, Jimmy?" asked Jackson. "De'll knows, sir," said Jimmy, "I reckon he's a furriner." "Try him in Irish, Jimmy," suggested Jackson. Jimmy tried a bit of this, but the minister only shrugged his shoulders and said, "Plait-il?" "Och!" exclaimed Jimmy, "he can't go Irish, sir. He's French to be sure!" "Send for the French cook," said Jackson, "and let him try if he can find out what the gentleman wants." The cook was hurried out from the kitchen, sleeves rolled up, apron on, and carving-knife in hand. The Portuguese minister, seeing the cook with his knife, rushed for the door, but Jimmy blocked his way. At Jackson's order, the cook began questioning the minister in French and relaying his answers to Jackson in English. At this juncture Secretary McLane arrived and at once presented the man formally to the President. Ever after, it is said, Jackson resented any allusion to the incident.[41]

The Eaton Malaria

For a time the Jackson administration was plagued by what Martin Van Buren called the "Eaton malaria." Jackson's Secretary of War, John Eaton, took up with an attractive brunette named Peggy O'Neale, daughter of a Georgetown tavern-keeper; and when her husband, a navy purser who spent most of his time at sea, committed suicide, Jackson advised Eaton to marry her. Eaton told Jackson that Peggy's reputation was none too good in Washington. "Well," said Jackson philosophically, "your marrying her will disprove these charges, and restore Peggy's good name."

Eaton married Peggy; but her name remained unrestored. Clergymen denounced her as a wicked woman, and the wives of Jackson's Cabinet members refused to have anything to do with "that hussy." Vice-President John C. Calhoun, whose wife was foremost among the Washington ladies blackballing Peggy, said that "the quarrels of women, like those of the Medes and Persians, admitted of neither inquiry nor explanation." Actually, he knew better; with political ambitions of his own, he was using his wife to disgrace Eaton, whose influence with Jackson he deeply resented.

Jackson remembered the slights to his beloved Rachel (who had died shortly after his election in 1828). Roused to wrath (particularly against the Calhouns) by the way Mrs. Eaton was being snubbed, he determined to stand by his "little friend Peg" to the end. "Mrs. Jackson," he told one of Peggy's critics, "to the last moment of her life, believed Mrs. Eaton to be an innocent and much injured woman." And he added: "Female virtue is like a tender and delicate flower; let but the breath of suspicion rest upon it, and it withers and perhaps perishes forever."

When two clergymen criticized the Eatons, Jackson invited them to a Cabinet meeting to discuss the subject. He opened the meeting by saying that Christians must constantly war against the meanness of calumny, then asked the ministers what they had to say. When the clergymen admitted there was no evidence to convict Eaton of improper conduct, Jackson snapped, "Nor Mrs. Eaton, either." "On that point," said one of the ministers, "I would rather not give an opinion." "She is as chaste as a virgin!" exclaimed Jackson angrily (leading Daniel Webster to remark, when he heard of this statement, "Age cannot wither her, nor time stale her infinite virginity").

Things reached an impasse. The ladies of Washington flatly refused to attend White House receptions where "Pothouse Peg," as they called her, was present. Emily Donelson, wife of Jackson's secretary (who became hostess for Jackson after Rachel's death), also refused to have anything to do with her and was sent packing. Only Martin Van Buren, a widower, and the British and Russian ministers, both bachelors, attended White House parties in honor of Mrs. Eaton. Finally Secretary of State Van Buren solved Jackson's problem by persuading Eaton to resign from the Cabinet, then resigning himself. The rest of the Cabinet (which included Calhoun men whom Jackson wished to get rid of) had to follow suit. Jackson then formed a Cabinet of loyal Jacksonians and made Eaton governor of Florida territory and Van Buren minister to England. "It is odd enough," Webster told a friend perspicaciously, "that the consequences of this dispute in the social and fashionable world are producing great political effects, and may very probably determine who shall be successor to the present Chief Magistrate." In 1832, Van Buren replaced Calhoun as Jackson's Vice-President; in 1837 he succeeded Jackson as President.[42]

Jackson in Florida

Jackson liked to boast that his foot "had never pressed foreign soil" and that, "born and raised in the United States, he had never been out of the country." One day when he made this boast, Mrs. Eaton said mischievously, "But how about Florida, General?" "That's so," admitted Jackson (who had invaded Florida in 1818 in pursuit of some Indians and had hoisted the American flag at St. Marks). "I did go to Florida when it was a foreign country; but I had quite forgotten that fact when I made the remark." "I expect, General," said Mrs. Eaton, "you forgot that Florida was foreign when you made the trip!" "Yes, yes, maybe so," said Jackson. "Some weak-kneed people in our own country seemed to think so." "Oh, well, General, never mind," said Mrs. Eaton. "Florida didn't stay foreign long after you had been there!" This little exchange with Mrs. Eaton was a favorite anecdote of Jackson's. Whenever he told it he would add: "Smartest little woman in America, sir; by all odds, the smartest!"[43]

Deserves Credit

When Congress assembled on December 7, 1829, Jackson sent in his first annual message, which attracted a great deal of attention. Meeting his old friend General Robert Armstrong the next day, Jackson said, "Well, Bob, what do the people say of my message?" "They say," replied Armstrong, "that it is first-rate, but nobody believes that you wrote it." "Well," said Old Hickory good-naturedly, "don't I deserve just as much credit for picking out the man who could write it?"[44]

Important Exceptions

In 1833, Jackson consulted a doctor in Philadelphia for pains in his side and bleeding of the lungs. "Now, Doctor," he told the physician after describing the symptoms, "I can do any thing you think proper to order, and bear as much as most men. There are only two things I can't give up; one is coffee, and the other is tobacco."[45]

Premeditated Madness

During the winter of 1833 and spring of 1834, friends of Nicholas Biddle, director of the Second Bank of the United States, and delegations of businessmen from various cities called on Jackson to protest his anti-Bank policy and tell him how damaging it was to the nation's economy. Jackson became weary of such callers and finally staged a dramatic outburst to discourage further visitations. When a delegation of businessmen from Philadelphia came to tell him they were insolvent, Jackson pretended to go into a towering rage. "Insolvent, do you say?" he yelled, jumping to his feet. "What do you come to me for, then? Go to Nicholas Biddle. We have no money here, gentlemen, Biddle has all the money. He has millions of specie in his vaults, at this moment, laying idle, and yet you come to *me* to save you from breaking. I tell you, gentlemen, it's all politics!" Shocked by Jackson's vehemence, the delegation quickly left the room, thinking he had lost his mind. When they were gone, Jackson settled back in his chair, reached for his pipe, and started chuckling. "They thought I was mad," he said contentedly. Commented an intimate associate of Jackson for forty years, "No man knew better than Andrew Jackson when to get into a passion and when not."[46]

Visitors from Baltimore

Some frightened Congressmen came running to the White House one day with rumors that a group of people from Baltimore were threatening to camp on Capitol Hill and stay there until Jackson restored government funds to the Bank of the United States. "Gentlemen," thundered Jackson, "I shall be glad to see this mob on Capitol Hill. I will fix their heads on the iron palisades around the square to assist your deliberations. The leaders I will hang as high as Haman to deter forever all attempts to control the legislature of the Congress by intimidation and design." Exit Congressmen in a hurry.

No mob laid siege to the Capitol; but a delegation of Baltimoreans did call on the President to protest his bank policy. "General," said the chairman of the group, "the committee has the honor to be delegated by the citizens of Baltimore, without regard to party, to come to you, sir, the fountain head, for relief. . . ." "Relief, sir!" cried Jackson. "Come not to me, sir! Go to the monster [Bank of the United States]! It is folly, sir, to talk to Andrew Jackson." "Sir," said the man, "the currency of the country is in a dreadful situation." "Sir, you keep one-sided company," retorted Jackson. "Andrew Jackson has fifty letters from persons of all parties daily on this subject. Sir, he has more and better information than you, sir, or any of you." "The people, sir . . .," interposed the man. "The people!" cried Jackson. "The people, sir, are with me!"[47]

Jackson and the Nullies

When a South Carolina Congressman tried to explain the position of the nullificationists in his state, Jackson told him bluntly: "Tell them that they can talk and write resolutions and print threats to their hearts' content. But if one drop of blood be shed there in defiance of the laws of the United States, I will hang the first man of them I can get my hands on to the first tree I can find." Afterward, South Carolina Senator Robert Hayne expressed doubt that Jackson would really hang anyone, but Senator Thomas Hart Benton sharply disagreed. "I tell you, Hayne," he said, "when Jackson begins to talk about hanging, they can begin to look for the ropes."[48]

As High as Haman

Once, toward the end of Jackson's life, Dr. Edgar, Presbyterian minister in Nashville, asked him: "What would you have done with Calhoun and the other nullifers if they had kept on?" Jackson's response was immediate. "Hung them, sir, as high as Haman! They should have been a terror to traitors to all time, and posterity would have pronounced it the best act of my life." A few days later, Jackson began reminiscing about his Presidency and suddenly asked Edgar: "What act in my Administration, in your opinion, will posterity condemn with the greatest severity?" Edgar suggested it might be the removal of deposits from the Bank of the United States. "Oh, no," cried Jackson. "Then it may be the specie circular?" "Not at all!" insisted Jackson. "What is it, then?" asked Edgar. "I can tell you," said Jackson, rising in his bed, with his eyes flashing, "I can tell you; posterity will condemn me more because I was persuaded not to hang John C. Calhoun as a traitor than for any other act in my life!"[49]

Slayer of Abel

Visiting the United States in the 1830's, British writer Harriet Martineau heard about a New England Sunday School teacher who asked her class the name of the slayer of Abel. "General Jackson," piped up one of her pupils.[50]

Martin Van Buren
1837–41

While the electoral votes for the eighth President of the United States were being counted in the presence of the two Houses of Congress, Senator Henry Clay remarked politely to Vice-President Martin Van Buren: "It is a cloudy day, sir!" Replied Van Buren: "The sun will shine on the 4th of March, sir!"[1] He was right. On inaugural morning, March 4, 1837, the sun shone brightly; there wasn't a cloud in the sky. But Van Buren, handpicked by Andrew Jackson to succeed him in the White House, was completely overshadowed by his predecessor at the inauguration. People listened respectfully to Van Buren's inaugural address, but when they caught sight of Jackson afterward, they gave him a tremendous ovation. "For once," remarked Senator Thomas Hart Benton, "the rising sun was eclipsed by the setting sun."[2]

Van Buren (1782–1862) was never a popular leader like Jackson. In New York, where he rose to political prominence, and in Washington afterward, he was primarily a party organizer, a political strategist, a manipulator of men, and a skilled wheeler-dealer, not a charismatic public figure like Old Hickory. Genial, suave, tactful, good-humored, and something of a dandy, he carefully avoided Jackson's forthrightness in public; and the moral obdurateness of John Quincy Adams was utterly foreign to his spirit. He came, in fact, to be known as a waffler; and the adjective "van-burenish" was coined to describe the kind of political evasiveness which he seemed to represent.[3] Van Buren, said John Randolph of Roanoke, "rowed to his object with muffled oars." None of the nicknames he received—"the Red Fox of Kinderhook," "the Little Magician," "the Flying Dutchman," "the American Talleyrand"—was especially complimentary. "Even his best friends," said a close acquaintance, "were apprehensive that he was overcautious and lacked the moral or political courage . . . to meet those exigencies which might require bold and decisive action."[4] The toast he proposed at the famous Jefferson birthday dinner in 1830 at which Jackson toasted Union and Calhoun states' rights was typical: "Mutual forbearance and reciprocal concessions. . . ."[5]

Even before Van Buren became President, the noun "non-committalism" had become popular in Washington for describing his customary public stance. Once, according to a widely circulated story, a Senator accepted a bet that he could trap Van Buren into committing himself to some positive belief. "Matt," he said, "it's been rumored that the sun rises in the East. Do you believe it?" "Well, Senator," replied Van Buren, "I understand that's the common acceptance, but as I never get up till after dawn, I can't really say." According to another popular yarn, two newspapermen saw Van Buren leaning against the railing of a Hudson River steamboat. One of them bet the other that he could smoke him out on some issue. "Fine day, isn't it, Mr. Van Buren?" he said tentatively. "Now that depends on what you mean by a fine day," was the response. "There are all sorts of fine days. This particular one. . . ." In his *Autobiography,* Van Buren good-naturedly mentions the first of these tales but, characteristically, neglects to comment on its authenticity.[6]

In July 1827, Van Buren made a puzzling speech about the tariff in Albany, New York. He was a New York Senator at the time, speaking to a group of businessmen seeking greater "promotion of the interests of wool growers and manufacturers." In his address, Van Buren (who disliked protectionism) first explained why he had been absent from the Senate on the day a tariff bill sponsored by Henry Clay had come up for a vote, then gave a rather involved explanation of what he thought about the bill's various provisions. After that, he stated his views on tariffs in general and concluded by declaring that he would support any tariff which was "temperate and wise and therefore salutary" in promoting "every branch of domestic production and industry. . . ." The audience applauded enthusiastically when he had finished, but afterward a man named

Wood turned to Van Buren's friend Benjamin Knower and said somewhat uncertainly, "Mr. Knower, that was a very able speech." "Yes, very able." There was a pause; and then Wood asked, "Mr. Knower, on which side of the tariff question was it?" Sighed Knower: "That is the very point I was thinking about when you first spoke to me, Mr. Wood."[7]

Once, when Van Buren was Jackson's Vice-President and presiding over the Senate, Whig leader Henry Clay decided to drive him into a corner. The Senate was protesting Jackson's policy of withholding government funds from the Bank of the United States at the time, and Clay resolved to force Van Buren to take issue with the President on the matter. In a long and impassioned speech about the calamitous effects of Jackson's policy on the nation's economy, Clay implored Van Buren to go to the President and beg him to spare the country from ruin by altering his bank policy. While Clay was talking, Van Buren listened attentively and seemed to be drinking in Clay's every word; the Senators began wondering how the Vice-President would react to Clay's eloquence. When Clay finally finished and dropped back into his seat, apparently overcome with emotion, Van Buren put down his gavel, asked one of the Senators to take his chair, and, with all eyes upon him, descended from the rostrum. But instead of turning around to address the chair himself, he walked down the aisle toward Clay. When he reached the Senator's desk he said, "Mr. Clay, may I borrow a pinch of your excellent snuff?" Astonished, Clay nodded mechanically and handed over his snuff-box. Van Buren took a pinch of snuff from the box, applied it to his nostrils, smiled, bowed, thanked Clay, and then walked calmly out of the Senate chamber.[8]

Jackson (who came to cherish Van Buren as a father does a son) vigorously denied that his friend was a trimmer. Van Buren was, he insisted, "one of the most frank men I ever knew . . . a true man with no guile." Recalling the days when the two of them were in the Senate together, he told a friend: "I had heard . . . about Mr. Van Buren, especially about his *non-committalism.* I made up my mind that I would take an early opportunity to hear him and judge for myself. One day an important subject was under debate in the Senate. I noticed that Mr. Van Buren was taking notes while one of the Senators was speaking. I judged from this that he intended to reply, and I determined to be in my seat when he spoke. His turn came, and he rose and made a clear, straight-forward argument, which, to my mind, disposed of the whole subject. I turned to my colleague, Major Eaton, who sat next to me. 'Major,' I said, 'is there anything non-committal about that?' 'No, sir,' said the major."[9]

Jackson had good reason for liking Van Buren. Shortly after Van Buren reached Washington to take up his duties as Jackson's Secretary of State, he called on Peggy Eaton and confided to her that he had been reading much and thinking deeply on the character of great men and had come to the conclusion that General Jackson was the greatest man that had ever lived—the only man among them all who was without a fault. "But don't tell General Jackson what I have said," he begged her. Of course Mrs. Eaton promptly told Jackson, who looked at her with tears in his eyes and said: "Ah, Madam, that man loves me; he tries to conceal it, but there is always some fixed way by which I can tell my friends from my enemies."[10]

Van Buren became President with the warm support of his popular predecessor, but his White House years were unhappy. He had not been in office long when the Panic of 1837 struck the nation's banks and produced a long and painful depression. When he ran for a second term in 1840, his enemies sneeringly quoted the boast he had made in his 1837 inaugural that the United States presented "an aggregate of human prosperity surely not elsewhere to be found."[11] They also accused him of living in luxury in the White House while people went hungry. Van Buren never understood the fury with which newspapers attacked him. "Why the deuce is it that they have such an itching for abusing me?" he once cried. "I try to be harmless, and positively good natured, & a most decided friend of peace."[12]

In 1840, the Whig Party (which had emerged in the 1830's to challenge the policies of the Jacksonian Democrats) beat Van Buren with William Henry Harrison. In 1844, Van Buren made an unsuccessful bid for the Democratic nomination and then settled down to farming and writing his memoirs. When the Free Soil Party, organized by anti-slavery men in 1848, asked him to run, he at first demurred; he was no longer eager to return to presidential politics. But he shared the Free Soilers' opposition to the expansion of slavery into the federal territories and felt duty-bound to accept the nomination. His supporters made much of his public-spiritedness. During the campaign Ben Butler, an old New York friend, made speeches for him emphasizing how happy the former President was in retirement running his farm in Lindenwald, New York. On one occasion, however, when he was telling an audience how Van Buren jumped over fences in his eagerness to show people his turnip patch, someone shouted: "Damn his turnips! What are his present opinions about the abolition of slavery?"

Van Buren's opinions no longer mattered. He failed to win a single electoral vote in 1848. In Virginia, the only southern state where he received any popular votes, he polled a total of nine votes. But when the Free Soilers cried fraud, one Virginian exclaimed, "Yes, fraud! And we're still looking for that son-of-a-bitch who voted nine times!"[13]

★   ★   ★

Friendly Weather

Once, when Van Buren was receiving guests at a White House levee, Henry Clay sidled up to him and whispered that it must be pleasant to be surrounded by so many friends. "Well," said Van Buren cautiously, "the weather is very fine."[14]

Self-Restraint

At a White House dinner a servant came rushing up to Van Buren and whispered, "The house is on fire!" Excusing himself, Van Buren went out to the kitchen and helped quench the blaze. On returning, he explained why he had left. When he finished, Henry Clay looked up at him and, putting his hand on his heart, said earnestly: "I am doing all I can to get you out of this house; but believe me, I do not want to burn you out."[15]

NINE

William Henry Harrison
1841

When the Whigs nominated William Henry Harrison (1773–1841) for President in 1839, Thomas Hart Benton, Democratic Senator from Missouri, sniffed disdainfully that "availability was the only ability sought by the Whigs."[1] The *Baltimore Republican* was even more derisive. "Give him a barrel of hard cider and a pension of two thousand a year," sneered the editor, "and, our word for it, he will sit the remainder of his days in a log cabin by the side of a 'sea coal' fire and study moral philosophy."[2] But the Whigs quickly transformed the slur into an asset, jubilantly launching one of the most colorful campaigns in American history: the log-cabin, hard-cider campaign of 1840.

Harrison was an unlikely log-cabin candidate. Son of a wealthy Virginia planter, he had gone to college; enlisted in the army and risen to major-general; fought in the Battle of Tippecanoe, against the Indians of the Northwest in 1811, and the Battle of the Thames, during the War of 1812; and served as Congressman and Senator from Ohio after leaving the army. He was living with his family on a beautiful estate in North Bend, Ohio, when he received the nomination. But the Whigs presented him to the voters as the "Farmer of North Bend," born in a log cabin, who had worked his way up from humble beginnings to high distinction in civil and military life by his own efforts and whose tastes and habits were far closer to those of the ordinary citizen than those of his Democratic opponent, Martin Van Buren, who was running for re-election. They also presented him as a military hero. His victory over the Indians in the Battle of Tippecanoe provided them with a nickname: "Tippecanoe" or "Old Tip." And his running mate, John Tyler of Virginia, gave them a euphonious campaign slogan: "Tippecanoe and Tyler Too." The only thing lacking was a party platform, but the omission was intentional. During the contest, Harrison made a few speeches here and there, but mainly he followed the advice Philadelphia banker Nicholas Biddle once gave Whig leaders before about Harrison: "Let him say not one single word about his principles, or his creed—let him say nothing—promise nothing. Let no Committee or Convention—no town meeting ever extract from him a single word, about what he thinks now, or what he will do hereafter. Let the use of pen and ink be wholly forbidden as if he were a mad poet in Bedlam."[3]

Harrison's managers, however, provided mad poets and created considerable bedlam themselves. They flooded the country with silly campaign songs and held riotous rallies everywhere. Across the land they sponsored noisy conventions, mass meetings, and colorful processions of people singing and shouting; log-cabin headquarters dispensing hard cider; campaign papers like the *Hard Cider Press, Old Tip's Broom, Tippecanoe,* and the *Log Cabin;* log-cabin handkerchiefs; log-cabin sunbonnets; log-cabin buttons; log-cabin teacups; log-cabin plates; log-cabin glee clubs; log-cabin songbooks; log-cabin anecdotes; log-cabin textbooks; Tippecanoe Tobacco; Tippecanoe Shaving Soap; Old Cabin Whiskey, produced by the E. C. Booz Distillery of Philadelphia; and lively dances like the Harrison Hoe-down and the Tippecanoe Quick Step.[4] The Log Cabin campaign became so rambunctious at times that John Quincy Adams wondered whether a civil war was at hand. Exulted a Whig editor: "Little did the . . . simpleton who proposed pensioning the Hero of the Thames with a Log Cabin and Hard Cider dream . . . that his taunt would raise such a tornado."[5]

The Log-Cabin campaign overwhelmed Van Buren and the Democrats. The Democrats called Harrison "General Mum" for evading the issues, referred to him as "Old Tip-ler" and "Granny Harrison," accused him of profanity, drunkenness, and loose living, and suggested spelling his name backwards ("Nosirrah!"); but when it came to pyrotechnics they could never seem to seize the initiative.[6] Most of the time they were busy defending Van Buren against the charge that he was an effete, snobbish aristocrat. The Whigs insisted that

Van Buren ate dainty food with gold spoons, perfumed his whiskers, wore a corset, rode in an "English coach" with liveried English servants, strutted and swaggered "like a crow in a gutter," and looked down on the plain folk of America.[7] They also circulated a story about the "log-cabin chap" who knocked at the White House at eight o'clock one morning and was told by "a fat servant" that he was there too early to see the President and should return at ten. Snorted the log-cabin boy: "I'll come here the 5th of March next at daylight—and I'll see the President. Old Tip is a mighty early riser—I never heer'd of his being ketched napping."[8] The Democrats tried their best to set people straight on Van Buren's lowly origins and his plain and simple habits, but it was of no avail. The Whigs simply chanted:

> Old Tip he wears a homespun coat
> He has no ruffled shirt-wirt-wirt
> But Mat he has the golden plate
> And he's a little squirt-wirt-wirt.

And they squirted tobacco juice through their teeth as they chanted "wirt-wirt."[9]

"General Harrison," said one prominent Whig, "was sung into the Presidency,"[10] But he won in November with more people voting than ever before. "Harrison comes in upon a hurricane," exclaimed John Quincy Adams after the election. "God grant he may not go out upon a wreck!"[11] Complained Harrison's wife: "I wish that my husband's friends had left him where he is, happy and contented in retirement."[12] But Harrison himself looked forward to the White House and expected to do great things there. "He is as tickled with the Presidency," Van Buren observed, "as a young woman is with a new bonnet."[13]

Just before Harrison took his oath of office, Daniel Webster prepared an inaugural address because he thought the General would be too busy to do one himself. But Harrison insisted on writing his own speech. "If I should read your inaugural address instead of mine," he told Webster, "everybody would know that you wrote it, and that I did not." Webster then offered to look over Harrison's manuscript and make some suggestions. Harrison rather reluctantly agreed, and the following day Webster started going over it. To his horror, he discovered that Harrison's speech dwelt mostly on Roman history, using the word "proconsul" many times, and had no more to do with American affairs than a chapter in the Koran. He spent many hours in his office that day, doing the best he could to Americanize Harrison's sentiments. When he got home that night, completely exhausted, he was late for dinner and apologized to his landlady. "That is of no consequence," she said, "but I am sorry to see you looking so worried and tired. I hope nothing has gone wrong. I really hope nothing has happened." Sighed Webster: "You would think that something had happened if you knew what I have done. I have killed *seventeen Roman proconsuls* as dead as smelts, every one of them!"[14]

Despite Webster's excisions, Harrison's inaugural address on March 4, 1841, took the sixty-eight-year-old General close to two hours to deliver. It was a cold and wintry day, and the crowd shivered, but Harrison stood bareheaded and without gloves or overcoat as he droned on and on and on. Later that month he contracted a chill that quickly became pneumonia, and on April 4 he was dead. His last words, perhaps intended for his Vice-President, John Tyler, were: "Sir, I wish you to understand the principles of the Government. I wish them carried out. I ask nothing more."[15] Harrison was a stout nationalist; Tyler, an equally stout states'-righter.

★ ★ ★

Great Father

In 1810, when Harrison, as Governor of Indiana Territory, was negotiating with Tecumseh just before the battle of Tippecanoe, he ordered a chair brought for the great Shawnee warrior. The man who brought it bowed and said, "Warrior, your father, General Harrison, offers you a seat." "My father!" exclaimed Tecumseh, lifting his long arms aloft. "The sun is my father, and the earth is my mother; and on her bosom will I recline!" And he stretched himself out on the ground.[16]

One of the People

A plain farmer called to see President Harrison one stormy day, while the latter was at dinner, and the servant made him wait in a room where there was no fire. Afterward Harrison rebuked the servant. "Why did you not show the man into the drawing room, where it is warm and comfortable?" The servant mumbled something about soiling the carpet, and Harrison said sternly: "Never mind the carpet another time. The man is one of the people, and the carpet and the house, too, belong to the people."[17]

Father of the House

"Let me introduce Mr. Williams of North Carolina to you, General," said a Cabinet member to President Harrison one day. "Mr. Williams is the oldest member of the House of Representatives and, you know, is called the Father of the House." "Mr. Williams," said Harrison, taking his hand and beaming, "I am glad to see the Father of the House, and the more so because you have a very unruly set of boys to deal with, as I know."[18]

TEN

John Tyler
1841–45

Vice-President John Tyler (1790–1862) was at home in Virginia, playing marbles with his boys (according to one story), when he heard of President Harrison's death. He had just lost in the game of "knucks" and was on his knees with his knuckles on the ground, ready to receive the penalty, when Fletcher Webster, son of Secretary of State Daniel Webster, rode up in hot haste and dismounted. Tyler got up at once and looked inquiringly at him. "Mr. President," exclaimed young Webster, "I have been instructed by the Secretary of State to deliver these dispatches to you without delay." Tyler glanced at the papers handed him and then cried, "My God, the President is dead!" "Yes, sir, Mr. President," said Webster, "the nation is in mourning." "Come, let us go into the house," said Tyler; and he began making arrangements to return to Washington.[1]

Not everyone believed that Tyler—the first Vice-President to become President upon the death of the incumbent— had succeeded to the prerogatives of a Chief Executive under the Constitution. In the House of Representatives, John McKeon of Pennsylvania introduced a resolution stipulating that Tyler's title should be "acting President." The resolution was defeated by a *viva voce* vote, but some Congressmen continued to look upon the Virginian as only an "acting" President. Tyler himself, however, claimed all the rights and privileges of the Chief Executive; and the precedent he set has been followed by every Vice-President who has succeeded to the Presidency.

Daniel Webster tried at first to dominate the new President. "Mr. President," he said at the first Cabinet meeting, "I suppose you intend to carry on the ideas and customs of your predecessor, and that this administration inaugurated by President Harrison will continue in the same line of policy under which it has begun." Tyler nodded slightly, wondering what was coming next, and Webster continued: "It was our custom in the cabinet of the deceased President, that the President should preside over us. Our custom and proceeding was that all measures whatever, however, relating to the administration were brought before the cabinet, and their settlement was decided by a majority—each member, *and the President, having one vote.*" For a moment Tyler did not know quite what to say. Then he exclaimed: "I beg your pardon, gentlemen. I am sure I am very glad to have in my cabinet such able statesmen as you have proved yourselves to be, and I shall be pleased to avail myself of your counsel and advice, but I can never consent to being dictated to as to what I shall or shall not do. I, as president, will be responsible for my administration. I hope to have your co-operation in carrying out its measures; so long as you see fit to do this, I shall be glad to have you with me—when you think otherwise, your resignations will be accepted."[2]

The resignations were not long in coming. Tyler was a states'-righter and strict constructionist; he took a narrow view of what the Constitution permits the federal government to do. The Whig program for tariffs, a national bank, and internal improvements (roads and canals) was anathema to him, and he rejected it *in toto.* As he vetoed one bill after another passed by the Whigs in Congress, he gradually alienated most of the leaders of the party which had elevated him to office. On September 11, 1841, every member of the Cabinet except Webster sent in his resignation. That afternoon Webster came to see Tyler and asked, "Where am I to go, Mr. President?" "You must decide that for yourself, Mr. Webster," replied Tyler. At this, Webster, who was anxious to continue negotiations he was carrying on with the British, exclaimed, "If you leave it to me, Mr. President, I will stay where I am." Tyler got up, extended his hand, and said warmly, "Give me your hand on that, and now I will say to you that Henry Clay is a doomed man."[3]

But Clay thought Tyler was the doomed man. He dismissed him

contemptuously as "a President without a party." Clay's Whig colleagues also called Tyler "His Accidency," an "Executive Ass," "the Accident of an Accident," and *a man destitute of intellect and integrity, whose name is the synonym of nihil.*" An influenza epidemic that swept the nation was dubbed "Tyler grippe."[4] And when Tyler, a widower, married a woman thirty years his junior, the Whigs circulated jokes about the mating of January and May. Tyler's new wife Julia was irked by Clay's taunt that her husband was a President without a party. "If it is a party he wants," she said, "I will give him a party." She did just that. On February 22, 1845, she and her husband gave a farewell party for a large but select group of people from the *beau monde;* and the White House, usually cold and somber, was alive with merriment and laughter for many hours. When one of the guests congratulated Tyler on this unusual gathering of beauty and fashion in the Executive Mansion, he quipped: "Yes, they cannot say now that I am a *President without a party!*"[5]

On the morning of March 4, 1845, Tyler prepared to leave Washington after James K. Polk's inauguration. The Potomac steamer was about to swing away from the wharf (which was crowded with people) when he suddenly arrived with his family, a retinue of slaves, and a pile of luggage. Just as the Tylers alighted from their carriages at the head of the wharf, the whistle sounded, the boat's bell rang, and the steamer began moving slowly off. Someone in the crowd yelled, "Hello! Hello! Captain, hold on there, ex-President Tyler is coming. Hold on!" But the captain, an old Henry Clay Whig, pulled his engine bell violently and shouted: "Ex-President Tyler be dashed! Let him stay!"[6] The Tylers finally managed to get back to their plantation in Virginia, where the former President continued to nourish his states'-rights views. During the Civil War he was a devoted Confederate.

★   ★   ★

In the Prime

Tyler's first wife died in 1842, and a year or two later the President began courting Julia Gardiner, daughter of a well-to-do New Yorker, who was considerably younger than he was. One day in March 1844, he was out for a ride with his old friend Henry A. Wise, Congressman from Virginia, and decided to tell him about his plan to marry Julia. "Have you really won her?" asked Wise, somewhat taken aback.

"Yes," said Tyler, "and why should I not?" "You are too far advanced in life to be imprudent in a love-scrape," said Wise cautiously. "How imprudent?" Tyler pressed him. "Easily," said Wise, "you are not only past middle age, but you are President of the United States, and that is a dazzling dignity which may charm a damsel more than the man she marries." "Pooh!" laughed Tyler. "Why, my dear sir, I am just full in my prime!"

Wise was still not convinced. To make his point stronger, he told Tyler the story of a Virginia planter who had decided to marry a much younger woman and asked his house slave, Toney, what he thought of the match. "Massa," said Toney, "you think you can stand dat?" "Yes, Toney, why not?" said the planter. "I am still strong, and I can now, as well as ever I could, make her happy." "Yes," said Toney doubtfully; "but Massa, *you* is now in *your* prime, dat's true; but when she is in *her* prime, where den, Massa, will *your* prime be?"

Tyler burst into laughter at Wise's story, but married Julia all the same. In the fall of 1847, Tyler and Wise met by accident on a riverboat, and Wise noticed that in the former President's baggage was a double-seated wicker baby carriage. "Aha!" said Wise, "it has come to that, has it?" "Yes," said Tyler; "you see now how right I was; it was no vain boast when I told you I was in my prime. I have a houseful of goodly babies budding around me. . . ." At the time he had two, but five more were to come. He had more children, in his two marriages, than any other President.[7]

Best Train

A year or two after he became President, Tyler decided to take a trip and sent his son Bob to order a special train. The railroad superintendent, a devout Whig, told Bob that he didn't run special trains for Presidents. "What!" cried Bob, "didn't you furnish a special train for the funeral of General Harrison?" "Yes," said the superintendent. "And if you will bring your father here in that shape, you shall have the best train on the road!"[8]

ELEVEN

James K. Polk
1845–49

James K. Polk (1795–1849) was a "dark horse." A deadlock between ex-President Martin Van Buren and Lewis Cass of Michigan at the Democratic convention in May 1844 led the delegates to turn to Polk on the ninth ballot. He had never been seriously regarded as presidential timber before that. When news of the nomination was sent from Baltimore to Washington by the new Morse telegraph, some people in Washington were convinced that Morse's invention was a failure because they simply couldn't believe what the telegraph reported.[1] "Polk!" exclaimed Governor R. P. Letcher of Kentucky. "Great God, what a nomination!"[2]

Polk was not exactly an unknown. He had been in Congress for seven consecutive terms and Governor of Tennessee for one; as Speaker of the House he was known for his conscientiousness ("Polk the Plodder").[3] But he had no large personal following; he had failed twice to regain his gubernatorial seat; and he was totally lacking in personal magnetism or even quiet charm. "The idea of Jem Polk being President of the United States!!!" exclaimed a Tennessee Congressman. "We are more disposed to laugh at it here than to treat it seriously."[4] "Who is James K. Polk?" exclaimed the Whig nominee, Henry Clay, sarcastically. Clay's question quickly became a slogan, so that during the 1844 campaign the Whigs went around crying, "Who is Polk?"[5] Even the Democrats found the question hard to answer at first. When a steamboat captain who was a loyal Democrat first heard the choice of the Baltimore convention, he shouted, "Hurrah for———What d'ye say his name is?"[6] "Polk," said Governor Letcher, "has no more chance to be elected than if he were dead and buried, and d———ned, as he will be in due time."[7]

Letcher was dead wrong. In a close election in which the tiny anti-slavery Liberty Party drew votes away from the Whigs, Polk beat the far better known Clay and became our eleventh President. He may have been a little man (he was known as the "Napoleon of the stump"), but he was big with plans for territorial expansion, and his ambitions had an enormous appeal at a time when many Americans thought it was their "manifest destiny" to take control of as much territory on the North American continent as possible.[8] Polk did what he could to make this destiny manifest while he was in the White House. He was "a short man with a long program."[9] He settled a boundary dispute with Britain over Oregon Territory quite peacefully; but he precipitated a war with Mexico over his territorial ambitions in the Southwest. When he left office, the United States was half again as large as when he became President.

Polk was not a popular President. Though he literally worked himself to death in the White House, and though, unlike most Presidents, he achieved just about all of his goals, his cold, formal, suspicious, and humorless nature made it impossible for people to warm to him. When he became President, he prepared a form letter notifying his Cabinet appointees that they must devote all their time and energy to the Polk administration and not be candidates "to succeed me in the presidential office."[10] During the Mexican War he quarreled with Generals Zachary Taylor and Winfield Scott because he thought their military exploits were encouraging them to have presidential ambitions. He also enjoyed putting down James Buchanan in front of the entire Cabinet. When Buchanan, Polk's Secretary of State, prepared a diplomatic letter for the President's signature, Polk read it over carefully, came across a passage he thought did not conform to standard diplomatic usage, and called Buchanan's attention to it at a Cabinet meeting. Buchanan insisted that Polk was in error and that the passage in question was correctly worded. Polk then bet Buchanan a basket of champagne that he was right and Buchanan wrong. Buchanan took him up on the bet and produced a bound letter-book which, he said, contained precedents for the form he had used in the letter. But after searching through the letter-book for some time, he finally had to admit that he could not find what he was looking for. Somewhat chagrined, he admitted that Polk had won the bet and promised to deliver the champagne as soon as possible. Polk refused to accept the champagne; he said he had only been joking. But he made a solemn entry in his diary afterward: "I record this incident for the purpose of showing how necessary it is for me to give my vigilant attention even to the form & details of my [subordinates'] duties."[11]

White House entertainments were cheerless affairs with the strait-laced Polk as host. Sam Houston said that Polk's main trouble was that he drank too much water.[12] White House visitors were rushed past the President as fast as they could be introduced and given a quick handshake, with an attendant droning in the background: "Gentlemen-who-have-been-presented-will-please-walk-into-the-East-room-don't-block-up-the-passage." On rare occasions Polk essayed the light touch. Once, for instance, he explained to some people how he handled the problem of handshaking. "I told them," he confided to his diary, "that I had found that there was great art in shaking hands, and that I could shake hands during the whole day without suffering any bad effects from it. They were curious to know what this art was. I told them that if a man surrendered his arm to be shaken, by some horizontally, by others perpendicularly, and by others again with a strong grip, he could not fail to suffer severely from it, but that if he would shake and not be shaken, grip and not be gripped, taking care always to squeeze the hand of his adversary as hard as he squeezed him, that he suffered no inconvenience from it. I told them also that I could generally anticipate when I was to have a strong grip, and that when I observed a strong man approaching I generally took advantage of him by being a little quicker than he was and seizing him by the tip of his fingers, giving him a hearty shake, and thus preventing him from getting a full grip upon me." Polk's auditors were amused by his exposition, but Polk ended up being deadly serious about it. There was "much philosophy," he decided, in what he had said: "though I gave my account of the operation playfully, it is all true."[13]

★　★　★

Specie

Polk, a good Jacksonian Democrat, opposed banks and paper currency and favored the exclusive use of gold and silver as a circulating medium. He used specie himself when paying his debts. In the summer of 1834, while traveling to Washington with his wife, he discovered one morning that he needed money and said, "Sarah, get some money out of the trunk. I haven't enough in my pocket to pay expenses during the day." A little irked, his wife opened a trunk and began riffling through its contents looking for some of the bags of specie packed in different places. "Don't you see," she said, "how troublesome it is to carry around gold and silver? This is enough to show you how useful banks are." "Sarah," cried Polk, "you've changed your politics then! But," he added, "all I want now is that money." Mrs. Polk finally turned the trunk upside down and dislodged a bag of specie, but she persisted in her views. "Why," she said, "if we must use gold and silver all the time, a lady can scarcely carry enough money with her."[14]

TWELVE

Zachary Taylor
1849–50

When a Whig politician first proposed Zachary Taylor (1784–1850) for President, the forthright old general scoffed: "Stop your nonsense and drink your whiskey!"[1] A little later he became enchanted with the idea. Though he had been a professional soldier for forty years and was utterly lacking in political experience, he began to envision himself as the candidate not of a party, but of the people as a whole. But he had to have a party; so he announced that he was "a Whig, but not an ultra-Whig."[2] Daniel Webster scornfully dismissed him as "a swearing, whiskey-drinking, fighting frontier colonel," but he was not being fair about it.[3] Taylor's only real vice was tobacco-chewing; he was known as a "sure shot spitter." Despite Webster's misgivings, the Whigs went ahead and nominated him for President in June 1848 (with Millard Fillmore as his running mate), sent him a letter of notification, and awaited his acceptance. They had to wait a long time. When the letter arrived, collect, at the post office in Baton Rouge, Taylor did not bother to pick it up; he was refusing to accept any unpaid mail at the time. Weeks passed before he received a duplicate letter from the chairman of the convention and replied with an official acceptance.[4]

As in 1840, the Whigs had a candidate in 1848 but no platform. They avoided issues and presented Taylor to the voters as a military hero. Not only had he served ably in the War of 1812, the Black Hawk War in Illinois (1832), and the Seminole War in Florida (1836–

37); he had also acquitted himself honorably at Palo Alto and the Resaca de la Palma in the early stages of the Mexican War (1846–48). And at Buena Vista in February 1847, he had achieved a glorious victory: with only 5,000 men he had defeated Mexican President Santa Anna's army of 20,000. But Taylor was no war-monger. "My life has been devoted to arms," he once said, "yet I look upon war at all times, and under all circumstances, as a national calamity, to be avoided if compatible with national honor." As for domestic policies, Abraham Lincoln summarized Taylor's views in a speech in the House of Representatives: "The people say to General Taylor: 'If you are elected, shall we have a national bank?' He answers, 'Your will, gentlemen, not mine.' 'What about the tariff?' 'Say yourselves.' 'Shall our rivers and harbors be improved?' 'Just as you please. If you desire a bank, an alteration of the tariff, internal improvements, any or all, I will not hinder you. If you do not desire them, I will not attempt to force them on you.' "[5]

Despite his nebulous political views, Taylor was enormously appealing to the plain people of America. He was no "Fuss and Feathers" like General Winfield Scott, the other Mexican War hero. His tastes and manners were simple and unaffected; his men referred to him affectionately as "Old Zach" and "Old Rough and Ready." His dress was as informal as his demeanor; he almost never wore a uniform or anything to indicate his rank. "He looks more like an old farmer going to market with eggs to sell than anything I can . . . think of," said one officer. "He wears an old oil cap," reported a man who saw him in Saltillo, Mexico, "a dusty green coat, a frightful pair of trousers and on horseback he looks like a toad."[6]

General Taylor's lack of pretension was legendary. He was "perfectly unaffected by his brilliant successes," said a Virginia officer, "plain and unassuming in his kind manners, mild and affable in his disposition, and kind and courteous in his demeanour. You feel at once comfortable and easy in his society. He paid me a visit the other day; I was sitting on a trunk writing at the time; I arose and offered him the seat, remarking that I had but a poor seat to offer him; oh, never mind, said he, all I am afraid of is that I will spoil the trunk, and he sat down and conversed in the most sociable and familiar manner for some time."[7] In November 1847, when Taylor, on leave, boarded a vessel bound for New Orleans, one of the first things he did was to have the sick and wounded soldiers on the ship placed in his stateroom, where they could be given proper care. After that, he hunted up a place in which to take a nap. When at supper time he failed to put in an appearance, some deckhands went looking for him. At length one of them found him sound asleep on some old mattresses in front of the boilers.[8] On another occasion, a young man assigned to an upper berth on a ship traveling down the Mississippi found, to his delight, that the lower berth was occupied by "Z. Taylor, Baton Rouge." After a lively chat with General Taylor, mainly about farming, he went up on deck for some air. When he returned, ready to retire, he found the lower berth empty and Taylor sleeping in the upper berth. With considerable hesitation, he took the lower berth himself that night and the next morning apologized for what had happened. "Pooh, pooh!" said Taylor, laughing, "don't you know I am not the youngest, and more used to hard fare than you are?"[9]

Even when on duty Taylor avoided pomp and circumstance. The story is told of two young second lieutenants, fresh from West Point and faultlessly attired, who on their first morning at Fort Smith, Arkansas, encountered a heavy-set man who looked like a farmer. "Good morning, old fellow!" they called out. "Good morning." "How's crops?" they asked. "Purty good." "Come on, take a drink with us." The old fellow joined them for a chat, though he did not drink anything himself, and when he got up to leave, one of the young men said: "Give our love to the old woman and the gals." Later that day, the two lieutenants, immaculate in full dress, went to headquarters to pay their respects to their commanding officer. To their chagrin, they found that he was the old farmer whom they had been teasing earlier that day. Taylor gravely acknowledged their salute and then introduced his wife and daughter. "Here," he said, "are the old woman and gal."[10]

Ulysses S. Grant, who served as a second lieutenant under Taylor during the Mexican War, reported that Taylor rarely wore his uniform and that one of the few occasions on which he did so turned into a comedy of errors. On May 11, 1847, according to Grant, Taylor was to meet with Commodore David Conner, flag officer of the naval squadron off the mouth of the Rio Grande. Knowing that American naval officers placed great emphasis on proper attire, Taylor thought it would be only courteous for him to receive Conner in full dress. He dug up an old uniform, brushed it up, put it on, added sword, epaulets, and sash, and awaited the Commodore's visit.

Meanwhile, Conner, fully aware of Taylor's aversion to wearing uniforms, had decided, as a courtesy, to meet the General in civilian clothing. "The meeting," said Grant, "was said to have been embarrassing to both and the conversation was principally apologetic." Afterward, Taylor threw his uniform away and vowed that he would never again resort to formalities.[11]

After a narrow victory in the 1848 election, Taylor traveled to Washington late in February, 1849, for his inauguration. There he was mistaken at first for John Boyle, a Navy Department clerk who bore a striking resemblance to the President-elect; when he tried to make a speech, people jeered, "Ah! Get out, John Boyle, you can't fool us!" But on discovering their error they gave him a noisy round of applause.[12] On March 5 (March 4 was a Sunday), Taylor gave a brief inaugural address, then launched his Presidency. He sent his first (and only) message to Congress on December 24. To the great amusement of the Democrats, the printed copies contained the sentence "We are at peace with all the nations of the world and the rest of mankind," quickly revised to read, "We are at peace with all the nations of the world, and seek to maintain our cherished relations of amity with them."[13]

Taylor found the Presidency tougher than the battle-field. "The President called to see me," reported Orlando Brown, head of the Bureau of Indian Affairs, in April 1850, "and in a conversation of several hours fully disclosed to me his feelings and his purposes. He spoke as a proud, a brave and a deeply injured man alone can speak of an unmerited wrong and unprovoked persecution. I listened to his recital of the annoyances by which he had been harassed, of the contumely that had been heaped upon him—of the contemptuous disparagements which were showered on him from high places, till my heart was sad and my eyes filled with tears. But when, almost with the eloquence, certainly with an equal depth of agony, of Lear, he spoke of his being exposed without defense to this pitiless storm, *I felt* like I could now see how keener than a serpent's tongue was the ingratitude of our race. But General Taylor is the unconquerable man. When he was through with the recital of his injuries, the soldier awoke within him and he exclaimed that he always kept his flag flying in front of his tent and would never strike it—that he had never turned a back to friend or foe and that by God he would not do it now."[14] But Taylor was President for only a little over two years. On July 4, 1850, at the laying of the cornerstone of the

Washington Monument, the sixty-five-year-old President overexposed himself to the heat, consumed iced milk and cherries (both of which disagreed with him), and developed acute gastroenteritis. A few days later he died and was succeeded by the far less engaging Millard Fillmore.

At the time the United States was facing a crisis over the status of slavery in the territories acquired from Mexico. Taylor, though a slaveowner, had opposed the extension of slavery and favored admitting California, and even New Mexico, into the Union as free states. Adamantly opposed to the Compromise of 1850, which Henry Clay and Daniel Webster sponsored as a means of placating the South, he gave them to understand that he would veto any such "omnibus bill." At the same time he made it crystal clear that he would put down promptly and forcefully any attempts at secession. When three southern Whig Congressmen came to his office to argue with him and began to talk of secession, Taylor exploded and told them angrily that "if it becomes necessary, in executing the laws, he would take command of the army himself, and that, if they were taken in rebellion against the Union, he would hang them with less reluctance than he had hung deserters and spies in Mexico!" After the irate Congressmen left, Senator Hannibal Hamlin entered Taylor's office and found him "rushing around the room like a caged lion," muttering and shaking his fist. "Did you see those damned traitors?" he exclaimed, adding that he would hang them and put himself at the head of the army if there were any attempts at secession.[15]

A week later, dining with Congressman Horace Mann, Taylor declared that the moment any of the southern states made a move toward secession, he would send a fleet to blockade their harbors, levy duties on all goods going into the South, and prevent any goods from coming out. "I can save the Union without shedding a drop of blood," he assured Mann. "It is not true, as reported in the North, that I said I would march an army and subdue them: there would be no need of any."[16]

★　★　★

Hominy

General Taylor was fond of hominy but did not like it made from musty corn. While stationed in Florida he discovered that his favorite horse, Claybank, had a keen nose for sweet corn, so he would let the sagacious animal loose among the sacks of corn provided for the army until he commenced gnawing a hole in a sack that pleased him. Taylor would patiently watch until he saw that Claybank had made a choice, then call his servants and have the horse stabled at once. "But," he would say, "as the animal has eaten a hole in the bag, take out a quart or so of the corn and make a dish of hominy."[17]

Judging Strangers

Once, during the Florida campaign, Taylor stopped off in a tavern at Newmansville with officers on his staff for a glass of beer. A young man on his way to report for duty entered the place and approached their table. Fresh from West Point, he wore a linen duster to protect his uniform; Taylor, as usual, was wearing a home-spun sack coat and a broad-brimmed straw hat. "Well, old man," said the young man, as he sat down, "how are the Indians now?" "I believe, sir," Taylor replied, "that they are giving considerable trouble." "They are, are they?" said the young man. "We will have to see to that. I am an army officer and I am on my way to take a hand. Have a glass of beer with me, Old Codger, you and your neighbors." Taylor and his companions rose, toasted the young man, and then boarded the stagecoach, leaving him alone in the tavern. A day or so later, when the young West Pointer reported for inspection, he faced the "Old Codger" in a colonel's uniform. Horrified, he stumbled through the ordeal and afterward asked some of the other officers what he could do to make amends. "Oh, with Colonel Taylor, just forget it," they told him. But the young man did not feel like letting the matter drop, so he went to Colonel Taylor's tent to apologize. "My young friend," said Taylor calmly, "let me give you a little piece of advice which may be of advantage to you. Never judge a stranger by his clothes."[18]

Inquisitive Old Fellow

During the Seminole War, a young officer who had just received his commission was ordered to join the army in Florida and report to Zachary Taylor, by now a brigadier general. After a tedious journey through the woods, however, he reached a tavern about fifty miles from headquarters and decided to stop there for a few days.

There were only two other people staying there. One of them, an oldish, shabby-looking fellow, with a black hat, minus part of the crown, and a piece of twine for a ribbon, was very inquisitive, and among other things asked the officer what excuse he intended to make for his delay in reporting to the General. "Oh," said the young man, "they say Taylor is a very easy old soul, and I can easily make up an excuse." On going to bed that night, he asked the landlord who the talkative old fellow was. "Why," said his host, "don't you know General Taylor?" About an hour later, at midnight, the landlord heard the tramp of a horse's feet, making fast tracks towards headquarters.[19]

Rough and Ready

Among the volunteers for the Florida campaign was a "gentleman's son" who, heartily sick of rainy weather, mud, and lack of shelter, went to his captain with his complaints, but, meeting with no particular sympathy, resolved to have a talk with General Taylor himself. When he reached the commander's headquarters, the General was pointed out to him, but he was incredulous. "*That* old fellow General Taylor?" he cried. "Nonsense!" Finally persuaded that such was the case, he marched up and rather patronizingly began his business. "General Taylor, I believe." "Yes, sir." "Well, General, I'm devilish glad to see you—am, indeed." The General nodded politely. "General," continued the young man, "you'll excuse me, but since I've been here I've been doing all I could for you—have, indeed; but the fact is, the accommodations are very bad—they are, indeed; mud, sir! *bleeged* to lie down in it, actually; and the fact is, general, I'm a *gentleman's son,* and not used to it!" Taylor expressed regrets that such annoyances should exist under any circumstances in a civilized army. "Well, but, general," said the young man, "what am I to do?" "Why, really," said Taylor, "I don't know, unless you take my place." "Well, now, that's civil—'tis, indeed," said the young man. "Of course don't mean to *turn you out,* but a few hours' sleep—a cot, or a bunk, or anything—would be so refreshing! Your place—where is it, general?" "O," said Taylor, "just drop down— *anywhere about here*—any place about camp will answer!" The young man was stunned for a moment; then he smiled and said, "Well, no wonder they call you 'Rough and Ready.'!" And amid the smiles of everyone around except Taylor himself he returned to his unit, prepared to take his chances with the weather.[20]

THIRTEEN

Millard Fillmore
1850–53

On July 10, 1850, the day after President Zachary Taylor's death, Vice-President Millard Fillmore (1800–74) took the oath of office as thirteenth President. Before long a story about the new President was circulating in Washington. Fillmore, it was said, decided that as President he ought to have a new carriage; so "Old Edward" Moran, a White House attendant, took him to see a handsome outfit which was being sold for a bargain because the owner was leaving the city. "This is all very well, Edward," said Fillmore, after looking it over carefully, "but how would it do for the President of the United States to ride around in a second-hand carriage?" "But, sure," said Old Edward, "your Ixcellency is only a sicond-hand Prisident!"[1]

Secondhand, commonplace, mediocre, undistinguished: these are the words that spring naturally to mind as one surveys Fillmore's brief rise from obscurity and quick descent into oblivion. "Fillmore," said one observer in 1843, "is a great man; but it takes pressure to make him show his highest powers."[2] The pressure, possibly, was never strong enough. "He had the peculiar faculty," said another observer, "of adapting himself to every position in which he served."[3] Fillmore opposed the institution of slavery; but he did not believe anything could be done to abolish it. "God knows," he once said, "that I detest slavery, but it is an existing evil, for which we are not responsible, and we must endure it, and give it such protection as is guaranteed by the constitution, till we can get rid of it without destroying the last hope of free government in the world."[4] As President, he strongly supported the Compromise of 1850, with its Fugitive Slave Act; by enforcing this law against courageous blacks seeking to escape to freedom he roused anti-slavery forces in the North to wrath, thereby contributing to the widening gulf between North and South.

While Fillmore was filling out General Taylor's term, his father, "Squire" Fillmore, a venerable-looking gentleman of eighty, came to visit the White House. When he was about to leave, he was invited to stay a few days longer. "No, no!" he cried. "I will go. I don't like it here; it isn't a good place to live; it isn't a good place for Millard; I wish he was at home in Buffalo."[5] He soon got his wish. In 1852, the Whigs denied Fillmore the chance to run on his own for President, and he returned to his home town. But early in 1855, as a preliminary to re-entering presidential politics, he joined the Order of the Star-Spangled Banner and participated in this nativist group's secret rites in the library of his home. When the ceremony was over, Charles McComber, who had presided over the initiation, declared solemnly: "Mr. Fillmore, you have taken this step which will certainly land you in the presidential chair at Washington." "Charles," replied Fillmore, "I trust so."[6] The following year he became the presidential candidate of the anti-Catholic, anti-immigrant Know-Nothing Party, but McComber's prediction turned out to be faulty; he lost handsomely in the election of 1856.

Fillmore himself was not especially nativist in outlook. So far as we know, he did not eat the Know-Nothing candy, drink the Know-Nothing tea, use Know-Nothing toothpicks, or read the Know-Nothing books and poems circulated by his party; and he certainly made no demagogic Know-Nothing appeals during the 1856 campaign. The year before, in fact, he had been presented to the Pope when visiting Rome. He was nervous beforehand about the possibility of having "to kneel and kiss the hand of the Pope, if not his foot"; but, to his immense relief, the Pope received him sitting, "neither offering hand or foot for salutation."[7] While Fillmore was President, Commodore Matthew Perry opened up Japan, and Congress adopted cheap postal rates; but Fillmore really could not take major credit for either of these accomplishments. Mrs. Fillmore did rather better: she installed the first bathtub in the Executive Mansion (in the face of severe public criticism), and White House bathtubs have been a Presidential perquisite ever since.

To his credit, Fillmore never overestimated himself. When he visited England in 1855, Oxford University offered him an honorary degree, but he at once declined it. "I have not the advantage of a classical education," he explained, "and no man should, in my judgment, accept a degree he cannot read." In refusing the honor, Fillmore may have been thinking of the jokes made when Andrew Jackson accepted an honorary degree from Harvard in 1833. But he also feared the ridicule which unruly students at Oxford were wont to heap on people receiving honorary degrees from the university. "They would probably ask," he said, "who's Fillmore? What's he done? Where did he come from? and then my name would, I fear, give them an excellent opportunity to make jokes at my expense."[8]

★ ★ ★

No Double-Header

When he became Comptroller of the State of New York in 1847, Fillmore decided to sell his law library to his partner Solomon G. Haven. A clerk listed the books, and Fillmore and Haven began negotiating a sale price. After considerable haggling they found they still had a disagreement of twenty-five cents per volume. "Mr. Haven," said Fillmore finally, "to settle this matter let us flip a coin. If it comes up heads, you will pay my price, if tails, you can have them at your price." "Agreed," said Haven. Fillmore groped in his pocket, came up with a large old-fashioned penny, and cried, "Haven, here's a go!" "No, no!" shouted Haven, rushing over with both arms extended. "Mr. Fillmore, you have been spending the last three weeks down at Albany with a political gang of cunning politicians, just long enough to learn their ways and tricks, and I want to examine that cent, to see if you have not got a double header." He then carefully examined Fillmore's coin, approved it, and handed it back. Fillmore threw the coin, it came up heads, and the deal was closed as he had wished.[9]

Franklin Pierce
1853–57

Franklin Pierce (1804–69), like James K. Polk, was a dark horse candidate. Not until the thirty-fifth ballot did he appear on the lists in the Democratic convention of 1852; nor did he win the nomination until the forty-ninth ballot. His wife, whose health was poor and who hated Washington, collapsed when she heard the news; and his little boy Bennie told his mother: "I hope he won't be elected for I should not like to be at Washington and I know you would not either."[1] Nathaniel Hawthorne, Pierce's classmate at Bowdoin College, wrote a campaign biography for his friend and expressed the opinion that Pierce "has in him many of the chief elements of a great ruler" and "is deep, deep, deep."[2] But in Pierce's New Hampshire hometown, the choice of the Baltimore convention was greeted by one man with the exclamation: "Wall, wall, dew tell! Frank Pierce for President! Neow Frank's a good fellow, I admit, and I wish him well; he made a good State's attorney, thar's no doubt about that, and he made a far Jedge, thar's no denying that, and nobody kaint complain of him as a Congressman, but when it comes to the hull Yewnited States I dew say that in my jedgment Frank Pierce is a-goin to *spread durned thin.*"[3]

The 1852 campaign was itself pretty darned thin. Pierce and his Whig opponent, General Winfield Scott, both accepted the Compromise of 1850 on slavery, and their supporters avoided raising serious issues during the campaign and concentrated instead on personalities.

The Democrats hailed Pierce as Andrew Jackson's successor ("Young Hickory of the Granite Hills") and praised his record as a "citizen soldier" during the Mexican War. They also dismissed Pierce's Whig opponent as a "carbuncle-faced old drunkard" who, as a professional soldier, was a pompous and potentially dangerous "military chieftain." The Whigs, for their part, belittled Pierce's military record, distributing with great glee a miniature book, only an inch high and a half inch wide, entitled *The Military Services of General Pierce.* They also made much of the fact that during the Mexican War he had fainted twice in action. During the battle of Contreras, Pierce had, in fact, been severely injured when his horse stumbled and fell on some rocks, but the Whigs didn't see it that way. The *Louisville Journal* reported that Pierce "tumbled from his horse just as he was getting into one fight, fainted and fell in the opening of a second, got sick and had to go to bed on the eve of a third, and came pretty near to getting into the fourth, missing it only by about an hour."[4]

The campaign became increasingly inane. When the Whigs grew tired of ringing changes on the "fainting-general" motif, they concentrated on a statement by one of Pierce's supporters that the Democratic candidate had once given a little boy "a whole cent" with which to buy a stick of candy. Anyone else, insisted the Whigs, would have given the lad a nickel; and they came up with a satirical "Ballad of the Stick of Candy" to commemorate Pierce's "reckless liberality." Another anecdote, to the effect that Pierce had once corrected his aged father's spelling of the word, "but," also came in for unending ridicule. Exclaimed the *Louisville Journal* sarcastically: "What political honors can be too lofty for the man who gave a cent's worth of candy to a boy who was a total stranger to him . . . and who could spell 'but' when he was just out of college!" During the Mexican War, according to the *Boston Atlas,* Pierce was ordered "to proceed to a certain place, and make a FEINT to attract the attention of the Mexicans. . . . Now, although General Pierce had progressed far enough in the spelling book to be able to tell his illustrious father how to spell b-u-t, yet he had . . . no idea of the difference between FEINT and FAINT. Accordingly he proceeded to the spot pointed out by his superior, tumbled from his horse, and commenced to FAINT. A soldier, seeing the maneuver, and not understanding military tactics, asked him what he was doing. 'OBEYING ORDERS,' promptly replied the General."[5]

Despite all the ridicule, Pierce won the election handily; but his triumph was soon followed by tragedy. On January 6, 1853, Pierce, his wife, and his son boarded the train in Boston for Concord, New Hampshire. But it had not gone very far before there was a sudden jolt and the car they were sitting in slipped off the track, toppled off the embankment, and rolled into a field below. Pierce and his wife were only slightly injured; but Bennie was caught in the wreckage and killed before their very eyes. The Pierces never really recovered from this terrible disaster. For weeks they tormented themselves with Calvinistic probings: was God punishing the President-elect because he had failed to attain a conviction of saving grace? Mrs. Pierce finally decided that God had taken Bennie so that her husband would have no family distractions to take him away from his grave responsibilities as President. But Pierce himself, interpreting the death of his boy as punishment for his sins, refrained from using the Bible at his inauguration. Instead, he broke a precedent by raising his right hand and affirming rather than swearing his loyalty to the U.S. Constitution.[6]

When it came to public issues, Pierce was known as a "doughface," that is, a "Northern man with Southern principles." He hated the abolitionists, insisted that the U.S. Constitution safeguarded property rights in slavery for all time, and had no objection to the expansion of slavery. In 1835, when he was in Congress, he once announced proudly that there was "not one in five hundred" in New Hampshire who supported the nefarious doctrine of abolition. John C. Calhoun challenged this assertion, producing an editorial claiming that a much larger proportion of people than that had signed anti-slavery petitions in the state. Pierce, visibly upset, chided the South Carolinian for citing a "worthless editor of an incendiary abolition publication" and insisted that antislavery petitions in his state were signed not by legal voters but by women and children, "who knew not what they did."[7] A few years later, hearing a rumor that his brother, a member of the New Hampshire legislature, would support some anti-slavery resolutions, he took a special train to Concord to remonstrate with him. "Ben," he cried, when he reached the state capital, "they tell me you are going to vote for the abolition resolutions. Now, I am not here, of course, to dictate to you; but if you vote for those resolutions . . . , you are no brother of mine; I will never speak to you again." His brother looked at him in astonishment and said: "You might have saved youself all this trouble, for I had no more

idea of voting for those resolutions than of knocking you down."
The brothers then warmly embraced.[8]

As President, Pierce favored acquiring Cuba as a new slave state.
He also strongly supported the Kansas-Nebraska Act which, by re-
pealing the Missouri Compromise and opening formerly free territory
to slavery, produced a bitter struggle in Kansas between pro-slavery
settlers and settlers wishing the territory to be free. With "Bleeding
Kansas," the nation took another giant step toward a bloody resolution of the conflict over slavery. Pierce, who sided with the pro-
slavery faction in Kansas, was deeply disappointed when the Democrats, having suffered losses in the Congressional elections of 1854,
denied him renomination in 1856. Asked what a President should
do after leaving office, he sighed: "There's nothing left . . . but to
get drunk."[9] He took his own advice for a time. But in 1860, when
his friends wanted him to run for President again, he adamantly
refused, suggesting his former Secretary of War, Jefferson Davis,
instead.

During the Civil War, Pierce supported the Union cause only
with grave reservations, denounced the Lincoln administration as
cruel, arbitrary, and oppressive, excoriated the Emancipation Proclamation as unconstitutional, and backed General George McClellan
for President in 1864. In New Hampshire, he became so unpopular
that a half century went by after his death in 1869 before the citizens
of Concord saw fit to erect a statue in his memory. During the
war, Nathaniel Hawthorne, against the advice of his publishers, dedicated one of his books to Pierce and included in it an open letter
to the former President full of praise. People like Ralph Waldo Emerson bought Hawthorne's book, but cut out both the letter and dedication before reading it.[10]

★   ★   ★

Loyalty

When news of Lincoln's death reached Concord, New Hampshire,
a mob of angry citizens gathered in front of Pierce's house demanding
proof of his loyalty because of his failure to join them in displaying
the American flag. Pierce hastily picked up a small flag, expressed
horror at the tragedy, and insisted it was not necessary "to show
my devotion for the Stars and Stripes by any special exhibition upon
the demand of any man or body of men. . . ." When he finished
speaking, the crowd dispersed.[11]

James Buchanan
1857–61

When James Buchanan (1791–1868) was minister to England, the State Department issued a circular instructing American officials abroad to perform their duties "in the simple dress of an American citizen" and to avoid ribbons, jewels, and gold lace. This put Buchanan on the spot. British officials advised him that if he did not wear the customary ceremonial dress he would be denied admittance to court balls and dinners and to the opening of Parliament. Buchanan tried to think of alternative garb: a military uniform like George Washington's or a plain blue coat with gold buttons embossed with the American eagle. Not having made up his mind what to wear by the time Parliament convened, he skipped the opening session. For this he was denounced by the British press for his "Republican ill manners" and for "American Puppyism." After much thought he finally hit upon a solution: he would simply carry a plain black-hilted dress sword when he appeared at Court. This did the trick. "As I approached the Queen," he reported with satisfaction, "an arch but benevolent smile lit up her countenance—as much as to say, you are the first man who ever appeared before me at Court in such a dress. I must confess that I never felt more proud of being an American."[1]

Buchanan was a gentleman of the old school. Distinguished-looking, faultlessly attired, and courtly-mannered, he looked, it was said, like a British nobleman of an earlier generation. An eye defect forced him to tilt his head slightly forward and sideways when engaged in conversation, which gave the impression of exceptional courteousness and sensitivity to others. He also had a passion for precision. For years he kept account books in which he conscientiously recorded every penny that passed through his hands. While he was minister to Britain for President Pierce, he kept a daily record of his valet's expenditures, including pennies spent for pins and suspenders buttons. Once he refused to accept a check for over $15,000 from a friend because there was an error of ten cents in it. And on one occasion when he was President he discovered that he had paid three cents too little for some food; the merchant receipted the bill as paid in full, but he sent him the three cents anyway.[2]

"Mr. Buchanan," James K. Polk wrote in his diary, "is an able man, but in small matters without judgment and sometimes acts like an old maid."[3] Still, in 1845 he made Buchanan his Secretary of State. Andrew Jackson registered a strong protest. "But, General," said Polk defensively, "you yourself appointed him minister to Russia in your first term." "Yes, I did," replied Jackson. "It was as far as I could send him out of my sight, and where he could do the least harm. I would have sent him to the North Pole if we had kept a minister there!"[4]

Buchanan, clearly, was not Jackson's type. Once, when Old Hickory was President, Buchanan paid a call at the White House with a lady he had befriended in England. Leaving her in the reception room downstairs, he went up to Jackson's private quarters and, to his horror, found the President unshaved and unkempt, wearing a dressing-gown, with his slippered feet on the fender before a blazing wood fire, and smoking a corncob pipe. Buchanan stated the object of his visit, and Jackson said he would be happy to meet the lady right away. With some diffidence, Buchanan then asked whether the President intended to change his attire. At this, Jackson got up, his long pipe in his hand, and, knocking the ashes out of the bowl, said sharply: "Buchanan, I want to give you a little piece of advice, which I hope you will remember. I knew a man once who made his fortune by attending to his own business. Tell the lady I will see her presently." Buchanan nodded meekly, left the room, and went downstairs to join his friend. A few minutes later Old Hickory entered the room cleanly shaved and wearing a black suit, went up to the woman, and greeted her with almost kingly grace. As she left the White House afterward she told Buchanan: "Your republican President is the royal model of a gentleman."[5]

Buchanan was a model gentleman himself. His entry into the White House in March 1857 dispelled the gloom that had settled over the place while the Pierces lived there. With Buchanan, a wealthy bachelor possessing Epicurean tastes, as Chief Executive, White House entertainments took on a festive note. A few weeks after his inauguration, the new President chided his liquor merchants for delivering champagne in small bottles. "Pints are very inconvenient in this house," he told them, "as the article is not used in such small quantities."[6] Buchanan was celebrated for serious drinking. "The Madeira and sherry that he has consumed would fill more than one old cellar," said journalist William Forney, "and the rye whiskey that he has 'punished' would make Jacob Baer's heart glad." Jacob Baer operated a distillery in Washington, and frequently Buchanan used his Sunday drive to church as an excuse for a trip to Baer's to pick up a ten-gallon cask of "Old J. B. Whiskey," which he regarded as the finest. He was amused when White House guests mistook the initials "J. B." for his own. "There was no head ache, no faltering steps, no flushed cheek" associated with Buchanan's drinking, said Forney. "Oh, no! All was as cool, as calm and as cautious and watchful as in the beginning. More than one ambitious tyro who sought to follow his . . . example gathered an early fall."[7]

Buchanan entered the White House hoping to quiet the storm over slavery. He even toyed with the idea that he might achieve the reputation of George Washington by his policies. But he had not been President long before Edwin Stanton of Ohio told him, "You are sleeping on a volcano. The ground is mined all around and under you and ready to explode, and without prompt and energetic action, you will be the last President of the United States." "Mr. Stanton," cried Buchanan, "for God's sake come in and help me!"[8] Buchanan thought slavery was evil, but without remedy, and blamed the abolitionists for the nation's troubles. He supported the Fugitive Slave Act, favored adding Kansas to the Union as a slave state, wanted to add slave territory to the United States by acquiring Cuba—by force, if necessary—and warmly endorsed the Dred Scott decision proclaiming that blacks were not citizens and that Congress could not prohibit slavery in U.S. territories. In 1860 he supported John Breckinridge, a slavery man from Kentucky, for President. But the Republicans won with Lincoln, and, as a result, shortly after the election the southern states started leaving the Union.

Buchanan was attending a dance in Washington when the news of South Carolina's secession arrived. Hearing some commotion outside the ballroom, he sent a young woman to see what was going on. In the hall outside she found a South Carolina Congressman running around gleefully, holding a telegram high over his head. "I feel like a boy let out of school," he shouted. "South Carolina has seceded!" The woman made her way back to the President. "South Carolina has seceded," she told him. Buchanan's face seemed to age on the spot. "Please—some one—won't some one call a carriage," he murmured in a husky voice. "I must go."[9]

During the secession crisis Buchanan seemed helpless and irresolute. He denied that states could secede from the Union, but—being a strict constructionist—he also denied that the federal government could do anything about it. His Cabinet, composed mainly of Southerners, began falling apart as one member after another resigned to cast his lot with the South. With a new Cabinet made up of Union Democrats, Buchanan took a somewhat stronger stand when it came to defending federal property in the seceded states. He also proposed amendments to the Constitution protecting slavery in the South as a solution to the crisis, but they were not adopted. By the time of Lincoln's inauguration he was at the end of his rope. "I am the last President of the United States," he told people.[10] To Lincoln he said frankly, "If you are as happy in entering the White House as I shall feel on returning to Wheatland [Pennsylvania], you are a happy man indeed."[11] As a Union Democrat he supported Lincoln's efforts to save the Union and spent his remaining years writing a defense of his own administration.

"I have always felt," said Buchanan shortly before his death in 1868, "and still feel that I discharged every public duty imposed on me constitutionally. I have no regret for any public act of my life, and history will vindicate my memory."[12] He was wrong; history (i.e., historians) never did vindicate him. In the North he was regarded as unimaginative, legalistic, and morally obtuse. And even the South, which he had championed so stoutly, looked on him with contempt. Many people agreed with a Pennsylvania judge who knew him well: "he was cut out by nature for a great lawyer, and I think was spoiled by fortune when she made him a statesman."[13]

★ ★ ★

Dismissal

Buchanan started out as a lawyer, and because of his skill in the courtroom he rose rapidly in his profession. In a typical case, he defended a man charged with threatening the life of another man. When the plaintiff took the stand, Buchanan asked him: "Well, sir, suppose you were a man of more nerve, a man not easily frightened by threats—put yourself in the position of a courageous man—would you have cared for the threat of my client?" "I am a man," replied the plaintiff, "of as much courage as anybody, sir." "Then," said Buchanan, "you were not frightened when my client threatened you?" "No, sir." "You are not afraid of him?" "No, I am not." "Well, then what did you bring this charge for? I move its dismissal." The court at once dismissed the case.[14]

Misfortune

In February 1860 some ladies came to the White House to pay their respects to the President. "Mr. Buchanan," said one of them just before they left, "we have looked all through this House—it is very elegant and well kept; but we have noticed one deficiency." "What is that, madam?" asked Buchanan. "That you have no lady of the house." "That, madam," said Buchanan, "is my misfortune, not my fault."[15]

SIXTEEN

Abraham Lincoln
1861–65

Abraham Lincoln (1809–65) was the first humorist to occupy the White House. "He could make a cat laugh!" exclaimed Bill Green.[1] "It was as a humorist that he towered above all other men it was ever my lot to meet," said another friend from Lincoln's youth.[2] H. C. Whitney, a lawyer who rode the circuit with Lincoln in Illinois, was struck by Lincoln's keen sense of the absurd: "He saw the ludicrous in an assemblage of fowls, in a man spading his garden, in a clothes-line full of clothes, in a group of boys, in a lot of pigs rooting at a mill door, in a mother duck teaching her brood to swim—in everything and anything."[3] During the Civil War, London's *Saturday Review* told its readers: "One advantage the Americans have is the possession of a President who is not only the First Magistrate, but the Chief Joker of the Land."[4] By the middle of 1863, several joke books—with titles like *Old Abe's Jokes, Abe's Jokes—Fresh from Abraham's Bosom,* and *Old Abe's Jokes, or, Wit at the White House*—were circulating in the North and spreading Lincoln stories, many of them spurious, far and wide; and there have been collections of Lincoln anecdotes in print ever since.[5]

Humor was unquestionably a psychological necessity for Lincoln, though—being a serious, not a solemn, man—he would not have put it quite that way. He once called laughter "the joyous, beautiful, universal evergreen of life," and he enjoyed droll stories the way some people enjoy detective novels.[6] But both as a lawyer and as a politician he also found amusing stories enormously helpful in putting across important points he wanted to make. And as President he used his gifts as a storyteller to put people at ease, to win them over to his point of view, or simply to get them off the point and out of his office without having to deny their requests in so many words. Humor, he once said, was "an emollient" that "saves me much friction and distress." A group of people who had gone to the White House seeking government jobs reported resignedly afterward that "the President treated us to four anecdotes." Humor was also important for Lincoln during the Civil War as a means of relaxing, getting away from his troubles for a moment, and refreshing his spirit. "I laugh," he told a friend in the darkest days of the war, "because I must not cry; that is all—that is all." Once, when a Congressman came to complain about something, Lincoln said, "Well, that reminds me of a story." Outraged, the Congressman growled that he hadn't come to the White House to hear jokes. "Now, you sit down!" exclaimed Lincoln; and he went on to explain how vital it was for him to relieve his cares from time to time with funny stories. On another occasion Ohio's Senator Benjamin Wade called to demand that General Grant, who was not doing very well before Vicksburg at the time, be fired at once. "Senator," said Lincoln, "that reminds me of a story—" "Yes, yes," said Wade impatiently, "That is the way it is with you, Sir, all *story, story!* You are the father of every military blunder that has been made during the war. You are on the road to hell, Sir, with this government, by your obstinacy, and you are not a mile off this minute!" Senator," said Lincoln gently, "that is just about the distance from here to the Capitol, is it not?"[7]

Lincoln's taste in jokes ran all the way from the lowly pun to the satirical anecdote. Like all lovers of the English language, he took keen pleasure in plays upon words. Once he was looking out the window of his law office in Springfield, Illinois, and saw a stately matron, wearing a many-plumed hat, picking her way gingerly across the muddy street. Suddenly she slipped and fell. "Reminds me of a duck," said Lincoln. "Why is that?" asked a friend. "Feathers on her head and down on her behind," said Lincoln.[8] His pun about Admiral Andrew H. Foote was equally corny. When Admiral Foote was put in charge of the South Atlantic squadron, Lincoln told Secretary of the Navy Gideon Welles to be sure the Admiral's ship was seaworthy. "How is it you are so particular?" asked Welles. "Why," chuckled Lincoln, "have I not placed my Foote in it?"[9] On another occasion, taking a walk in Washington with Secretary of State William H. Seward, he noticed a store sign bearing the name of the proprietor, T. R. Strong, in bold letters. "T. R. Strong," murmured Lincoln, "but coffee are stronger." Seward smiled and made no reply. "We don't see how he could reply after so atrocious a thing as that," commented the newspaper which reported the story.[10]

But Lincoln's humor ordinarily rose above the level of puns. He particularly enjoyed teasing solemn people. To a temperance committee calling to tell him that Union defeats were "the curse of the Lord" on a drunken army, Lincoln (who was a teetotaler) could not resist remarking that it was "rather unfair on the part of the curse, as the other side drank more and worse whiskey than ours did."[11] He treated some Chicago ministers who came to give him advice the same way. When they told him they brought "a message to you from our Divine Master" about his slavery policy, Lincoln said it was "odd that the only channel he could send it by was the roundabout route of that awful wicked city of Chicago!"[12] He had some fun, too, with a pompous Austrian count who wanted to obtain a position in the Union army. In making his request, the Austrian harped on the fact that his family was ancient and honorable and that he bore the title of count. With a twinkle in his eye, Lincoln finally patted him on the shoulder and said, "Never mind, you shall be treated with just as much consideration for all that. I will see to it that your bearing a title sha'n't hurt you."[13]

Lincoln's humor wasn't always gentle. Sometimes he used it to point up a blunt truth. Asked once how large the Confederate army was, he said, "About 1,200,000 men." When his questioner expressed amazement, Lincoln explained: "Well, whenever one of our generals is licked he says he was outnumbered three or four to one, and we have 400,000 men."[14] He also could not help making wry remarks about General George B. McClellan, whose extreme caution in pursuing military campaigns drove Lincoln almost crazy. Once, when a man from a northern city asked him for a pass to Richmond, Lincoln exclaimed: "My dear sir, if I should give you one, it would do you no good. You may think it very strange, but there are a lot of fellows who either can't read or are prejudiced against every man who takes a pass from me. I have given McClellan, and more than 200,000 others, passes to Richmond, and not one of them has gotten there!"[15] A little later, greatly irked by McClellan's inactivity, he wrote: "Dear

General, if you do not want to use the army I would like to borrow it for a few days."[16] Lincoln gave as good as he got, too, when he felt like it. When McClellan, irritated by one of Lincoln's orders requiring detailed reports to the White House, sent him a telegram saying, "We have just captured six cows. What shall we do with them?" Lincoln answered: "Milk them."[17]

Lincoln, one reporter decided, was "a master of satire, which at times was as blunt as a meat-ax, and at others as keen as a razor."[18] In a speech in Congress opposing the Mexican War, he said that people who denied it was a war of aggression reminded him of the Illinois farmer who said, "I ain't greedy 'bout land. I only want what jines mine."[19] In another speech he ridiculed the sanctimonious sentiments of the expansionists: "Young America is very anxious to fight for the liberation of enslaved nations and colonies, provided, always, that they have land. As to those who have no land, and would be glad of help, he considers they can wait a few hundred years longer."[20] He once told of a Congressman who, having opposed the War of 1812 and come under heavy criticism, said, when asked to oppose the Mexican War: "I opposed one war; that was enough for me. I am now perpetually in favor of war, pestilence, and famine."[21] He also enjoyed telling people about the old loafer who said to him "I feel patriotic," and when asked what he meant, exclaimed, "Why, I feel like I want to kill somebody or steal something!"[22] Once a Senator came to the White House, furious about what he regarded as unfair distribution of patronage, and let loose a flood of profanity on the President. When he had finished, Lincoln said calmly, "You are an Episcopalian, aren't you, Senator?" "Yes, sir, I belong to that church." "I thought so," said Lincoln. "You Episcopalians all swear alike. But Stanton is a Presbyterian. You ought to hear him swear!" Lincoln, who rarely used intemperate language himself, was frequently criticized for not being a church member, so he was doubtless amused at hearing profanity from the orthodox.[23]

Lincoln laughed at himself as well as at other people. When Senator Stephen A. Douglas called him a "two-faced man," Lincoln said: "I leave it to my audience. If I had another face, do you think I would wear this one?"[24] He joked about his homely looks again while speaking to a convention of newspaper editors in Bloomington, Illinois. Pointing out that he was not an editor and therefore felt out of place at the meeting, he said: "I feel like I once did when I met a woman riding on horseback in the wood. As I stopped to let her pass, she also stopped and looked at me intently, and said, 'I do believe you are the ugliest man I ever saw.' Said I, 'Madam, you are probably right, but I can't help it.' 'No,' said she, 'you can't help it, but you might stay at home.' "[25] Lincoln also enjoyed telling about the grouchy old Democrat who walked up to him and said, "They say you're a self-made man," and when Lincoln nodded, snapped, "Well, all I've got to say is that it was a damned bad job."[26]

Lincoln combined a sense of fun with high seriousness. As President, he showed himself to be shrewd, thoughtful, selfless, dedicated, strong-willed, resourceful, compassionate, and extraordinarily magnanimous. The burdens he bore during the Civil War were far heavier than those of most American Presidents, yet he carried out his responsibilities with remarkable patience and determination. Though his critics could not always see it, he remained steadfastly true throughout the war to his basic objectives: restoration of the Union (which he regarded as a magnificent experiment in government of, by, and for the people) and the abolition of slavery (which he regarded as utterly incompatible with democracy). Anxious to get the very best men, civilian and military, he could find to help him in realizing these objectives, he did not mind if they personally held him in contempt. When someone told him that his Secretary of War, Edwin Stanton, had called him a damned fool, he said lightly, "If Stanton said I was a damned fool, then I must be one, for he is nearly always right and generally says what he means."[27] Stanton came to hold Lincoln in high esteem; but some of the Radical Republicans never did. They found it hard to understand that in pursuing his objectives—preserving the Union and emancipating the slaves—Lincoln had to proceed cautiously to avoid alienating the border slave states (thus driving them to secession) and offending northern public opinion (which was by no means sympathetic to abolitionism at first). He also thought it important to synchronize his policies with progress on the battlefield (which came slowly at first) if he was to avoid making futile and perhaps even counterproductive gestures.

No president has been vilified the way Lincoln was during the Civil War. He was attacked on all sides: by abolitionists, Negrophobes, states'-righters, strict constructionists, radicals, conservatives, armchair strategists, and by people who just did not like his looks or resented his storytelling. From the day of his inauguration to the day of his assassination the invective was unrelenting. Among other things, Lincoln was called an ape, a baboon, a buffoon, a clown, a usurper, a traitor, a tyrant, a monster, an idiot, a eunuch, a bigot, a demagogue, a lunatic, a despot, a blunderer, a charlatan, and a bully. One New York newspaper regularly referred to him as "that hideous baboon at the other end of the avenue" and said that "Barnum should buy and exhibit him as a zoological curiosity." The *Illinois State Register* called him "the craftiest and most dishonest politician that ever disgraced an office in America." *"Honest Abe, forsooth!"* sneered one editor. "Honest Iago! Benignant Nero! Faithful Iscariot!" Even his hometown paper joined the chorus: "How the greatest butchers of antiquity sink into insignificance when their crimes are contrasted with those of Abraham Lincoln!"[28] And all but three or four words failed an angry Louisiana letter-writer named Pete Muggins when he contemplated Lincoln: "God damn your god damned old hellfired god damned soul to hell god damn you and god damn your god damned family's god damned hellfired god damn soul to hell and good damnation god damn them and god damn your goddamn friends to hell."[29] No wonder Lincoln said, when asked how it felt to be President, "You have heard about the man tarred and feathered and ridden out of town on a rail? A man in the crowd asked how he liked it, and his reply was that if it wasn't for the honor of the thing, he would much rather walk."[30] In saying this, however, Lincoln was thinking not of the abuse heaped on him but of the terrible loss of life on the battlefield and the heartbreakingly slow progress being made toward the achievement of his objectives. He had enjoyed politics immensely before he became President and had been eager, too, to hold the highest office in the land. But in the White House, he said, instead of glory he found only "ashes and blood."[31]

The theater, like humorous stories, lightened the cares of office for Lincoln. He had a special fondness for Shakespeare and experienced exquisite pleasure one evening at seeing the veteran actor James Hackett play Falstaff in a Washington theater. He was so delighted with the performance that he wrote a letter of congratulation afterward. Hackett, flattered by such attention from the President of the United States, turned the letter over to the *New York Herald,* which reprinted it, accompanied by savage comments. Greatly embarrassed, Hackett wrote Lincoln to apologize. "Give yourself no uneasiness on the subject . . . ," Lincoln responded. "I certainly did not expect to see my note in print; yet I have not been much shocked by the comments upon it. They are a fair specimen of what has occurred to me through life. I have endured a great deal of ridicule, without much malice; and have received a great deal of kindness, not quite free from ridicule. I am used to it." For Lincoln, the pleasure of seeing Hackett do Falstaff far outweighed the pain of abuse from the *Herald.* But even this pleasure was short-lived. A little later Hackett sought a government job, but when Lincoln was unable to give him one he turned against the President and joined the ranks of the Lincoln-haters.[32]

Lincoln's love of Shakespeare grew out of his love of fine writing. As a young man he read and re-read the King James Bible, Aesop's *Fables,* Shakespeare, John Bunyan, Daniel Defoe, and Robert Burns, and he worked hard to improve his own vocabulary, grammar, and lucidity of expression. By the time he became President, he had developed a distinguished prose style of his own: simple, clear, precise, forceful, rhythmical, poetic, and at times majestic. When Vicksburg surrendered in July 1863, and the Mississippi River was open again, he told the country: "The Father of Waters again goes unvexed to the sea."[33] It is hard to imagine any other President writing such a stunning sentence—or penning such masterpieces of prose as the Gettysburg Address (which even H. L. Mencken called "genuinely stupendous")[34] and the First and Second Inaugural Addresses.

John Adams, Jefferson, Theodore Roosevelt, and Wilson all possessed unusual literary skills; but at his best Lincoln towered above them all. He was the only President ever to be called a literary artist. Jacques Barzun, in fact, has called him a "literary genius."[35] In their multi-volumed biography of Lincoln appearing in 1894, John Nicolay and John Hay, who had worked for him, had this to say: "Nothing would have more amazed him while he lived than to hear himself called a man of letters; but this age has produced few greater writers."[36] Ralph Waldo Emerson ranked Lincoln with Aesop in his lighter moods, but when it came to serious moments he said this of the Civil War President: "The weight and penetration of many passages in his letters, messages, and speeches, hidden now by the very closeness of their application to the moment, are destined to a wide fame. What pregnant definitions, what unerring common-sense, what foresight, and on great occasions what lofty, and more than national, what human tone! His brief speech at Gettysburg will not easily be surpassed by words on any recorded occasion."[37]

At Gettysburg on November 19, 1864, Edward Everett, famed for his oratory, spoke for close to two hours, while Lincoln took up only a couple of minutes. Afterwards, Everett took Lincoln's hand and said: "My speech will soon be forgotten; yours never will be. How gladly would I exchange my hundred pages for your twenty lines!"[38]

★   ★   ★

Good Lies

Once, when young Lincoln was reading Aesop's *Fables* aloud, his cousin Dennis Hanks remarked, "Abe, them yarns is all lies." "Mighty darn good lies, Denny," retorted Lincoln.[39]

Military Tactics

During the Black Hawk Indian War of 1832, Lincoln was captain of a militia company, but, completely unfamiliar with military procedures, he made many blunders. One day, marching with a front of over twenty men across a field, he wanted to pass through a gate into the next field. "I could not for the life of me remember the proper word of command for getting my company endwise," Lincoln recalled years later. "Finally, as we came near I shouted: 'This company is dismissed for two minutes, when it will fall in again on the other side of the gate.' "[40]

Out of Sight

When young Lincoln joined the Sangamon (Illinois) militia during the Black Hawk War, his colonel was a little fellow about four feet three inches tall. Abe himself was unusually tall; but he tended to walk with a slouch in those days. The colonel dressed him down for sloppy posture. "Come, Abe," he cried, "hold up your head; high, fellow!" "Yes, sir," said Abe. "High, fellow," persisted the colonel. "Higher!" Abe straightened up, stretched his neck, and said, "So, sir?" "Yes, fellow," said the colonel, "but a little higher." "And am I always to remain so?" asked Abe. "Yes, fellow, certainly!"

exclaimed the colonel. "Then," said Abe with a sad look, "good-bye, colonel, for I shall never see you again!"[41]

End in View

"One day," according to Lincoln's friend and fellow circuit-rider Ward Lamon, "when we were attending court at Bloomington, Illinois, I was wrestling near the courthouse with someone who had challenged me. In the scuffle, I made a large rent in the rear of my trousers. Before I had time to change, I was called into court to take up a case. Since I had on a short coat, my misfortune was apparent, and one of the lawyers started a subscription paper, which was passed from one member of the bar to another, to buy me a pair of pants. Several put down ridiculous subscriptions, and finally the paper was laid in front of Lincoln. Glancing over it, he immediately wrote after his name, 'I can contribute nothing to the end in view.' "[42]

Too Lazy to Stop

One day when Lincoln was handling a case in an Illinois courtroom, Judge David Davis held up a long bill in chancery drawn up by a usually sluggish attorney. "Astonishing, ain't it, Lincoln?" he called out. "It's like the lazy preacher that used to write long sermons," drawled Abe. "He got to writin' and was too lazy to stop!"[43]

Worst Way

Lincoln attended his first ball in Springfield because he wished to see Mary Todd. "Miss Todd," he said, "I should like to dance with you the worst way." Afterward Mary told a friend: "He certainly did!"[44]

Slow Horse

Called out of town on an important case, Lincoln hired a horse from a livery stable. When he returned a few days later he took the horse back to the stable and asked the owner: "Keep this horse for funerals?" "No, indeed," replied the man indignantly. "Glad to hear it," said Lincoln, "because if you did the corpse wouldn't get there in time for the resurrection."[45]

Contempt of Court

"I was never fined but once for contempt of court," a court clerk revealed. "Davis fined me five dollars. Mr. Lincoln had just come in, and leaning over my desk had told me a story so irresistibly funny that I broke out into a loud laugh. The Judge called me to order, saying, 'This must be stopped. Mr. Lincoln, you are constantly disturbing this court with your stories.' Then to me: 'You may fine yourself five dollars.' I apologized but told the Judge the story was worth the money. In a few minutes the Judge called me over to him. 'What was that story Lincoln told you?' he asked. I told him, and he laughed aloud in spite of himself. 'Remit your fine,' he ordered."[46]

Sense of Direction

In 1846, Lincoln ran for Congress as a Whig and was opposed by Peter Cartwright, the eloquent Methodist evangelist, who was running as a Democrat. During the campaign, Lincoln attended a religious meeting where Cartwright was preaching. After his sermon, Cartwright declared, "All who desire to lead a new life, to give their hearts to God, and go to Heaven, will stand." A sprinkling of men, women, and children stood up. Then Cartwright cried: "All who do not wish to go to hell will stand!" At this, everyone stood up except Lincoln. Then said Cartwright in his gravest voice: "I observe that many responded to the first invitation to give their hearts to God and go to heaven. And I further observe that all of you save one indicated that you did not wish to go to hell. The sole exception is Mr. Lincoln, who did not respond to either invitation. May I inquire of you, Mr. Lincoln, where are you going?" Lincoln got up slowly and said quietly: "I came here as a respectful listener. I did not know I was to be singled out by Brother Cartwright. I believe in treating religious matters with due solemnity. I admit that the questions propounded by Brother Cartwright are of great importance. I did not feel called upon to answer as the rest did. Brother Cartwright asks me directly where I am going. I desire to reply with equal directness: I am going to Congress." The meeting quickly broke up.[47]

Not a Know-Nothing

When his friend Joshua Speed wrote to ask Lincoln in August 1855 what he thought about the new American (Know-Nothing) Party, Lincoln responded: "I am not a Know-nothing. That is certain. How could I be? How can anyone who abhors the oppression of negroes, be in favor of degrading classes of white people? Our progress in degeneracy appears to me to be pretty rapid. As a nation, we began by declaring that *'all men are created equal.'* We now practically read it 'all men are created equal, *except negroes.'* When the Know-nothings get control, it will read 'all men are created equal, except negroes, *and foreigners and Catholics.'* When it comes to this, I shall prefer emigrating to some country where they make no pretense of loving liberty—to Russia, for instance, where despotism can be taken pure, and without the base alloy of hypocrisy."[48]

Too Big to Cry

A few minutes after the Illinois legislature elected Stephen A. Douglas rather than Lincoln Senator in 1858, the latter was asked by a friend, "How do you feel?" Said he: "I feel like the boy who stubbed his toe; I am too big to cry and too badly hurt to laugh."[49]

Holds His Hat

When Lincoln came out to the platform erected over the steps of the eastern portico of the Capitol to be sworn in as President, he was carrying the manuscript of his speech, a cane, and his tall silk hat. The cane he put under the table, but he didn't know what to do with the hat. Senator Stephen A. Douglas quickly stepped forward, took the hat, and returned to his seat. "If I can't be President," he said to one of Mrs. Lincoln's cousins, "I can at least hold his hat."[50]

Cowardly Lion

When W. C. Reeves of Virginia advised Lincoln to give up Forts Sumter and Pickens and other federal property in the southern states,

Lincoln said: "Do you remember the fable of the lion and the wood-man's daughter?" Reeve said he did not, and Lincoln proceeded to tell him the story. "Aesop," he said, "writes that a lion was very much in love with a woodman's daughter. The fair maid referred him to her father. The lion applied for the girl. The father replied: 'Your teeth are too long.' The lion went to a dentist and had them extracted. Returning, he asked for his bride. 'No,' said the woodman. 'Your claws are too long.' Going back to the dentist, he had them drawn. Then he returned to claim his bride, and the woodman, seeing that he was unarmed, beat out his brains." Concluded Lincoln: "May it not be so with me, if I give up all that is asked?"[51]

Something for Everybody

One day Lincoln was ill and not inclined to listen to people nagging him for jobs. Just as one of these pests had seated himself for a long interview, the President's physician happened to enter the room. Lincoln, holding out his hands, asked him, "Doctor, what are those blotches?" "That's varioloid, or mild small-pox," said the doctor. "They're all over me," said Lincoln. "It is contagious, I believe?" "Very contagious, indeed," said the doctor. Lincoln's visitor got up at this point and exclaimed, "Well, I can't stop now, Mr. Lincoln. I just called to see how you were." "Oh! don't be in a hurry, sir," said Lincoln pleasantly. "Thank you, sir," said the visitor hastily; "I'll call again." And he headed for the door. "There is one good thing about this," remarked Lincoln as the man left; "I now have something I can give everybody."[52]

Hair on a Pumpkin

A great bore from Philadelphia repeatedly encroached on Lincoln's time, until Lincoln figured out a way to get rid of him. The next time he called, Lincoln interrupted his conversation, walked over to a wardrobe in the corner of the room, and, taking a bottle from the shelf, said to the man, who was bald, "Did you ever try this stuff for your hair?" "No, sir," said the man, "I never did." "Well," said Lincoln, "I advise you to try it and I will give you this bottle. If at first you don't succeed, try, try again. Keep it up. They say it will make hair grow on a pumpkin. Now take it and come back in eight or ten months and tell me how it works." Somewhat non-

plussed, the man took the bottle and left. When Justice Carter of
the Supreme Court of the District of Columbia entered the room
shortly afterward, he found Lincoln convulsed with laughter.[53]

Sicker

A delegation urged Lincoln to appoint their man commissioner to
the Sandwich Islands. He was not only competent, they said; he
was also in delicate health, so the climate there would be good for
him. "Gentlemen," sighed Lincoln, "I am sorry to say that there
are eight other applicants for that place, and they are all sicker
than your man."[54]

Needs No Office

Some Republicans met with Lincoln to seek a port-collectorship for
their man. "Mr. President," said their spokesman, "we have come
here today to present our distinguished townsman to your favorable
consideration. He is preëminently qualified for the position—not only
for his administrative ability, but also for his invincible loyalty and
attachment to Republican principles. No honors, sir, could be showered on him that could elevate him higher in the estimation of his
fellow-men." "Gentlemen," said Lincoln with a smile, "it gives me
much gratification to hear the praise bestowed. Such a man needs
no office; it can confer on him no additional advantage, or add prestige
to his well-earned fame. You are right, Mr. Chairman, 'No honors
could be showered on him that would elevate him higher in the
estimation of his fellow-man.' To appoint so good and excellent a
gentleman to a paltry place like this would be an act of injustice
to him. I shall reserve the office for some poor politician who needs
it."[55]

Done Enough

A woman imperiously demanded a colonel's commission for her
son. "Sir," she told Lincoln, "my grandfather fought at Lexington,
my father fought at New Orleans, and my husband was killed
at Monterey." "I guess, madam," said Lincoln, "your family has
done enough for the country. It's time to give somebody else a
chance."[56]

Bigger Than I Am

Some weeks after the 1860 election, Springfield banker John W. Bunn met Senator Salmon P. Chase coming out of Lincoln's law office in Springfield. "You don't want to put that man in your cabinet," he told Lincoln. "Why do you say that?" Lincoln asked. "Because," said Bunn, "he thinks he is a great deal bigger than you are." "Well," said Lincoln, "do you know of any other men who think they are bigger than I am?" "I don't know that I do," said Bunn, "but why do you ask?" "Because," said Lincoln, "I want to put them all in my cabinet."[57]

Burn It and Write Again

One day Secretary of War Stanton complained to Lincoln of a major-general who had accused him of favoritism in extremely abusive language. Lincoln suggested writing him a sharp rejoinder. "Prick him hard!" he said. Stanton at once wrote out a strongly worded letter, then showed it to the President. "Right! Right!" cried Lincoln approvingly. "Just it! Score him deeply! That's first rate, Stanton." But when Stanton folded the letter and put it in an envelope, Lincoln interrupted him. "What are you going to do with it?" he asked. "Send it," said Stanton, surprised at the question. "Nonsense!" exclaimed Lincoln. "You don't want to send that letter. Put it in the stove. That's what I do when I have written a letter while I am angry. It's a good letter, and you've had a good time writing it and feel better. Now, burn it, and write another letter."[58]

Stray Kittens

Once, while visiting the army's telegraph hut in Washington, Lincoln saw three tiny kittens wandering around and mewing as if lost. He picked up one of them and said, "Where is your mother?" "The mother is dead," someone told him. "Then," said Lincoln, petting the little one, "she can't grieve as many a poor mother is grieving for a son lost in battle." Gathering the other two kittens in his hands, he put them on his lap, stroked their fur, and, according to General Horace Porter, said gently, "Kitties, thank God you are cats, and can't understand this terrible strife that is going on." And to Colonel Theodore Bowers he said, "Colonel, I hope you will see that these poor little motherless waifs are given plenty of milk and treated kindly." On several occasions afterward Porter noticed Lincoln fondling these kittens. "He would smooth their coats," according to Porter, "and listen to them purring their gratitude to him." A curious sight it was, Porter thought, "at an army headquarters, upon the eve of a great military crisis in the nation's history, to see the hand which had affixed the signature to the Emancipation Proclamation and had signed the commissions from the general-in-chief to the lowest lieutenant tenderly caressing three stray kittens."[59]

Bootblack

A foreign diplomat, according to Lincoln folklore, came upon Lincoln while he was polishing his shoes. "What, Mr. President," he cried, "you black your own boots?" "Yes," said Lincoln, "whose do you black?"[60]

More Light, Less Noise

At the outset of the Civil War, when the newspapers were giving Lincoln all sorts of gratuitous advice, the correspondent of a New York paper called to propose a plan for conducting the war. Lincoln listened patiently for a while, then said: "Your New York papers remind me of a little story. Some years ago, there was a gentleman traveling through Kansas on horseback. There were few settlements and no roads and he lost his way. To make matters worse, as night came on, a terrific thunderstorm arose and peals of thunder and flashes of lightning shook the earth and momentarily illuminated the scene. The terrified farmer finally got off his horse and began to lead it along as best he could by the flickering light of the lightning flashes. All of a sudden, a tremendous crash of thunder brought the man to his knees in terror and he cried out: 'Oh Lord! If it's all the same to you, give us a little more light and a little less noise!' "[61]

Abraham Is Joking

Lincoln's favorite story among the many circulating about him concerned two Quaker ladies who were discussing Lincoln and Jefferson Davis. "I think Jefferson will succeed," said the first Quaker. "Why does thee think so?" asked the second. "Because Jefferson is a praying man," said the first. "And so is Abraham a praying man," said the second. "Yes," said the first, "but the Lord will think Abraham is joking."[62]

Clean-Shaven

John Ganson of Buffalo, beardless and bald, was a Democrat who supported Lincoln in Congress but was disturbed by the bad news from the front. One day he made a formal call on the President to discuss the state of the country. "Though I am a Democrat," he told Lincoln, "I imperil my political future by supporting your war measures. I can understand that secrecy may be necessary in military operations, but I think I am entitled to know the exact conditions, good or bad, at the front." Lincoln looked at him earnestly for a moment or two and then exclaimed: "Ganson, how clean you shave!" That ended the interview.[63]

Lincoln Testifies

According to a popular tale (undoubtedly spurious), Lincoln once appeared before a Senate committee to defend his wife against charges of treason. "We had just been called to order by the chairman," one of the Senators is supposed to have recalled, "when, at the foot of the committee table, his hat in hand, his form towering, was Abraham Lincoln. No one spoke, for no one knew what to say. At last the caller spoke slowly, with control, though with a depth of sorrow in his tone of voice: 'I, Abraham Lincoln, President of the United States, appear of my own volition before this committee to say that I, of my own knowledge, know it is untrue that any member of my family holds treasonable communication with the enemy.' Having attested this, he went away as silent and solitary as he had come. We sat for some minutes speechless. Then, by tacit agreement, no word being spoken, the committee dropped all considerations of the rumors that the wife of the President was betraying the Union."[64]

Plucking Thistles

An old lady, grateful to Lincoln for releasing her husband from the army to support the family, had tears in her eyes as she said, "Good-bye, Mr. Lincoln; I shall probably never see you again till we meet in heaven." Deeply moved, Lincoln took her hand and, following her to the door, said: "I am afraid with all my troubles I shall never get to the resting-place you speak of; but if I do, I am sure I shall find you. That you wish me to get there is, I believe, the best wish you could make for me. Good-bye." Afterward, he remarked to his friend Joshua Speed, "It is more than many can often say, that in doing right one has made two people happy in one day. Speed, die when I may, I want it said of me by those who know me best, that I have always plucked a thistle and planted a flower when I thought a flower would grow."[65]

Methuselah

One day an old man asked for a pardon for his son. "I am sorry," said Lincoln, gently but firmly, "I can do nothing for you. Listen to this telegram I received from General Butler yesterday: 'President Lincoln, I pray you not to interfere with the courts-martial of the army. You will destroy all discipline among our soldiers.' " The old man's face fell; but when Lincoln saw his hopeless despair, he cried: "By jingo! Butler or not Butler, here goes!" He wrote an order and showed it to the old man: "Job Smith is not to be shot until further orders from me—A. Lincoln." "Why, I thought it was a pardon," said the father disconsolately. "You may order him to be shot next week." "My old friend," said Lincoln, "I see you are not very well acquainted with me. If your son never dies until orders come from me to shoot him, he will live to be a great deal older than Methuselah."[66]

Handsomest

Pennsylvania's Thaddeus Stevens frequently criticized Lincoln for granting too many pardons, but one day he brought a woman from his own state to the White House to plead the case of a boy condemned for sleeping at his post. Lincoln listened attentively to her story, then turned to Stevens. "Now, Thad," he said, "what would you do in this case, if you happened to be President?" Stevens didn't enjoy being cornered; but he replied that because of extenuating circumstances he would certainly pardon the boy. Lincoln then reached for a piece of paper, wrote on it, and handed it to the woman. "Here, madam," he said, "is your son's pardon." Stevens escorted the grateful woman to the outer door of the White House, where she turned to him and exclaimed: "I knew it was a lie! I knew it was a lie!" "What do you mean?" asked Stevens. "When I left home yesterday," she said, "my neighbors told me that I would find Mr. Lincoln an ugly man. It was a lie; he is the handsomest man I ever saw in my life!"[67]

Leg Cases

A Judge Holt came to Lincoln one day with the case of a soldier who had thrown down his gun in the middle of a battle and hidden behind a stump until the shooting was over. When tried for cowardice, he had no defense. Testimony at the court-martial revealed that he had no father or mother living, no children, and, as he constantly stole from his comrades, no friends either. "Here," said Judge Holt, "is a case which comes exactly within your requirements. He does not deny his guilt, he will serve the country better dead than living, as he has no relations to mourn for him, and he is not fit to be in the ranks of patriots." Lincoln deliberated for a while and then turned to Holt. "Well, after all, Judge," he said, "I think I'll have to put this with my 'leg cases.' " "Leg cases?" cried the Judge. "What do you mean by 'leg cases,' sir?" "Why, Judge," said Lincoln, "do you see those papers crowded into those pigeonholes? They are cases that you call by that long name, 'cowardice in the face of the enemy,' but I call them for short my 'leg cases.' I put it to you, and I leave it for you to decide for yourself: if Almighty God gives a man a cowardly pair of legs, how can he help their running away with him?"[68]

Weighty Men

A dozen or more leading Wilmington businessmen called on Lincoln one day. They told him they represented the "weighty men" of Delaware and had come to discuss ways and means of winning the war. After the chairman of the delegation had finished his little speech, Lincoln asked: "So you are the weighty men of Delaware? All from New Castle County?" "Yes, all from the same city." "Well," said Lincoln mischievously, "did it ever occur to you gentlemen that there was danger of your little state tipping up during your absence?"[69]

Road Runner

Lincoln enjoyed the description of the Congressman who led the race when Union soldiers streamed back to Washington after their defeat by the Confederates at Bull Run in July 1861. "I never knew but one fellow who could run like that," he said. "He was a young man out of Illinois who had been sparking a girl much against the wishes of her father. In fact, the old man took such a dislike to him that he threatened to shoot him if he ever caught him on the premises again. One evening the young man learned that the girl's father had gone to the city, and he ventured out to the house. He was sitting in the parlor with his arm around the girl's waist and then he suddenly spied the old man coming around the corner of the house with a shotgun. Leaping through the window into the garden, he started down the path at the top of his speed like greased lightning. Just then a jackrabbit jumped up in the path in front of him. In about two leaps the boy overtook the rabbit. Giving it a kick that sent it high in the air, he yelled, 'Git out of the road, gosh dern you, and let somebody run that knows how!' "[70]

Exaggeration

A general sent Lincoln a glowing report of having killed hundreds of Confederates in battle which closed by saying, "and our loss was twelve men killed, wounded, and captured." This reminded Lincoln of the fellow who used to lecture about his travels abroad but got his figures all out of proportion not only to the facts but also to one another. A friend who traveled with him kept advising him not to stretch his statements and figures too far. Admitting that his enthusiasm sometimes carried him into exaggerations before he realized it, the lecturer asked his friend, who always sat behind him on the platform, to pull his coattails whenever he saw him getting too worked up and drifting into hyperbole. In his next lecture he had occasion to tell about a tall building he had seen in Europe. "And that building," he said excitedly, "was a mile and a half long; and really it must have been a mile high!" Just then his friend pulled his coattails. While he was trying to collect his wits and get his statement back to normal, someone in the audience yelled: "And how *wide* was that building, please?" Thoroughly confused by now and determined to make amends for his previous exaggerations, the lecturer said quickly: "Oh, *just about a foot!*"[71]

Lincoln and Holmes

During the Confederate attack on Fort Stevens, near the northern corner of the District of Columbia, Lincoln journeyed to the front to inspect Union defenses. The task of showing him around fell to young Oliver Wendell Holmes, Jr., aide to the commanding general. When Holmes pointed out the enemy in the distance, Lincoln, with his high plug hat, stood up to look. A snarl of musketry fire came from the enemy trenches. Grabbing the President by the arm, Holmes dragged him under cover, shouting, "Get down, you fool!" When he realized what he had said, he was sure that disciplinary action would be taken. But to his immense relief, Lincoln said to him just before leaving, "Good-bye, Captain Holmes. I'm glad to see you know how to talk to a civilian."[72]

How to Charge

Once when Lincoln was in the War Department an officer who was in a big hurry slam-banged into him, then offered "ten thousand pardons" when he saw who it was. "One is enough," smiled Lincoln. "I wish the whole army would charge like that!"[73]

Grant's Whiskey

A temperance committee visited Lincoln, according to the *New York Herald* (November 26, 1863), and asked him to fire General Grant. Surprised, Lincoln asked, "For what reason?" "Why," said the spokesman for the group, "he drinks too much whiskey." "Well," said Lincoln, "I wish some of you would tell me the brand of whiskey that Grant drinks. I would like to send a barrel of it to every one of my other generals."

Asked whether the *Herald* story was accurate, Lincoln said, "No, I didn't happen to say it—but it's a good story, a hardy perennial. I've traced that story as far back as George II and General Wolfe. When certain persons complained to George that Wolfe was mad, George said, 'I wish he'd bite some of the others!' "[74]

Them Three Fellows

Once Lincoln was telling Senator John B. Henderson of Missouri about the great pressure being brought on him by the Radical Republicans to issue an emancipation proclamation. He didn't think the time was ripe for it and was annoyed by the persistence of three men in particular: Senators Charles Sumner and Henry Wilson of Massachusetts and Thaddeus Stevens of Pennsylvania. "Henderson," he said, "did you ever attend an old field [country] school?" "Yes," said Henderson. "Well," said Lincoln, "I did, and a funny thing occurred one day. You know, we had no reading books, and we read out of the Bible. The class would stand up in a row, the teacher in front of them, and read verses, turn about. This day we were reading about the Hebrew children. As none of us were very good readers, we were in the habit of counting ahead and each one practicing on his particular verse. Standing next to me was a red-headed, freckled-faced boy, who was the poorest reader in the class. It so fell out that the names of the Hebrew children appeared in his verse. He managed to work through Shadrach, fell down at Meschach, and went all to pieces at Abednego. The reading went on, and in due course of time came round again, but when the turn came near enough for the boy to see his verse, he pointed to it in great consternation, and whispered to me, 'Look! there come them three d——ed fellers again!' And there," said Lincoln, pointing out of the window, "come those three same fellows." And sure enough, there were Wilson, Sumner, and Stevens, coming up the walk.[75]

Emancipation

On September 21, 1862, Lincoln summoned his Cabinet to the White House for a special session. "The President was reading a book and hardly noticed me as I came in," Secretary of War Stanton wrote later. "Finally he turned to us and said: 'Gentlemen, did you ever read anything of Artemus Ward? Let me read a chapter that is very funny.' " Lincoln then read aloud something by humorist Ward entitled "A High Handed Outrage at Utica." Furious at what he regarded as "buffoonery" on Lincoln's part, Stanton almost got up and left. But Lincoln read on until the end of the piece and then laughed heartily. Everyone else was silent. "Gentlemen," said Lincoln disappointedly, "why don't you laugh? With the fearful strain that is upon me night and day, if I did not laugh I should die, and you need this medicine as much as I do." Then he reached into his tall hat on the table, took out a paper, and said: "I have called you here upon very important business. I have prepared a little paper of much significance. I have said nothing to anyone, but I have made a promise to myself—and to my Maker. I am now going to fulfil that promise." He read in a clear voice: "On the first of January in the year of our Lord, 1863, all persons then held as slaves in any state or designated part of a state the people whereof shall then be in rebellion against the United States, shall be then, and thenceforth and forever free." Stanton was overwhelmed. He got up, took Lincoln's hand, and said, "Mr. President, if reading a chapter of Artemus Ward is a prelude to such a deed as this, the book should be filed among the archives of the nation and the author canonized!"

At noon on January 1, 1863, the final Proclamation was taken to Lincoln. As it lay before him, he twice picked up his pen and then put it down. Turning to Secretary of State Seward, he said, "I have been shaking hands since nine o'clock this morning, and my right arm is almost paralyzed. If my name ever goes into history, it will be for this act, and my whole soul is in it. If my hand trembles when I sign the Proclamation, all who examine the document hereafter will say, 'He hesitated.' " He then took up the pen again and slowly and firmly wrote, "Abraham Lincoln."

Some time later Lincoln told Francis B. Carpenter, the artist who painted a picture commemorating the event, that he regarded the Emancipation Proclamation as "the central act of my administration, and the great event of the nineteenth century." When Colonel McKaye of New York reported that he had found enormous affection for Lincoln among freedmen on the coast of North Carolina, the President was deeply moved. "It is a momentous thing," he told McKaye, "to be the instrument, under Providence, of the liberation of a race."[76]

Gettysburg

On the morning of Lincoln's departure for Gettysburg to dedicate the National Cemetery there, his aides were afraid he would not be on time for the train. "You fellows remind me of the day they were going to hang the horse thief," Lincoln told them. "The road to the hanging place was so crowded with people going to the execution that the wagon taking the prisoner was delayed. As more and more people crowded ahead the prisoner called out, 'What's your hurry? There ain't goin' to be any fun till I get there!' "[77]

Preferred Disease

In June 1864, Lincoln was nominated for a second term. About the only way he could be defeated, his friends told him, was if General Grant took Richmond and decided to run for President against him. "Well," said Lincoln, "I feel very much like the man who said he didn't want to die particularly, but if he had to die that was precisely the disease he would like to die of."[78]

Cold Feet

Visiting a soldiers' hospital in Washington, Lincoln came across a soldier who was even taller than he was. When he caught sight of the lad, he stopped in amazement and then, extending his hand, said: "Hello, comrade, do you know when your feet get cold?"[79]

Precedent

In February 1865, President Lincoln and Secretary of State Seward met with three Confederate commissioners at Hampton Roads, Virginia, to discuss peace. Since Jefferson Davis insisted on the recognition of Southern independence, Lincoln had no real hope for the meeting, but he did not want to overlook any chance for peace. At the conference Lincoln made it clear he would make no bargains with armed forces warring against his government. One of the Confederates pointed out that Charles I had negotiated with people in arms against his government. Lincoln said wryly: "Upon questions of history, I must refer you to Mr. Seward, for he is posted in such things, and I don't profess to be; but my only distinct recollection of the matter is, that *Charles lost his head.*"[80]

Lawful Prize

On April 10, 1865, official news of Lee's surrender produced a flood of victory celebrations in Washington. A crowd of some three thousand people, headed by a brass band, marched to the White House. Lincoln came out to read some remarks he had jotted down to commemorate the historic occasion. As he finished reading each page he let it fall to the ground; his son Tad picked it up, shouting, "Give me another paper!" When Lincoln finished, he said, "I propose closing up this interview by having the band perform a particular tune which I will name. Before this is done, however, I wish to mention one or two little circumstances connected with it. I have always thought 'Dixie' one of the best tunes I ever heard. Our adversaries over the way attempted to appropriate it, but I insisted yesterday that we fairly captured it. I presented the question to the Attorney-General, and he gave it as his legal opinion that it is our lawful prize. I now request the band to favor me with its performance." The band then played "Dixie" and followed it up with "Yankee Doodle."[81]

Last Day

After lunch on his last day in the White House, Lincoln signed a pardon for a soldier sentenced to be shot for desertion. "I think," he said, "the boy can do us more good above ground than under ground." He also approved an application for the discharge of a rebel prisoner who had taken an oath of allegiance. "Let it be done," he wrote on the petition. And he met with Nancy Bushrod, who had come to the White House to tell the President of her plight. She and her husband Tom, she said, had been slaves on a plantation near Richmond until the Emancipation Proclamation was issued, after which they came to Washington. Tom joined the army, leaving Nancy with twin boys and a baby girl. At first his army pay came regularly every month; then, abruptly, it stopped coming. She trudged all over the city looking for work but without any success. Could the President help her get Tom's pay? "You are entitled to your soldier-husband's pay," Lincoln assured her. "Come this time tomorrow and the papers will be signed and ready for you." Tears filled Nancy's eyes as she started to leave, but Lincoln called her back. "My good woman," he said gently, "perhaps you'll see many a day when all the food in the house is a single loaf of bread. Even so, give every child a slice and send your children off to school." With that, he bowed, said Nancy, "lak I wuz a natchral bawn lady," and she left him in a glow.[82]

Theater Party

On the fatal night, April 14, 1865, Lincoln did not want to go to the theater. He had seen the play, *Our American Cousin,* once before and was not anxious to see it again. He tried to get out of going, but Mrs. Lincoln had her heart set on it. "It has been advertised that we will be there," Lincoln told White House guard Colonel William H. Crook, "and I cannot disappoint the people. Otherwise I would not go. I do not want to go." As he left, he said, "Good-bye, Crook." This puzzled the guard. Ordinarily the President said, "Good-night."[83]

SEVENTEEN

Andrew Johnson
1865–69

Andrew Johnson's presidency was a failure, but Johnson (1808–75) himself was in many respects an impressive figure. The only tailor ever to occupy the White House, he was fiercely proud of his craft. The only southern Senator to oppose secession, he bore the contempt and hatred of secessionists in Tennessee and elsewhere with courage and defiance. And the only President ever to be impeached, he behaved with dignity and restraint during the ordeal of trial by the U.S. Senate.

Johnson, who had no schooling, was apprenticed to a tailor at the age of ten. Though he rose rapidly in life after entering politics he never forgot his humble origins. "Andy Johnson," said people in East Tennessee, "never went back on his raisin'."[1] Johnson made his own clothes until he went to Washington as a Congressman. Even after he became President he almost never passed a tailor shop without dropping in for a chat. He also liked to stop and talk with mechanics whom he met on the street. "Adam, the Father of the race, was a tailor by trade," he told a meeting of mechanics in his hometown, Greenville, Tennessee, in May 1843, "for he sewed fig-leaves together for aprons. Tubal Cain was an artificer in brass and iron; Joseph, the husband of Mary, the mother of Jesus, was a carpenter by trade, and the probability is strong that our Savior himself followed the same."[2]

When Johnson was Governor of Tennessee (the "Mechanic Governor") he made a suit of clothes for the Governor of Kentucky (who had been a blacksmith) and received a homemade shovel and pair of tongs in return. In Congress he once had an angry exchange with Jefferson Davis over appropriations for the military academy at West Point, which Davis had attended. When Johnson said it was wasteful to spend so much money to employ high-priced "experts" to teach at West Point, Davis cried sarcastically: "Can a blacksmith or a tailor construct the bastioned fieldworks opposite Matamoros?" "I am a mechanic," replied Johnson angrily, "and when a blow is struck, on that class, I will resent it. I know we have an illegitimate, swaggering, bastard, scrub aristocracy which assumes to know a great deal, but which, when the flowing veil of pretension is torn off, is seen to possess neither talents nor information on which one can rear a useful superstructure."[3] Johnson always believed it was a minority of southern aristocrats who were responsible for secession, and he denounced them bitterly for deceiving and misleading the masses of people. "If Johnson were a snake," growled one secessionist leader, "he would hide himself in the grass and bite the heels of the children of rich people."[4] When Jefferson Davis became President of the Confederacy, Johnson exclaimed: "When I look at his gallant services, finding him first in the military school of the United States, educated . . . at the expense of his country— taught to love the principles of the Constitution; afterwards entering its service fighting beneath the Stars and Stripes, . . . I cannot understand how he can be willing to hail another banner, and turn from that of his country; . . . if I could not unsheathe my sword in vindication of the flag of my country . . . I would return the sword to its scabbard; I would never sheathe it in the bosom of my mother; never! never! never!"[5]

In the Senate, Johnson, a good Jacksonian Democrat, blasted secession as "hell-born and hell-bound."[6] To secessionists he was a "southern traitor," and there were many threats on his life when he returned home after Lincoln's inauguration.[7] As his train pulled into Liberty, Virginia, en route to Tennessee, an armed mob rushed into the car where he was sitting. One man yelled, "Are you Andy Johnson?" "I am," said Johnson. "Then I am going to pull your nose," said the man. As he reached out to do so, Johnson drew his revolver, forced the mob out of the car, and, as the train pulled out of the station, shouted: "I am a Union man!"[8] At Lynchburg, another mob dragged him out of the train, kicked him, spit on him, and was about to hang him, when an old man in the crowd shouted: "His neighbors at Greenville have made arrangements to hang their Senator on his arrival. Virginians have no right to deprive them of that privilege!" The mob then decided to let him go, and he proceeded to Tennessee.[9]

In Knoxville, Memphis, and Nashville, Johnson was hanged and shot in effigy; wherever he went he was jeered at, insulted, and threatened. But he refused to be intimidated. No sooner had he reached home than he began stumping the state to fight the movement for secession. At Kingsport, where he presented his Unionist views in a church, he put his revolver on the pulpit before commencing to speak, so there were no incidents. At Rogersville, while he was speaking in the courthouse, some armed men marched in and demanded that the meeting be halted. But Johnson cried: "I have been a Democrat all my life and accustomed to the rule of the majority. If a majority of this crowd want me to stop speaking, I will stop. If a majority want me to continue, I will speak on, regardless of you and your company." The majority of the audience sided with Johnson, so he finished his talk without further trouble.[10] At Knoxville, where he made an impassioned speech for the Union, one observer exclaimed: "I had never seen him so cool, so determined, so eloquent, and so impressive in bearing. . . . As he appeared before the large assemblage . . . and appealed with burning words for the preservation of the Union, my heart—all hearts—turned towards him. . . ."[11]

Johnson's efforts to keep Tennessee in the Union were in vain. In June 1861, Tennessee voted to join the Confederacy, and Johnson had to flee the state. But after Union forces seized western and central Tennessee in 1862, Lincoln made him military governor of the state. Soon afterward Johnson persuaded the legislature to rescind the ordinance of secession and to end slavery in the state forever. In June 1864, when Johnson was nominated for Vice-President to run with Lincoln on the National Union Party ticket, people who disliked Lincoln made fun of Johnson as well. "The age of statesmen is gone," said the *New York World* of the Lincoln-Johnson ticket; "the age of rail splitters and tailors, of buffoons, boors and fanatics has succeeded. . . . In a crisis of the most appalling magnitude requiring statesmanship of the highest order, the country is asked to consider the claims of two ignorant, boorish, third-rate backwoods lawyers for the highest stations in the Government. Such nominations, in such a conjuncture, are an insult to the common sense of the people. God save the Republic!"[12] Despite Lincoln's forebodings of defeat, the Lincoln-Johnson ticket won handily in November. On the day of the inauguration—March 4, 1865—Johnson was ill. He wanted to skip the inaugural ceremony, but Lincoln persuaded him to attend. To steady his nerves he drank some whiskey beforehand, talked too much and rather incoherently during the proceedings, and was ever afterward unfairly called a "drunken tailor" by his enemies. But Lincoln stoutly defended him. "I have known Andrew Johnson for many years," he told his associates. "He made a bad slip the other day, but you need not be scared; Andy ain't a drunkard."[13]

When Johnson became President after Lincoln's assassination in April 1865, the Radical Republicans, knowing of his dislike for southern aristocrats, had high hopes of him. "Johnson, we have faith in you," Senator Ben Wade of Ohio told him. "By the gods, there will be no trouble now in running the government." Extremely pleased, Johnson replied: "Robbery is a crime; rape is a crime; murder is a crime; *treason* is a *crime* and *crime* must be punished. The law provides for it and the courts are open. Treason must be made infamous and traitors must be impoverished."[14] Nevertheless, it soon became clear that Johnson favored a milder reconstruction policy than that desired by the Radical Republicans in Congress, and that he was not willing to go as far as the latter in disfranchising former Confederate leaders and in guaranteeing the freedmen their full rights as citizens. During the Congressional elections of 1866, Johnson toured the East and Midwest to rally support for his views on reconstruction. But the "swing around the circle," as it was called, was an egregious failure. During the tour Johnson got into shouting matches with people in the audience and upset even his supporters by his unruly behavior in public. The result was that the Radicals won an overwhelming victory at the polls that fall, instituted a new reconstruction program for the South over Johnson's vetoes, and passed a Tenure of Office Act limiting the President's power to remove people from office.

Johnson regarded the Tenure of Office Act as unconstitutional (and the Supreme Court so ruled in 1926); but in February 1868, when he dismissed his Secretary of War, Edwin Stanton, who was working closely with the Radicals, the House of Representatives

voted to impeach him for "high crimes and misdemeanors." Johnson
exploded when he heard the charges against him. "Impeach me for
violating the Constitution!" he exclaimed "Damn them! Haven't I
been struggling ever since I have been in this chair to uphold the
Constitution they trample under foot!" When one of his friends suggested using patronage to persuade some of the Senators to vote
for acquittal, he exclaimed: "How would I feel after acquittal if I
had bought it? How would I feel if my conscience told me that I
owed my acquittal to bribery? I will do nothing of the kind. I will
not seek to use any unfair means for my vindication."[15] In the end,
after a trial lasting more than two months, Johnson was only narrowly
vindicated. Seven Republican Senators deserted their party to vote
with the Democrats for acquittal, with the result that Johnson's
enemies failed by only one vote to secure the necessary two-thirds
for conviction. When Chief Justice Salmon P. Chase, who presided
at the trial, announced the acquittal, Colonel William Crook, Johnson's bodyguard, ran all the way from the Capitol to the White
House to report the news. "Mr. President," he cried, as he entered
the library where Johnson was sitting with some friends, "You are
acquitted!" Everyone jumped up to congratulate Johnson, who, with
tears in his eyes, sent for whiskey so they could all drink a toast
to victory. When Crook told Mrs. Johnson, who was ill upstairs,
she said: "Crook, I knew he would be acquitted. I knew it."[16]

After leaving the White House in March 1869, Johnson returned
to Greenville. Anxious to prove that he had been in the right all
along, he ran for Congress later that year. He lost the election, but
tried again in 1872 and again lost. Finally, in 1874, the Tennessee
legislature elected him to his old office as U.S. Senator, and he returned to Washington in March 1875. When he walked into the
Senate Chamber shortly after noon on Friday, March 6, there was
an embarrassed silence for a moment or two and then handshakes
from both friends and former foes alike; and a little page came over
to hand him a bouquet of flowers.[17] Afterward, a friend called on
him at his quarters in the Willard Hotel on Pennsylvania Avenue
and observed that his present lodgings were not nearly as spacious
as those he had once occupied further up the avenue. "No," said
Johnson, "but they are more comfortable."[18]

★   ★   ★

Breaches

At the close of the Civil War, Johnson returned to Raleigh, North
Carolina, where he had been brought up, to attend the unveiling
of a monument erected to the memory of his father. In his address,
he said, "I have returned to the South and to the place of my boyhood,
to try, if possible, to heal the *breaches* made by war." An old woman
in the crowd, who had known Johnson in the old days, exclaimed:
"Bless his dear heart, he's going to come back and open up a tailor-
shop!"[19]

Ulysses S. Grant
1869–77

For a military hero, Ulysses S. Grant (1822–85) was singularly mild-mannered and pacific. He disliked hunting, shunned profanity, abhorred cruelty to animals, hated the sight of blood, and was sickened by the spectacle of a bullfight in Mexico. He never read a book on military strategy or tactics, moreover, and he enjoyed military pomp and circumstance or wearing full-dress uniforms no more than Zachary Taylor. As he told Bismarck after the Civil War while attending a military review in his honor at Potsdam: "I am more of a farmer than a soldier. I take little or no interest in military affairs."[1] This was, to be sure, an exaggeration. Still, it is a fact that when he met the second Duke of Wellington he said, innocently enough, "They tell me, my Lord, that your father was also a military man."[2]

As a young man Grant was not eager for a military career. When his father told him he had been appointed to a cadetship at the Military Academy at West Point, he said, "I won't go." "I think you will," said his father, and that settled the matter.[3] Grant did only fair work at the Academy, hoped that Congress would abolish the institution, and graduated twenty-first in a class of thirty-nine. He saw his first action during the Mexican war and performed creditably enough, but was utterly without enthusiasm for the war. The Mexican War, he said afterward, was "one of the most unjust wars ever waged by a stronger against a weaker nation. It was an instance of a republic following the bad example of European monarchies, in not considering justice in their desire to acquire additional territory."[4] After the war he was assigned duty at frontier posts in Oregon and California and could not afford to take his family with him. Homesick, lonely, and bored, he turned to drink, and after one spectacular episode—which involved driving three horses in tandem at breakneck speed down the street with their buggies careening behind them—he was asked to resign his commission. After that, his road went steadily downhill, from farming (on a little farm near St. Louis that he called "Hard Scrabble") to peddling firewood, collecting rents, and, finally, clerking in a leather goods store operated by his brothers in Galena, Illinois.

The Civil War (which Grant thought came as a punishment for America's sins in Mexico) brought the shy, modest, matter-of-fact, colorless Midwesterner to life. When Lincoln called for volunteers in April 1861, Grant at once offered his services. He helped raise a company of volunteers in Galena, took it to Springfield, and worked a few weeks there helping organize Illinois volunteer regiments. One regiment, rowdy and insubordinate, was turned over to Grant by the Governor of Illinois. Two politicians presented Grant to the soldiers after making long, flowery speeches; when they finished, the men started shouting, "Grant!" "Grant!" "Colonel Grant!" "Speech!" Grant stepped forward, wondering what to say, waited for the noise to abate, then gave his first Civil War order: "Go to your quarters!" Someone told him, "They're an unruly lot. Do you think you can manage them?" "Oh, yes," said Grant quietly, "I can manage them." He could and did.[5] A few days later, when one of the regiment's leading troublemakers came back from town drunk, defiant, and spoiling for a fight, Grant walked over to him and felled him with a blow. Then he had him tied to a post. "For every minute I stand here," the man shouted at Grant, "I'll have an ounce of your blood!" Grant turned to a sergeant and said, "Put a gag in that man's mouth." A few hours later, Grant untied the bully with his own hands. "Now salute me," he said, "and go to your quarters." The man saluted dejectedly and walked away without another word.[6]

Not long after Grant established order in his regiment, he took it into action against a rebel camp headed by Colonel Thomas Harris in northern Missouri. As the regiment neared Harris's camp, according to Grant, "my heart kept getting higher and higher until it felt to me as though it was in my throat. I would have given anything then to have been back in Illinois, but I had not the moral courage to halt and consider what to do; I kept right on. When we reached a point from which the valley below was in full view I halted. The place where Harris had been encamped a few days before was still there and the marks of a recent encampment were plainly visible, but the troops were gone. My heart resumed its place. It occurred to me at once that Harris had been as much afraid of me as I had been of him. This was a view of the question I had never taken before; but it was one I never forgot afterwards. From that event to the close of the war, I never experienced trepidation upon confronting an enemy, though I always felt more or less anxiety. I never forgot that he had as much reason to fear my forces as I had his. The lesson was valuable."[7]

"I cannot spare this man," Lincoln exclaimed to critics of Grant the following year. "He fights."[8] The famous message Grant sent in February 1862 to the Confederate commander of Fort Donelson in Tennessee proposing an armistice—"No terms except an unconditional and immediate surrender can be accepted. I propose to move immediately upon your works"—caused him to be nicknamed "Unconditional Surrender Grant" by the northern public (and "Victor" and "Caesar" by his wife).[9] A little later another pithy statement of his passed into folklore: "I propose to fight it out on this line if it takes all summer."[10] Exclaimed Lincoln happily: "When General Grant once gets possession of a place he seems to hang onto it as if he had inherited it."[11] After Shiloh (a bloody battle, but a victory for Grant) he was made commander of all Union forces in Tennessee, and after Vicksburg, his greatest campaign, he was given command of all the western armies. In March 1864, he was called to Washington, made a lieutenant general, and placed in command of all the armies in the field. When the unprepossessing and somewhat shabby-looking Grant registered at Willard's in Washington, the clerk was about to assign him to a fifth-floor room at the back of the hotel when someone in the lobby recognized him. "Why, *General* Grant," he cried, "we didn't expect you till—" With a gasp of surprise, the clerk quickly reassigned his customer to better quarters.[12]

Grant's prescription for military success was simple and straightforward. "Find out where your enemy is," he said. "Get at him as soon as you can. Strike at him as hard as you can, and keep moving on." When General George G. Meade asked him, "What shall I do if the enemy pushes me here?" pointing to a place on the map where his line seemed weak, Grant pointed to a spot a mile away and said, "Push him there."[13] Grant had a superstition about retreating or retracing his steps. Even as a young man, if he walked past a house he was trying to locate he would never go back but would always keep on walking until he came to a crossroad, then work his way back to the house by a new route. As Civil War commander he was similarly resistant to retreating; he hammered stubbornly away at the enemy and wore him down by sheer attrition. This method of winning battles produced such horrendous bloodshed that for a time he was called "Grant the Butcher" in the northern press. But after the Confederate surrender at Appomattox in April 1865, he emerged as a national hero. "Well, Ulysses," his mother said calmly after the war, "you've become a great man, haven't you?" and went back to her sewing.[14] Grant's behavior when he met with General Robert E. Lee to discuss terms of surrender in the Appomattox Court House was characteristic. He was plainly, even sloppily, attired, got off the point several times to reminisce about the old days before the war, and refused Lee's proffer of his sword as a token of surrender. He also let the Confederate officers keep their horses, remarking that they would need them for the spring plowing when they got home.

After the war, Congress made Grant a full general—the first since George Washington—and the public showered him with ovations and gifts, all of which he accepted quietly but gratefully. The 10,000 boxes of cigars he received after Fort Donelson had turned him into a heavy cigar-smoker; the postwar gifts developed in him a taste for elegant living. "Since Richmond's capitulation," grumbled Horace Greeley's *Tribune* on February 23, 1866, "the stern soldier has spent his days and eke his nights, in conjugating the transitive verb *to receive.*"[15] The greatest gift was of course the Presidency. In 1864, when his name was first mentioned for President, Grant told a political delegation, "I should like to be mayor of Galena . . . to build a new sidewalk from my house to the depot."[16] By 1868, however, his ambitions had grown to the point where he accepted the Republican nomination in May almost as a matter of course with the statement, "Let us have peace."[17] At the height of his popularity when he became President in March 1869, he seemed to be just the man the country needed at the helm in the difficult postwar years.

Grant's Presidency was a disaster. He appointed so many old friends to office that Charles Sumner told the Senate the country was suffering from "a dropsical nepotism swollen to elephantiasis."[18] After that, Grant never passed the Massachusetts Senator's house without shaking his fist. Told once that Sumner didn't believe in the Bible, he growled, "No, he didn't write it."[19] But Sumner was not Grant's only critic. Even friends of the administration were shocked by the scandals that punctuated Grant's years in office, though they knew that he was personally honest. In his last annual message to Congress Grant ruefully admitted that his Presidency was not all that it should have been. Once out of office he went on a world tour and was surprised to find himself a celebrity everywhere. In 1880, he made an unsuccessful bid for a third term; several years later, having invested his money unwisely, he was reduced to poverty. By this time he was suffering from cancer of the throat and, desperate for money, began writing articles on his Civil War campaigns for the *Century Magazine*. At this point Mark Twain intervened and gave him a generous contract for writing his memoirs. They were published shortly after his death to great acclaim and compared as military reminiscences to Caesar's *Commentaries*.

As Grant lay dying in his home in Mt. McGregor, New York, in 1885, Rev. J. P. Newman, a popular Methodist minister, with the encouragement of Grant's family, began visiting his bedside. Before long he was quoting biblical remarks, supposedly made by Grant, for the newspapers. At one point, when Grant became unconscious for a time, Newman sprinkled water over him, then announced to the press that the general had been converted and baptized. A little later the doctor succeeded in reviving Grant, and Newman exclaimed: "It is Providence. It is Providence." "No," said the doctor, "it was the brandy."[20] Shortly before he died, Grant told his doctor how years before, on the way to a reception in his honor, he had been caught in a shower and shared his umbrella with a stranger. The stranger, it turned out, was going to the reception too. "I have never seen Grant," he remarked, as the two walked down the street, "and I merely go to satisfy a personal curiosity. Between us, I have always thought that Grant was a very much overrated man." "That's my view also," Grant told him.[21]

*   *   *

Bargainer

When Grant was about eight years old a neighbor owned a colt which he very much wanted. Grant's father offered twenty dollars for it, but the neighbor demanded twenty-five. Grant was so anxious to have the colt that he begged his father to buy the animal anyway. The father said the colt was only worth twenty dollars, but if the neighbor wouldn't sell it for that, to offer twenty-two and a half, and if that did not work to offer the twenty-five. Young Grant at once mounted a horse and went for the colt. When he got to the neighbor's house, he told him: "Papa says I may offer you twenty dollars for the colt, but if you won't take that, I am to offer twenty-two and a half, and if you won't take that, to give you twenty-five." The story of these negotiations quickly spread around town, and it was a long time before Grant heard the last of it.[22]

Cleaning the Stables

When Grant was a little boy, his father took him one day into the stable, where a row of cows stood in their uncleaned stalls. "Ulysses," said he, "the stable window is pretty high for a boy, but do you think you could take this shovel and clean out the stable?" "I don't know, father," said Grant; "I never have done it." "Well, my boy," said his father, "if you will do it this morning, I'll give you this bright silver dollar," and he patted Grant on the head and held a silver dollar before his eyes. "Good," said Grant, "I'll try," and went to work. He "tugged and pulled and lifted and puffed," Grant said many years later, and when he had finished the job his father gave him the silver dollar, saying, "That's right, Ulysses, you did it splendidly, and now I find you can do it so nicely, I shall have you do it *every morning all winter.*"[23]

Fancy Dress

After graduating from West Point, Grant bought a new uniform, donned it, and set off proudly for Cincinnati on horseback. When he reached the city, a barefooted little boy, wearing a dirty shirt and ragged pants held up by suspenders, caught sight of him and yelled: "Soldier! will you work? No, sir—ee; I'll sell my shirt first!" This taunt upset Grant; and in his hometown he had another deflating experience. One day a rather dissolute stableman began parading around the streets, wearing a pair of sky-blue nankeen pantaloons, just the color of Grant's uniform trousers, with a strip of white cotton sheeting sewed down the outside seams in imitation of Grant's. The townspeople enjoyed the joke; Grant didn't. After that, he never really enjoyed wearing fancy dress uniforms. Even after he became a lieutenant general, he liked to go around in a private's blouse with his three stars stitched to the shoulders.[24]

Julia

One day Grant arrived at the home of Julia Dent, the woman he was courting, and found the family all dressed up and ready to leave for a neighborhood wedding. Grant was invited to go along; he rode in a buggy with Julia. On the way they came to an overflowing creek and a rickety bridge. "Do you think it safe, Ulysses?" asked Julia fearfully. "Why, of course it's safe," said Grant. "Oh, I'm afraid," said Julia. "I'm terribly afraid." "Now, now, don't be frightened," said Grant. "I'll take care of you." "I'm going to cling to you," she declared, "no matter what happens," and she clasped his arm with both hands. After they got safely across the bridge, Julia said, "Well, I clung to you, didn't I, Ulysses?" "You certainly did," he replied; and after a moment's silence he turned to her and said, "How would you like to cling to me for the rest of your life?" They were married in August 1848.[25]

Stanton and Grant

After the capture of Vicksburg, Lincoln sent Grant to Chattanooga to take command there. As the train bearing Grant and his staff stopped at the railroad station in Indianapolis, Secretary of War Edwin Stanton, who had come from Washington to meet Grant, entered. Grasping the hand of Dr. Kittoe, the staff surgeon, he exclaimed, "How are you, General Grant? I knew you at sight from your pictures."[26]

Rank

Once, after Grant had been made supreme commander, Secretary of War Stanton imperiously demanded an explanation of an order

he had given. "I think I rank you in this matter, Mr. Secretary,"
said Grant quietly. "We shall have to see Mr. Lincoln about that,"
said Stanton. "All right," said Grant. "Mr. Lincoln ranks us both."
They went to the White House. "Won't you state your case, General
Grant?" said Stanton. Replied Grant: "I have no case to state; I
am satisfied as it is." Stanton then stated his case. Said Lincoln:
"You and I, Mr. Stanton, have been trying to boss this job, and
we have not succeeded very well with it. We have sent across for
Mr. Grant, as Mrs. Grant calls him, to relieve us, and I think we
had better leave him alone to do as he pleases."[27]

Loses Temper

Horace Porter, who was on Grant's staff in 1864, reported that Grant
lost his temper only once while he was with him. One day Grant
and his staff, riding along a Virginia road, came upon a teamster
who was beating his horse over the head. Grant was furious; he
jumped out of the saddle, seized the man by the throat and shook
him fiercely. And before he rode away he ordered him to be tied
to a post for six hours.[28]

Grant and Twain

When Mark Twain was still a relatively unknown writer, he was
introduced to General Grant. As the two shook hands, Twain
couldn't think of a thing to say, and Grant maintained his usual
taciturnity. At last Twain stammered, "General, I'm embarrassed;
are you?"[29]

Post-Appomattox

In the spring of 1869, Robert E. Lee was in Baltimore on some
railroad business, received word that Grant would like to see him
at the White House, and called on him for a chat. It was the first
time the two had met since Appomattox; but the meeting did not
last long. At one point, referring to Lee's attempt to promote the
building of a railroad, Grant remarked, "You and I, General, have
had more to do with destroying railroads than building them." Lee
did not find the remark amusing and did not smile. It was impossible

for him to exchange jests about war with the man who had beaten him.[30]

Two Tunes

Grant was so tone-deaf that he had difficulty keeping step when his company at West Point marched to music. Once, when he was President, he had to attend a concert. Afterward someone asked him if he had enjoyed the music. "How could I?" he asked. "I know only two tunes. One of them is 'Yankee Doodle' and the other isn't."[31]

Dining with the Queen

In 1877, when General and Mrs. Grant, together with their nineteen-year-old son Jesse and General Adam Badeau, were in England, Queen Victoria invited them to dinner at Windsor Castle. When they arrived at the castle on the afternoon of June 26, they were taken to elegant apartments. Soon afterward, Sir John Cowell, Master of the Queen's Household, appeared and explained that Jesse and General Badeau were not to dine at Her Majesty's table, but in another room with "the Household." Immediately after dinner they would be presented to the Queen. Jesse at once balked at this arrangement; he said he would not eat with the servants and that if he could not sit at the Queen's table he would return to London. Cowell was apologetic; large dinners made the Queen giddy, he said, so she tried to keep her dinners as small as possible. Besides, he added, the Prime Minister of England, as well as foreign diplomats, dined with the Household unless especially invited to sit with the Queen.

But Jesse was stubborn; he absolutely refused to dine with the Household. With General Badeau he went down to Grant's room to tell him about it. There they found the Duchess of Roxburgh, one of the ladies-in-waiting, talking with Mrs. Grant. The Duchess assured Jesse that the Household consisted of important people: ladies-in-waiting like herself as well as gentlemen-in-waiting. But Jesse said he considered them all servants anyway, in a sense—that he would not dine with them and was going to pack his bags, walk back to the station, and perhaps have supper at some little eating place near it. Sir John Cowell was on the verge of hysteria. He begged Jesse to remain until the Queen, out for a drive, returned and the matter could be brought to her attention. General Grant broke in to say that if he were in his son's place he would react the same way; why invite the boy to dine with the Queen if he had to eat in some other dining room?

The Grants dressed for dinner and waited. The Queen returned, Cowell conferred with her, and he came back, much relieved, with the news that she would be pleased to have Jesse at her table. So Jesse dined with the Queen after all. But the conversation at the table was not especially scintillating. Her Majesty spoke most of the time with her son, Prince Leopold, and with Princess Beatrice, her daughter, in a low tone of voice. She did, though, at one point, remark to Mrs. Grant that her duties as royal sovereign were arduous. Replied Mrs. Grant stoutly: "Yes, I can imagine; I, too, have been the wife of a great ruler." After dinner, the Queen retired, and the Grants stayed up late playing whist with the lords and ladies.[32]

Cable for Grant

The Army of the Potomac was holding its annual meeting when it heard that Grant was being entertained by Queen Victoria at Windsor Castle. Not realizing that all such communications were supposed to pass through the ambassador of one's own country to the foreign minister of another country, the old soldiers cabled a warm message to General Grant, care of Queen Victoria, Windsor Castle, England. According to the *New York Times,* which reported the incident, a messenger boy arrived at Windsor Castle during the night and rang the front doorbell. Her Majesty called out the window, "Who is there?" The messenger boy shouted: "Cable for General Grant. Is he staying at this house?"[33]

NINETEEN

Rutherford B. Hayes
1877–81

Rutherford B. Hayes (1822–93) was prouder of having been a soldier than of having been President. "I am more gratified by friendly references to my war record," he wrote toward the end of his life, "than by any other flattery." And he added: "I know that my place was a very humble one—a place utterly unknown in history. But I also am glad to know that I was one of the good colonels."[1] When the Civil War came, Hayes volunteered at once; he participated in several engagements, was praised by Grant for "conspicuous gallantry," and rose to the rank of major general.[2] Ever afterward he enjoyed being addressed as "General Hayes." Being Governor of Ohio and even President of the United States did not afford him nearly as much pleasure.

As President, Hayes was, in fact, called "His Fraudulency," "Ruther*fraud* B. Hayes," and "the Usurper" for a time. Many Democrats felt that he had not come by his office fairly and squarely and that Samuel J. Tilden, the Democratic candidate, had really won the election of 1876. During the election, both parties had resorted to fraud in the South (still partly occupied by federal troops), with the result that the House of Representatives appointed an electoral commission to decide the outcome. Voting along strict party lines, the commission gave Hayes the victory by one electoral vote; many people were outraged. During the election crisis Hayes received many threatening letters, and one evening someone even fired a bullet into his house while he was at dinner. When he finally started for Washington on March 1, 1877, he was not sure the Democrats would accept his Presidency. On leaving Columbus, Ohio, he told a crowd assembled to see him off that "perhaps" he would "be back immediately." Not until dawn on March 2, when he reached Harrisburg, Pennsylvania, did he receive a telegram announcing that the Democrats had agreed not to contest his election further. When people in his car began cheering the news, he admonished them, "Boys, boys . . . you'll waken the passengers."[3]

In his inaugural address, which the Democrats boycotted, Hayes noted the unusual circumstances under which he had come into office and promised to be as non-partisan as possible as President: "He who serves his country best serves his party best."[4] As President, he followed a policy of conciliation toward the South, appointing so many Democrats to office and backing so many bills for internal improvements in the South that northern newspapers began protesting the "looting of the treasury for the former rebels."[5] Even so, in 1878, the House of Representatives, controlled by the Democrats, launched an investigation of Hayes's election; there was talk of removing him from office because of the corrupt voting uncovered. Queried about this possibility, Hayes said, "Who is to take my place?" "Mr. Tilden," was the reply. "Mr. Tilden will be arrested and shot," said Hayes angrily. "He cannot attempt to take possession of the White House without being shot. That means civil war and in that event we will whip them badly." Later he explained more calmly what he meant: "Such schemes cannot be carried out without war. I swore to preserve the Constitution of the United States, and will deliver the Executive Office in its integrity to my successor. They can impeach me in the House of Representatives and try me in the Senate. There is no other way in which I will recognize any attempt of Congress to remove me. . . . I should defend my office and the independence of the Executive against any intruder."[6] In the end, the Democrats stopped contesting Hayes's election; Democratic leader Abram Hewitt acknowledged that his administration "was creditable to all concerned and was far better than four years of unrest which we should undoubtedly have had if Tilden had occupied the office of President."[7]

Hayes's Presidency was generally lackluster. "It may be asked whether this man of destiny has any marked peculiarities," said a friend. "I answer none whatever. Neither his body nor his mind runs into rickety proportions."[8] One biographer insisted that Hayes possessed an insatiable intellectual curiosity, but his evidence rested largely on the fact that Hayes greeted acquaintances with the words, "Well, what do you know?"[9] Hayes sought the middle way; he had an abhorrence of "ultras." "Virtue," he decided, after reading Aristotle, "is defined to be *mediocrity,* of which either extreme is vice."[10] Bankers applauded his sound-money policy, pious people his temperance views, and civil-service reformers his efforts to reduce the spoils system. But when he went after the notorious New York customshouse, spoilsman Roscoe Conkling denounced him bitterly in the Senate and climaxed his remarks by declaring that "when Dr. Johnson said that patriotism was the last refuge of a scoundrel, he ignored the enormous possibilities of the word *refawr-rm.*"[11]

With the Hayeses in the White House morning prayers and nightly "hymn sings" were the rule; profanity, tobacco, and liquor vanished. People blamed Mrs. Hayes ("Lemonade Lucy") for the ban on liquor, but Hayes took the credit himself. He had long been a temperance man, though not a prohibitionist, and at the first official White House function, a dinner for two Russian Grand Dukes, wine was served; but it was never served again. "It seemed to me," Hayes explained, "that the example of excluding liquors from the White House would be wise and useful, and would be approved by good people generally. I knew it would be particularly gratifying to Mrs. Hayes to have it done."[12] He hoped, too, that it would keep temperance people in the Republican party and induce members of temperance organizations to vote Republican. But some Republicans thought it was too high a price to pay for votes. After one official dinner, Secretary of State William M. Evarts remarked dolefully: "It was a brilliant affair; the water flowed like champagne."[13] Even Republican Congressman James A. Garfield of Ohio, not exactly a tippler, sneered that he had attended "a State dinner at the President's wet down with coffee and cold water."[14] For a time it seemed that a sympathetic White House steward was trying to get around the ban on liquor by putting frozen punch made of Santa Croix rum into the oranges served at official banquets. "This phase of the dinner," according to one reporter, "was named by those who enjoyed it 'the Life-Saving Station.'" But after leaving the White House, Hayes firmly denied that there had ever been any "Life-Saving Stations" at his and Lucy's parties. "The joke of the Roman punch oranges was not on us," he insisted, "but on the drinking people. My orders were to flavor them *rather strongly* with the same flavor that is found in Jamaica rum! This took! There was not a drop of spirits in them! This was certainly the case after the facts alluded to reached our ears. It was refreshing to hear 'the drinkers' say with a smack of the lips, 'Would they were hot!' "[15]

Hayes had never intended to run for a second term. "I am heartily tired of this life of bondage, responsibility, and toil," he told his wife. Lucy heartily agreed: "I wish it was at an end."[16] When William Dean Howells and his wife visited the White House in May 1880, Mrs. Howells told the President, "Well, you will soon be out of it." "Yes," rejoined Hayes, "out of a scrape, out of a scrape."[17] As his administration neared its end, he was pleased to note that the acrimony surrounding his elevation to high office had given way to general approval of his conduct by the people he thought counted most. "Coming in," he wrote in his diary, "I was denounced as a fraud by all the extreme men of the opposing party, and as an ingrate and a traitor by the same class of men in my own party. Going out, I have the good will, blessings, and approval of the best people of all parties and sections."[18]

After returning to private life, Hayes quickly slipped into obscurity and was soon forgotten by most people. New York lawyer Chauncey Depew met him one day in front of a fruit display in a fancy grocery store and after a cordial greeting said to the groceryman, "That is ex-President Hayes. Don't you want to meet him?" Replied the grocer: "I am not interested in him, but I have the finest collection of pears in the city and want to sell you some."[19] Toward the end of his life, Hayes began wondering whether he had been too Puritanical. "In avoiding the appearance of evil," he reflected, "I am not sure but I have sometimes unnecessarily deprived myself and others of innocent enjoyments."[20] He found too that he could joke about it. One day he got up to speak ruddy with poison ivy, and told his audience: "When your eyes met mine a suspicion arose in your minds which I assure you is without foundation. I have not forsaken my temperance principles and practice. Appearances, I admit, are against us. But in truth it is not whiskey but poison ivy which did it."[21]

★   ★   ★

By Way of Richmond

In 1864 Ohio Republicans asked General Hayes to run for Congress. Hayes agreed, but made it clear that if elected he would not take his seat in the House unless the war was over. During the campaign his supporters urged him to take a leave and return to Ohio. "I have other business just now," he told them. "Any man who would leave the army at this time to electioneer for Congress ought to be scalped." After a lively campaign in which his supporters utilized such slogans as "Our Candidate Is a Hero" and "Hayes Loves His Country and Fights for It," Hayes won the election. His friends then urged him to resign his commission to take his seat. One of them wrote from Washington asking him if he was coming to town. Replied Hayes: "I shall never come to Washington until I can come by way of Richmond." He took his seat in December 1865.[22]

White House Exit

When Hayes was President the White House was small and cramped for space. At a diplomatic dinner one evening the British minister's wife told Mrs. Hayes that she had to leave early and wanted to sneak out unobtrusively by a side door. Mrs. Hayes asked her son to help out. "Of course," the son recalled many years later, "I had explored the White House from cellar to attic and knew every door and passageway. There was not a single side or back door available. The ground floor was then simply a basement, where coal, old furniture and other odds and ends were stored. I recalled a door near the coal-bin, and led her through the dark musty basement and let her out of this door. She was very jolly and laughed heartily over the escapade."[23]

TWENTY

James A. Garfield
1881

James A. Garfield (1831–81) was a good party man; he played the game by the rules. A skilled debater, spellbinding orator, and efficient parliamentarian, he enjoyed his work in the House of Representatives, where he served as Congressman from Ohio between 1863 and 1880. In June 1880 he went to the Republican presidential convention in Chicago committed to the candidacy of his Ohio colleague John S. Sherman. But the "Stalwart" faction of the party, headed by Senator Roscoe Conkling (who was pushing Grant for a third term), and the "Half-Breed" faction (which was backing Garfield's friend James G. Blaine) soon became hopelessly deadlocked. When, at one point, Garfield challenged a Conkling resolution and was cheered by the delegates, "Lord Roscoe" thought the Ohioan was making a bid for the nomination himself. Grabbing a newspaper, he wrote a sarcastic note on the margin and sent it over to him: "I congratulate you on being the dark horse."[1]

Conkling turned out to be right. Though Garfield stubbornly refused to push his own cause, there was a stampede toward him on the thirty-sixth ballot, on which he came out the winner. After receiving the nomination, he sat apparently stunned for a moment. Then he cried, "Get me out of here," to one of the Ohio delegates, and the two pushed their way through the crowd to the street outside. But a group of people already gathered to greet him there tore off the top of the public hack ordered for him before the driver could get the horses moving. After Garfield left, the convention picked Chester A. Arthur (an ally of Stalwart Conkling in New York) as his running mate to appease the Stalwarts.[2]

Garfield's campaign biographies made much of a dramatic speech he was supposed to have given in April 1865. He was in New York City, they reported, when news of Lincoln's assassination arrived. Seeing angry crowds gather in the streets and head for the offices of the anti-Lincoln *New York World* in an ugly mood, and fearful of what might happen, the Ohio Congressman stepped forward, with a small flag in his hand, beckoned to the mob, lifted his right arm, and cried: "Fellow citizens! Clouds and darkness are round Him! His pavilion is dark waters and thick clouds of the skies! Justice and judgment are the establishment of his throne! Mercy and truth shall go before His face! Fellow citizens! God reigns, and the Government at Washington still lives!" Garfield's words held the crowd spellbound. People, it was said, "stood riveted to the ground with awe, gazing at the motionless orator, and thinking of God and the security of the Government at that hour. . . . What might have happened had the surging and maddened crowd been let loose, none can tell. The man for the crisis was on the spot, more potent than Napoleon's guns at Paris." It was a good story. Unfortunately, it was apocryphal.[3]

The 1880 campaign was in some ways humiliating for Garfield. One of the main issues was whether he had been involved in the scandals that tarnished Congress during the Grant administration. Among other things, the Democrats charged that in 1868 he had accepted a bribe of $329 from the Crédit Mobilier, a corrupt construction company involved in the building of the Union Pacific Railroad. A Congressional investigating committee had decided in 1873 that there was no conclusive evidence that Garfield ever took bribes for political favors, and Garfield himself published a thirty-page pamphlet defending himself; but suspicions lingered which were revived in 1880. By September, the figure 329 began appearing throughout the country: on sidewalks, streets, doors, fences, walls, posts, on the steps of Garfield's home in Washington, on hats, napkins, and even, according to one amused Republican, "on underclothing and the insides of shoes."[4] Garfield won the election despite the attacks on his character, but seems not to have taken much pleasure in victory. He called the Presidency "a bleak mountain."[5] He also looked tired and worn at the inauguration, in contrast to his predecessor,

Hayes, who, according to Benjamin Harrison, looked "sweet and lamblike."[6]

In his inaugural address, Garfield paid lip service to civil-service reform but also sought peace with the Stalwarts (who opposed reform) by making it clear that he would consult them on appointments. He even considered the possibility of a Cabinet post for his Stalwart enemy Roscoe Conkling. "If it seems best to make the tender," he said to Blaine (to whom he had promised the State Department), "what would you say to exchanging seats—you for the Treasury, he for State?" Blaine's reply was blunt: "His appointment would act like strychnine upon your administration—first, bring contortions and then be followed by death." Garfield promptly dropped the idea.[7] For years Garfield had taken the spoils system for granted, but when he became President the pressure of office-seekers drove him to distraction. "My God!" he cried shortly after taking office, "what is there in this place that a man should ever want to get into it?"[8] He took pleasure, though, in appointing General Lew Wallace to office. He had intended sending him to Paraguay, but after reading *Ben-Hur,* he decided to send him to Constantinople, where he might be inspired to write another exciting book about biblical times.[9]

The spoils system was Garfield's undoing. At the same time that he was trying to please everyone (it was, John Hay decided, his chief defect), a man named Charles J. Guiteau was pestering the State Department for an appointment as consul in Paris. In mid-May 1881 he managed to corner James G. Blaine, who—trying to escape—cried angrily, "Never speak to me again about the Paris consulship!" But Guiteau persisted, saying that the new President was sure to want a new man in Paris, and finally Blaine sighed, "Well, if he will . . . ," waved him off, and got away.[10] A few weeks later, when Garfield, accompanied by Blaine, went to the Baltimore and Potomac railroad station in Washington to take a train to Massachusetts, Guiteau was waiting for him. As Garfield entered the waiting room, Guiteau fired two shots at him, then ran out of the station and shouted, "I am a Stalwart and Arthur is President now!" "My God! What is that?" gasped Garfield as he sank to the floor. Guiteau was seized by policemen, and Garfield was carried back to the White House, where he lingered near death for weeks.[11] Late in August, a *Washington Star* reporter, interviewing Garfield's doctor, D. W. Bliss, said that "some people say that prayer has saved the President." Bliss snapped: "They may think so. In my opinion it was whiskey," and added irritably, "I have received a number of letters today abusing me for using stimulants."[12] To escape the Washington heat Garfield was moved to a seaside cottage in New Jersey early in September. There he died on September 19, eighty days after the shooting. Guiteau was tried, sentenced to death, and hanged on June 30, 1882.

Garfield's assassination produced a nationwide demand for civil-service reform. "The assassination of Mr. Garfield," said the *New York Evening Telegraph*, was a natural "outcome of the debased and debasing machine politics that this nation has suffered from ever since the war closed. . . ."[13] Across the country there were rallies for reform at which Garfield's portrait was prominently displayed. People who had formerly been lukewarm about the late President also tended to think better of him in retrospect. Exclaimed Henry Adams impatiently: "The cynical impudence with which the reformers have tried to manufacture an ideal statesman out of the late shady politician beats anything in novel-writing."[14] It is ironic that Garfield's successor, Chester A. Arthur, commonly regarded as a political hack, did better in office than had Garfield.

★   ★   ★

Thirty-Minute Speech

Garfield, a professional orator, knew when to stop talking. Once he was in Nashua, New Hampshire, sharing the platform with Eugene Hale, Congressman from Maine, who spoke for over two hours. The crowd became impatient and began calling for Garfield, who, when his turn came, proposed that the audience remain for exactly thirty minutes more. He then delivered a half-hour speech which was so rousing that the audience asked for more. But he did not continue.[15]

Bow Wow

When Charles Dickens was in the United States, Garfield attended his lectures and enjoyed them thoroughly. During one reading of *A Christmas Carol*, when Dickens came to the words "Bless his heart: it's Fezziwig again!" a dog in the building suddenly responded

with a series of double-bass barks. This not only brought the house
down; it also amused Dickens so much that he found it hard to
continue. For months afterward, whenever Garfield met anyone who
had attended the Dickens lecture, he greeted them with the cry,
"Bow! wow! wow!"[16]

Chester A. Arthur
1881–85

When Garfield died and Chester A. Arthur (1830–86) became President in September 1881, one prominent Republican exclaimed: "Chet Arthur President of the United States. Good God!"[1] His chagrin was understandable. Arthur had never held elective office until he became Vice President; he was known largely as a "Gentleman Boss" closely associated with Roscoe Conkling's New York political machine. "Arthur for President!" former President Hayes wrote, almost in disbelief, in his diary. "Conkling the power behind the throne, superior to the throne!"[2] For the *New York Times* Arthur was "about the last man who would be considered eligible to that position, did the choice depend on the voice either of a majority of his own party or of a majority of the people of the United States."[3]

Arthur, who liked to be called "General" after his Civil War rank, was a "spoilsman's spoilsman."[4] A few months before Garfield's assassination, speaking at a Republican banquet in New York, he had shocked reformers by his levity about politics. The banquet was in honor of Stephen W. Dorsey, Secretary of the Republican National Committee, and Arthur began his speech by teasing the Republican notables there about the methods used during the 1880 campaign, especially in Indiana. "I don't think we had better go into the minute secrets of the campaign, so far as I know them," he said playfully, "because I see the reporters are present, who are taking it all down; and, while there is no harm in talking about some things after the election is over you cannot tell what they may make of it, because the inauguration has not yet taken place. . . . Still, if I should get to going about the secrets of the campaign, there is no saying what I might say to make trouble between now and the 4th of March." After a few more remarks along this line, accompanied by cheers, laughter, and applause from the banqueters, Arthur got to Dorsey. "The first business of the convention," he said, "was to carry Indiana, and Mr. Dorsey was selected as the leader of the forlorn hope to carry Indiana. That was a cheerful task." The crowd roared with laughter, and Arthur went on: "Indiana was really, I suppose, a Democratic State. It has always been put down in the book as a State that might be carried by close and careful and perfect organization and a great deal of—" Here he paused; and there were immediate cries from the audience of "soap" (purchased votes), followed by more laughter. "If it were not for the reporters I would tell you the truth," continued Arthur, "because I know you are intimate friends and devoted adherents to the Republican party." He sat down. When it came time for Henry Ward Beecher to speak, the eloquent Brooklyn preacher announced that he was not present as a clergyman and that it was a good thing for some people in the audience that he wasn't. The crowd roared with delight at this, and a little later the meeting broke up amid general hilarity.[5] But when reports of Arthur's remarks appeared in the newspapers the following day, many people were extremely upset. "The cynicism of this, coming from such a veteran Machinist as Mr. Arthur, was not surprising," said E. L. Godkin, editor of *The Nation,* "but people were rather shocked . . . when they remembered that it was from the lips not of Mr. Conkling's 'lieutenant' in this city, but of the Vice-President-elect of the United States."[6]

When Arthur became President, however, Governor Foster of Ohio predicted that people "will find that Vice-President Arthur and President Arthur are different men."[7] He seemed to be right. Arthur's brief inaugural address received much praise; his break with his old associates in machine politics surprised and pleased his critics; and his warm support for civil-service reform (which Conkling called "snivel service") led many people to revise their opinions of the former spoilsman drastically. Said Mark Twain: "I am but one in 55,000,000; still, in the opinion of this one-fifty-five millionth of the country's population, it would be hard to better President Arthur's Administration."[8] Even Godkin found words of praise for Arthur; but Arthur's former associates were disgruntled. "He isn't 'Chet' Arthur any more," said one spoilsman sadly, "he's the President."[9] "Why, General," said a New York Republican when Arthur refused him a political favor, "if you were still president of the New York County Republican Committee, you would be here right now asking for this very thing." "I certainly would," agreed Arthur; "but since I came here I have learned that Chester A. Arthur is one man and the President of the United States is another."[10] Conkling, needless to say, was not impressed. "I have but one annoyance with the Administration of President Arthur," he sneered, "and that is, in contrast with it, the Administration of Hayes becomes respectable, if not heroic."[11]

Arthur not only pleased reformers by his break with the spoils system; he also delighted Washington society by his hospitality. He had the White House renovated before moving in and transformed it from the gloomy mansion of Hayes's and Garfield's days into a bright, lively, sociable place where good liquor and excellent food became the rule and serious as well as popular music could be heard on occasion. With his fastidious attire, impeccable manners, and affable but dignified demeanor, Arthur came to be known as "the prince of hospitality" and even as something of a dandy.[12] "It is not that he is handsome and agreeable—for he was both *long ago*," said one admirer, "but it is his ease, polish and perfect manner that make him the greatest society lion we have had in many years."[13] Since Arthur's wife had died just before he became President, his sister acted as White House hostess; she was just as popular among Washington *bon vivants* as Arthur himself. Arthur was not the most diligent of Presidents; the social side of the Presidency was just about the only aspect of it that he really enjoyed. "President Arthur," a White House clerk once confided, "never did today what he could put off until tomorrow."[14] He was frequently late to meetings; but he always carried a "property basket" with him, filled with official-looking documents, to give the impression that he had been hard at work.[15]

Arthur won much good will while he was in the White House; but he never became enormously popular, so most Americans were ready to see him retire in 1885. He had little support for renomination in 1884: reformers still were not quite sold on him; the Half Breeds continued to regard him as a Stalwart; and the Stalwarts regarded him as a renegade. But Arthur had no serious designs on the nomination anyway. He suffered from Bright's disease and his health had steadily declined during the last months of his Presidency. Queried about his plans for the future, he said, "Well, there doesn't seem anything else for an ex-President to do but to go into the country and raise big pumpkins."[16] He went to New York City, not the country, after leaving the White House, and died the following year of a massive cerebral hemorrhage at the age of fifty-six.

★ ★ ★

Sideboard

After Arthur became President he had the White House cleaned, repaired, and refurnished. Before he got through he had loaded twenty-four wagons with stuff accumulated there through the years (including a pair of Lincoln's trousers, a badly worn hat of John Quincy Adams's, and an ancient portmanteau of Abigail Adams's), which was all sold at auction. One of the things he disposed of was a sideboard which had been presented to "Lemonade Lucy" Hayes by the Women's Christian Temperance Union because she refused to serve liquor in the White House. A Washington saloon-keeper bought the sideboard and kept it in a prominent place, loaded with liquors, in his barroom on Pennsylvania Avenue.[17]

TWENTY-TWO

Grover Cleveland
1885–89, 1893–97

Seconding the nomination of the short and chubby Grover Cleveland (1837–1908) for President at the Democratic convention in June 1884, General Edward S. Bragg cried: "They love Cleveland for his character, but they love him also for the enemies he has made!"[1] What kind of enemies? Corrupt politicians in Buffalo, for one. As Mayor of that city, Cleveland had turned down so many crooked appropriation measures proposed by the city council that he came to be known as the "veto mayor" and as "His Obstinacy, Grover of Buffalo." Tammany Hall spoilsmen, for another. As Governor of New York, the "buxom Buffalonian" (who loved his food and beer) refused to accept bills passed by the state legislature to benefit Tammany's friends, handing down one veto after another from his desk in Albany.

Cleveland was called "ugly-honest," that is, truculently honest. When people coming to Albany seeking favors began whispering to him, he would answer them in a loud voice that everyone around could hear. And when an office-seeker whined, "Don't I deserve it for my party work?" Cleveland would say coldly, "I don't know that I understand you."[2] His "you-be-damnedness" became famous.[3] So did his hard work. One newsman sighed that Governor Cleveland "remains within doors constantly, eats and works, eats and works, and works and eats."[4] Once someone asked Samuel J. Tilden, "What sort of man is this Cleveland?" "Oh," said Tilden in his squeaky voice, "he is the kind of man who would rather do something badly for himself than to have somebody else do it well."[5]

But Cleveland was by no means all work and no play. Sometimes he took time off to play poker on Sunday afternoons. "My father used to say that it was wicked to go fishing on Sunday," he once explained, "but he never said anything about draw-poker."[6] He also liked his beer; and as a young man he spent plenty of time drinking, singing, and chatting in the beer-gardens of Buffalo. In 1870, when he ran for district attorney of Erie County, he and his friendly opponent, Lyman K. Bass, agreed to drink only four glasses of beer daily. But after they had met a few times on warm summer evenings to talk things over, they decided that their ration was too skimpy and so began to "anticipate" their future supply. A few evenings later, Bass suddenly exclaimed: "Grover, do you know we have anticipated the whole campaign?" Cleveland nodded sorrowfully. The next night, however, both of them brought huge tankards to the saloon, christened them "glasses," and had no problem with the ration after that.[7]

Cleveland continued to enjoy his beer after becoming Governor, but he also put in long hours at his desk. He was hard at work in Albany when news arrived that the Democrats had nominated him for President. "They are firing a salute, Governor, for your nomination," said one of his associates, hearing a distant cannon boom. "That's what it is," said someone else. "Do you think so?" said Cleveland thoughtfully. "Well, anyhow, we'll finish up this work."[8] After the nomination, reporter William C. Hudson was assigned the task of preparing a campaign document setting forth Cleveland's achievements as Mayor of Buffalo and Governor of New York. Going through Cleveland's state papers and public addresses, he was struck by how frequently Cleveland had referred to public officers as trustees of the people. He finally came up with a slogan—"Public Office is a Public Trust"—and with great glee showed it to the candidate. "Where the deuce did I say that?" asked Cleveland doubtfully. "You've said it a dozen times publicly, but not in those few words," explained Hudson. "That's so," said Cleveland. "That's what I believe. That's what I've said a little better because more fully." "But this has the merit of brevity," Hudson pointed out, "and that is what is required here. The question is, will you stand for this form?" "Oh, yes," said Cleveland. "That's what I believe. I'll stand for it and make it my own." Within a few hours the country was ringing with the statement: "Governor Cleveland's greatest phrase: 'Public Office is a Public Trust.' "⁹

During the campaign, Joseph Pulitzer's *New York World* listed four good reasons for endorsing Grover of Buffalo: "1. He is an honest man; 2. He is an honest man; 3. He is an honest man; 4. He is an honest man."¹⁰ Since Cleveland's Republican opponent, James G. Blaine, had been involved in railroad scandals, Republican reformers (called "Mugwumps") decided to desert their party and vote for Cleveland instead. Then, out of the blue, a Buffalo newspaper revealed "A Terrible Tale" about Cleveland: as a young bachelor in Buffalo he had become involved with Maria Halpin, an alcoholic widow, and fathered a child by her. "Tell the truth," said Cleveland quietly when his campaign managers came to him in despair.¹¹ Fresh revelations of Blaine's secret railroad dealings diverted public attention from the Halpin story; but when Democratic leaders showed Cleveland documents purporting to besmirch Blaine's private life, he refused to make use of them. "Are the papers all here?" he asked. Assured that they were, he tore them to bits, threw them into a waste basket, and ordered them burned. "The other side can have a monopoly of all the dirt in this campaign," he declared.¹² Meanwhile, Republican torchlight parades chanted, "Ma, ma, where's your pa? Gone to the White House, ha, ha, ha!" Though shocked by the Halpin story, the Mugwumps decided to stick with Cleveland. As one of them put it: "We are told that Mr. Blaine has been delinquent in office but blameless in private life, while Mr. Cleveland has been a model of official integrity, but culpable in his personal relations. We should therefore elect Mr. Cleveland to the public office which he is so well qualified to fill, and remand Mr. Blaine to the private station which he is admirably fitted to adorn."¹³

Reformers were pleased with their choice in 1884. After Cleveland was installed in office and confronted with a flood of hungry Democratic office-seekers, he stubbornly refused to make unworthy appointments. "Well," he growled to one Democratic politician seeking handouts for his constituents, "do you want me to appoint another horse thief for you?"¹⁴ But he found "the d——d everlasting clatter for offices" almost unbearable. It "makes me feel like resigning," he sighed.¹⁵ To his physician he once lamented, "Oh, Dr. Kean, those office-seekers! They haunt me in my dreams!"¹⁶ Haunted as well by the thought of an overactive federal government, he pored over Congressional legislation searching for possible vetoes. In four

years he issued no fewer than 413, more than twice the number of
veto messages which his twenty-one predecessors, from Washington
to Arthur, had sent to Congress. He was called the "Veto President,"
and many children were taught to sing, "A fat man once sat in a
President's chair, singing Ve-to, Ve-to, With never a thought of trouble or care, singing Ve-to, Ve-to."[17]

Cleveland's first term in office met with general approval. Civil-
service reformers liked what he was doing; businessmen praised his
emphasis on sound money, economy, and efficiency in government.
"I was against you, Mr. President," a Chicago clergyman told him.
"I labored diligently among my flock and prayed that you might
be overthrown, but now—" "I like that," interrupted Cleveland;
"I like that *but now,* especially. Go on!"[18] Despite the friends he
made among voters, Cleveland lost his bid for re-election in 1888
to Benjamin Harrison of Indiana. He claimed that there was "no
happier man in the United States" than he when he left the White
House, but his wife was sure he would return to it.[19] "Now, Jerry,"
she told one of the White House servants on the morning of Harrison's inauguration, "I want you to take good care of all the furniture
and ornaments in the house, and not let any of them get lost or
broken, for I want to find everything just as it is now, when we
come back again." "Excuse meh, Mis' Cleveland," said Jerry in some
astonishment, "but jus' when does you-all expec' to come back,
please—so I can have everything ready, I mean?" "We are coming
back just four years from today," Mrs. Cleveland replied confidently.[20] She was right. In 1892, Cleveland whipped Harrison and
returned, with more pleasure than he had anticipated, to Jerry's
care.

Cleveland's pleasure was short-lived; his second term was a stormy
one. The Panic of 1893 touched off a long and harrowing depression,
accompanied by widespread unemployment, labor unrest, agitation
in the farm belt, and the rise of Populism. Cleveland was stubbornly
honest, enormously conscientious, and politically courageous, but
he was also narrow and unimaginative, unable to grasp social realities
and utterly baffled by mass misery. According to a popular story,
a lean and hungry man came to the White House one day, got
down on his hands and knees, and began chewing the grass. "What
are you doing?" asked Cleveland, seeing him from a window. "I'm
hungry and have to eat grass," replied the man. "Why don't you

go around to the back yard?" asked Cleveland. "The grass is longer there."[21]

When Cleveland left the White House in 1897 he was one of the most unpopular men in the country. He retired to Princeton, New Jersey, deeply dejected over having lost the love and confidence of the American people. One day a friend came by for a visit; his fine setter dog, excluded at the door, found another entrance into the house. When the dog came trotting triumphantly into the drawing-room and put his cold muzzle on the former President's hand, the friend rushed over to expel him. "No, let him stay," cried Cleveland. "He at least likes me."[22]

As the years passed people began to think more kindly of Grover of Buffalo. He had, after all, stood for honesty and integrity in government at a time when it was important to do so, and some of his vetoes were unquestionably justified. Once, when Cleveland was reminiscing with a friend about his White House days, he paused for a moment and then exclaimed: "Do you know that I ought to have a monument over me when I die?" "I am sure of that, Mr. President," said the friend, "but for what particular service?" "Oh!" returned Cleveland, "not for anything I have ever done, but for the foolishness I have put a stop to. If you knew the absurd things proposed to me at various times while I have been in public life, and which I sat down—and sat down hard—upon, you would say so too!"[23] His last words before his death in June 1908 were: "I have tried so hard to do right."[24]

★ ★ ★

Rum, Romanism, and Rebellion

In 1884, when Cleveland was running for President against Republican Senator James G. Blaine, he needed the votes of Irish-Americans in New York City to win. The Blaine forces spread rumors that Cleveland hated Catholics and played up the fact that Blaine's mother was an Irish Catholic. Then Rev. Samuel D. Burchard, a Presbyterian Minister, unexpectedly spoiled things for Blaine. Shortly before the election, Blaine went to the Fifth Avenue Hotel in Manhattan to meet some Protestant ministers who supported him; and Burchard, greeting the Republican candidate on their behalf, announced: "We expect to vote for you next Tuesday. We are Republicans and don't propose to leave our party and identify ourselves with the party whose antecedents have been Rum, Romanism, and Rebellion!" The Democrats saw his blunder at once and flooded New York City with flyers quoting the remark. Contemporary observers were convinced that Blaine lost thousands of Catholic votes as a result, so that Burchard's crack helped elect Cleveland.[25]

Burglars

Cleveland continually quarreled with the Senate but got along well with the House of Representatives. One night, according to a popular story, he was awakened by his wife. "Wake up at once!" she cried urgently, "there are burglars in the house!" "No, my dear," said Cleveland sleepily. "In the Senate maybe, but not in the House."[26]

Greetings

At one of President Cleveland's formal receptions a man named Decker appeared. As he approached the President in the receiving line he gave Colonel Williams (the President's aide) his name, adding that it was an easy one to pronounce and remember. The Colonel then presented him to the President. "Happy to meet you, Mr. Cracker," beamed Cleveland. "Happy to meet you, Mr. Baker," said Mrs. Cleveland. "Mr. Sacker," said Miss Bayard, also in the receiving line, doubtfully. "Happy to meet you, Mr. Black," said Mrs. Whitney, who was standing next to Miss Bayard. As Mr. Decker left, he took another look at his calling card to make sure of what his name really was.[27]

TWENTY-THREE

Benjamin Harrison
1889–93

One day in the fall of 1856, when Benjamin Harrison (1833–1901) was hard at work in his law office, some Republican friends dropped by and asked him to speak at a political gathering in the street outside. Harrison refused. He needed time, he said, to prepare a speech. But his friends persisted; and when he continued to say no, they simply picked him up, carried him downstairs, and deposited him on a box in front of the crowd. Then one of them introduced him grandiloquently as the grandson of President William Henry Harrison. Quick as a flash, young Ben cried out: "I want it understood that I am the grandson of nobody. I believe that every man should stand on his own merits."[1] Years later, when he was running for President, he was still exasperated by references to his grandfather; but to no avail. During the 1888 campaign Democratic cartoonists pictured him as a little fellow standing in the shadow of his grandfather's gigantic beaver hat, while the Republicans campaigned for him with the song "Grandfather's Hat Fits Ben!"[2]

Harrison was a Senator from Indiana when he received the Republican nomination for President in 1888. The *Des Moines Register* praised him as "calm, cool, deliberate, polished, candid, dignified and strong," but most people found him something of a cold fish.[3] His handshake, it was said, was "like a wilted petunia."[4] One of Harrison's friends, before introducing some people to him, warned them beforehand: "Don't think he means to insult you; it is his

way!"[5] Speaker of the House Thomas B. ("Czar") Reed was invited
to "board the Harrison bandwagon" just before the 1888 nomination,
but he cried, "You should say 'ice wagon,' " and added: "I never
ride in an ice-cart."[6] Still, some people liked Harrison's style. The
owner of the boarding house in Washington where Harrison lodged
found the Senator's frosty independence a matter for commendation.
"You know," he said, "I like . . . Harrison, and I'll tell you why.
At dinner frequently a group of Senators (whom I shall not name)
pass Harrison by without speaking, as though they didn't care a
d——n for him. But what I liked about Harrison was, that he didn't
seem to care a G—d d——n for them."[7]

Harrison was an effective public speaker who could move masses
of people with his oratory. In face-to-face encounters, though, he
had a way of turning people off. One afternoon several years before
he became President, he was leaving Indianapolis to make a campaign
speech in another Indiana city, and his friend General John C. New
saw him off at the railway station. "Now, Ben," said New as they
parted, "I know you'll capture them with your speech, but for God's
sake be a human being down there. Mix around a little with the
boys after the meeting." A few days later, when the two met again,
Harrison confessed: "John, I tried it, but I failed. I'll never try it
again. I must be myself."[8] But "being himself" created a hardship
for Harrison's campaign workers. On a railroad campaign in Illinois,
Harrison made a series of speeches which roused audiences to great
enthusiasm. Each time he held a reception afterward, however, people
came away, after shaking hands with him, silent and downcast. Noticing this, one of Harrison's supporters began pulling the bell-rope
to start the train again the very minute Harrison ended a speech.
Chided for rushing Harrison away from each town that way, he
explained: "Don't talk to me. I know my business. Benjamin Harrison
had the crowd red-hot. I did not want him to freeze it out of them
with his hand-shaking."[9]

On occasion, Harrison's cool imperturbability amazed and discom-
fited his friends and associates. On election eve in November 1888,
they were struck by his seeming unconcern when early returns from
New York were unfavorable. "Cheer up, everybody," Harrison told
them. "This is no life and death affair. I am very happy here in
Indianapolis and will continue to be if I'm not elected. Home is a
pretty good place." He seemed interested only in Indiana and followed the returns from every Hoosier county with great interest.

Toward eleven o'clock, however, he finally said, "This last bulletin settles it. We've got Indiana." And he added; "That's enough for me tonight, then. My own State is for me. I'm going to bed." The next morning a friend who had called at midnight to congratulate him asked him why he had retired so early. "Well," he explained, "I knew that my staying up would not change the result if I were defeated, while if elected I had a hard day ahead of me. So I thought a night's rest was best in any event."[10]

In December, Senator Stanley M. Quay of Pennsylvania, chairman of the Republican National Committee, went to Indianapolis to congratulate Harrison on his victory and discuss Cabinet selections with him. To his surprise, he found Harrison disposed, "in true Presbyterian fashion (for he was a pious man) to believe that Providence had been on the Republican side." Taking Quay's hand, the President-elect said fervently: "Providence has given us the victory!" "Think of the man!" exclaimed Quay to a journalist friend afterward. "He ought to know that Providence hadn't a damn thing to do with it." Harrison, he added, "would never know how close a number of men were compelled to approach the penitentiary to make him President."[11] Harrison himself was of course incorruptible; he was, in fact, "ugly honest," like Cleveland. But the 1888 election was a close one, and the Democrats charged corruption in the key state of New York, which had gone Republican. When Harrison became President, moreover, he found that he could not name his own Cabinet; his party managers "had sold out every place to pay the election expenses."[12]

Harrison's Presidency was famous mainly for high tariffs, a Treasury surplus, and lavish spending by Congress on veterans' pensions and special-interest projects. When the Democrats criticized what they called the "Billion Dollar Congress," Speaker Reed retorted: "This is a billion-dollar country!"[13] Harrison's reputation for unapproachability continued undiminished during his four years in the White House. "You may be interested in knowing that we have one of the smallest Presidents the United States has ever known," Walter Wellman of the *Chicago Tribune* told Judge Walter Q. Gresham. "He is narrow, unresponsive and, oh, so cold! . . . There are bitter complaints. . . . Senators call and say their say to him, and he stands silent. . . . As one Senator says: 'It's like talking to a hitching post!' "[14] Senator Thomas Platt called Harrison the "White House Iceberg." "Outside the White House and at a dinner," said

Platt, "he could be a courtly gentleman. Inside the Executive Mansion, in his reception of those who solicited official appointments, he was as glacial as a Siberian stripped of his furs. During and after an interview, if one could secure it, one felt even in torrid weather like pulling on his winter flannels, galoshes, overcoat, mitts and earlaps."[15]

One day Captain A. H. Reed, a one-armed Civil War veteran, visited Harrison to talk about appointments in the third Minnesota district. No sooner had he commenced discussing problems there than the President cut him off. "Oh, I know all about the political conditions up there," Harrison told him impatiently: "much better than you." "Do you mean to tell me," asked Reed incredulously, "that you know more about the political conditions in my home district where I have lived all my life than I do?" "Certainly," replied Harrison. "You have only the narrow personal interest view and do not comprehend the real situation." "Then I have nothing more to say," exclaimed Reed. "Good day, Mr. President." And he stalked out of the room and told his friends outside: "He's a damned icicle." Everyone agreed: Harrison had a knack for "doing the right thing in the wrong way."[16]

Democratic cartoonists depicted "little Ben" (he was only five feet six inches tall) as a tiny pigmy standing in the shadow of his grandfather's gigantic hat. Some Republicans also questioned his stature. One man went day after day to see him, and day after day the President's secretary got rid of him on one pretext or another. Finally the frustrated office-seeker went to the White House determined not to be turned away again. To his peremptory demand that he see the President, the secretary insisted, "I'm sorry, sir, but the President cannot be seen." "Can't be seen!" exclaimed the enraged visitor. "My God! Has he got as small as that?"[17]

★ ★ ★

Despicable Temptation

Shortly after President Harrison had decided to nominate Justice David J. Brewer of Kansas for the U.S. Supreme Court, Kansas Senator Preston B. Plumb came to the White House to suggest Brewer for the Court. He was extremely aggressive about it. He paced the floor, used strong language, and even threatened retaliation in the Senate if he did not have his way. Harrison was highly offended by Plumb's manner and finally bowed him out of the office without revealing his plans. But after Plumb had left he put the finishing touches on the nomination and sent it to the Senate. "I think," he said afterward, "I think one of the great moral victories of my life came when I put that commission back on my desk after Plumb had left, and conquered a despicable temptation to tear it up and throw it in the wastebasket."[18]

Grasps Situation

"I grasp the situation," said President Harrison after listening a while to an eager office-seeker. "That's just the trouble," complained the man. "What I want is for you to let go of the situation so that I can grasp it."[19]

Serving Out Term

"We want a new postmaster at Wabash," said an Indianan. "For what reason?" asked President Harrison. "The incumbent is a Democrat," was the reply. "That can hardly be considered a sufficient cause for a change," said Harrison. "Well, sir," exclaimed the Indianan, "when we were beating about the woods looking for votes, if I remember correctly, the principal reason for turning Mr. Cleveland out of office was that he was a Democrat." "That may be," said Harrison after thinking it over for a moment, "but if I remember correctly, Mr. Cleveland was permitted to serve out his term, and I guess that is about the privilege we shall have to grant your postmaster."[20]

TWENTY-FOUR

William B. McKinley
1897–1901

William B. McKinley (1843–1901) was the polar opposite of Benjamin Harrison. Harrison could do a man a favor, it was said, and make an enemy; McKinley could refuse a favor and make a friend. "He had an innate dignity," said Senator Robert La Follette, "and at the same time a warm sympathetic nature."[1] When Senator George F. Hoar of Massachusetts came to the White House to protest the decision to annex the Philippines, McKinley asked him how strongly he felt about the matter. "Pretty pugnacious, I confess, Mr. President," exclaimed Hoar. McKinley took his hand and assured him, "I shall always love you, whatever you do."[2] On another occasion an angry Congressman stormed into McKinley's office to complain about something, but when he came out afterwards he told his friends, somewhat resignedly, "I don't know a blamed word he said, but it's all right, boys." Once, when McKinley asked Senator Shelby M. Cullom whether he would be angry if he overruled him on the appointment of an Illinois man whom the Senator was pushing, Cullom confessed: "Mr. President, I could not get mad at you if I tried."[3] Speaker Tom Reed was frankly envious: "My opponents in Congress go at me tooth and nail, but they always apologize to William when they are going to call him names. . . ."[4]

McKinley's handshake was famous. To save wear and tear on his right hand at receptions, the President developed what came to be called the "McKinley grip." In receiving lines, he would smile as a man came by, take his right hand and squeeze it warmly before his own hand got caught in a hard grip, hold the man's elbow with his left hand, and then swiftly pull him along and be ready to beam on the next guest.[5] McKinley's remarkable memory for faces and names was also well known and highly appreciated. Once, while waiting for ceremonies to begin at the dedication of a monument at the Antietam battlefield, he walked over to the edge of the platform and called down to an old veteran in blue, "Hello, comrade, I saw you in the crowd at Gettysburg last month when I spoke there, didn't I?" Astonished, the veteran exclaimed, "Yes, but how did you recognize me?" Queried about his memory afterward, McKinley shrugged it off: "Oh, I don't know, it just comes naturally."[6]

Senator "Billy" Mason said that when McKinley couldn't give a man the office he sought he looked so unhappy about it that the office-seeker went away filled with sympathy for the President. Sometimes McKinley soothed the feelings of a disappointed caller by taking the flower out of his buttonhole and pinning it to the other man's lapel. Once he had to refuse a labor leader some favor, and the man was deeply offended. McKinley told him how sorry he was; then, shaking hands with him, asked if he was married. When the man said he was, McKinley took a carnation from his coat and handed it to him, saying, "Give this to your wife with my compliments and best wishes." Completely mollified by this gesture, the man smiled and said as he left, "I would rather have this flower from you for my wife than the thing I came to get."[7] McKinley was tactful even with children. One afternoon his secretary George Cortelyou's two boys came to the White House to meet the President. McKinley shook hands with them, chatted a bit, and then, as they turned to go, gave the carnation in his lapel to the older boy while the younger looked on enviously. But right away McKinley took a fresh carnation from a vase nearby, put it in his buttonhole for a moment, then gave it to the younger boy. Years later Cortelyou's son recalled his first lesson in tact and diplomacy from McKinley.[8]

McKinley's solicitude for his ailing wife, Ida, was the talk of the town. Ida was a semi-invalid, subject to headaches and epileptic seizures, and her dependence on "the Major," as she called her husband, was heavy. She covered the walls of the house with pictures of him because, she said, "he's a dear good man and I love him."[9] McKinley, for his part, always kept her in mind. When he was Governor of Ohio, he breakfasted with her each morning, then walked across the street to the State Capitol and, before entering the building, stopped, turned, and waved to her. And promptly at three every afternoon he stopped whatever he was doing, opened the window in his office, waved a white handkerchief, and waited for her to wave back. As President he abandoned the rule that the President escorted the wife of the Secretary of State to the dinner table, insisting on escorting Ida instead and sitting next to her. If, perchance, she had a seizure at one of these dinners or at a reception, he continued the conversation as if nothing had happened. William Howard Taft, chatting with the McKinleys at dinner one day, asked the President for a pencil so he could make a note of what they were discussing. As McKinley reached into his pocket for the pencil, "a peculiar hissing sound" came from Mrs. McKinley. McKinley quickly picked up a napkin, dropped it over her face, handed the pencil to Taft, and continued talking. When Mrs. McKinley recovered a few moments later, she resumed her part in the conversation where she had left off.[10]

There is irony in all this: McKinley, the kind and gentle President, is remembered primarily for taking the nation into the Spanish-American War. Having seen action in the Civil War, he was no war lover. "I have been through one war," he said on the eve of our war with Spain. "I have seen the dead piled up, and I do not want to see another." "We want no wars of conquest," he told the American people in his inaugural address on March 4, 1897; "we must avoid the temptation of territorial aggression. Wars should never be entered upon until every agency of peace has failed; peace is preferable to war in almost every contingency."[11] Shortly after entering the White House, he told Carl Schurz: "Ah, you may be sure that there will be no jingo nonsense under my administration."[12] But there was plenty of "jingo nonsense" abroad in the land during McKinley's Presidency, and in the end he succumbed to it himself.

In the beginning, McKinley hoped to act as mediator between Spain and the Cuban rebels fighting for independence. But it was not to be. The pressure for military intervention by war hawks like Theodore Roosevelt was unremitting. TR called McKinley a "white-livered cur" for holding back; the Hearst papers excoriated him day after day for cowardice; and people hissed his name, tore his picture off walls, and even burned him in effigy in some cities.[13] An angry Senator burst into the State Department one day and started yelling: "By ———! Don't your President know where the war-declaring power is lodged? Well tell him, by ———! that if he doesn't do something, Congress will exercise the power and declare war in spite of him!"[14] McKinley was extremely sensitive to public opinion— Senator Joe Cannon said he kept his ear so close to the ground that it was full of grasshoppers—so that finally, in April 1898, he asked for and obtained authority from Congress to intervene in Cuba.[15] During the war that followed, McKinley became a devout expansionist himself and, like other promoters of empire, criticized anti-imperialists as short-sighted isolationists.

When the war began, McKinley was extremely vague about the location of the Philippines, but quickly learned his geography and warmly supported the idea of taking them from Spain when the war ended. "We are all jingoes now," said the *New York Sun;* "and the head jingo is the Hon. William McKinley."[16] Though annexation was followed by a bloody insurrection in the Philippines which took more than three years to quell, McKinley had no difficulty in his bid for re-election. Not only did he win in 1900 by the largest plurality up to that time; he also began his second term amid feelings of good will in the nation at large.

On September 5, 1901, attending the Pan-American Exposition in Buffalo, McKinley made an address denouncing isolation and urging the expansion of American foreign trade. The following day he planned to hold a reception in the Temple of Music. George Cortelyou, however, thought the President was needlessly exposing himself to possible danger and wanted to cancel the reception. "Why should I?" asked McKinley. "No one would wish to hurt me." Cortelyou then argued that since McKinley could only greet a few people in the ten minutes allotted for the reception, others might be offended at not getting to shake hands. "Well," said McKinley, "they'll know I tried, anyhow." Cortelyou sighed, added another man to the Secret Service staff, and hoped for the best.[17]

The following afternoon, McKinley began using his famous hand-shake on a long line of people in the Temple of Music. Before he had greeted many an anarchist named Leon Czolgosz approached the President with a revolver concealed in a handkerchief and fired two shots at him. Horrified, people nearby grabbed the assassin, knocked him down, and pinned him to the floor. McKinley slumped into a chair, looked up at the scuffle, and cried, "Don't let them hurt him." Then he gasped: "My wife—be careful, Cortelyou, how you tell her—oh, be careful!" And as he was being carried to a little hospital nearby he sighed: "It must have been some poor misguided fellow." A few days later, when it was clear that the end was near, McKinley said quietly, "It is God's way. His will, not ours, be done," and repeated some lines from his favorite hymn, "Nearer my God, to Thee." He then embraced his wife, who exclaimed: "I want to go, too. I want to go, too." "We are all going," murmured McKinley. "We are all going." They were his last words.[18]

★   ★   ★

Streetcar Scene

One evening President McKinley was having a hard time deciding which of two equally competent men to appoint to an important diplomatic post. Suddenly he recalled an incident that had occurred on a stormy night many years before. He had boarded a streetcar and taken the last empty seat at the rear. At one point an old washerwoman carrying a heavy basket boarded the car, and stood forlorn in the aisle. One of the men whom McKinley was now considering for the post had been sitting right in front of the old lady, but shifted his newspaper in such a way as to seem not to see her. McKinley went down the aisle, picked up the basket of washing, and led the old lady back to his seat. The man with the newspaper, looking down, did not see this. "The candidate never knew," said McKinley's friend Charles G. Dawes, who reported the story, "that this little act of selfishness, or rather this little omission of kindness, had deprived him of that which would have crowned his ambition of a lifetime."[19]

Hatband

One evening shortly after McKinley's inauguration, Chicago editor H. H. Kohlsaat was chatting with the President. During a lull in the conversation the latter, with a whimsical smile, asked, "What are you thinking about?" "I was wondering," replied Kohlsaat, "if you would be wearing the same-sized hatband in a year from now." "Do you think I am in danger of a swelled head?" asked McKinley. "You would be more than human if you were not influenced by the adulation paid you by 98 per cent of your callers," said Kohlsaat. "Not more than 2 per cent can tell you the truth." "Well," said McKinley, "if you see evidence of an expansion, please tell me."

About a year later the two were sitting in the same room smoking when McKinley suddenly said, "Have you seen any evidences of my hatband expanding?" "No," admitted Kohlsaat, "but I am still watching it!"[20]

Football

Neither McKinley nor his friend, Cleveland industrialist Mark Hanna, knew anything about football when they attended a Princeton-Yale game and so were completely bewildered throughout. McKinley kept asking Hanna what was going on, but Hanna admitted he understood as little about the game as McKinley. Finally McKinley told Hanna that he felt like the country boy who said, "They didn't have no game; they got into a scrap and kept fightin' all the time when they ought to have been playin' ball."[21]

TWENTY-FIVE

Theodore Roosevelt
1901–9

Theodore Roosevelt (1858–1919) was without doubt the most energetic of all our Presidents. And the most ebullient. And the most athletic. He was, Henry Adams decided, "pure act."[1] After visiting the White House, John Morley, British essayist and biographer, concluded that Roosevelt was "an interesting combination of St. Vitus and St. Paul." To Joseph Bishop, one of Roosevelt's newspaper friends, he exclaimed: "My dear fellow, do you know the two most extraordinary things I have seen in your country? Niagara Falls and the President of the United States—both great wonders of nature!"[2]

TR seemed to possess limitless vitality, indomitable courage, and indestructible will; and he was a passionate devotee of the strenuous life. "Get action," he advised; "do things; be sane; don't fritter away your time; create, act, take a place wherever you are and be somebody; get action."[3] Roosevelt wanted his fellow countrymen to "hit the line and hit it hard," and set an astonishing example of line-hitting himself.[4] Reported Rudyard Kipling, after spending some time with the President: "I curled up in the seat opposite, and listened and wondered, until the universe seemed to be spinning around and Theodore was the spinner."[5] But French ambassador Jean-Jules Jusserand had a tougher time with TR. He joined the President for two sets of tennis one day; then TR suggested a bit of jogging; and after they had jogged on the White House lawn a while, they had a workout with the medicine ball. After that, TR turned to his guest and asked, "What would you like to do now?" "If it's just the same with you, Mr. President," sighed Jusserand, "I'd like to lie down and die."[6]

The child, in TR's case, was not father to the man. As a boy, Teedie, as he was called, was weak and sickly, with a puny body, poor eyes, and an asthmatic cough. When he was ten, his father took him aside and told him: "Theodore, you have the mind but you have not the body. . . . You must *make* your body."[7] A humiliating encounter with four boys on a stagecoach reinforced the point: when the boys began teasing him, he found he couldn't take on even one of them alone. *"I'll make my body,"* he resolved. He began working out in a gym which his father installed for him on the second floor of their home in New York City and continued working out for the rest of his life.[8] He took boxing lessons, studied judo, learned to ride and shoot, played tennis, took long hikes, climbed the Matterhorn, hunted big game in Africa, explored Brazil, and fought in the Spanish-American War. He also became a cowboy.

In September 1883, Roosevelt visited the Dakota Badlands, fell in love with the cattle business, acquired two ranches, and became a gentleman cowhand. The cowboys chuckled over "Four Eyes" at first. Amused by his mild expletives—"By Godfrey!"—they were in stitches when they heard him say, the first time he took part in a roundup, "Hasten forward quickly there!" The phrase was, for a time, a byword in the Badlands.[9] But the cowboys soon learned to take TR seriously. He spent almost forty hours in the saddle with them without complaint; he gradually acquired the professional skills of a good cowboy; and he handled a barroom tough just the way he should be handled. When he dropped in at a hotel in Mingusville one night after spending the day looking for lost horses, a shabby character with a cocked pistol in each hand accosted him in the lobby (which was also the barroom) and cried: "Four Eyes is going to treat!" TR sat down by the stove and tried to ignore him, but the pistol-packing bully persisted. "Maybe you didn't hear me," he yelled. "I said Four Eyes is gonna treat!" At this point Roosevelt got up, as if to comply, and then, as he later told it, "struck quick and hard with my right just to one side of the point of his jaw, hitting with my left as I straightened out, and then again with my right." The man fell, and on his way down hit his head against the bar and was knocked unconscious. He was dragged outdoors and deposited in a shed; the next day, when he came to, he hurriedly left town.[10] "That four-eyed maverick," said one old cowhand of Roosevelt, "has sand in his craw a-plenty."[11] Years later, when TR was recruiting men to fight with him in Cuba, he had no trouble finding volunteers in the Wild West.

TR loved war as well as sports; he regarded the two as moral equivalents. He was, in fact, just about the only President we have ever had who (at least in his younger days) looked upon war as a good thing in itself. "No triumph of peace," he insisted, "is quite so great as the supreme triumphs of war."[12] He admired soldierly virtues and wanted to restore "the fighting edge" to the American spirit.[13] "Every man," he once wrote, "who has in him any real power of joy in battle knows that he feels it when the wolf begins to rise in his heart; he does not then shrink from blood or sweat or deem that they mar the fight; he revels in them, in the toil, the pain, and the danger, as but setting off the triumph."[14] Throughout the 1880s and 1890s, TR hankered for a war. Whenever there was a crisis in U.S. relations with other countries, he diligently beat the drums for war and hoped for a flare-up. But he not only wanted the United States to go to war; he also wanted to get into the war himself. The two always went together for Roosevelt. He was steadfastly true to what may be called the "TR principle": one volunteers for action in the wars one advocates, regardless of profession, social standing, health, age, or political position. After all, what fun is there—especially if one is an important person—in arranging vicarious valor? "My power for good," Roosevelt pointed out, "would be gone if I didn't try to live up to the doctrines I have tried to preach."[15]

But TR had to wait a long time for his war. In 1886 he hoped for a fight with Mexico over a border incident and offered to organize his "harum-scarum" ranch hands into a cavalry battalion; but the war never came. In 1892, a quarrel with Chile fired his hopes again. Roosevelt, a friend reported, "goes about hissing through his clenched teeth. . . . For two nickels he would declare war himself . . . and wage it sole."[16] "Do you remember," Mrs. Roosevelt asked a friend amusedly some years later, "how we used to call Theodore the Chilean Volunteer and tease him about his dream of leading a cavalry charge?"[17] But the Chilean crisis, too, passed. Friction with Great Britain in 1895 roused TR's belligerency once more. "This country needs a war," he told his friend Henry Cabot Lodge; and he pointed out that a war with Britain might well result in the acquisition of

Canada.[18] But the fighting, not the acquiring, was what really roused
his spirit. Unfortunately, the United States and England settled their
differences peacefully so TR was cheated once more out of combat.

In 1897, TR became Assistant Secretary of the Navy in the McKinley administration and fell in love with his work at once. "The Secretary is away," he wrote a friend one day, "and I am having immense
fun running the navy."[19] But he was more than ever eager for the
United States (and TR) to get into a shooting war. This time things
looked promising. The United States had been wrangling with Spain
ever since 1895, when the Cubans had revolted against Spanish rule;
when TR entered the Navy Department, relations between the two
nations were extremely strained. TR, who had favored American
intervention in Cuba almost from the beginning, was impatient with
President McKinley for his lack of truculence. McKinley, he complained, had "the backbone of a chocolate eclair."[20] But he did not
despair. "We will have this war for the freedom of Cuba," he insisted
in an after-dinner speech in Washington, "in spite of the timidity
of the commercial interests." As he spoke he looked right at Senator
Mark Hanna, the Cleveland industrialist, who opposed war; and
someone next to Hanna whispered wryly: "Now, Senator, may we
please have that war?"[21]

In April 1898, TR finally got his war. When the United States
declared war on Spain, he ran excitedly around the Navy Department
for a week or two like a little boy on roller skates; then he resigned
his post, volunteered for action, was commissioned a lieutenant colonel, and helped organize a cavalry unit of cowboys and college men
to fight in Cuba. The press had a good time thinking up nicknames
for the regiment—"Teddy's Terrors," "Teddy's Texas Tarantulas,"
"Roosevelt's Rough 'Uns"—and finally settled on "Roosevelt's
Rough Riders."[22]

In Cuba, at long last, TR saw the action he had dreamed of for
years and acquitted himself bravely, even heroically, on the battlefield.
"Gentlemen," he cried, during the attack at Kettle Hill (which he
called the "San Juan charge"), "the Almighty God and the just
cause are with you. Gentlemen, charge!" To some reluctant troopers,
he exclaimed: "Are you afraid to stand up when I am on horseback?"
As he told it later: "I waved my hat and we went up the hill with
a rush. . . . I killed a Spaniard with my own hand"; he added,
"like a jackrabbit." And when the operation was over, he cried:
"Look at those damned Spanish dead." "The charge itself was great

fun," he said afterward. "Oh, but we have had a bully fight!"[23] Roosevelt's combat experience amounted to one week's campaign in Cuba and one hard day of fighting, but it was enough to make him a national hero. When the war was over he published a book about his experiences entitled *The Rough Riders.* The story that the publisher had to order a special supply of the letter "I" from the type foundry is apocryphal. But the comment Irish humorist Finley Peter Dunne put into the mouth of his character Mr. Dooley was not. TR, said Mr. Dooley in his Irish accent, should have called his book *Alone in Cubia.* For TR, of course, the Cuban campaign was no matter for mirth. "San Juan," he said two decades later, "was the great day of my life."[24]

San Juan made TR a popular hero. After the war, when he was stumping New York State as candidate for Governor, he took seven Rough Riders with him and had a bugler sound the cavalry charge before each speech. "You have heard the trumpet that sounded to bring you here," he told voters in one town. "I have heard it tear the tropic dawn when it summoned us to fight at Santiago." After winning the election and taking office in 1899, he alienated Republican leaders by sponsoring a civil-service law and a tax on corporation franchises. Speaking of his relations with the Republican state machine, he once explained: "I have always been fond of the West African proverb: 'Speak softly and carry a big stick, you will go far.' " Anxious to get rid of the independent young Governor, party leaders began talking of kicking him upstairs into the Vice-Presidency. When he heard about it, TR at once announced: ". . . under no circumstances could I or would I accept the nomination for the Vice-Presidency." But when he made a speech for McKinley's renomination at the Republican convention in June 1900, the delegates went wild and enthusiastically picked him as McKinley's running mate. TR accepted the nomination; but Republican National Chairman Mark Hanna was glum. "Don't any of you realize," he cried, "that there's only one life between this madman and the White House?" He was horrified when "that damned cowboy," as he called TR, became President upon McKinley's death in September 1901, but he gradually came to like him.[25]

Soon after TR became President, one worried citizen beseeched him not to let his fighting spirit plunge the United States into war: "What!" cried Roosevelt earnestly, "a war, and I cooped up here in the White House? Never!"[26] Roosevelt did not exactly remain cooped up in the White House; but his seven and a half years in office were devoid of armed conflict. He did throw his weight around on the international scene: mediated in a war between Japan and Russia; sent the U.S. Navy on a cruise around the world; and supported a revolution in Panama to further his plans for building an interoceanic canal there. But there were no wars or even serious rumors of war during his Presidency. There was plenty of excitement nonetheless. "No President has ever enjoyed himself as much as I have enjoyed myself," admitted Roosevelt when it was all over, "and for the matter of that I do not know of any man of my age who has had as good a time. . . ."[27] He invited the distinguished black educator Booker T. Washington to dinner in the White House and was castigated by southern Democrats. He tried to have the inscription "In God We Trust" removed from U.S. coins (where it had been put in 1864) as both unconstitutional and sacrilegious and was blasted as impious. He got into a big fight with people he called "nature fakers"—that is, people who wrote sentimentally about wildlife—and was charged with cruelty to animals. He sent his annual message to Congress in 1906 in simplified spelling and produced outrage in that august body. ("Nuthing escapes Mr. Rucevelt," wrote the *Louisville Courier-Journal.* "No subject is tu hi fr him to takl, nor to lo for him to notis.")[28] He sprang a surprise antitrust suit on J. P. Morgan's Northern Securities Company in 1902, producing astonishment and indignation in that high and mighty captain of finance. "If we have done anything wrong," Morgan loftily told TR, "send your man to my man and they can fix it up." "That can't be done," TR told him, and went on with the action. Afterward he said that Morgan seemed to view the President of the United States as a "big rival operator" rather than as the elected representative of the American people and that it was time he learned differently.[29] (Morgan was a reluctant learner; when TR headed for big game in Africa after leaving office in 1909, the banking tycoon is said to have cried: "Health to the lions!")[30]

TR was one of America's most assertive Presidents. Not only did he believe that the U.S. Constitution empowered the federal government to act vigorously in the general welfare; he also believed in the centrality of the executive branch in the American system. When he ran for a third term in 1912 on the Progressive Party (Bull Moose) ticket, he called for a "New Nationalism"—that is, a national government which exercised broad powers to govern the country in the interest of the people as a whole. In October 1912, while campaigning in the West, he was shot by a crazy man in Milwaukee. "He pinked me," TR exclaimed; but he insisted on riding to the city auditorium to give his speech anyway. "I have a message to deliver," he told his associates, "and I will deliver it as long as there is life in my body." He gave his speech with a bullet hole in his chest, undressed and bleeding, and then was rushed to the hospital.[31]

TR lost his bid for a third term in 1912, went on an exploring expedition in Brazil, and returned to harass the administration of Woodrow Wilson. When the Great War broke out in Europe in the summer of 1914, he clamored for action again and offered to raise a volunteer division to fight with the Allies in Europe. Though thousands of young men volunteered to serve in a TR unit, President Wilson stubbornly refused to approve the idea, arguing that the ex-President was too old and too much of a show-off to be of any use in the European conflict. Marshal Joffre, hero of the battle of the Marne, urged Wilson to commission Roosevelt; French Premier Georges Clemenceau also strongly backed TR's request. "There is in France," he wrote Wilson, "one name which sums up the beauty of American intervention. You must know, Mr. President, that more than one of our *poilus* has asked, 'But where is Roosevelt?' Send them Roosevelt. It will gladden their hearts."[32] But Wilson remained adamant, while Roosevelt (who called the President a "Byzantine logothete") dreamed of being shut up in the same room with Wilson and boxing with him. "I am the only one he has kept out of war," he said bitterly.[33]

On July 4, 1917, when the first American troops arrived in Paris and paraded through the streets, the French people on hand cheered enthusiastically: *"Vive les Teddies!"*[34] Though Roosevelt was not with them, he took enormous satisfaction in knowing that all four of his sons were in the service. But when his son Quentin, a pilot in the air force, was shot down and killed behind enemy lines in 1918, the heart seemed to go out of TR. His health declined rapidly thereafter, and he was reduced to invalidism. He died suddenly on January 5, 1919, shortly after composing an article for a newspaper, and his son Archie, home on sick leave, cabled his brothers in France the incredible news: "THE LION IS DEAD."[35]

★   ★   ★

Student

As a student at Harvard, TR talked so much in class that one professor finally shouted: "See here, Roosevelt, let me talk. I'm running this course."[36]

Teacher

While at Harvard, TR taught Sunday School for a while at Christ Church, but he was too muscular a Christian for the vestrymen there. One day a boy came to class with a black eye. He admitted he had been in a fight, and on Sunday, too. A bigger boy had been pinching his sister, he said, and he got into a fist fight with him. "You did perfectly right," said TR and gave him a dollar. The vestrymen thought this was going too far and let TR go.[37]

Boxer

Once, when he was boxing at Harvard, time was called on a round, so Roosevelt dropped his guard. At that moment his opponent landed a heavy blow on his nose, which spurted blood. When people in the gallery started booing and hissing, TR raised his arm to command silence. "It's all right," he cried, his arm still in the air; then, pointing to the timekeeper, he said: "He didn't hear him." With his nose bleeding, he walked up to his opponent and shook hands.[38]

Polo

In 1888, while he was living in Oyster Bay, Long Island, TR organized a polo team. To get more action in the game he reduced the team from four men to three. He got action all right; he received many injuries while playing and on occasion was knocked senseless. At first his wife was upset by his accidents. Gradually, however, she came to understand his zest for rough riding and began accepting his injuries with equanimity. When he came home one afternoon with a gory cut on his head, she said sharply: "Theodore, I do wish you'd do your bleeding in the bathroom. You're spoiling every rug in the house!"[39]

TR and the Texan

In the Dakota Badlands, most of the men accepted TR as an equal despite his toothbrush and his habit of shaving. But one man, a surly Texan, considered him a "dude" and went out of his way to pick on him. TR laughed at first and let it go; but eventually it dawned on him that the Texan regarded him as a coward as well as a "dude" and that he had better correct that impression. One evening, when the man was being particularly offensive, TR strode up to him and exclaimed, "You're talking like an ass! Put up or shut up! Fight now, or be friends!" Startled, the Texan stared, his shoulder dropped a little, and he shifted his feet. "I didn't mean no harm," he said. "Make it friends." And they did.[40]

The Maverick

One day, while TR was riding over the range with one of his ablest cowpunchers, they came upon a "maverick," a two-year-old steer which had never been branded. They lassoed him at once and built a fire to heat the branding-irons. It was the rule among cattlemen that a "Maverick" belonged to the ranchman on whose range it was found. This particular steer therefore belonged to Gregor Lang, not to TR, for Lang claimed the land on which TR and his cowboy were riding. When the cowboy began to apply the red-hot iron, TR said, "It's Lang's brand—a thistle." "That's all right, boss," said the cowboy, "I know my business." "Hold on!" cried TR, "you're putting on my brand." "That's all right," said the cowboy. "I always put on the boss's brand." "Drop that iron," said TR quietly, "and go to the ranch and get your time. I don't need you any longer." The cowpuncher was amazed. "Say," he cried, "what have I done? Didn't I put on your brand?" "A man who will steal *for* me will steal *from* me," said TR; "you're fired." The man rode away. A day or so later the story was all over the Badlands.[41]

Damned Little Dude

TR became a member of the New York Assembly at the age of twenty-three, and was at first regarded by the other members as a kind of dude. One afternoon he was taking a walk and stopped at a saloon for a beer. At the bar he met another Assemblyman, John

Costello, drinking with two of his cronies. "Won't mama's boy catch cold?" sneered Costello when he saw the young aristocrat. When TR ignored him, Costello called him a "damned little dude." At this point, TR took off his glasses, put them in his pocket, and knocked Costello down with one blow. Then he floored one of Costello's cronies with a swift second punch. The third man quickly retreated. "Go wash yourself," TR told Costello. "And then join me for a beer." Costello did as he was ordered. Later, as he was leaving to continue his walk, TR said, "When you are in the presence of gentlemen, behave like a gentleman!"[42]

Damnedest Ass

When TR first served under Colonel Leonard Wood during the Spanish-American War, he was inexperienced in military discipline. One day he treated his squadron to a beer as a reward for their improvement in drill. That evening Wood remarked casually at supper that "of course, an officer who would go out with a large batch of men and drink with them was quite unfit to hold a commission." TR kept silent at the time; but later he visited Wood in his tent and confessed to what he had done. "I wish to say, sir," he told Wood, "that I agree with what you said. I consider myself the damnedest ass within ten miles of this camp. Good night."[43]

Jaws

One day at Havana harbor, Cuba, TR decided to take a swim in the Caribbean. He wanted to inspect the wreck of the *Merrimac,* some three hundred yards out to sea, and persuaded an unenthusiastic lieutenant, Jack Greenway, to go with him. They had scarcely entered the water when General Fitzhugh Lee, who had climbed up on the parapet of Fort Morro, began to yell at them. "Can you make out what he's trying to say?" asked TR, still swimming. "Sharks," said Greenway, wishing he was back on shore. "Sharks?" said TR, blowing out a mouthful of water and punctuating his words with strokes. "They—won't—bite. I've—been—studying them—all my life—and I never—heard of one—bothering a swimmer. It's all—poppycock." Just then a big shark showed up alongside the swimmers; it was soon joined by several others. But TR paid them no attention. Meanwhile General Lee continued shouting and gesticulating. Finally the swimmers reached the *Merrimac,* which TR eagerly examined while his companion kept thinking of sharks and hoping they would get back to shore unharmed. "After a while," Greenway said afterward, TR "had seen enough, and we went over the side again. Soon the sharks were all about us again, sort of pacing us in, as they had paced us out, while the old general did the second part of his war dance. He felt a lot better when we landed, and so did I."[44]

How He Did It

At one of the Rough Rider reunions, a Dakota cowboy who had been an excellent soldier in Cuba greeted TR, then told him he was glad the judge had let him out in time to come to the party. TR asked what had happened. "Why, Colonel," said the man, "don't you know I had a difficulty with a gentleman, and . . . er . . . well, I killed the gentleman. But you can see that the judge thought it was all right or he wouldn't have let me go." "How did it happen?" asked TR, with some concern. "How did you do it?" Thinking TR was interested in the technique, the ex-puncher answered: "With a .38 on a .45 frame, Colonel."[45]

Like Sheep to Slaughter

During his campaign for the governorship of New York in 1898, the hero of San Juan toured the state in a special train accompanied by seven Rough Riders. At every stop, a bugler would sound the cavalry charge, and TR would step forward to speak. At one point in the tour, ex-Sergeant Buck Taylor was called on to address the crowd at a station. "I want to talk to you about mah colonel," Taylor began. "He kept ev'y promise he made to us and he will to you. When he took us to Cuba he told us . . . we would have to lie out in the trenches with the rifle bullets climbing all over us, and we done it. . . . He told us we might meet wounds and death and we done it, but he was thar in the midst of us, and when it came to the great day he led us up San Juan Hill like sheep to slaughter and so he will lead you!"[46]

Seth

At the time of the presidential election of 1900 the West was William Jenning Bryan's territory, so TR faced some unfriendly crowds when campaigning there. At one gathering, where an old cowboy friend named Seth was in the audience, he expected a lot of heckling, but to his surprise the people were unusually well-behaved. After the meeting was over, he complimented the chairman on the fact that there had been no interruptions. "Interruptions!" exclaimed the chairman. "Well, I guess not! Seth sent around word that if any son of a gun peeped he'd kill him."[47]

Bully Fight

In Chicago in August 1901, Vice-President Roosevelt decided to attend services in a Dutch Reformed Church on Sunday morning, and journalist H. H. Kohlsaat took him to a small church on the West Side. En route TR pulled a pink sheet out of his pocket and said, "There was a prize-fight last week. I did not want to attract attention by reading it at the breakfast-table in the hotel." But he hadn't finished reading the fight report when the carriage reached the church, so he put it back in his pocket. He and Kohlsaat entered the church while the minister was praying. The usher looked curiously at TR; when the prayer ended, Kohlsaat introduced him to TR, and they were shown into the front pew. During the singing of a hymn, the usher stepped up to the minister and told him who was in the congregation. Roosevelt sang the hymns louder than anyone else, made the responses in a vigorous voice, and listened with pleasure to the sermon, which was based on the text "Be ye doers of the word and not hearers only."

At the close of the sermon the pastor said, "We are honored by having with us today a fellow member of our church, the Vice-President of the United States, Theodore Roosevelt. I am going to ask him to speak to us." TR jumped up at once, mounted the pulpit, and began talking about the text of the morning. While he was talking, he threw his fists right and left, with uppercuts and undercuts. At one point he ran to the farther side of the pulpit and struck out with such vehemence that he frightened a child of two or three in the front pew; the child began screaming. Tremendously embarrassed, the mother picked up the child and started to leave. "Sit down, please, madam," interposed TR. "Don't go out. I have six of them of my own at home, and I am used to crying children!" The woman resumed her seat, but the child continued to yell until TR was finally obliged to stop talking. He left the pulpit and shook hands with everyone in the congregation. Outside a crowd of people cheered him and Kohlsaat as they got into their carriage and started off. A block or two from the church TR pulled the pink sheet out of his pocket and began reading once more about the fight. "By George," he cried, "that was a bully fight. Sorry I missed it!"[48]

Alice

One day while a friend was visiting Roosevelt in the White House, TR's young daughter Alice kept popping in and out of the office interrupting them. "Theodore," the friend finally complained, "isn't there anything you can do to control Alice?" Said TR firmly: "I can do one of two things. I can be President of the United States or I can control Alice. I cannot possibly do both."[49]

Roosevelt's Rambles

TR's enthusiasm for exercise led to the formation of a "tennis cabinet" made up of friends from Congress, the diplomatic corps, and Cabinet members. But some of TR's friends found it hard to keep up with him. When the new British ambassador, Sir Mortimer Durand, took his first hike with the President, he turned out, according to TR, to be a "bad walker and wholly unable to climb." Durand saw it differently. "We drove out to a wooded valley with streams running through it," he recalled, "and he then made me struggle through bushes and over rocks for two hours and a half, at an impossible speed. My arms and shoulders are still stiff with dragging myself up by roots and ledges. At once place I fairly stuck, and could not get over the top till he caught me by the collar and hauled at me."

Jean-Jules Jusserand, the French ambassador, did better than Durand. "Yesterday," he wrote, "President Roosevelt invited me to take a promenade with him this afternoon at three. I arrived at the White House punctually, in afternoon dress and silk hat, as if we were to stroll in the Tuileries Garden or in the Champs Elysées. To my surprise, the President soon joined me in a tramping suit, with knickerbockers and thick boots, and soft felt hat, much worn. Two or three other gentlemen came, and we started off at what seemed to me a breakneck pace, which soon brought us out of the city. On reaching the country, the President went pell-mell over the fields, following neither road nor path, always on, on, straight ahead! I was much winded, but I would not give in, nor ask him to slow up, because I had the honor of *La belle France* in my heart. At last we came to the bank of a stream, rather wide and too deep to be forded. I sighed in relief, because I thought that now we had reached our goal and would rest a moment and catch our breath, before turning homeward. But judge of my horror when I saw the President unbutton his clothes and heard him say, 'We had better strip, so as not to wet our things in the Creek.' Then I, too, for the honor of France, removed my apparel, everything except my lavender kid gloves. The President cast an inquiring look at these as if they, too, must come off, but I quickly forestalled any remark by saying, 'With your permission, Mr. President, I will keep these on, otherwise it would be embarrassing if we should meet ladies.' And so we jumped into the water and swam across."

Once, just as TR and a friend were starting out on a hike, there was an explosion in a nearby quarry; rocks flew into the air like hailstones. "Aha!" cried TR gleefully. "We are going right there!"

"You must always remember," sighed British diplomat Cecil Spring Rice, an old friend of the Roosevelts, "that the President is about six."[50]

Seduction and Rape

In 1903, the Roosevelt administration made an agreement with Colombia which granted the United States a canal zone across the province of Panama in return for a payment of $10 million and an annual rental fee. The U.S. Senate quickly ratified the treaty but the Colombian Senate, hoping for better terms, unanimously rejected it. Furious over the rejection, TR encouraged the Panamanians to revolt and, when they did, saw to it that a U.S. warship was on hand to prevent the landing of Colombian troops on the Isthmus. On November 6, the United States recognized the Republic of Panama and twelve days later signed a treaty authorizing the construction of a canal there. At a Cabinet meeting a few days later TR started to give a detailed legal analysis of American rights in the Isthmus. "Oh, Mr. President," Attorney General Philander Knox interrupted, "do not let so great an achievement suffer from any taint of legality." TR persisted, however, and when he was finished asked the Cabinet whether he had answered all the charges and successfully defended himself. "You certainly have, Mr. President," Elihu Root assured him. "You have shown that you were accused of seduction and you have conclusively proved that you were guilty of rape."[51]

Court-Martial

One day young Quentin Roosevelt and his pals focused mirrors in such a way as to flash sunlight through the windows of the State-War-Navy Building where people were working. A protest was promptly sent to the President, who sent his personal aide, Captain Archie Butt, off with a message for the boys. "I've just heard," Butt told them, "that they're going to signal something from the top of the War Building." Delighted, the boys went out to look. A little later a man appeared on the roof of the building and signaled the following message with a flag: "YOU, UNDER TREES, ALL OF YOU. ATTACK ON THIS BUILDING MUST IMMEDIATELY CEASE HALT STOP. CLERKS CANNOT WORK. GOVERNMENT BUSINESS INTERRUPTED. REPORT WITHOUT DELAY TO ME FOR YOU KNOW WHAT. THEODORE ROOSEVELT." When the boys filed into the President's office, he held a sham court-martial, pronounced them guilty, and gently reprimanded them.[52]

Posing

TR and John Singer Sargent spent two afternoons trying to find a suitable place in the White House to serve as the background for a painting of the President. They tried pose after pose in place after place, but none was satisfactory. Sargent, of course, was anxious to capture the real Roosevelt in the right surroundings, but TR was not deeply concerned about it and became increasingly tired of the search. Finally, as the two descended a staircase, he stopped at the bottom, rested his elbow on the newel, and turning to his companion, said hopelessly, "Well, Sargent, we had better give it up. We're after the impossible." "Don't move, Mr. President!" exclaimed Sargent quickly. "Don't move! We've got it!" And they had.[53]

TR Gets Some Pointers

Shortly before leaving the White House in March 1909, TR began making plans for a hunting trip to Africa. Hearing that a famous English big-game hunter was in the United States, he invited him to come to Washington to give him some pointers. After a two-hour conference with TR, the Englishman came out of the President's office in a daze. "And what did you tell the President?" asked a curious bystander. "I told him my name," said the wearied visitor.[54]

Resting

When Warrington Dawson, the United Press man who covered TR's 1909 African trip, returned to the United States, he sought an interview with Corinne Robinson, TR's younger sister, to give her a firsthand account of it. But when Dawson said that TR spent his evenings resting, Mrs. Robinson was incredulous. "I have never known my brother Theodore to rest," she said. Dawson then explained what he meant. At night, he said, TR and his companions would sit around the campfire and talk first about the day's hunting; then the conversation would branch out to cover medieval history and literature, astronomy, perhaps the question of whether Louis XVII escaped from the Temple, then European politics and socialism. Exclaimed Mrs. Robinson, greatly relieved, "Yes, I can accept, now, your original statement that my brother Theodore rested!"[55]

Royal Funeral

In 1910, President Taft appointed TR special ambassador of the United States at the funeral of Edward VII. "The President," Archie Butt, now Taft's aide, told his sister-in-law, "has named Mr. Roosevelt to represent us at the King's funeral. With him and the Kaiser present, it will be a wonder if the corpse gets a passing thought."

TR, in fact, played a fairly subdued role at the funeral. The only man in ordinary evening dress, he spent his time placating the French foreign minister, Stephen Pinchon (whose clothes were "stiff with gold lace"), who complained that the coach assigned to him and TR was an ordinary carriage while the royalty had glass coaches. Never having heard of a glass coach, "excepting in connection with Cinderella," TR was quite satisfied with the handsome vehicle assigned to them and persuaded Pinchon to get in. Pinchon then complained that "ces Chinois" were to precede them in the procession. TR said that anyone as gorgeously attired as the Chinese should go first, but Pinchon did not think the remark was funny. The final straw for Pinchon was the fact that a prince—and a minor one at

that—was put into the carriage with the representatives of two repub-
lics: a Persian prince whom TR described as "a deprecatory, inoffen-
sive-looking Levantine." Pinchon slammed himself into the left rear
seat and flung his arms protectively over the right rear seat, indicating
that TR, not "ce Perse," would have the place of honor. The Persian
prince meekly climbed in and sat opposite TR and Pinchon, "looking
about as unaggressive," according to Roosevelt, "as a rabbit in a
cage with two boa constrictors." Pinchon continued to complain
that "toutes ces petites royautés" ("all these unimportant royalties"),
even "le roi du Portugal" ("the King of Portugal"), were preceding
them in the procession, but TR begged him not "to make a row at
a funeral."

Afterward, the Kaiser said to TR, "Call upon me at two o'clock;
I have just 45 minutes to give to you." "I will be there at two,
your Majesty," said TR, "but, unfortunately, I have but 20 minutes
to give you."[56]

Important Conversation

At a Chicago press conference during the 1912 presidential campaign,
TR took Edward B. Clark, *Chicago Evening Post* reporter, aside
for a long whispered conversation. Afterward, newsmen surrounded
Clark, dying of curiosity. "Well," said Clark, "you'll hardly believe
this, but it's true. TR knows I am an amateur ornithologist, as he
is. It seems that yesterday morning at Sagamore Hill, his house in
Oyster Bay, he saw what he believes to be a hermit thrush, and he
wanted my opinion whether it could have been. He described the
bird in detail." Clark said he told TR it might have been a hermit
thrush, but he doubted it very much. This was in the midst of one
of the fiercest political battles in American history.[57]

Small Enough

At Sagamore Hill, TR and naturalist William Beebe used to play
a little game together. After an evening of talk, they would go out
on the lawn and search the skies until they found the faint spot of
light-mist behind the lower lefthand corner of the Great Square of
Pegasus. Then they would recite:

> That is the Spiral Galaxy in Andromeda.
> It is as large as our Milky Way.

> It is one of a hundred million galaxies.
> It consists of one hundred billion suns,
>   each larger than our sun.

Then TR would grin at Beebe and say, "Now I think we are small enough! Let's go to bed!"[58]

Heavenly Choir

On TR's first day in heaven, the story goes, he told St. Peter: "Your choir is weak, inexcusably weak! You should reorganize it at once." St. Peter at once assigned him the task of reorganization. "Well," said TR, "I need ten thousand sopranos, ten thousand altos, and ten thousand tenors." "But what about the basses?" "Oh," said TR, "I'll sing bass."[59]

Promise

Toward the end of TR's life, his sister Corinne visited him in the hospital, and they talked about his future in case his health improved. "Well, anyway," said TR finally, "no matter what comes, I have kept the promise that I made to myself when I was twenty-one." "What promise, Theodore?" his sister asked. "I promised myself," said TR, bringing his right fist down on the arm of his chair, "that I would work *up to the hilt* until I was sixty, and I have done it. I have kept my promise, and now, even if I should be an invalid . . . , or if I should die [snapping his fingers], what difference would it make?" "Theodore," said his sister, "do you remember what you said to me nearly a year ago when you thought you were dying in this same hospital? You said that you were glad it was not one of your boys that was dying at the time in this place, for *they* could die for their country. Do you feel the same way now?" "Yes," said TR, "just the same way. I wish that I might, like Quentin, have died for my country." "I know you wish it," said his sister, "but I want to tell you something. Every one of us . . . would, I feel sure, if our country were in peril, be willing to bare our breasts to any bullet, could we, by so doing, protect and save our country. . . . The difference, Theodore, between you and the majority of us is that you not only are willing and anxious to *die* for your country, but that you *live* for your country every day of your life."[60]

TWENTY-SIX

William Howard Taft
1909–13

One evening in January 1908, Secretary of War William Howard Taft (1857–1930) and his wife Helen dined at the White House with the Roosevelts and some of their friends. After dinner they all went to the library on the second floor for a chat. But TR sat down in an easy chair, threw his head back, closed his eyes, and began chanting: "I am the seventh son of a seventh daughter. I have clairvoyant powers. I see a man standing before me weighing about 350 pounds. There is something hanging over his head. I cannot make out what it is; it is hanging by a slender thread. At one time it looks like the Presidency—then again it looks like the Chief Justiceship." "Make it the Presidency!" exclaimed Mrs. Taft. "Make it the Chief Justiceship!" cried Taft.[1] It ended up being both: the Presidency in 1908 and the Chief Justiceship in 1921. But Taft neither wanted nor enjoyed the Presidency; the happiest years of his life were those he spent on the Supreme Court from 1921 to 1930. "Presidents come and go," he once said, "but the Court goes on forever."[2]

Taft simply was not a good politician. He was careless about names, for one thing. When he headed the War Department, he saw eight reporters just about every day; but for all of his affability and jolly good nature he never learned any of their names or the names of the newspapers they represented. One day Colonel W. R. Nelson, owner of the *Kansas City Star,* came to Washington on business and had occasion to see Taft. During the conversation he mentioned

Dick Lindsay. "Lindsay?" said Taft blankly. "Dick Lindsay? Who's he?" "Why," said Nelson, dumbfounded, "he's my Washington correspondent. I understand from him that he comes in to see you every day. Don't you know him?" "Never heard of the name," said Taft frankly. Later, after Lindsay succeeded in convincing Nelson that he had not been malingering and actually did see the Secretary of War every day, the *Star* proprietor returned home with his liking for Taft considerably diminished. Lindsay, for his part, went to Taft's office the next day, pounded on the desk, and cried: "Take a good look at me, will you, Mr. Secretary? I want you to be able to remember what I look like, so that the next time you talk to my boss you will be able to describe me. I'm Lindsay, of the *Kansas City Star!*" Highly amused, Taft pounded his fists on the arms of his chair and roared. But he never did get to know the names of the other seven reporters.[3]

The contrast with TR, when it came to names, was striking. One reporter had occasion to see both men in action in 1912. At a reception for Roosevelt in Wyoming (just before TR threw his hat in the ring again), the reporter, seeing a great admirer of the Rough Rider approaching, asked TR in a low voice whether he remembered the man. "No," TR whispered back, "I can't recall him." "He's been at the White House and lunched with you," said the reporter. "His name is Watson." "Oh yes," said TR. "I know who he is now. How many children has he?" "Five, no, he has six—another was born just a few days ago." When Watson reached Roosevelt, the latter grasped both his hands, pumped them heartily up and down, and exclaimed, "My dear fellow, I'm so glad to see you again. I shall never forget the delightful hour we spent together in Washington. How are those five, oh no, I believe you have six children now?" Watson (who was a popular and influential figure in Wyoming politics) left happy and smiling; and when TR tried for a third term in 1912 he supported him enthusiastically. A few months later, the same correspondent went to Seattle with Taft and stood by his side as the reception line moved along. At one point he recognized an old Taft admirer approaching and quickly whispered, "Mr. President, there's a man approaching whom you certainly remember?" "No, I don't," said Taft. "What his name?" The reporter told him. Taft repeated it reflectively and then said, "No, I don't seem to place him." When the man's turn came, Taft took his hand in a friendly way and beamed on him as he said, "They tell me I ought to remember you, but bless my soul, I cannot recall you at all." Extremely irritated, the man, a prominent politician in the state of Washington, left the reception determined not to support Taft in the campaign.[4]

Taft was tactless as well as forgetful. He hurt the feelings of TR, his best friend and heartiest supporter, shortly after his election as President in November 1908. TR had chosen Taft to succeed him in the White House and during the campaign had watched over him carefully and given him sage advice on politics. Taft's brother, Charles P., had managed finances for the campaign, but it was really TR who made Taft the nominee and got him elected. Yet after the election, Taft told TR, "I owe a great deal to you, Theodore, and I want to take this opportunity of saying so." TR nodded expectantly, and Taft continued: "Yes, in thinking over the whole campaign I am bound to say that I owe my election more to you than to anybody else, *except my brother Charley.*" Somewhat miffed, TR grumbled afterward: "He puts money above brains."[5] A little later Taft again displayed his genius for saying the wrong thing. When a reporter, referring to the hard times following the Panic of 1907, asked him what would be the outcome of high unemployment, Taft answered resignedly, "God knows!" All he meant was that Taft didn't know; but the remark was spread far and wide, and in cold print it seemed to reveal a heartless indifference toward people out of work. For a long time afterward, working people called him "God-knows Taft."[6]

Carelessness about names and tactless remarks did not of course destroy Taft's Presidency. His accomplishments during four years in office were modest but respectable: establishing the parcel-post and postal-savings services, creating the Department of Labor, extending the civil service, launching more antitrust suits than Roosevelt (without in any way checking the inexorable movement toward consolidation of American industry), and continuing TR's campaign to conserve America's natural resources. But it can hardly be said that Taft made much of a mark on the course of events here or abroad. He was too easygoing and conservative, moreover, to generate much popular excitement, while his administration seemed dull when compared to that of the frenetic TR. Most people, including Taft himself, were happy to see him leave the White House in 1913.

Taft's size may have had something to do with his style. Tall and heavy (though well-proportioned), he was the biggest man ever to occupy the White House. He weighed between 300 and 350 pounds most of the time and had to have a special bathtub constructed for him when he took up residence in the White House. Once, when he was Governor-General of the Philippines, he cabled Secretary of War Elihu Root from Manila, "Took long horseback ride today; feeling fine." Root at once cabled back: "How is the horse?"[7] When he visited the Panama Canal, shortly after its completion, his engineer host saw fit to reinforce a dining-room chair with steel. Taft was grateful; it gave him a great feeling of security, he said, during his visit.[8] He was, people said, the politest man in Washington: on street-cars he would rise and give his place to three women. One day, according to a popular story, he decided to go swimming at Beverly Bay, Massachusetts, donned one of the largest bathing suits ever manufactured, and plunged into the water. Shortly afterward, one of his neighbors suggested to a friend that they go bathing. "Perhaps we'd better wait," said the friend cautiously. "The President is using the ocean."[9] A reporter once asked him precisely how much he weighed. "I won't tell you," he boomed. "But you know that when someone asked Speaker Reed that, he replied that no true gentleman would weigh more than two hundred pounds. I have amended that to three hundred pounds."[10]

Perhaps because of his weight, "Big Bill" Taft was essentially lazy; he had a way of dozing off during conferences, Cabinet meetings, White House dinners, and on public occasions, to the great embarrassment of his friends and aides. After one White House dinner for Cabinet members, Taft called for some music on the Victrola but fell sound asleep during the first selection. When he woke up, he called for the "Prize Song" from *Die Meistersinger,* but fell asleep again before the record could be put on. His Attorney General, George W. Wickersham, then impishly suggested the sextet from *Lucia di Lammermoor,* since "it will awake anyone but a dead man." But it failed to rouse Taft, and Wickersham sighed: "He must be dead." At the opera one evening, Taft's military aide Archie Butt agonized through an entire act, hoping the President would wake up when the lights came on at intermission so the audience would not see the Chief Executive sleeping through a command performance. Fortunately he did awaken. On another occasion Taft fell asleep during a funeral at which he was a front-row mourner. And once he was deep in sleep during a campaign tour of New York City in an open car.[11]

Taft was badly defeated when he ran for re-election in 1912. Of the three candidates—Wilson, Roosevelt, and Taft himself—he got the fewest votes. Many people tried to cheer him up afterward by telling him, "I voted for you," and Taft told a friend: "Whenever any one says that to me, I have an almost uncontrollable desire to say, 'Well, my friend, you are one of a select but small body of citizens whose judgment I heartily concur in and admire.' "[12] But he was philosophical about his defeat. "I have one consolation," he reflected after the returns were in. "No one candidate was ever elected ex-President by such a large majority."[13]

★ ★ ★

Large Party

As a young lawyer, Taft once visited a small town on legal business. When he finished he found it was hours until the next train was due. After inquiries at the station, however, he learned that a fast train was due in an hour but did not stop at this particular town. Taft had an inspiration. Mindful of his 300 pounds, he sent a wire to the division superintendent: "Will No. 7 stop here for a large party?" When the train stopped, Taft climbed aboard and told the astonished conductor: "You can go ahead; I am the large party."[14]

A Ripping Good Time

While Taft was Governor-General of the Philippines, he had occasion to appear at the court of Czar Nicholas. As he and his wife alighted from their carriage at the imperial palace, there was a loud ripping sound; the seam of his trousers had burst. There was no time to return to the hotel for a change of clothes. Mrs. Taft rose to the emergency; she borrowed needle and thread from a lady-in-waiting and quickly sewed up the rent. Fearful that her hasty stitches might not hold during the audience, Taft moved crabwise before the Czar and on leaving backed out of the room.[15]

Mr. Taft

One day a man called on Lawrence Lowell, president of Harvard University, and found he had been called to Washington on business. "The President is in Washington," Lowell's secretary told the caller, "seeing Mr. Taft."[16]

Woodrow Wilson
1913–21

Woodrow Wilson (1856–1924) was a devout predestinarian. Son of a Presbyterian minister and theology professor, as a boy he thoroughly absorbed the teachings of his father and grew up with a fervent belief in religious destiny: his own, America's, and the world's. On receiving the Democratic nomination for President at Baltimore in 1912, he declared: "I am a Presbyterian and believe in predestination and election. It was Providence that did the work at Baltimore." After the election he told William F. McCombs, chairman of the Democratic National Committee: "Before we proceed I wish it clearly understood that I owe you nothing." Surprised, McCombs reminded him of his services during the campaign, but Wilson exclaimed: *"God ordained that I should be the next President of the United States. Neither you nor any other mortal could have prevented that!"*[1]

Wilson never doubted that he was a foreordained agent, "guided by an intelligent power outside himself," with important work to do in the world.[2] For him the League of Nations, his most famous enterprise, was not simply a human contrivance for ordering international relations; it represented God's will and, in rejecting it, the United States was trying futilely to resist its Providential destiny. As Wilson told some friends toward the end of his life: "I have seen fools resist Providence before, and I have seen their destruction. . . . That we shall prevail is as sure as God reigns."[3] To Raymond Fosdick, a former League official, he exclaimed, with tears in his eyes, a few weeks before his death in 1924: "You can't fight God!"[4]

Calvinists may bear tidings of great joy, but they are not usually very cheerful about it. Wilson struck most people as being cold, reserved, distant, and aloof, not to say vain and self-righteous. William Allen White said that Wilson's handshake was "like a ten-cent pickled mackerel in brown paper"; and many people were put off by his habit of busily polishing his glasses while they were talking to him.[5] It is true that Wilson enjoyed vaudeville, told dialect jokes with verve, and sang "Oh, You Beautiful Doll" when courting his second wife. It is true also that he confessed to carrying a "volcano" around inside him and insisted that he possessed a cheery Irish nature as well as a stern Covenanter temperament.[6] Nevertheless, his austere demeanor produced respectful admirers, not affectionate disciples, and he once complained that though he wanted people to love him he knew they never would. He was christened Thomas Woodrow Wilson and called "Tommy" as a boy; but he eventually dropped the Thomas, and not even his intimates called him "Woody" when he came of age. Once, though, when he was campaigning in the Middle West, someone in the audience yelled, "That was a good one, Woody!" Overcome with delight, Wilson said to the newsman accompanying him, "Did you hear, Mr. Thompson? They called me Woody!" But it was the exception, not the rule.[7]

Wilson was like Lincoln in his deep sense of Providential design in the world, but, far surer than Lincoln of God's will, he tended toward inflexibility and even intolerance when he had made up his mind on issues. Even as a college student in a debating society he could not bring himself to participate in a debate on the tariff after drawing the affirmative side; protectionism was just too wicked to contemplate. While president of Princeton he got into a bitter quarrel with the graduate dean; and when a faculty friend, seeking peace, gently reminded him, "There are two sides to every question," he replied icily, "Yes—the right and the wrong."[8] "I am sorry for those who disagree with me," he once told a political associate; asked why, he replied, "Because I know they are wrong."[9] He was not a good listener. When Walter Hines Page, ambassador to England during World War I, came to Washington to report on the situation there, he found it impossible to get Wilson to listen to any opinions at variance with his own. When Page persisted, Wilson "sprang up, stuck his fingers in his ears, and, still holding them there, ran out of the room."[10]

Still, for all his limitations, Wilson was probably the most influential man ever to occupy the White House. The foreign policy he developed during World War I has unquestionably had profound effects on the course of American (and thus world) history. He made world pacification—the achievement of world peace by collective action—the primary objective of American foreign policy. He was convinced that it was America's duty—and its destiny—to take the lead in organizing the "peace-loving nations" to uphold world order. And ever since his day, the belief that world pacification should occupy a central place in America's foreign policy has played a crucial part in shaping the country's perception of what is necessary, desirable, and possible in the world of nations.

Wilson's hatred of war and love for peace were deep-seated. Though he never doubted that the United States must enter World War I if the Allies needed its help in order to win, he took the American people into the war only with great reluctance. On the eve of American entry, he called for "peace without victory," that is, a peace that would not result in a mere division of spoils by the victors. At the same time he also agonized over the question of whether it was possible for a nation like the United States to participate in a major war without being brutalized by it. To the *New York World*'s Frank Cobb, he confided his doubts. "What else can I do?" he asked Cobb. "Is there anything else I can do?" According to Cobb, Wilson "was uncanny that night. He had the whole panorama in his mind. . . . He began to talk about the consequences to the United States. He had no illusions about the fashion in which we were likely to fight the war. He said that when a war got going it was just war and there weren't two kinds of it. It required illiberalism at home to reinforce the men at the front. We couldn't fight Germany and maintain the ideals of Government that all thinking men shared. He said we would try it but it would be too much for us. 'Once lead this people into war,' he said, 'and they'll forget there ever was such a thing as tolerance. To fight you must be brutal and ruthless, and the spirit of ruthless brutality will enter into the very fibre of our national life, infecting Congress, the courts, the policeman on the beat, the man on the street.' . . . He thought the Constitution would not survive it; that free speech and the right of assembly would go. He said a nation couldn't put its strength into a war and keep its head level; it had never been done. 'If there is any alternative, for God's sake, let's take it,' he exclaimed."[11] The next day, when he delivered his war message to Congress and was greeted with a standing ovation, he said to Joseph Tumulty, his private secretary: "Think what it was they were applauding. My message today was a message of death for your young men. How strange it seems to applaud that."[12]

To organize the nations of the world for a just and lasting peace, Wilson formulated his famous Fourteen Points and went to Paris himself to join England's David Lloyd George, France's Georges Clemenceau, and Italy's Vittorio Orlando in writing the Treaty of Versailles. His blunders—ignoring the U.S. Senate, which had to ratify the treaty, and the Republicans who dominated the Senate after the 1918 elections—are well known. So are his clashes with his associates in Paris, who felt, with some justification, that Wilson's view of the world did not accord with the harsh realities. "God gave us his Ten Commandments, and we broke them," said Clemenceau skeptically. "Wilson gave us his Fourteen Points—we shall see."[13] According to Lloyd George, "It was part of the real joy of these conferences to observe Clemenceau's attitude toward Wilson during the first five weeks of the Conference. . . . If the President took a flight beyond the azure main, as he was occasionally inclined to do without regard to relevance, Clemenceau would open his great eyes in twinkling wonder, and turn them on me as much as to say: 'Here he is off again.' I really think that at first the idealistic President regarded himself as a missionary whose function was to rescue the poor European heathen from their age-long worship of false and fiery gods. . . . His most extraordinary outburst was when he was developing some theme—I rather think it was connected with the League of Nations—which led him to explain the failure of Christianity to achieve its highest ideals. 'Why,' he said, 'has Jesus Christ so far not succeeded in inducing the world to follow His teaching in these matters? It is because He taught the ideal without devising any practical scheme to carry out his aims.' Clemenceau slowly opened his dark eyes to their widest dimension and swept them round the Assembly to see how the Christians gathered around the table enjoyed this exposure of the futility of their Master."[14]

In the end, the Versailles treaty did incorporate some of Wilson's principles; but it also made important concessions to *realpolitik.* "I think I did as well as might be expected," said Lloyd George afterward, "—seated as I was between Jesus Christ and Napoleon Bonaparte."[15] But Wilson made concessions himself; he "talked like Jesus Christ," Clemenceau snorted afterward, "but acted like Lloyd

George."[16] Wilson did not enjoy acting like Lloyd George; and he was disappointed by the treaty's scaling down of his ideals. Nevertheless, he took heart from the fact that the League of Nations (whose covenant he drafted himself) was made an essential part of the final settlement. The League, he thought, could in due time rectify the injustices of the treaty itself.

Having compromised in Paris, Wilson was in no mood for more compromises when he submitted the treaty to the Senate in January 1919. "The stage is set," he announced, "the destiny disclosed. It has come about by no plan of our conceiving, but by the hand of God which led us into this war."[17] Wilson's chief enemy in the Senate, Republican Henry Cabot Lodge, Chairman of the Senate Foreign Relations Committee, saw more of Wilson's hand in it than God's; determined to get his own hand into it as well, he formulated a set of reservations to be added to the treaty. If Wilson had been willing to accept these reservations, or even others somewhat less stringent, he probably would have obtained Senate ratification. But to one Senator he exclaimed: "Accept the Treaty with the *Lodge* reservations! Never! Never! I shall never consent to adopt any policy with which that impossible name is so prominently identified."[18] When Senator T. S. Martin of Virginia expressed doubts that the necessary two-thirds majority could be mustered for the treaty without reservations, Wilson snapped: "Martin! Anyone who opposes me in that, I'll crush!"[19]

Lodge's tactics in fighting Wilson were maddening; he accused him of selfishness and a lust for power (terrible charges for an idealist like Wilson to hear) and made fun of his prose style ("As an English production it does not rank high. It might get by at Princeton but certainly not at Harvard").[20] Still, many supporters of the League felt that it was absolutely necessary for the President to accept some reservations to get the treaty ratified, so they strongly urged him to compromise with the reservationists. French ambassador Jusserand made a special trip to Washington to assure Wilson that France and Britain were willing to accept the treaty with reservations demanded by an important group of Senators, but to his disappointment Wilson exclaimed: "Mr. Ambassador, I shall consent to nothing. The Senate must take its medicine."[21] Senator Gilbert M. Hitchcock, the Democratic leader, also interceded. "Mr. President," he said, "it might be wise to compromise with Lodge on this point." "Let Lodge compromise," said Wilson. "Well, of course," said Hitchcock, "he must compromise also, but we might well hold out the olive branch." "Let Lodge hold out the olive branch," said Wilson. Even Mrs. Wilson put pressure on the President.[22] "For my sake," she cried, "won't you accept these reservations and get this awful thing settled?" "Little girl," said Wilson gently, "don't you desert me; that I cannot stand." And he explained: "Better to go down fighting than to dip your colors to dishonorable compromise."[23]

In both Senate votes—on November 19, 1919, and on March 19, 1920—Wilson's supporters stood firm and helped defeat the treaty with reservations. Just before the final vote, Democratic Senator H. F. Ashurst of Arizona exclaimed: "As a friend of the President, as one who has loyally followed him, I solemnly declare to him this morning: If you want to kill your own child because the Senate straightens out its crooked limbs, you must take the responsibility and accept the verdict of history."[24] And after the final vote, Senator Frank B. Brandegee, one of Wilson's opponents, told Lodge: "We can always depend on Mr. Wilson. He never has failed us."[25]

The United States did not join Wilson's League; but the principles on which it was based continued to animate American foreign policy-makers and were finally embodied in the United Nations in 1945. Wilson did not live to see the triumph of his principles, but he never doubted that they would win out in the end. While touring the country to win popular support for the League in September 1919, he had a stroke and returned to Washington semi-paralyzed. When Republican Senator Albert Fall of New Mexico visited him in the White House to check on his health and said piously, "Well, Mr. President, we have all been praying for you," Wilson responded ironically: "Which way, Senator?"[26] He was happy, though, that during the 1920 presidential campaign James M. Cox, Democratic candidate, spoke out for the League; and his opinion of the Republican candidate, Warren G. Harding, who opposed it, was exceedingly low. During the campaign, a book appeared attempting to prove that Harding came of mixed blood, and Joseph Tumulty hurried to the White House to tell Wilson. "Governor," he exclaimed, "we've got 'em beat! Here's a paper which has been searched out and is absolutely true, showing Harding has Negro blood in him. This country will never stand for that!" But Wilson told him: "Even if that is so, it will never be used with my consent. We cannot go into a man's genealogy; we must base our campaign on principles, not on back-stair gossip. That is not only right but good politics. So I insist you kill any such proposal."[27]

When Harding won in 1920, Wilson insisted on attending his inauguration despite his own frail condition. "The Senate fell down on me," he remarked, "but I am not going to let it see me fall down."[28] On inauguration day he went to the Capitol to sign a few bills just passed. Then he received a joint committee of the two Houses, as was the custom, which came to notify him that Congress had completed its business and was ready to adjourn unless the President had any further message to communicate. The spokesman of the committee was Senator Lodge. "Mr. President," said Lodge, "we have come as a committee . . . to notify you that the Senate and the House are about to adjourn and await your pleasure." "Senator Lodge," returned Wilson, "I have no further communication to make. I thank you. Good morning." And after giving Lodge an icy stare he left.[29]

Care

Wilson enjoyed repeating a retort his father made to a fellow townsman in Augusta, Georgia, when Wilson was a little boy. His father, wearing an old alpaca coat, was seated in his buggy driving a well-groomed gray mare down the street when one of his parishioners called to him, "Doctor, your horse looks better groomed than yourself." "Yes," said Wilson's father, "I take care of my horse; my congregation takes care of me."[30]

False Glamor

When Wilson was president of Princeton University, the mother of one of his students begged him to make the college a coeducational institution. "Why?" he asked her. "To remove the false glamor with which the two sexes see each other," she replied. "My dear Madam," said Wilson, "that is the very thing we want to preserve at all costs!"[31]

Good of the College

As president of Princeton, Wilson insisted on high academic standards. He once told a man pleading the case of a boy who had failed the entrance examination, "I want you to understand that if the angel Gabriel applied for admission to Princeton University and could not pass the entrance examinations, he would not be admitted. He would be wasting his time." To a woman whose son had been expelled for cheating, who said she had to have an operation and would die if her boy was not reinstated, he said: "Madam . . . , you force me to say a hard thing, but, if I had to choose between your life or my life or anybody's life and the good of this college, I should choose the good of this college."[32]

Hanging Around College

After resigning as president of Princeton, Wilson went into politics and became Governor of New Jersey. One of his favorite stories was about two laboring men who heard him speak at Newark. "That's a smart guy," said one of them. "He's smart as hell," said the other. "What I don't see is what a fellow as smart as that was doing hanging around a college so long."[33]

Agreeable to Undertaker

When Wilson was Governor of New Jersey, he received a phone call from Washington notifying him that one of the New Jersey Senators, a good friend of his, had just died. Stunned, Wilson cancelled all his appointments for the day. A few minutes later he received a call from a New Jersey politician. "Governor," said the man, "I would like to take the Senator's place." "Well," said Wilson, shocked by the man's haste, "you may quote me as saying that's perfectly agreeable to me if it's agreeable to the undertaker."[34]

Ain't Good-Looking

During Wilson's 1912 presidential campaign, his associates frequently heard people say, "Well, he may be all right, but he ain't good-looking." One day the journalist Charles Willis Thompson asked Wilson what he thought of a certain political associate; to his surprise, Wilson said, "Well, he may be all right, but he ain't good-looking." Seeing the effect of his statement, Wilson smiled and said: "So you have heard them say that too, have you?" "Yes," said Thompson, "but we didn't think you had." "I've caught it several times as I passed by," said Wilson. "It reminds me of a thing that happened when I was running for Governor. I stopped in front of a billboard that had my picture on it. As I looked at it I became conscious of two working men who had stopped and were staring at me. One

of them said to the other, 'Bill, damned if them two ain't enough
alike to be twins.' "[35]

Advocates Chewing Tobacco

In a 1912 campaign speech, Wilson stressed the need for thinking
things through. To underscore his point, he described a group of
men sitting around in a country store conferring about the affairs
of the neighborhood and spitting tobacco juice into a sawdust box.
"Whatever may be said against the chewing of tobacco," said Wilson
(who neither chewed nor smoked), "this at least can be said for it,
that it gives a man time to think between sentences." The next day
a brief, garbled account of the speech appeared in the newspapers
with the headline "Advocates The Chewing of Tobacco." A few
days later, to Wilson's dismay, a prominent tobacco firm began
quoting him in advertisements appearing in several New York
newspapers.[36]

Disappointment

Wilson liked to tell of an incident in Staunton, Virginia, his hometown, where he received a great ovation after his election as President
in 1912. While he was addressing a large crowd of people, a small
boy pushed and shoved his way to the front until he stood right in
front of the speaker, shouting: "Where is it? Where is it?" Wilson
stopped his speech and said good-naturedly, "Well, my boy, I guess
I'm it." "Shucks," cried the boy disgustedly, "I thought it was a
dogfight."[37]

Pudd'nhead Wilson

Wilson admired Mark Twain. When his presidential train passed
through Hannibal, Missouri, he ordered a three-hour stopover so
he could visit some of Twain's boyhood haunts. Approaching one
of the townsmen, he said, "I'm a stranger in these parts. Could
you tell me where Tom Sawyer was supposed to live?" "Never heard
of him," said the man. "Well, how about Huck Finn?" persisted
the President. "Never heard of him nuther," said the man. The
President tried once more. "How about Pudd'nhead Wilson?" he

asked. The man's face lighted up. "I heard of him all right," he exclaimed. "In fact, I even voted for the durn fool."[38]

Speeches

Once a Cabinet member praised Wilson for his short speeches and asked him how long it took to prepare them. "It depends," Wilson told him. "If I am to speak ten minutes, I need a week for preparation; if fifteen minutes, three days; if half an hour, two days, if an hour, I am ready now."[39]

Making Faces

Riding along a country road near Washington one day, accompanied by a Secret Service man, President Wilson passed a small boy by the roadside. "Did you see what that boy did?" Wilson asked his companion. "No sir," said the Secret Service man; "what did he do?" "He made a face at me," said the President gravely. The Secret Service man was shocked. But the President smiled and said, "Did you see what I did?" "No, sir." "Well," said the President with a mischievous look, "I made a face right back at him!"[40]

Bungalow

A man who had something of "great importance" to say sought an interview with the President. Afterward Secretary of State Bainbridge Colby asked Wilson, "What impression did he he make on you, Mr. President?" "That of a bungalow," said Wilson shortly. "How is that?" asked Colby. "No upper story," said Wilson.[41]

Germans

On weekends during World War I, President Wilson often made trips down the Potomac on the presidential yacht *Mayflower* with his wife and friends. One Sunday morning they decided to visit a small Chesapeake island called Tangier that was inhabited by fishermen and their families. When they landed, the village streets were deserted. The only persons in sight were an old man and a child. "Hi! Grandpa," called Wilson's Secret Service guard. "Say, mister," said the old man, "who is that feller with his woman?" "That's

Mr. Wilson," said the Secret Service man, "the President of the United States." "Great lovin' hands o' God a' Mighty!" exclaimed the islander. "Everybody thought you was Germans and went to hide inside!" When word got around that it was the President instead of the Kaiser's sailors, the villagers came out to welcome them. They explained that during the War of 1812 the British had occupied their island and used it as a base for preparing their attack on Baltimore, so they were afraid that the Germans had landed to do the same.[42]

Honeymoon

Wilson's first wife, Ellen, died in 1914. The following year the President met and fell deeply in love with Edith Bolling Galt, and the two were married in December 1915. One day, during their honeymoon, they took a drive in the country and stopped to take a walk. When they returned to the automobile, the President's shoes were muddy. "If you'll put your foot on the running board I'll clean it," offered the chauffeur. Wilson accepted. His bride looked down at her feet. "My shoes are not muddy," she said. "I was more careful. But I have a lace untied." "May I tie it for you?" asked Colonel Starling, the Secret Service man. Mrs. Wilson nodded and rested her foot on his trouser leg, raising the skirt of her handsomely tailored suit to reveal a shapely ankle. When Starling set her foot back on the ground she smiled at him and said, "You make a very neat bow." Then Starling noticed the bridegroom, who was standing by the car, staring straight ahead with his jaws moving up and down in cold anger, and he quickly retreated to the Secret Service car. For the next two weeks Wilson refused to speak to him.[43]

Commander-in-Chief

One day after the Armistice, Wilson accompanied General John J. Pershing on a tour of inspection in France. Commenting on the efficiency of the American soldier's equipment, Pershing picked up a folding tent pole from one soldier's outfit and explained how it worked. When he was finished, he threw the pole down on top of the soldier's carefully laid-out equipment. "Are those boys not likely to be inspected further after we have passed?" Wilson asked Pershing. "Yes, sir, they may be." "One other thing, General," continued Wilson. "I am the commander-in-chief of the army and authorized to give you orders, am I not?" "Certainly, sir." "Then, General," said Wilson, "you will replace that tent pole as you found it." With a smile, Pershing knelt, folded the tent pole, and put it in its proper place. Afterward some of the soldiers watching insisted that the President winked at them.[44]

By-Laws

In Paris, the strain of the Versailles Conference wore Wilson down; eventually he contracted a violent case of the then-deadly influenza. Joseph Tumulty, his private secretary, cautioned him against over-work and warned him that if he did not let up he might wreck his constitution. "Constitution!" exclaimed Wilson. "Why, man, I'm already living on my by-laws!"[45]

One Country Enough

When Germany finally accepted the armistice terms, Wilson said to Joseph Tumulty, "Well, Tumulty, the war's over, and I feel like the Confederate soldier General John B. Gordon used to tell of, soliloquizing on a long, hard march, during the Civil War: 'I love my country and I am fightin' for my country, but if this war ever ends, I'll be dad-burned if I ever love another country!' "[46]

Wilson and Ten Commandments

When Wilson died and went to heaven, according to a popular story, he encountered Moses while traversing the golden streets of New Jerusalem. "You are Mr. Wilson, are you not?" asked Moses. "I am." "I am very sorry for you," said Moses. "Why so?" asked Wilson. "Weren't you Woodrow Wilson, President of the United States?" "I was." "And didn't you issue the Fourteen Points for the settlement of the Great War?" "I did." "Well," said Moses, "I am sorry for you, because they have done such dreadful things to your Fourteen Points." "For the matter of that," returned Wilson, "I should advise you to go back to the earth and see what they have done to your Ten Commandments."[47]

TWENTY-EIGHT

Warren G. Harding
1921–23

Warren Gamaliel Harding (1865–1923) once confessed: "I like to go out into the country and bloviate."[1] In Ohio, when Harding was a young man, to bloviate meant to loaf around, chat with people, and in general enjoy oneself. For Harding the politician bloviating turned out to mean making long-winded speeches stuffed with shabby ideas, stale clichés, and awkward neologisms.

A former small-town Ohio newspaper editor, Harding thought he had a way with words. He did, but it was the wrong way. He gave intransitive verbs direct objects: "we must prosper America first." He left transitive verbs dangling bewilderedly without direct objects: "I would like the government to do all it can to mitigate." He used clumsy words of his own making, like "re-revealment." He was a master of banal wisdom: "Despite all the deprecation I cannot bring myself to accept the notion that the inter-relation among our men and women has departed." And he had a passion for alliteration that led him at times into an orgy of word-mongering. "Progression," he once said, "is not proclamation nor palaver. It is not pretense nor play on prejudice. It is not of personal pronouns, nor perennial pronouncement. It is not the perturbation of a people passion-wrought, nor a promise proposed."[2]

H. L. Mencken was fascinated by what he called "Gamalielese." It was, he thought, the worst English he had ever encountered. "It reminds me," he wrote, "of a string of wet sponges; it reminds me of tattered washing on the line; it reminds me of stale bean soup, of college yells, of dogs barking idiotically through endless nights. It is so bad that a sort of grandeur creeps into it. It drags itself out of a dark abysm . . . of pish, and crawls insanely up the topmost pinnacle of posh. It is rumble and bumble. It is flap and doodle. It is balder and dash."[3]

In a speech in Boston in May 1920, Harding, wallowing in alliterative delights, came up with the word "normalcy," which was a perfectly good word, though that is not why Harding used it; he was simply mispronouncing "normality." "America's present need," he said, "is not heroics but healing, not nostrums but normalcy, not revolution but restoration, not agitation but adjustment, not surgery but serenity, not the dramatic but the dispassionate, not experiment but equipoise, not submergence in internationality but sustainment in triumphant nationality."[4] Reporters picked up "normalcy," editorial writers commented on it, and the Republicans coined the phrase "Back to Normalcy" to use during the 1920 campaign. By "normalcy," Harding meant an earlier, simpler, nineteenth-century America in which the small town was the heart of American life and village virtues prevailed throughout the land. But Harding himself displayed no small-town virtues as President. He invited his cronies to poker games in the White House, at which liquor flowed freely despite Prohibition. He also arranged clandestine meetings with his mistress, Nan Britton, and provided secret financial support for her baby.

Harding had no illusions about himself, for he had never really wanted to be President. "I am a man of limited talents from a small town," he once admitted. To Nan he exclaimed: "I'm in jail, and I can't get out. I've got to stay." And when Senator Frank B. Brandegee (who thought Harding was "the best of the second-raters") asked him how he liked being President, he cried: "Frank, it is hell! No other word can describe it."[5] "Jud," he once lamented to one of the White House secretaries, "you have a college education, haven't you? I don't know what to do or where to turn in this taxation matter. Somewhere there must be a book that tells all about it, where I could go to straighten it out in my mind. But I don't know where the book is, and maybe I couldn't read it if I found it! And there must be a man in the country somewhere who could weigh both sides and know the truth. Probably he is in some college or other. But I don't know where to find him. I don't know who he is, and

I don't know how to get him. My God, this is a hell of a place for a man like me to be!"[6] Harding's grasp of economic realities was, in fact, infirm. He once told a reporter that "the United States should adopt a protective tariff of such a character as will help the struggling industries of Europe to get on their feet."[7]

Still, Harding did his best. Though no integrationist, he made a speech in Alabama advocating civil rights for blacks which Negro educator J. Wilson Pettus called the "most notable and courageous expression on the race question made by any President of the United States since Lincoln."[8] He sponsored a disarmament conference of the Big Powers in Washington and was pleased by the fact that, for the time being, there was a halt in the arms race. He was also decent enough to pardon Eugene Debs, the high-minded Socialist leader jailed by the Wilson administration for opposing World War I; he even invited Debs to the White House for a friendly chat. Some of Harding's Cabinet appointments were good. But although Harding himself was honest, some of the men he appointed to high office turned out to be crooks. Perhaps his father was right: "Warren," he said, "it's a lucky thing you were not born a girl, because you can't say no."[9] Alice Roosevelt Longworth put it differently. "Harding was not a bad man," she said. "He was just a slob."[10]

In the summer of 1923, distressed by stories of graft and corruption among his friends and associates, Harding left Washington for a vacation and speechmaking tour. In San Francisco he had a heart attack and was put to bed in the Palace Hotel. There, on the evening of August 2, his wife began reading an article about him entitled "A Calm View of a Calm Man." "That's good," said Harding at one point. "Go on. Read some more."[11] Moments later he was dead. In a courteous gesture the following year the Democratic convention passed a resolution that "Our party stands uncovered at the bier of Warren G. Harding"; but "bier" was changed to "grave" to avoid offending the Prohibitionists.[12]

★ ★ ★

Church-Goer

On Sunday mornings President Harding rode horseback. It was White House guard Colonel Edmund W. Starling's duty to see that he got back to the White House in time to attend church with Mrs. Harding. Harding was not much of a church-goer, but the "Duchess," as he called his wife, insisted that "Wurr'n" put in an appearance. "Colonel," Harding told Starling one morning, "let's take that path." "If we do," said Starling, "we won't be back in time to go to church." "I know it," sighed Harding; "your memory is too damn good!"[13]

Will Rogers

When Will Rogers visited the White House, Harding told him, "This is the first time I ever got to see you without paying for it."[14]

Amnesty

One day journalist Lincoln Steffens visited President Harding to urge amnesty for people imprisoned during World War I for their antiwar activities. "Make peace at home," Steffens told Harding. "We've got it abroad. Let all the prisoners who are in jail fighting for labor, for peace, for—anything. Let 'em all out, with a proclamation, you and the governors." "That's all right for fellows like you and me," said Harding mildly, "but—but They won't let me do it." He then brought up the case of Socialist leader Eugene Debs. "I am going to pardon Debs," he told Steffens. "I have put that over, but a general amnesty?" He shook his head. Then he had an idea. "I'll tell you what I'll do," he said. "I'll make you a fair, sporting proposition. You get my Cabinet and I'll do it. No. You get Hoover and—my Secretary of Labor, and I'll get the rest myself, and we'll do it." Steffens rushed out hopefully, but soon returned with emphatic refusals from Hoover and the Secretary of Labor. Harding laughed long and loud. Then he showed Steffens a typewritten paper he had in his hand. "Here, look at this." It was a statement his Attorney General had dictated for Debs to sign when he was pardoned. Steffens called it a "dirt-eating promise," and Harding agreed. "What would you do about that?" he asked. Steffens said he wouldn't pardon any man who would subscribe to such a statement. Harding nodded. "I thought so," he muttered; and he crumpled up the paper and threw it away. A few days later he pardoned Debs without any humiliating conditions.[15]

TWENTY-NINE

Calvin Coolidge
1923–29

Shortly after midnight on August 3, 1923, the news of President Harding's death reached Vice-President Calvin Coolidge (1872–1933) in Plymouth Notch, Vermont, where he was spending his summer vacation. "Guess we'd better have a drink," said Coolidge, after a call was put through to Washington to find out whether Coolidge's father, a notary public, could swear his son in as President. Accompanied by Vermont Congressman Porter Dale, railway mailman L. L. Lane, and editor Joseph Fountain of the *Springfield Reporter,* Coolidge went down to the general store to celebrate. "Moxie, sasparella [sic], cream, cherry, and raspberry soda," announced the girl behind the counter. "Moxie," said Coolidge. Downing his drink, he pulled an old change purse out of his pocket, fumbled around in it until he found the coin he was looking for, and plunked it down on the counter. It was a nickel. Congressman Dale blinked and quietly picked up the rest of the check. A little later Coolidge's father administered the oath of office by the light of a kerosene lamp; then Coolidge went back to bed. The next morning, as he came out of the house to start his journey to Washington, he noticed that one of the stone steps leading to the porch was slightly out of place. "Better have that fixed," he told his father.[1]

The country "wanted nothing done" while Coolidge was in the White House, someone said, "and he done it."[2] "Coolidge!" exclaimed H. L. Mencken. "A remarkable man, a really *remarkable* man. Nero fiddled while Rome burned, but Coolidge only snores."[3] In 1924, Coolidge ran for President on his own and defeated the Democratic candidate by a landslide. The Republican campaign slogan was "Keep Cool and Keep Coolidge." The word "cool" did not mean hip, groovy, "with it," or keen, as it did some years later. It meant the precise opposite: calm, imperturbable, serene, even somnolent. Coolidge was truly cool in this sense. After moving into the White House, he put a rocking chair out on the front porch and sat there evenings smoking cigars. He did less work and made fewer decisions than just about any other President. "His chief feat during five years and seven months in office," said Mencken, "was to sleep more than any other President—to sleep more and say less. Wrapped in magnificent silence, his feet upon his desk, he drowsed away the lazy days. He was no fiddler like Nero; he simply yawned and stretched. And while he yawned and stretched the United States went slam-bang down the hill—and he lived just long enough to see it fetch up with a horrible bump at the bottom."[4]

Not for nothing was Coolidge nicknamed "Silent Cal." Alice Roosevelt, Theodore Roosevelt's daughter, gleefully circulated someone's remark that he looked as if he had been weaned on a pickle.[5] When he smiled, someone said, "the effect was like ice breaking up in a New England river."[6] Every time he opened his mouth, someone else said, a moth flew out.[7] Coolidge could indeed be a man of few or no words if he so chose. During the 1924 campaign, eager reporters sought him out. "Have you any statement on the campaign?" asked one. "No," replied Coolidge. "Can you tell us something about the world situation?" asked another. "No." "Any information about Prohibition?" "No." Then, as the disappointed reporters started to leave, Coolidge said solemnly: "Now, remember—don't quote me." Just before returning to Washington from a trip to California he was interviewed on the radio. Asked if he had a message for the American people, he paused for a moment, then said: "Goodbye." Coolidge knew what he was about. "If you don't say anything," he once explained, "you can't be called on to repeat it."[8]

Coolidge's record as President, according to Mencken, was "almost a blank. No one remembers anything that he did or anything that he said."[9] Mencken erred. Many of the things Coolidge said became famous. His statement as Governor of Massachusetts during the Boston police strike of 1919—"There is no right to strike against the public safety by anybody, anywhere, any time"—brought him nationwide attention and helped pave the road to the Vice-Presidency.[10] His supposed remark as President when queried about canceling Allied war debts from World War I—"They hired the money, didn't they?"—was widely quoted and approved.[11] His announcement that "the business of America is business" also brought him acclaim. But when, after he said in August 1927, "I do not choose to run for President in 1928," the Republicans nominated Herbert Hoover at the 1928 convention, Coolidge seemed to be somewhat put off. He was lucky, though, for the economy went into a tailspin shortly after he left the White House. Before leaving office, he gave Hoover advice on how to get rid of long-winded visitors: "If you keep dead still they will run down in three or four minutes."[12]

In retirement, Coolidge wrote his autobiography; and in 1930 he had a daily newspaper column in which he put forth such words of wisdom for the Great Depression as the following:

> Our banking system is not yet perfect.
> Public officers are not infallible.
> The future may be better or worse.
> Raising tax rates does not now seem to be popular.
> The final solution for unemployment is work.[13]

In 1933, he died suddenly of a heart attack. When *New Yorker* writer Dorothy Parker was told that Coolidge was dead, she exclaimed: "How can they tell?"[14]

In some ways, Coolidge was more important in anecdote than in actuality. Even while he was in the White House, stories about his close-mouthedness, shrewd horse sense, and stinginess began accumulating. Some of them are spurious; but many of them are delightfully authentic. And it is a fact that, with his nasal twang, he could pronounce the word "cow" in four syllables.[15]

★   ★   ★

Cal Gets a Penny

During the presidential campaign of 1880, little Cal asked his dad for a penny to buy some candy. His father told him it looked as though a Democrat was going to win in November, and, if so, there would be hard times and it would be necessary to economize. Several days later Republican James A. Garfield won by a slim margin.

"As soon as the news reached our town," Coolidge said later, "I went to my father and told him the result indicated we were to continue a Republican administration, and with that prospect in view I was able to secure the advance of the sum I asked."[16]

Coolidge's Dad Praises Him

Coolidge's father once reminisced: "It always seemed as though Cal could get more sap out of a maple tree than any other boy I knew."[17]

Gastronomist

When Coolidge was a student at Amherst College, he ate his meals in a boardinghouse for three dollars and a half a week. A big black cat occasionally prowled around the dining room. One evening the main dish was hash. When Cal was served, he looked critically at his plate for a few seconds and then called the waiter in. "Bring me the cat," he said. The waiter brought the cat in, spitting and clawing. Taking a look at her, Coolidge murmured "Thank you," and began eating the hash.[18]

Young Athlete

Coolidge was once asked, "What part did you take in college athletics?" His response: "I held the stakes."[19]

Cal Goes A-Courting

"That's a likely gal," Cal's grandmother said of Grace Goodhue. "Why don't you marry her?" "Mebbe I will, Grandma," responded Cal. A few days later he turned up at the Goodhue home. "Hello, Calvin," said Mr. Goodhue when he came upon Cal reading a magazine in the living room, "what are you doing in Burlington? Got some business here?" "No," was the reply. "Came up to marry Grace." "Why, have you spoken to her yet?" "No, I can wait a few days if it's any convenience to you."[20]

Coolidge's Socks

One afternoon, shortly after marrying Cal, Mrs. Coolidge saw him coming home from his law office carrying an odd-looking and ancient russet-colored bag. When he opened it for her, she found it crammed with men's socks, all in need of repair. Mrs. Coolidge counted them; there were fifty-two pairs. After mending them, she asked whether he had married her just to get his stockings darned. "No," he said quite seriously, "but I find it mighty handy."[21]

No Cure

Shortly after her wedding, Mrs. Coolidge was talked by a salesman into paying eight dollars for a medical book called *Our Family Physician*. Afterward she had misgivings about spending so much money, so she said nothing to her husband about it but simply left the book on the parlor table. One day she took a look at it and found that her husband had written on the flyleaf: "This work suggests no cure for a sucker."[22]

Coolidge Pie

Mrs. Coolidge used to tell the story of her first attempt to make apple pie "such as mother used to make." It was so tough that neither she nor Cal got very far with it at dinner. Later in the evening, some friends dropped in and Coolidge insisted they have some pie. Somehow they managed to eat it all up. When they were finished, Coolidge exclaimed: "Don't you think the Road Commissioner would be willing to pay my wife something for her recipe for pie crust?"[23]

Gossiper

Coolidge was having his hair cut in a small Vermont barbershop that had only one chair. The town doctor entered, sat down to wait, and said, "Cal, did you take the pills I gave you?" Coolidge said nothing for a minute or two and then answered: "Nope!" A little later the doctor asked: "Are you feeling any better?" Another long silence, then: "Yup!" His haircut finished, Coolidge started to leave, when the barber hesitatingly asked, "Aren't you forgetting something, Mr. Coolidge?" A bit sheepishly Coolidge replied, "I'm sorry; I forgot to pay you. I was so busy gossiping with the doctor it just slipped my mind."[24]

Abstinence

A Baptist preacher who dined with the Coolidges before leading a revival meeting ate almost nothing, saying that abstinence improved his preaching. After hearing him preach Coolidge told his wife: "Might as well have et."[25]

Dissenter

Once, when Coolidge was in the Massachusetts legislature, a member noted for his long-winded speeches gave a lengthy and tiresome address in support of some measure. The speech included a series of affirmations, all beginning with the words "Mr. Speaker, it is . . ." After he sat down, Coolidge rose and said, "Mr. Speaker, it is not!" Everyone laughed, and the measure was killed.[26]

Looks Up the Law

One time while Coolidge was president of the Massachusetts Senate, two Senators got into an angry debate during which one told the other to go to hell. Furious, the latter called on Coolidge to do something about it. "I've looked up the law, Senator," Coolidge told him, "and you don't have to go there."[27]

Coolidge Treats

Coolidge had just been elected Governor of Massachusetts when Bill, an old friend of the family, stopped by, saying he wanted to be the first newspaper correspondent to congratulate the Governor-elect. A relative of the Coolidges let Bill in the house, explaining that Coolidge would be down in a few minutes. Coolidge appeared and, after greetings, the hospitable relative said, "Cal, aren't you going to give Bill a drink?" At this, Coolidge fished a fistful of keys out of his pocket, deliberately selected two, and opened a closet door with one and a trunk inside the closet with the other. Raising the lid of the trunk, he lifted out the top tray, setting it on the floor behind him, extracted a bottle from the depths of the trunk, procured a small glass, pulled the cork slowly, poured a modest drink, carefully recorked the bottle, replaced it in the trunk, put the tray in place, locked the trunk, and locked the closet door. A little later, another newspaperman, Jim, arrived to congratulate the Governor-elect. Jim, Bill, and Cal chatted for a moment, until Coolidge's relative asked Cal if he wasn't forgetting Jim. Again, Coolidge went through the ceremony of procuring the bottle. Carefully he filled a glass, handed it to Jim, and, as he recorked the bottle, explained: "Bill's had his."[28]

Hometown Visit

During Coolidge's first visit to Northampton, where he had practiced law a number of years, after becoming Governor, an elderly gentleman who hadn't kept up with the news said to him on the street. "How d'ye do, Mr. Coolidge. I ain't seen ye about lately." "No," said Coolidge, "I've been out of town."[29]

Coolidge's Explanation

When Coolidge was Vice-President, his successor as Governor of Massachusetts, Channing Cox, paid him a visit. Cox asked how Coolidge had been able to see so many visitors a day when he was Governor, but always leave the office at 5:00 P.M., while Cox himself found he often left as late as 9:00 P.M. "Why the difference?" he asked. "You talk back," said Coolidge.[30]

On Sunday Golf

As Vice-President Coolidge was as uncommunicative as ever, although he was forced to attend numerous dinners At one of these he listened for some time to a discussion of the morality of playing golf on Sunday. Finally his hostess asked him his opinion, and he replied: "I had a grandmother. She was a Baptist. She didn't."[31]

Social Register

Right after he became Vice-President, Coolidge received a dinner invitation from a resident of Washington. He called in his secretary to ask him if he knew the gentleman. The secretary did not and said he could not find the name listed in the *Social Register.* "No conclusion can be drawn from that," said Coolidge. "I've been in it myself only half an hour."[32]

The Wrong Vice-President

While he was Vice-President, Coolidge and his wife lived at the Willard Hotel in Washington. One evening a fire alarm brought all the guests to the lobby. Even after the little fire was under control, they were detained by the firemen. Coolidge finally became impatient and started upstairs, but he was halted by the fire marshal. "Who are you?" the marshal asked. "I'm the Vice-President," said Coolidge. "All right, go ahead," said the marshal. But Coolidge had only gone a step or two when he was halted a second time. "What are you Vice President of?" the marshal demanded suspiciously. "I am the Vice-President of the United States," said Coolidge. "Come right down," snapped the fire chief. "I thought you were Vice-President of the hotel."[33]

Cousin

"Howdy, Cal!" "Howdy, Newt!" The man in the wagon passed on, waving his whip. "Cousin of mine," Vice-President Coolidge explained to a friend visiting Plymouth Notch. "Haven't seen him for twenty years."[34]

Laying a Cornerstone

As Vice-President, Coolidge was once asked to preside at the laying of a cornerstone for a public building. He turned the customary spadeful of earth. The workmen laid the stone. The crowd waited for the customary oratory, but none came. Finally, the master of ceremonies requested a few words from the Vice-President. Coolidge thought for a moment; then, pointing to the spadeful of earth he had thrown up, he said, "There's—a—mighty fine fishworm," and walked off to his waiting limousine.[35]

On Dining Out

At one of the many dinners Coolidge attended as Vice-President, Alice Roosevelt Longworth is said to have remarked: "I guess going to all these parties must bore you. Why do you go?" "Well," said Coolidge, "a man must eat."[36]

The Lady Loses

The best story about Coolidge's taciturnity, told by his wife, concerns the society woman who said, as she sat down next to him at a dinner party, "You must talk to me, Mr. Coolidge. I made a bet today that I could get more than two words out of you." "You lose," said Coolidge.[37]

First Paycheck

A messenger from the Treasury Department delivered President Coolidge's first paycheck in person and made something of a ceremony out of it. "Call again," Coolidge told him.[38]

Self-Confidence

Some years after he became President, Coolidge had his portrait painted by Charles Hopkinson. During the sitting, Hopkinson, desperate to bring some animation into the President's Vermont-granite features, decided to inquire into one of the great crises in Coolidge's life. "Mr. President," he said, "what was your first thought when you heard that Harding had died?" Without any change of expression, Coolidge twanged: "I thought I could swing it."[39]

Leaves It to the Convention

During the 1924 convention, Republican leaders asked Coolidge to name his candidate for Vice-President. Coolidge said he guessed the convention could do that. "It did in 1920," he added, "and it picked a durned good man."[40]

Broad-Minded

To a suggestion that a well-known captain of industry be placed in Coolidge's Cabinet, an associate of Coolidge objected: "But Mr. President, that fellow's a son of a bitch." "Well," said Coolidge, "don't you think they ought to be represented, too?"[41]

Sin

According to the most famous Coolidge story, Coolidge attended church alone one Sunday because his wife was unable to go. When he returned, she asked whether he had enjoyed the sermon. "Yes," he said. "And what was it about?" "Sin," said Coolidge. "But what did he *say?*" his wife persisted. "He was against it," said Coolidge. Mrs. Coolidge once said, however, that this was such a good story "it is almost a pity to refute it," while Coolidge himself remarked that it would be funnier if it were true.[42]

Cigar Bands

Once New Jersey's Senator Frelinghuysen was a guest at the Executive Mansion. As he sat chatting with his host, he mentioned that he had had some fine Havana cigars made especially for Coolidge in Cuba, but that, unfortunately, there had been some delay in securing the lithographed bands bearing the initials "C. C." that were to go around them. "Well, Joe," said the President, "you know I don't smoke the bands."[43]

Hospitality

Knowing that Coolidge was a good judge of cigars, engineer John Hays Hammond sent him a box of particularly fine ones and received a note of appreciation from the President. The next time he was in the White House he found Coolidge smoking a cigar which had the familiar aroma of Hammond's own brand. As Hammond sat down, Coolidge opened a drawer of his desk and held out a box of cigars. Hammond leaned over and eyed it critically; one glance convinced him that Coolidge had taken literally Vice-President Tom Marshall's witticism about the country's need for a five-cent cigar. So he smiled and said, "No thank you." Coolidge grinned, dipped into his desk again, and brought out Hammond's gift box. "Come to think of it, you sent me these," he said. "Try one." Hammond gratefully accepted.[44]

Boston

A guest at a White House reception once eased up to President Coolidge and said, "Mr. President, I'm from Boston!" Replied Coolidge: "You'll never get over it."[45]

Coolidge Becomes Irritated

A White House luncheon guest was belaboring her pet enemy, an ambassador of whom Coolidge thought highly. She went on and on: the man was crude, uncultured, ignorant, and boorish. About this time, Tige, an old black cat, sauntered into the room and began rubbing itself lazily against the table leg. The President turned to the person on his right and said in a voice quite audible to the shrewish woman on his left: "This is the third time that cat has stopped at this table."[46]

Feeding the Cat

At one of his breakfasts for politicians Coolidge carefully poured his coffee and cream into a saucer; a few of his guests politely did the same. Then, as they waited for Coolidge to take a gulp, he smiled slightly, leaned over, and put the saucer on the floor for his cat.[47]

Alice in Wonderland

In May 1928, Clarence S. Brigham, executive head of the American Antiquarian Society, lunched at the White House, bringing with him the original manuscript of *Alice in Wonderland,* which he had just purchased. Finding that *Alice* was a favorite of Coolidge's, Brigham explained that the first edition, issued in 1865, not being entirely to the author's liking, had been suppressed. "Suppressed?" exclaimed the President. "I didn't know there was anything off-color in *Alice!*"[48]

Fine Carpet

Ruth Hanna McCormick, wife of Illinois Senator Medill McCormick, anxious to secure a federal judgeship for a prominent Chicagoan of Polish descent, as part of her campaign of persuasion arranged for a group of Chicago Poles to call on the President. The delegation was ushered into the President's office and stood in stony silence while Coolidge sat there staring rather gloomily at the floor. Finally Coolidge said, "Mighty fine carpet there." His visitors all smiled and nodded expectantly. "New one—cost a lot of money," Coolidge continued. His visitors smiled even more expansively. "She wore out the old one," concluded the President, "trying to get you a judge." That ended the interview.[49]

Sleep

Coolidge slept about eleven hours a day; he went to bed at ten and got up between seven and nine o'clock. In the afternoon he always took a nap lasting from two to four hours: from one-thirty to three-thirty or four and sometimes to four-thirty or five. One afternoon a White House staff member had to awaken him from his nap. When he opened his eyes, he grinned and said: "Is the country still here?" Coolidge used to argue that it was in the national interest for him to take long afternoon naps because he couldn't be initiating anything while alseep. One evening when he went to the theater to see the Marx brothers in *Animal Crackers,* Groucho spied him in the audience and cried, "Isn't it past your bedtime, Calvin?"[50]

Same Old Cal

When Coolidge was a young man, a friend tried to borrow five dollars from him but was turned down. Many years later the friend was taking a tour of the White House and ran into President Coolidge. Again he tried to borrow five dollars and again was turned down. His eyes wide with admiration, he exclaimed, "Well, I got to say one thing for you, Cal. Success hasn't changed you one bit!"[51]

Will Rogers Meets Cal

Just before Will Rogers first met President Coolidge, one of his friends said, "I'll bet you can't make Cal laugh in two minutes." "I'll bet he laughs in 20 seconds," said Will. Then came the introduction: "Mr. President, this is Mr. Will Rogers; Mr. Rogers, President Coolidge." Will held out his hand, looked confused, then said, "Excuse me, I didn't quite get the name." And a grin spread over Coolidge's face.[52]

Send Bill to England

One day while the White House was being repaired, Coolidge found his way to the attic, where the architect and the contractor were looking at the rafters and girders. The architect pointed out the bad condition of the timbers charred from the fire the British had set during the War of 1812. He insisted they be replaced; but he wanted to know whether to do it with wood or with the more expensive steel beams. Coolidge carefully examined the charred wood, then turned to the contractor and said: "All right. Put in the steel beams and send the bill to the King of England."[53]

Senator Borah

According to a popular (but spurious) story, Coolidge was riding in his car through Rock Creek Park in Washington one day and spied Senator William Borah, the great Republican independent from Idaho, on horseback. They chatted for a moment. Then, as Borah rode away, Coolidge chuckled: "Must bother the Senator to be going in the same direction as the horse!"[54]

Hobby

"What is your hobby?" a woman asked him. "Holding office," drawled Coolidge.[55]

Portrait

One day a friend called on Coolidge. After he and the President had shaken hands, Coolidge motioned him to follow. They went into the hall, up a flight of stairs, and into a room, where the President unlocked a door, shoved it open, flipped on a light, and stepped back. The friend found himself confronted by a painting of the President which was so bad that he couldn't think of anything whatever to say. There was a moment of silence. Then Coolidge said, "That's what I think, too," flipped off the light, and led his friend back downstairs.[56]

Honorary Depositor

Jimmy Reynolds, former treasurer of the Republican National Committee, was elected vice-president of a Washington bank. He came to see President Coolidge and told him about his good fortune. "Mr. President," he said, "you know the success I had in securing funds for the Republican Party. I did not ask for any recognition or thanks at the time and I do not ask for any now. But it would do me an enormous amount of good and be a feather in my cap if you would become a depositor in my bank. Will you do it?" Coolidge puffed at his cigar; finally, after several minutes of silence, he said: "Couldn't you make me an honorary depositor?"

Coolidge did make a deposit in the bank. Some time later he was strolling past it with an old Boston friend when they suddenly heard a terrific noise from within. "What in hell is that noise?"

cried the friend. Unruffled, Coolidge drawled, "That deposit of mine drawing interest."[57]

Conversationalist

One afternoon the Coolidges were with a party of friends on the presidential yacht *Mayflower*. A moving-picture cameraman was trying to get some shots of the group for a silent newsreel. "Look pleasant," he told the President, "and for Heaven's sake, say something—anything; good morning or howdy do!" To which Coolidge remarked dryly, as he assumed his stage face, "That man gets more conversation out of me than all Congress."[58]

Careful Giver

Coolidge was not a generous giver, but he always tried to do the right thing. One day he walked up to the desk of Ira R. T. Smith, Chief of Mails at the White House, and handed him a box of cigars, saying, "Have some tobaccah." Then he walked on down to the desk of Nelson Webster, the disbursing officer, and repeated the performance. Afterward, Smith and Webster compared notes and found that Coolidge had taken the trouble to find out what price each of them paid for their cigars. Webster smoked twenty-five-centers and got twenty-five-cent cigars from Coolidge; Smith smoked ten-centers, so that's what he got. Both boxes, though, came from the large collection of gift cigars sent to the President, which were stacked up in his study.[59]

Cheese Sandwiches

Colonel Edmund W. Starling, Secret Service guard for the President, took afternoon walks with Coolidge. When they returned, Coolidge would take Starling to the butler's pantry and make two sandwiches of Vermont cheese, one for himself and one for Starling. He cut the cheese carefully and measured the sandwiches one against the other; if they weren't equal, he would shave off a little more cheese to make them balance. Then he would give one to Starling, and they would sit down and eat them. The cheese, said Starling, was as strong as a billygoat. One day Coolidge said, "I'll bet no other

President of the United States ever made cheese sandwiches for you.'
"No," said Starling. "It's a great honor." Added Coolidge gloomily:
"I have to furnish the cheese too."[60]

Fishing

Having learned from Colonel Starling to enjoy fishing, the President
became an ardent fisherman. One day he lost a fish he had been
playing and said, "Damn!" Then he turned to Starling and, with a
shy smile, said: "Guess I'm a real fisherman now. I cussed."

Coolidge always wore gloves fishing, and when he fished at his
vacation place in South Dakota he wore white kid gloves. But Mrs.
Coolidge made such fun of him that he went back to a darker shade.

When he fished he just held the rod. Bait was put on for him,
and any fish he caught were likewise taken off the hook for him.
The Secret Service men complained bitterly when it fell to their
lot to perform this function, which they did not consider a part of
their duty of protecting the President.

Once a man caught some fish from the stream in front of Coolidge's
house in South Dakota. "They are my fish," said Coolidge, and
sent a Secret Service man to get them.

One of Coolidge's favorite angling places was the River Brule.
Once a newspaper reporter asked him how many fish there were
in the river. Coolidge said the waters were estimated to contain
about 45,000 trout. "I haven't caught them all yet," he added, "but
I've intimidated them."[61]

Satisfied

A famous architect visiting the White House admired its architectural
beauty at great length. After listening to him for some time, Coolidge
said: "Suits me."[62]

Short Skirt

On the *Mayflower* once, according to Mrs. Coolidge, a young society
lady whom Coolidge liked sat down opposite him on the deck. At
that time fashion dictated that women's skirts should be short, and
hers was entirely in the mode. As she took her chair, she tried to
arrange it to cover her knees and obviously had trouble doing so.

Finally, the President, taking his cigar out of his mouth, remarked, "What *yeou* need, young lady, is a rug!"[63]

Short Speech

During Coolidge's return from an American Legion convention in Omaha, his train stopped for coal and water at a small town on the way to St. Louis and a large crowd gathered to see him. Colonel Starling went into the President's private car and found him seated on a big lounge, his elbows on a table, his hands cupped about his chin, fast asleep. Starling tapped him on the shoulder and said, "Mr. President, there are about twenty-five hundred people waiting to see you." Without a word, Coolidge got up, smoothed his hair, straightened his jacket, and followed Starling to the observation platform. He gave the people his official smile, and they applauded. Then Mrs. Coolidge appeared and got an even bigger ovation. Then the local master of ceremonies shouted: "Now, you folks keep quiet. I want absolute silence. The President is going to address us." Silence ensued, "All right," said the man, turning to the President, "Mr. President, you may speak now." Just then there was a hiss of air as the brakes were released, and the train began to roll gently out of the station. The President, still smiling, raised his hand to the crowd and said: "Goodbye."[64]

The Rake

Before Coolidge left the White House, his Vermont neighbors decided to recognize his devotion to the old family farm where he had spent his boyhood by giving him a handmade rake. The orator who presented the rake in an elaborate ceremony dwelt at length on the qualities of the hickory wood from which it was made. "Hickory," he said, "like the President, is sturdy, strong, resilient, unbroken." Then he handed the rake to Coolidge, and the audience settled back for his speech of acknowledgment. Coolidge turned the rake over, looked at it carefully, and said: "Ash."[65]

Retirement

Shortly after he left the White House, Coolidge was called on to fill out a card to accompany the payment of his annual dues to the National Press Club. He filled in his name and address and then, on the line provided for "Occupation," he wrote "Retired." After a moment's thought, he wrote on the line labeled "Remarks": "Glad of it."[66]

The Passing Cars

A newspaperman visited Coolidge in Plymouth Notch, Vermont, after he had left the White House. As they sat on the porch, watching the automobiles roll by, the newsman remarked, "It must make you proud to see all these people coming by here, merely to look at you sitting on the porch. It shows that although you are an ex-President you are not forgotten. Just look at the number of cars!" "Not as many as yesterday," replied Coolidge. "There were sixty-three then."[67]

Standing Up

A woman who heard Coolidge speak at Madison Square Garden in October 1932, rushed up to him afterward and exclaimed: "Oh, Mr. Coolidge, what a wonderful address! I stood up all through it!" "So did I," said Coolidge.[68]

Greetings

Some Amherst alumni attending a conference in Madrid decided to have a reunion of Amherst men in Spain, so they sent Coolidge, class of 1895, a cable asking him to send a message to be read at the dinner. To make sure that Coolidge knew he could say as much as he pleased they made it clear that there would be no cable charges. Sixty-five people attended the dinner, and at the climax of the evening the ex-President's name was announced, to a burst of applause. When the applause had subsided, the chairman read the message: "Greetings. Calvin Coolidge."[69]

Academic World

Soon after Arthur Stanley Pease resigned as president of Amherst College, the president of the alumni society called on Coolidge in Northampton and told him he led the list of those mentioned for the post. Coolidge shook his head. "Easier to control a Congress than a college faculty," he said.[70]

Red Dressing

At a luncheon party given by the Coolidges, the guests began discussing the question of whether the United States should recognize the Soviet Union. When the discussion got a bit heated, Mrs. Coolidge diplomatically changed the subject. Indicating two containers, she said, "One is French dressing and the other is Russian." "I'll take the one that isn't red," said the ex-President.[71]

Depression

Just before the 1932 election, actor Otis Skinner said, "Oh, Mr. Coolidge, I wish it were you that we were going to vote for in November. It would be the end of this horrible depression." "It would be the beginning of mine," replied Coolidge.[72]

THIRTY

Herbert Hoover
1929–33

Herbert Hoover (1874–1964) became President in March 1929, with a reputation for unusual intelligence, energy, efficiency, and humanitarian concern. A wealthy mining engineer who turned to public service during World War I, he headed the Commission for Relief in Belgium, 1914–19, served as director of Woodrow Wilson's Food Administration, and managed European relief at the end of the war. "He is certainly a wonder," exclaimed young Franklin D. Roosevelt, "and I wish we could make him President of the United States. There couldn't be a better one."[1] Both parties claimed him; but he decided he was a Republican and served as Secretary of Commerce for both Harding and Coolidge. Coolidge called him, a bit waspishly, the "wunduh boy," but he was more commonly known as the "Great Engineer."[2] When he entered the White House in March 1929, the stock market was booming, and the country seemed headed for increasingly higher levels of productivity as well as more affluence for many of its citizens. "The poorhouse is vanishing among us," said Hoover cheerily in 1928. "We in America today are nearer to the final triumph over poverty than ever before in the history of the land. . . . We shall soon with the help of God be in sight of the day when poverty will be banished from this nation."[3]

A few months after this millenial statement came the Great Crash. "WALL STREET LAYS AN EGG," screamed a *Variety* headline on October 30, 1929. The collapse of the stock market was followed by the Great Depression, which far exceeded in length and severity every previous economic setback that the country had experienced. To bolster the sagging morale of the American people as the depression deepened, Hoover and his Cabinet members issued a series of hopeful statements about the economic situation:

> Any lack of confidence in the economic future or the basic strength of business in the United States is foolish [November 1929].
> Let us be thankful that we are getting back on our feet again [February 1930].
> The nation will make steady progress in 1930 [January 1, 1930].
> The crisis will be over in sixty days [March 1930].
> Normal conditions should be restored in two or three months [May 1930].
> I am convinced we have now passed the worst [May 1930].
> The worst is over without a doubt [June 1930].
> Courage and resource are already swinging us back on the road to recovery [August 1930].
> We have hit the bottom and are on the upswing [September 1930].

In 1931 Edward Angly collected a long list of optimistic forecasts made by President Hoover and his associates in a book entitled *Oh Yeah?*[4] Even former President Coolidge was bothered by the situation. "The country," he announced in January 1931, "is not in good condition." And in another famous statement analyzing the country's plight, he explained: "When a great many people are unable to find work, unemployment results."[5]

Though Hoover took more action than any previous President had taken during a depression, he simply could not seem to get on top of the situation. One day, when ex-President Coolidge was visiting the White House, Hoover outlined the latest measures he had sponsored to promote recovery and said that he could not understand why his efforts were so disappointing or why his critics were growing so rapidly in numbers and vehemence. "You can't expect to see calves running in the field," said Coolidge, "the day after you put the bull to the cows." "No," said Hoover wearily, "but I would expect to see contented cows."[6] During Hoover's last year in office a fanciful story gained wide popular currency. One day, it went, Hoover was walking down the street with Andrew Mellon, his Secretary of the Treasury. He suddenly stopped and said, "Andy, I came out this morning without a cent in my pocket. Lend me a nickel, will you? I want to call up a friend." "Here's a dime," offered Mellon. "Call up both of them!"[7] Will Rogers also told a story about the man who bit into an apple and found a worm and cried: "Damn Hoover!"[8]

In 1932, Hoover took a special train to Philadelphia to throw out the first ball for the World Series. He hoped that his presence at the game would display to the public his calm confidence in the state of the Union and lift the nation's spirits. But the cameraman wanted shots of the President throwing out the ball before the game, and Hoover ended by posing for so many pictures that the game finally started without him. That evening, it suddenly occurred to a press association man that he had never actually seen the ball thrown. He went back to the President's car and, sure enough, he was right. At some point while being photographed Hoover had dropped the ball into his pocket; he never got around to making his ceremonial gesture. To reporter Richard L. Strout the incident typified Hoover's good intentions but poor performance as President.[9]

After his defeat by Franklin Roosevelt in November 1932, Hoover went to Florida to do some sailfishing. After a successful catch, he and his party boarded a special train at West Palm Beach to return to Washington. While waiting for the train to start, Hoover stepped out on the observation platform to listen to a string orchestra which was entertaining the crowd that had gathered to see him off. When the leader of the orchestra saw Hoover, he took off his hat and made a sweeping bow. Hoover, who was shy about such things and easily embarrassed, tried not to notice. He moved his right shoulder awkwardly up and down and jingled the keys in one of his pockets. Just then the train began to move and the orchestra leader beckoned to his musicians. Instantly they came to attention and started playing a well-known tune: "Happy Days Are Here Again." It had been the Roosevelt campaign theme song.[10]

Hoover settled down in California after leaving office; shortly afterward he and his wife were hosts to a debating team from an Australian university. One young Australian, unfamiliar with U.S. electoral procedures, tried to say something nice to the former President about his recent loss at the polls. "Really, Mr. Hoover," he said, "we Australians were dreadfully sorry to hear of your defeat in the last election. Tell me, sir, did you keep your seat?" At this the glum expression on Hoover's face dissolved. Breaking into hearty laughter and slapping his knee, he cried: "Yes, indeed, young man, but that's about all I kept!"[11]

★ ★ ★

No TR

Hoover was in China during the Boxer uprisings at the turn of the century and on one occasion rescued a trapped Chinese child in the line of gunfire. Years later, his political backers wanted to release to the press a dramatic account of the incident. Hoover read the story they had prepared, slowly tore the sheet into tiny fragments, and dropped them into a wastebasket. "You can't make a Teddy Roosevelt out of me," he told them.[12]

Prompt Payment

When Hoover was in charge of Belgian relief work before the United States entered World War I, he crossed the English Channel many times between London and Belgium. It took a full day to make the trip, so three meals were served on the boat. At breakfast on one of his last crossings, he asked the steward to keep a record of his expenses and collect payment for them at the end of the trip. The steward hesitated, shifted from one foot to the other, and finally blurted out: "Damn sorry, sir, but when the last boat was torpedoed the passengers got drowned. We may be sunk at any moment, so I must collect after each meal."[13]

Call the Dog

At one point during the war Hoover hurried to Berlin to protest U-boat sinkings of the Belgian Relief Commission's ships. A high German naval official assured him that it would never happen again. Hoover replied with a parable. "Your Excellency," he said, "there was a man once who was annoyed by a snarling dog. He went to see the owner and asked him to muzzle the dog. 'There is no need of that,' said the owner, 'the dog will never bite you.' 'Maybe,' said the man. 'You know the dog will not bite me. I know the dog will not bite me. But does the dog know?' " "Pardon me one moment, Herr Hoover," said the official. "I will telephone at once the dog." And he did so.[14]

Surrender

While Hoover was in Paris directing European relief after World War I, an American officer came to him and told him a curious story. Civil War was raging in Dalmatia, he said, and he and two doughboys had gotten caught in a crossfire on a mountain road above Cattaro. Upon investigating, they learned that the entrenched armies, perhaps a thousand guerrillas in all, were willing to call the battle off, but neither of the commanding generals wanted to lose face by surrending first. The American finally told them that they could both surrender to the United States with their honor intact. In drawing up the formal surrender statement, however, he began to worry about involving the United States in a foreign quarrel and wrote in "United States Food Administrator" (Hoover's title, 1917–19) instead. Followed then a surrender ceremony, during which he collected swords from the two generals; then he put the soldiers to work loading trucks. Afterward, he said, he became concerned about whether he had embarrassed Hoover by using his name, so he had come to Paris to explain things to him. With a straight face, Hoover asked what had happened to the swords. The officer told him he still had them. In that case, said Hoover, if the officer would give him one and keep the other as a souvenir of the Dalmatian peace he had arranged, the episode would be considered closed. Later Hoover wrote the officer that he was "of the stuff that had made America a great country."[15]

Hoover's English

In July 1923, Hoover wrote a few powerful paragraphs for President Harding's Independence Day address, announcing the voluntary abolition by industry of the twelve-hour day and the eighty-four-hour week. His language was so different from the rest of the speech that Harding stumbled over the passage when reading it. While the audience was applauding the announcement, Harding whispered to Hoover, who was sitting on the platform, "Damn it, Hoover, why don't you write the same English as I do?"[16]

White House Visitors

On May 28, 1932, three children came to the White House door. They had hitchhiked from Detroit to ask the President to help bring

their father home. Their father, it turned out, had been jailed for
stealing an automobile while looking for work. Hoover reacted sym-
pathetically to their plea. "I know there must be good in a man
whose children are so well behaved and who show such loyalty and
devotion to him," he told his visitors. "I will use my good office.
You may go home happy." He gave each of the children a little
gift and then told them: "Now run along and go straight home.
Dad will be waiting there for you." After they left, he summoned
one of his aides and told him, "Get that father out of jail immediately." The aide wanted permission to give the facts to the reporters,
but Hoover agreed only to the barest announcement. "Let's not argue
about it," he said. "That will be enough. That is all I will say about
it. Now we will get back to work."[17]

Hoover Laughs

As the Hoovers entered the room for a Cabinet dinner during their
second year in the White House, the naval aide announced, "The
President and Mrs. Coolidge." Even Hoover laughed at this.[18]

Celebrities

After Hoover left the White House, his name was no longer a household word. Once, according to a popular story, he vacationed in a
small Canadian resort. When he signed the hotel register the clerk
was obviously impressed. "Any relation to G-Man Hoover?" he
asked. When Hoover said no, he tried again. "How about the Hoover
who makes those vacuum cleaners?" Again the former President
said no. "Oh, well," said the clerk, "no harm done. We do get a
kick, though, out of entertaining relatives of real celebrities!"[19]

Dropping Jugs

Referring to politicians who pay lip service to American principles
while violating them in practice, Hoover once said: "All this reminds
me of the small girl who said, 'Mother, you remember the beautiful
jug you said has been handed down to us from generation to generation?' Mother replied, 'Yes, Ann, what of it?' And Ann answered
solemnly, 'This generation has dropped it.' "[20]

Stories about Presidents

In 1938, Raymond Moley, former FDR aide, accidentally met Hoover on a train traveling from California to New York; they decided to dine together. As the steward stopped by the table, he said in a confidential tone of voice, "Do you think that Mr. Hoover would like to hear the latest story about Mr. Roosevelt?" Hoover glowered at the menu. "I don't like stories about Presidents," he snapped.[21]

THIRTY-ONE

Franklin D. Roosevelt

1933–45

"Look out you don't make the mistake of liking Roosevelt," warned a New York Republican leader when a friend of his was making plans to call on Governor Franklin D. Roosevelt (1882–1945). "I've seen people taken in by it." "By what?" asked the friend. The Republican leader hesitated a moment, then burst out: "By a perfectly grand political personality, you fool!"[1]

For a long time some people thought that all Franklin Roosevelt had was a grand personality. "He is," wrote Walter Lippmann in a famous column for the *New York Herald Tribune* in January 1932, "a pleasant man who, without any important qualifications for the office, would very much like to be President." When Roosevelt read Lippmann's comments, he grinned, turned over a page, noted a headline—"Ubangi Natives Arriving Today"—and read aloud from the article: "All have wooden discs in their lips and will fill a vaudeville engagement here." Commented FDR: "I could suggest one political writer for the same circuit. His comments have about the same relation to actuality—interesting and perhaps pleasing to some, but just as distorted as the faces of those savages."[2] Roosevelt was right; Lippmann's assessment fell short of the mark. Roosevelt was more than a charmer. As Governor of New York he had shown himself to be thoughtful, energetic, compassionate, and open to experiment when it came to coping with the Great Depression. And as President he was to display remarkable gifts for leadership in a time of crisis.

Despite his conservative background as a country squire in Hyde Park, New York, Roosevelt enjoyed breaking precedents and shattering traditions. He thought that dramatic gestures on his part would raise morale and help pull the country out of the slump. Thus after receiving the Democratic nomination for President in the summer of 1932, he flew to Chicago to give the first acceptance speech ever made to a party convention. "You have nominated me and I know it," he told the delegates, "and I am here to thank you for the honor. Let it . . . be symbolic that in so doing I broke traditions." He went on to pledge himself to "a new deal for the American people."[3] Immediately after taking office in March 1933, he proclaimed a national bank holiday in order to stop runs on the banks and give the Treasury Department time to devise measures for saving the nation's banking system. He broke another precedent by having members of his Cabinet sworn in before their relatives and friends in the White House. He appointed the first woman, Frances Perkins, to hold a Cabinet office. He teased the Daughters of the American Revolution about their obsession with their roots. "Remember, remember always," he told the D.A.R., "that all of us, and you and I especially, are descended from immigrants and revolutionists."[4] On the eve of the Republican national convention in 1940, he suddenly appointed two prominent Republicans, Henry Stimson and Frank Knox, to his Cabinet. He also brushed aside the unwritten law against a third term in 1940 and went on in 1944 to run for a fourth. "If anyone says that's unorthodox," he once told Frances Perkins, "lay it onto me. They already have me tagged. But it's doing the country good."[5]

FDR's New Deal was itself precedent-breaking. In its efforts to cope with the Great Depression, the federal government under Roosevelt took measures to help the poor and jobless for the first time in American history. Not only did it provide for direct relief to the needy; it also created a variety of jobs for the unemployed. "While it isn't written in the Constitution," said Roosevelt, "nevertheless it is the inherent duty of the Federal Government to keep its citizens from starvation."[6] The New Deal sponsored major programs for putting industry and agriculture back on their feet; it also undertook responsibility on a large scale for social justice by sponsoring such measures as unemployment insurance, old-age pensions, wages and hours legislation, slum clearance, and low-income housing projects. And since all of these programs cost money, government spending (and unbalanced budgets) under the New Deal became an important factor in shaping the national economy. World War II enormously enhanced the fiscal role which the federal government had assumed under the New Deal, and government spending on a large scale has remained basic to the American system ever since.

Some Americans regarded the New Deal as too innovative. Roosevelt's critics talked ominously about "radicalism" and "socialism," and even "communism," in New Deal policies. But Roosevelt wanted to reform, not transform, the American system, with the result that the New Deal never went nearly as far as leftists, in and out of Congress, wanted it to go. Once, when the Tennessee Valley Authority was being attacked as socialistic, FDR exploded to Adolf Berle: "Why do we have to be 'socialist' or 'capitalist'? The United States is a big enough country to have several systems going at once. It has brains and tolerance enough to accommodate them. We don't have to force everything into some doctrinaire model."[7] When Upton Sinclair, author of a grandiose scheme called End Poverty in California (EPIC), was running for governor of California in 1934, some of Roosevelt's associates were afraid that the Sinclairites would win. "Well, they might be elected in California," said Roosevelt calmly. "Perhaps they'll get E.P.I.C. in California. What difference, I ask you, would that make in Duchess county, New York, or Lincoln county, Maine? If it has fatal consequences in one place, it has little effect upon the rest of the country. If a new, apparently fanatical program works well, it will be copied. If it doesn't, you won't hear of it again."[8] Roosevelt's Secretary of Labor, Frances Perkins, was undoubtedly right: Roosevelt "took the status quo in our economic system as much for granted as his family. They were a part of his life, and so was our system; he was content with it. He felt that it ought to be humane, fair, and honest, and that adjustments ought to be made so that the people would not suffer from poverty and neglect, and so that all would share."[9] A young reporter once tried to pin FDR down. "Mr. President," he asked, "are you a Communist?" "No," said Roosevelt. "Are you a capitalist?" "No." "Are you a socialist?" "No." Then the young man asked him what his philosophy was. "Philosophy?" The President seemed puzzled. "Philosophy? I am a Christian and a Democrat—that's all."[10]

Roosevelt's approach to problems tended to be personal rather than theoretical. He took to the radio for periodic "Fireside Chats" with the American people, in which he liked to discuss basic policies in terms of concrete people and dramatic events. British economist John Maynard Keynes emerged from a conference with Roosevelt keenly disappointed at the President's lack of interest in economic theory. "Men and women are becoming mere units in statistics," Roosevelt once lamented. "This is not human progress."[11] To an economist who had been talking too abstractly for his taste he exploded: "People aren't cattle, you know!"[12]

One of Roosevelt's first orders after becoming President was that, if people in trouble telephoned the White House for help, someone on his staff was to talk to them and figure out some way of providing assistance. After Roosevelt's death, his wife Eleanor received many letters from people telling her how in the worst days of the Great Depression they had called the President and received immediate help. When civil works projects for putting the unemployed to work were being set up, someone brought to Roosevelt's attention the plight of artists who were out of work and suggested including them in the program. "Why not?" was Roosevelt's response. "They are human beings. They have to live. I guess the only thing they can do is paint and surely there must be some public place where paintings are wanted." Years later, painter George Biddle had this to say: "You know, it is strange. Roosevelt has almost no taste or judgment about painting, and I don't think he gets much enjoyment out of it; yet he has done more for painters in this country than anybody else ever did—not only by feeding them when they were down and out; but by establishing the idea that paintings are a good thing to have around, and that artists are important."[13] Once, when Roosevelt was driving in New Bedford, Massachusetts, a young woman suddenly broke through his Secret Service guard and handed him a note. She was a textile worker who had been receiving $11 a week; but recently she had suffered a 50 percent wage cut. "You are the only man that can do anything about it," her note said. "Please send somebody from Washington up here to restore our minimum wages because we cannot live on $4 or $5 or $6 a week."[14] On the night he died in April 1945, a young soldier who was in a group gathered around the White House said to Frances Perkins: "I felt as if I knew him. . . . I felt as if he knew me—and I felt as if he liked me."[15]

Roosevelt carried his personal approach to problems into international affairs after the United States entered World War II. He was the first President to travel widely around the world to attend interna-

tional conferences, and he enjoyed immensely the face-to-face encounters with notables in other lands. Before he flew to Teheran
in 1943 to confer with Winston Churchill and Joseph Stalin, he
was enormously curious about the Soviet dictator and told a friend
that he thought he could handle "the old buzzard." But when he
first met Stalin, the latter was stiff, solemn, cold, and uncommunicative. Roosevelt did everything he could to cut through Stalin's icy
reserve, but for three days he made no headway whatsover. Finally,
on the fourth day, he decided on a new tactic. On his way to the
conference room that morning, he told Frances Perkins afterward,
he caught up with Churchill and had just a moment to say to him,
"Winston, I hope you won't be sore at me for what I am going to
do." Churchill shifted his cigar and grunted. When they got into
the conference room, Roosevelt put his plan into effect. "I talked
privately with Stalin," he said afterward. "I didn't say anything that
I hadn't said before, but it appeared quite chummy and confidential,
enough so that the other Russians joined us to listen. Still no smile.
Then I said, lifting my hand up to cover a whisper (which of course
had to be interpreted), 'Winston is cranky this morning, he got up
on the wrong side of the bed.' A vague smile passed over Stalin's
eyes, and I decided I was on the right track. As soon as I sat down
at the conference table, I began to tease Churchill about his British-
ness, about John Bull, about his cigars, about his habits. It began
to register with Stalin. Winston got red and scowled, and the more
he did so, the more Stalin smiled. Finally Stalin broke out into a
deep, hearty guffaw, and for the first time in three days I saw light.
I kept it up until Stalin was laughing with me, and it was then
that I called him 'Uncle Joe.' He would have thought me fresh
the day before, but that day he laughed and came over and shook
my hand."[16]

Like other Presidents who exerted forceful leadership at critical
junctures in American history, Roosevelt was the recipient of both
passionate adoration and blind hatred. Roosevelt jokes—and jokes
about his wife, Eleanor, who was always on the go—abounded. Some
of them Roosevelt enjoyed; others he regarded as beneath contempt.
His favorite cartoon showed a little girl running to tell her mother
standing in front of a fashionable home: "Look, mama, Wilfred wrote
a bad word!" The word on the sidewalk was "Roosevelt."[17] And
his favorite story was about the commuter from Westchester County,
a Republican stronghold, who always walked into his station, handed

the newspaper boy a quarter, picked up the *New York Herald Tribune,* and then handed it back as he rushed out to catch his train. Finally the newsboy, unable to contain his curiosity any longer, asked his customer why he only glanced at the front page. "I'm interested in the obituary notices," the man told him. "But they're way over on page twenty-four, and you never look at them," said the boy. "Boy," said the man, "the son of a bitch I'm interested in will be on page one!"[18]

★ ★ ★

Cleveland's Wish

When Roosevelt was a little boy, his father took him to Washington, where he shook hands with President Cleveland. "I'm making a strange wish for you, little man," said Cleveland, placing his hand on the boy's head, "a wish I suppose no one else would make. I wish for you that you may never be President of the United States."[19]

The Great Chase

One afternoon when he was a student at Harvard, Roosevelt left a late class, rushed back to his quarters for his suitcase, and boarded a streetcar for South Station, where he intended to take the train to New York. En route to the station, the streetcar developed trouble, and the motorman stopped to investigate. Roosevelt grabbed his bag, abandoned the car, and started out on foot. His watch said he had four minutes to catch his train. He started to run. Just then he rammed into a little Italian boy coming out of an alley; they both went down, and the boy began bawling. The boy's mother stuck her head out of the window above and started screaming in Italian. Roosevelt tried to quiet the boy and explain to the woman what had happened, but utterly without success.

What to do? In desperation, he pulled a dollar bill out of his pocket and waved it toward the boy. It would, he thought, "create a diversion." Instead, it was "like a red flag to a bull." The boy grabbed it, crumpled it up, and flung it in the gutter, yelling, "You great big ——— ——— ———!" By this time windows were going up and faces appearing everywhere looking into the street. Roosevelt bent over to pick up the dollar. Everyone started shouting at him; it looked as though he was taking the money away from the little boy. Roosevelt then picked up his suitcase and started walking away. Two or three men came out on the street and began following him. He began running. They began chasing him. A police whistle shrilled. One person after another joined the chase until Roosevelt had a mob of people in pursuit.

Roosevelt finally reached South Station. Running as he had never run before, he dashed into the station just as the gate for his train was being shut. But he got through another gate and headed down the tracks for the New York train. "There he is!" screamed one of his pursuers, running into the station. "Stop him! Stop him!" When Roosevelt reached his train it was already moving out of the station. But with a last frantic dash, he tossed his suitcase onto the rear platform, caught at the handrail, and, with the help of a brakeman, dragged himself onto the car. He collapsed in the last seat and sat there gasping for a few minutes. For a while he was afraid that police would take him off at the first stop; but nothing happened, so he completed his journey without any further mishaps.

Afterward Roosevelt reflected on his experience. "I had bumped into a human situation," he told a friend many years later, "and I had failed to play my part in it. I remember I said to myself: 'The whole trouble was that I didn't solve the problem. I tried to dodge it by creating a diversion. That doesn't work. I'll never try that again!' "[20]

Adams's Forecast

The Roosevelts, who moved to Washington in 1913, visited the aging historian Henry Adams from time to time. One day, when Roosevelt was discussing some of his problems in the Navy Department, Adams suddenly stopped him and exclaimed: "Young man, I have lived in this house many years and seen the occupants of the White House across the square come and go, and nothing you minor officials or the occupant of that house can do will affect the history of the world for long!"[21]

Wartime Austerity

During World War I, the Roosevelts tried hard to comply with Food Administrator Herbert Hoover's plan to conserve food. Mrs. Roosevelt's food-saving program was eventually singled out by the

Food Administration as "a model for other large households." But an interview she gave a *New York Times* reporter produced hilarity all over Washington. "Mrs. Roosevelt," reported the *Times,* "does the shopping, the cooks see that there is no food wasted, the laundress is sparing in her use of soap, each servant has a watchful eye for evidence of shortcoming on the part of others; and all are encouraged to make helpful suggestions in the use of 'left overs.' " The *Times* also quoted Mrs. Roosevelt: "Making ten servants help me do my saving has not only been possible but highly profitable."

When FDR read the *Times* story, he wrote his wife, who was in Campobello at the time, "All I can say is that your latest newspaper campaign is a corker and I am proud to be the husband of the Originator, Discoverer, and Inventor of the New Household Economy for Millionaires. Please have a photo taken showing the family, the ten co-operating servants, [and] the scraps saved from the table. . . . I will have it published in the Sunday Times." Tremendously upset, Mrs. Roosevelt wrote back: "I do think it was horrid . . . to use my name in that way and I feel dreadfully about it because so much is not true and yet some of it I did say. I will never be caught again that's sure and I'd like to crawl away for shame."[22]

A Little Bomb

Toward the end of May 1919, the Roosevelts were returning home from a dinner party when a bomb exploded outside the home of Attorney General A. Mitchell Palmer with an impact that damaged the Roosevelt house across the street. The Roosevelts rushed home to see if their son James was all right. They found him standing half asleep by the window, confused by the uproar. Roosevelt hugged him so tightly that he remembered it for years; but Mrs. Roosevelt said calmly, "Whatever are you doing out of bed at this hour, James? Get yourself to bed." When the boy asked what had happened, she said, "Turn right over and go to sleep. It's just a little bomb!" For years after that, in moments of excitement in the Roosevelt household, someone was likely to quote her: "It's just a little bomb."[23]

Illness

In the summer of 1921, FDR was stricken with polio. Though he worked hard for years to regain the use of his legs, he never walked

again without the aid of braces and two canes. Being carried around
or pushed in a wheelchair became a normal part of his life; but he
never complained about his handicap and rarely mentioned it to
his friends and associates. When asked whether things worried him,
however, he did say at times, "If you had spent two years in bed
trying to wiggle your big toe, after that anything else would seem
easy!"

In 1928, when FDR was running for Governor of New York,
Frances Perkins was impressed by the aplomb with which he accepted
the fact that he had to be carried over a fire escape into a hall in
New York City's Yorkville district to deliver a speech. FDR, she
observed, "had accepted the ultimate humility which comes from
being helped physically. He had accepted it smiling. He came up
over that perilous, uncomfortable, and humiliating 'entrance,' and
his manner was pleasant, courteous, enthusiastic. He got up on his
own braces, adjusted them, straightened himself, smoothed his hair,
linked his arm with his son Jim's, and walked out on the platform
as if this were nothing unusual."[24]

Casket

In the summer of 1929 Mrs. Roosevelt, visiting Montreal with her
two youngest boys, received a curious telegram from her husband:
"Hope you had a good trip. What shall I do with your casket?"
Mrs. Roosevelt puzzled over this for some time, until finally it dawned
on her that she had forgotten one piece of luggage: a lunch basket.
The typographical error was a family joke for many years, quoted
whenever members of the family were planning trips.[25]

Alcoholic Plants

While he was Governor of New York, FDR enjoyed mixing drinks
for the daily cocktail hour and liked to press a second, and even a
third, drink on any guest who was at all willing. His usual remark,
on noticing an empty glass, was, "How about another little sippy?"
At one party he insisted on refilling State Supreme Court Justice
Samuel Rosenman's glass with a second drink. Rosenman was not
a drinker; he had found it difficult to finish the first cocktail. So
instead of downing the second, he waited until he thought no one
was looking and then poured it into one of the flowerpots in a corner
of the room.

A few evenings later FDR turned to Rosenman during the cocktail hour and said: "You know, Sam, a peculiar thing has been happening to the plants in the Executive Mansion. Some time ago, the leaves of some of them began to change their color. Whitehead [the steward] got worried about them and asked one of the experts from the Department of Agriculture to come over and take a look at them. The expert said he had never seen such a strange condition before, and would like to take the plants over to his laboratory for analysis of the soil. The report has just come back, and what do you think they found? They found that the soil was filled with a large percentage of alcohol. Whitehead is thoroughly mystified as to where we ever got that kind of soil." As everyone laughed, Rosenman owned up. "Well, Governor," he said, "if you don't want to lose all your plants, you'd better pass me up on seconds." After that FDR always did.[26]

Pleasing Eleanor

When Roosevelt was getting his Cabinet together, labor leaders suggested several men for the post; but he appointed Frances Perkins instead. She was the first woman to serve in a President's Cabinet. According to a story circulating in Washington, Mrs. Roosevelt commiserated with her husband over the bad hour he must have had with the labor leaders when he told them he had already made up his mind to appoint Perkins. "Oh, that's all right," FDR was said to have replied, "I'd rather have trouble with them for an hour than trouble with you for the rest of my life!"[27]

The President and the Justice

A day or so after his inauguration in March 1933, Roosevelt learned that former Supreme Court Justice Oliver Wendell Holmes, Jr. was celebrating his ninety-second birthday and insisted on paying his respects. "We face grave times," he told the Justice. "What is your advice?" "Form your ranks," said Holmes, "and fight!" Of FDR, Holmes said later: "A second-class intellect—but a first-class temperament!"[28]

A Trade

When it came to appointments, FDR, like all Presidents, sometimes had to make deals to get what he wanted. When Senator "Cotton

Ed" Smith of South Carolina was blocking Rexford Tugwell's confirmation as Undersecretary of Agriculture, Roosevelt won Smith over by naming one of his men a U.S. marshal. It turned out that the man had once been charged with homicide; so the next time he saw Tugwell, Roosevelt announced merrily, "Today I got you in trade for a murderer!"[29]

A Man

Once Mrs. Roosevelt began a speech to a group of women with the words, "I was talking with a man the other day, and he said. . . ." After she explained the man's views, one of the women, impressed by the analysis, asked, "Who was that man you talked to?" "Franklin," said Mrs. Roosevelt.[30]

Proper Address

Though FDR knew and loved the British, he had no patience with the arrogance that British officialdom sometimes displayed. One day Secretary of the Treasury Henry Morgenthau brought him a letter from the British Chancellor of the Exchequer addressed simply to "Mr. Henry Morgenthau," with no official title. Concerned with the content of the dispatch, Morgenthau had overlooked the omission; but FDR noticed it at once. When Morgenthau showed him the answer he had prepared, he said, "The substance of it is all right, Henry, but you have made a mistake." Somewhat flustered, Morgenthau asked, "What have I done?" Said Roosevelt: "It should be addressed to Mr. ———, with no title, just the way your letter was addressed." Needless to say, the next message from the Chancellor of the Exchequer was properly addressed to the Secretary of the Treasury.[31]

Dreadful Person

One day Senator Huey P. Long, the Louisiana demagogue, lunched with the Roosevelts at Hyde Park; the President placed Long on his right so that they could discuss some legislation. Roosevelt's mother (who, according to Eleanor Roosevelt, could whisper louder than anyone Eleanor ever knew when she wanted to be heard) was on the opposite end of the table. Suddenly, for a moment or two, there was a lull in the conversation. At that instant Roosevelt's mother placed her hand to her mouth and in her piercing whisper said to the man next to her: "Who is that AWFUL man sitting next to my son?"[32]

Ickes and Hopkins

During the Great Depression, FDR's relief program was handled by two agencies: the Works Progress Administration (WPA) and the Public Works Administration (PWA). WPA, headed by Harry Hopkins, concentrated on small projects which could provide quick employment for the jobless; PWA, under Secretary of the Interior Harold Ickes, handled long-term public works. But from the beginning, Hopkins and Ickes clashed over the division of duties. Hopkins thought Ickes moved too slowly, while Ickes thought Hopkins was promoting WPA at the expense of PWA, was getting more than his fair share of the available funds, and was encroaching on Ickes's domain. At one point Ickes told FDR that Hopkins's activities were putting PWA out of business, and FDR told him not to be childish. "I responded hotly," Ickes wrote in his diary the next day. "I never thought I would talk to a President of the United States the way I talked to President Roosevelt last night."

At a Cabinet meeting in May 1936, FDR cautioned Ickes against running down Hopkins's WPA when he appeared before the Senate Appropriations Committee to discuss the work of PWA. "It was clear as day that the President was spanking me hard before the full Cabinet . . . ," lamented Ickes afterward. "All the other members appeared to be embarrassed, but I could see Henry Morgenthau stealing a covert glance at me from time to time. Doubtless he enjoyed the spanking very much." After the meeting, Ickes tried to see FDR privately, but Secretary of Labor Frances Perkins got in ahead of him and took up all of the President's remaining time. Ickes went back to his office in a fury, sat down, wrote a letter of resignation, and sent it over to the White House. The next day, when he saw FDR at lunch, the President looked at him reproachfully and handed him a handwritten memorandum: "Dear Harold— 1. P.W.A. is not 'repudiated.' 2. P.W.A. is not 'ended.' 3. I did not 'make it impossible for you to go before the committee.' 4. I have not indicated lack of confidence. 5. I have *full* confidence in you. 6. You and I have the same big objectives. 7. You are needed, to carry on a big common task. 8. Resignation *not* accepted! Your affectionate friend, Franklin D. Roosevelt." Completely mollified, Ickes reflected: "What could a man do with a President like that! Of course I stayed."[33]

Pershing

Roosevelt once took a call in the White House from a person who identified himself as Pershing. Knowing that John J. Pershing, the World War I general, had recently died, Roosevelt replied impishly, "There's no one in, but this is Jesus Christ and I'll leave word you called." It turned out to be Warren Pershing, the general's son.[34]

Taking No Chances

Roosevelt enjoyed driving around the Hyde Park area with old friends. One day he took speechwriter Sam Rosenman and Postmaster General Jim Farley to show off a new road he had had built in the backwoods. The road was not as good as he had expected, and, as the car neared the bottom of a hill, he accidentally hit the accelerator instead of the brake. The car careened around a curve at a terrific speed before he brought it to a screeching halt. Turning around, he found Farley almost in a faint and Rosenman crossing himself. Laughing, Roosevelt asked his Jewish friend what in the Lord's name he was doing. "Driving with you," said Rosenman, "I'm taking no chances!" Roosevelt roared with laughter; it became one of his favorite stories.[35]

Fanny Hurst

The novelist Fanny Hurst, who had been on a reducing cure just before being invited to the White House, arranged with Marvin McIntyre, one of Roosevelt's secretaries, to be slipped into the President's office so she might astound him with the change in her appearance. Roosevelt looked up curiously as she suddenly appeared, motioned to her to make a slow turn around in front of him, and then commented: "The Hurst may have changed, but it's the same old fanny."[36]

Roosevelt and Mencken

At a meeting of the Gridiron Club in Washington on December 8, 1934, both Roosevelt and H. L. Mencken delivered addresses to the assembled newspapermen. Mencken came first; he gave a brief but thoroughly anti–New Deal speech. When Roosevelt's turn came, he referred with a grin to "my old friend Henry Mencken," then launched into a diatribe against the American press that stunned his audience. He accused newsmen of "stupidity" and "arrogance"; he also said that most editors and reporters were so ignorant that they couldn't pass college entrance examinations. As his attack continued, Mencken's face got redder and redder and the chill among the journalists colder and colder. Gradually it dawned on them that Roosevelt was simply quoting from Mencken's essay "Journalism in America"; they began to eye the red-faced Baltimorean with amusement. When the President finished and was wheeled out of the banquet hall, he stopped with a smile to shake Mencken's hand.[37]

Flat Denial

Campaigning for re-election in 1936, Roosevelt had to prepare a speech to deliver in Pittsburgh. Four years earlier he had spoken there advocating drastic government economy. Now he wanted to defend government spending. He asked his adviser Sam Rosenman to figure out some way of making this about-face without appearing too inconsistent. Rosenman thought it over for a few days and finally told him: "I think, Mr. President, that I have found a way out." "What is it, Sam?" asked Roosevelt eagerly. "Deny that you made a speech in Pittsburgh in 1932."[38]

Fitness Test

When Roosevelt was thinking of giving Joseph P. Kennedy a position in his administration, the latter said he would like to be ambassador to England; he was intrigued, he said, by the idea of being the first Irishman to hold that post. Roosevelt was so amused at the idea that he almost fell out of his wheelchair. "Joe," he said, "would you mind stepping back a bit, by the fireplace perhaps, so I can get a good look at you?" Puzzled, Kennedy did so. Then Roosevelt said, "Joe, would you mind taking your pants down?" Astonished, Kennedy undid his suspenders and dropped his trousers. "Someone who saw you in a bathing suit once told me something I now know to be true," said Roosevelt. "Joe, just look at your legs. You are just about the most bowlegged man I have ever seen. Don't you know that the ambassador to the Court of St. James has to go through an induction ceremony in which he wears knee britches and silk stockings? Can you imagine how you'll look? When photos of our new ambassador appear all over the world we'll be a laughing stock. You're just not right for the job, Joe." "Mr. President," said Kennedy, "if I can get the permission of his majesty's government to wear a cutaway coat and striped pants to the ceremony, would you agree to the appointment?" "Well, Joe," said Roosevelt, "you know how the British are about tradition. There's no way you are going to get permission, and I must name a new ambassador soon." "Will you give me two weeks?" begged Kennedy. Roosevelt finally agreed to that. Kennedy pulled up his pants and left. Within two weeks he returned with the permission he sought from the British government, and Roosevelt made the appointment.[39]

The Hyde Park Cataclysm

A visit by the King and Queen of England to Hyde Park in the summer of 1939 was punctuated by a series of accidents. During dinner, a rickety table behind a screen suddenly collapsed under the weight of dishes with a crash that momentarily drowned out all conversation. "Oh," cried FDR, "this is just an old family custom. Think nothing of it." Dinner over, the guests repaired to the library, and the butler approached carrying a huge serving tray laden with drinks. As he started down the steps leading into the room, he missed his footing. The tray hurtled into space and the butler bounced after it. When he had cleaned up the mess on the floor and sneaked guiltily out of the room, FDR roared with laughter, turned to the King, and said: "Well, there's number two! What next? These things usually come in threes!"

The following day, FDR invited his guests over to Val-Kill Cottage for tea and a dip in the pool. After his own swim, he sat down for a while on the edge of the pool, then decided to move to the lawn. Instead of asking the Secret Service men to carry him, he thought he would strike out on his own. He began propelling himself backward by planting his palms downward and raising his own weight toward where he wanted to go. After about five self-starting elevations, he landed *kerplunk* in the middle of a huge tray of assorted delicacies, cold tea, cracked ice, and broken glass. "Say," he cried, "why didn't somebody yell?" Then, grinning broadly, he turned to the King and said: "Didn't I tell you there would be a third? Well, now I can relax; the spell is broken." FDR enjoyed telling about the "Hyde Park Cataclysm," as he called it. "Really," he would say, "it's as funny as a crutch."[40]

Raising Taxes Again

President Roosevelt was frequently a guest aboard Vincent Astor's yacht, the *Nourmahal.* Once he was invited to take a cruise on it in wintertime. "Well, I hope you aren't putting that big thing in commission just for me," Roosevelt protested. "The *Nourmahal* is in commission all year round, Mr. President," replied Astor. "Well, in that case," said Roosevelt, "I guess we'll have to raise taxes on the rich again."[41]

Never Had It So Good

During the 1940 presidential campaign, Roosevelt met a friend and asked him how he intended to vote. "Republican," said the man. "How come?" asked Roosevelt. "Is the third term bothering you?" "No," answered the man, "that's not it at all. It's just that I voted Republican the first time you ran . . . and I voted Republican the second time you ran . . . and I am going to vote Republican again, because I seem to have never had it so good!"[42]

Monotonous

At a White House dinner just before FDR's third inauguration, Chief Justice Charles Evans Hughes and Roosevelt discussed arrangements for the administration of the oath at the Capitol. "Mr. President," said Hughes, "after I have read the oath and you have repeated it, how would it do for me to lean forward and whisper: 'Don't you think this is getting just a little monotonous for both of us?'"[43]

Sweet and Gentle

In 1943, the Roosevelts entertained Madame Chiang Kai-shek for a few days at the White House. Mrs. Roosevelt's first impression was that China's First Lady was a "sweet and gentle character." At the time, labor leader John L. Lewis was threatening a coal strike, and FDR asked her how China would deal with such a man. Mme Chiang did not say a word; instead, she lifted her hand and slid it across her throat. Afterward Roosevelt said to his wife: "Well, how about your sweet and gentle character?"

On another occasion Mme Chiang told the President not to get up when she left the room. "My dear child," he said, "I couldn't stand up if I had to."[44]

In Prison

During World War II Mrs. Roosevelt went to visit a Baltimore prison with Maury Maverick of Texas, who was in charge of prison industries and wanted her to see the salvage work being done there. In order to fit the trip into her schedule, Mrs. Roosevelt had to leave the White House very early that morning without informing her husband. On his way to the office that day, Roosevelt called to his wife's secretary and asked where Eleanor was. "She is in prison, Mr. President," said the secretary. "I'm not surprised," said Roosevelt, "but what for?"[45]

Tease

FDR was a great tease. Once, during World war II, he decided to have a little fun with Francis Biddle, his Attorney General and a great civil libertarian. Just before Biddle arrived for a conference, FDR told some of his aides: "You know, Francis is terribly worried about civil liberties—especially now. He has been on my neck asking me to say that the war will not curtail them too much. Now don't laugh and give me away, but I'm going to hand him a little line." When Biddle entered the room, FDR turned to him with a solemn look on his face and said sternly: "Francis, I'm glad you came. All of us have just been discussing here the question of civil liberties in the war, and I have finally come to a decision to issue a proclamation—which I am going to ask you to draft—abrogating so far as possible all freedom of discussion and information during the war.

It's a tough thing to do, but I'm convinced that it's absolutely necessary and I want to announce it in this speech we are working on now." Biddle looked thunderstruck for a moment. Then he launched into an impassioned argument against Roosevelt's proposal. After he had gone on for about five minutes, FDR and everyone else in the room suddenly burst out laughing. At this point Biddle, to his immense relief, realized that the President was pulling his leg.[46]

Nothing To Conceal

Winston Churchill had the habit of leaving his work at any hour, climbing into a hot tub, and afterward walking around the room in the buff. Once, during a stay at the White House, he was circling the room without his clothes on when there was a knock at the door. "Come in, come in," he cried. FDR appeared; seeing Churchill undressed, started to back out. "Come in, Mr. President!" boomed Churchill, throwing out his arms. "The Prime Minister of Great Britain has nothing to conceal from the President of the United States!" Harry Hopkins, FDR's top adviser during World War II, was fond of recounting this incident. Churchill himself vigorously denied its authenticity; but Grace Tully, FDR's private secretary, insisted that the President had told her about the encounter and added: "You know, Grace, I just happened to think of it now. He's pink and white all over."[47]

Civil War Expert

On the last evening of the Quebec Conference in 1944, FDR gave a farewell dinner for Churchill and top American and British staff members. During it he began telling a Civil War story. As he spoke Churchill's secretary entered and handed his chief a message which the Prime Minister, glasses perched on the end of his nose, began to read. While Churchill was engrossed in the dispatch, FDR made some reference to the battle of Antietam in 1863. "It was 1862," barked Churchill without looking up. He was a Civil War buff, and this was not the only time that he corrected the President on some detail of that conflict.[48]

Good Speeches

Whenever Churchill was a guest at the White House, FDR complained that the Prime Minister kept him up too late at night. But he enjoyed the lively conversations all the same. At Yalta, Roosevelt grumbled that one lengthy session was "Winston's fault because he had made too many speeches." "Yes, he did," said James F. Byrnes, "but they were good speeches." Roosevelt chuckled and acknowledged: "Winston doesn't make any other kind."[49]

Fourth-Term Imperative

Mrs. Nesbitt, official housekeeper for the White House, believed in "plain foods, plainly prepared," and Mrs. Roosevelt went along with the idea. But FDR quickly tired of the White House fare. "I'm getting to the point where my stomach positively rebels," he complained, "and this does not help my relations with foreign powers. I bit two of them today." Though he repeatedly made suggestions for more exciting menus, none of them was ever adopted. One day, in the late summer of 1944, chatting with his daughter Anna and his secretary Grace Tully, he suddenly exclaimed: "You know, I really want to be elected to a fourth term." The two women waited for a momentous pronouncement. Then: "I want to be elected to a fourth term, so I can fire Mrs. Nesbitt!" FDR was re-elected; but Mrs. Nesbitt stayed on.[50]

Quandary

At a Cabinet meeting one day Roosevelt gleefully told the story about an American marine who, ordered home from Guadalcanal, was disconsolate because he hadn't killed even one of the enemy. He stated his case to his superior officer, who said: "Go up on that hill over there and shout: 'To hell with Emperor Hirohito!' That will bring the Japs out of hiding." The marine did as he was ordered. Immediately a Japanese soldier came out of the jungle, shouting, "To hell with Roosevelt!" "And of course," said the marine, "I could not kill a Republican."[51]

Atom Bomb

In January 1945, Roosevelt arranged to bring his son James back from service in the South Pacific so he could be present at the fourth inauguration. At one point James told his father that, although the Americans were winning the war in the Pacific, they still had a lot of fighting to face and that since the invasion of Japan, in particular, was bound to be bloody, he could not be sure he would ever return to see his father again. "James," said Roosevelt softly, "there will be no invasion of Japan. We will have something that will end our war with Japan before any invasion takes place." James asked what it was, but his father said, "I am sorry; even though you are my son, I cannot tell you. Only those who need to know, know about it. But it is there, it is something that we can use and will use if we have to, something we certainly will use before you or any of our sons die in an invasion of Japan." He then smiled and said, "So you come back to me, son."[52]

Harry S. Truman
1945–53

On April 12, 1945, Vice-President Harry S. Truman (1884–1972) dropped by Speaker Sam Rayburn's office for a late afternoon drink. As Rayburn mixed the drinks he said that Steve Early, the White House press secretary, had left a message asking the Vice-President to call at once. When Truman got him on the phone, Early said, "Please come right over as quickly and quietly as you can." Truman left at once for the White House, thinking that President Roosevelt "wanted me to do some special piece of liaison work with the Congress"; when he arrived he was ushered into Mrs. Roosevelt's sitting room. "Harry," said Mrs. Roosevelt, putting her arm on Truman's shoulder, "the President is dead." Stunned, Truman was silent for a moment. Then he asked, "Is there anything I can do for you?" Shaking her head, Mrs. Roosevelt said, "Is there anything *we* can do for *you?* For you are the one in trouble now."[1] The following day, after he had taken his oath of office, Truman told reporters: "Boys, if you ever pray, pray for me now. I don't know whether you fellows ever had a load of hay fall on you, but when they told me yesterday what had happened, I felt like the moon, the stars and all the planets had fallen on me." "Good luck, Mr. President," cried one reporter. "I wish you hadn't called me that," sighed Truman.[2]

Truman became President twenty-three years after he entered Missouri politics on the local level with the backing of Kansas City boss Tom Pendergast. In 1934 he was elected to the Senate with the help of the corrupt Pendergast machine. No one questioned Truman's honesty and integrity; Pendergast himself called him "the contrariest cuss in Missouri." But critics questioned his connection with a graft-ridden political machine. "When you're in politics, you've got to be elected," Truman once said defensively. "You can't be unless the people who control the votes are for you. But when you have a good reputation and are a good vote getter, the people who control the votes are more likely to be for you." In the Senate Truman was a warm supporter of FDR's New Deal legislation, and when the United States entered World War II he headed a Senate committee investigating war contracts that saved the nation's taxpayers billions of dollars. In the spring of 1944 Washington newspapermen rated Truman as second only to FDR in his contribution to the war effort.[3]

Truman loved the Senate. He was reluctant to leave it to run for Vice-President. At the Democratic convention in July 1944, when Democratic National Committee Chairman Robert E. Hannegan told him FDR wanted him as his running mate, Truman exclaimed: "Tell him to go to hell." Hannegan argued with him. "Bob, look here," said Truman. "I don't want to be Vice-President. I bet I can go down the street and stop the first ten men I see and that they can't tell me the names of two of the last ten Vice-Presidents of the United States." A little later several other Democratic leaders joined Hannegan in putting pressure on Truman. "The President wants you to be Vice-President," said one of them. "I don't believe you," said Truman. About this time the phone rang and Hannegan answered it. FDR was on the line. "No," Hannegan told him, "he hasn't agreed yet." Then FDR said in a tone of voice loud enough for Truman to hear: "Well, tell him if he wants to break up the Democratic Party in the middle of the war, that's his responsibility." Turning to Truman Hannegan said: "Now what do you say?" "My God!" exclaimed Truman, and caved in at once. After the election he occasionally sat in on Cabinet meetings and chatted with the President a few times. But until the day of FDR's death it seems never to have occurred to him that he might some day be President himself.[4]

Like most Presidents, Truman enjoyed a brief honeymoon with Congress, the press, and the public after taking office. He impressed people as being plain, simple, unpretentious, and down-to-earth, and they had no great expectations for his Presidency. After Roosevelt, indeed, some people found it difficult to think of him as a President at all. Shortly after assuming his presidential duties, Truman telephoned Jesse Jones, a former Secretary of Commerce who was a friend of his, and said: "Hello, Jesse, the President has sent John Snyder's name to the Senate for confirmation as Federal Loan Administrator." "Did the President make that appointment before he died?" Jones wanted to know. "No—," said Truman, with emphasis, *"he* made it just now."[5] Events moved swiftly during Truman's early months in the White House as the war with Germany and Japan came to an end and the cold war with Russia commenced. The vexations and frustrations stemming from the radically new world conditions generated by World War II produced surprise, disappointment, and increasing discontent among the American people, so that by Truman's second year the honeymoon was definitely over. In the fall of 1946 the Republicans captured both houses of Congress, and many Democrats began to regard the President as a liability.

Truman's off-the-cuff remarks and the letters he dashed off in the heat of the moment added to the general turmoil surrounding his administration. As an old army artilleryman, proud of his World War I service, Truman couldn't resist saying of the U.S. Marines: "They have a propaganda machine that is almost equal to Stalin's." After a tussle with labor leader John L. Lewis he said he wouldn't appoint him "dogcatcher." When a Louisiana Congressman who had been a vituperative critic of Truman's policies wrote a pious letter suggesting a nationwide "appeal to Almighty God for guidance and wisdom in what I believe to be the Gethsemane of our existence," Truman shot back: "I am extremely sorry that the sentiments in your letter were not thought of before November 7, when the campaign in your State, Utah, North Carolina, Illinois and Indiana was carried on in a manner that was as low as anything I've ever seen and I've been in this game since 1906."[6] But it was when his daughter Margaret gave a singing recital in Washington and music critic Paul Hume roasted her the next day in the *Washington Post* that Truman (a fairly good pianist himself) penned the hottest letter of his career, dropping it in a mailbox when he set out for his morning walk. "I have just read your lousy review buried in the back pages," he told Hume. "You sound like a frustrated old man who never made a success, an eight-ulcer man on a four-ulcer job and all four ulcers working. I never met you, but if I do you'll need a new nose and a supporter below. Westbrook Pegler, a guttersnipe, is a gentleman compared to you. You can take that as more of an insult than a reflection on your ancestry." There was an uproar, of course, when Truman's letter was made public; but in the end the majority of people who wrote the White House about it approved of Truman's doughty defense of his daughter.[7]

Some people, though, thought Truman's language was too salty for a President. Truman could not resist throwing an occasional "hell," "damn," or "s.o.b." into his public comments if he felt strongly about something. When newspaper columnists began criticizing his appointments and suggesting people he should fire, he blew up. "Everyone is telling me who I should have on my staff and in my Cabinet," he exclaimed in an after-dinner speech in Washington. "No s.o.b. is going to dictate to me who I'm going to have!" Afterward Mrs. Truman reprimanded him severely for talking that way in public. But several days later one of his aides rushed into his office with the news that a prominent Washington clergyman had defended the President, saying that "under similar provocation, he might have said the same thing." Truman beamed; then, turning solemn, he said: "I just wish that the rector would go talk to my wife!"[8]

Despite a steady barrage of criticism, Truman became increasingly self-confident, and even cocky, as he familiarized himself with the duties and responsibilities of his office. "If you can't stand the heat," he said, "stay out of the kitchen." He kept two mottoes on his White House desk. One said: "The buck stops here." The other quoted Mark Twain: "Always do right. This will gratify some people and astonish the rest."[9] In foreign affairs he sponsored the Marshall Plan for European economic recovery, the Truman Doctrine to contain Russian expansion, and the North Atlantic Treaty Organization (NATO). On the domestic front he proposed the "Fair Deal," a series of measures extending the New Deal and guaranteeing civil rights for America's black citizens. "Now, nobody should have any more doubt," said one Republican leader angrily. "Not even President Roosevelt ever asked so much at one sitting. It is just a case of out–New Dealing the New Deal."[10] As Truman's popularity, measured by polls, dropped steadily throughout 1946 and 1947, he became the butt of bad jokes and nasty quips: "To err is Truman"; "What would Truman do if he were alive?"; "Don't shoot our piano player; he's doing the best he can."[11]

By 1948, Democratic leaders were casting about for someone other

than Truman to run for President, while the Republicans were looking forward confidently to taking over the White House after the
November election. Even Truman's mother-in-law thought it was
a waste of time for Harry to seek re-election. After the Republicans
nominated Governor Thomas E. Dewey of New York for President,
with every expectation of victory, the Democrats met amid great
gloom in Philadelphia to make their choice. "The Party might as
well immediately concede the election to Dewey," said the *New York
Post,* "and save the wear and tear of campaigning." Signs in Convention Hall summed up the feeling of most delegates: "I'M JUST MILD
ABOUT HARRY." "If Truman is nominated," said the writers of one
syndicated newspaper column, "he will be forced to wage the loneliest
campaign in recent history." When Truman appeared at the convention, his supporters released fifty doves from a Liberty Bell made
of flowers as a symbol of peace. But one of the doves bumped into
the balcony and fell dead to the floor. "A dead pigeon," exclaimed
one delegate, looking up at Truman. The "Dixiecrats," hostile to
Truman's civil-rights program, left the party to nominate their own
candidate; so did the "Progressives," who were hostile to Truman's
foreign policy. When the Democrats, finding no alternative, ended
by giving the nomination to Truman after all, *Fortune* declared:
"The prospects of Republican victory are now so overwhelming that
an era of what will amount to one party may well impend."[12]

Truman's spunk was aroused. He was absolutely certain he could
win. He made a rip-roaring speech at the convention, called the
Republican-controlled Congress back into session to tackle inflation
and the housing crisis, and planned a cross-country tour in which
he would lambaste the Republican Congress at every turn. "Mow
'em down!" Vice-Presidential nominee Alben Barkley told him. "I'm
going to give 'em hell!" Truman promised him.[13] He did just that.
Everywhere he went, he tore into the Republicans with ridicule and
scorn. "When I called them back into session in July, what did
they do?" he cried. "Nothing. The Congress never did anything
the whole time it was in session. If the Republicans win, they'll
tear you to pieces." "Give 'em hell, Harry!" came a cry from the
crowd in Chicago. "I have good news for you," Truman shouted
back. "We have the Republicans on the run. We are going to win!"
But no one believed him. Reporters "laughed hysterically," according
to his daughter, when he announced he would sweep the nation.
Editors, columnists, radio commentators, political savants, and pro-

fessional pollsters all predicted a substantial victory for Dewey. On the eve of the election, one magazine cover read: "WHAT DEWEY WILL DO." Another pictured Dewey and his wife on a small vessel with the caption: *The next President travels by ferry boat over the broad waters of San Francisco Bay.* "[14]

On election night, November 2, the first scattered returns showed Truman leading. "But this is only an early lead," one radio commentator explained. "He cannot win—his early lead will fold up." But the lead continued as the hours passed. About midnight, however, radio commentator H. V. Kaltenborn announced over the air: "Mr. Truman is still ahead but these are returns from a few cities. When the returns come in from the country the result will show Dewey winning overwhelmingly." Then came the news that Dewey had won in New York. A Kansas City friend, Tom Evans, called Truman at his hotel in Excelsior, Missouri, to tell him he had to carry either Ohio, Illinois, or California in order to win. "Tom," said Truman, "don't call me any more. I'm going to bed." "What the hell do you mean?" cried Evans. "Just that," said Truman. "I'm going to carry all three states so don't call me anymore. I'll be over at eight in the morning." At 4:00 A.M., one of Truman's Secret Service men burst into his room and told him to listen to Kaltenborn. Truman turned on the radio and learned he was over two million votes ahead, but that Kaltenborn was still insisting: "I don't see how he can be elected. The election will be decided in the House." At 4:30 A.M., Evans called Truman again. This time he found him up and in a happy mood. "I'm coming over at six to celebrate," he told Evans. Dewey finally conceded at 11:14 A.M. Stunned by his defeat, Dewey later said he felt like the man who woke up to find himself inside a coffin with a lily in his hand and thought: "If I'm alive, what am I doing here? And if I'm dead, why do I have to go to the bathroom?"[15]

Truman could not help chortling over his comfortable victory. At St. Louis, on his way to Washington, he held up for reporters a copy of the *Chicago Tribune* with its morning headline: "DEWEY DEFEATS TRUMAN." He also had fun imitating H. V. Kaltenborn's staccato-voiced prediction of Democratic defeat. Back in the capital, he found a sign in front of the *Washington Post* building which read, "Mr. President, we are ready to eat crow whenever you are ready to serve it." "I was supremely confident of your defeat," Truman's friend George Allen confessed after the election. "So was everybody else," said Truman. "But you're the first one who's admitted it."[16] Soon after his re-election, however, Truman decided not to run again. "If you don't like the heat, get out of the kitchen," he told a friend, using one of his favorite phrases. "Well, that's what I'm doing."[17] His second term was, if anything, more tumultuous than the first, what with the outbreak of the Korean War in 1950 and the rise of McCarthyism (with its assertion that the nation was honeycombed with subversives) at about the same time. In April 1951 Truman removed General Douglas MacArthur from his command of UN forces in Korea for repeatedly criticizing the administration's policy of avoiding fighting in China. This produced a storm which lasted many months and calls for impeachment. The moon, stars, and all the planets were still falling on the man from Missouri when he returned to private life in January 1953.

Just before he left the White House, Truman told Margaret: "Your dad will never be reckoned among the great. But you can be sure he did his level best and gave all he had to his country. There is an epitaph in Boothill Cemetery in Tombstone, Arizona, which reads, 'Here lies Jack Williams; he done his damnedest.' What more can a person do?"[18] After the inauguration of Dwight D. Eisenhower on January 20, 1953 the Trumans returned to Independence, Missouri; the next day the former President took his usual morning walk. When a reporter asked what was the first thing he had done when he walked into his house the night before, Truman said simply: "I carried the grips up to the attic."[19] A few weeks later, the Trumans stopped in San Francisco, en route to Hawaii, to have dinner with George Killion, head of the steamship company on whose liner they were to travel. The chauffeur got them into the right neighborhood but picked the wrong house. Truman rang the bell and "an unmistakably Republican-looking gentleman," as he put it, opened the door. "Does Mr. Killion live here?" asked Truman. "No," said the man; then he gave Truman a closer look and added: "By the way, I hope your feelings won't be hurt—but you look exactly like Harry Truman." "I hope yours won't either," replied Truman, "but I *am* Harry Truman."[20]

In retirement, Truman wrote his memoirs, lectured at universities, and continued making speeches for the Democrats. In 1960, he campaigned for John F. Kennedy, who was running against Richard M. Nixon, and, as of old, succeeded in rousing a storm. Speaking in San Antonio, he said that any Texan who voted for Nixon ought "to go to hell." With great indignation, the chairman of the Republican National Committee at once wired Kennedy: "This registers the strongest protest possible at the despicable campaign tactics of your colleague and cohort, Harry S. Truman. . . . Such profanity in your campaign is outrageous." Nixon himself also protested; Truman's language, he said, was a menace to American children. Shortly afterward, Kennedy spoke in Detroit. "I have to be careful of what I say in view of what Vice-President Nixon said," he told the crowd. "There may be children here." Columnist George Dixon humorously conjured up a "dire picture" of "impressionable little ones innocently repeating Trumanisms and having their little mouths washed out with bourbon." And an apocryphal Truman story made the rounds. After the birth of his first grandchild, it was said, the former President told his daughter: "When he gets older, I'm going to teach him to talk." "The hell you are!" said Margaret.[21]

"Some of the Presidents were great and some of them weren't," said Truman in an interview on April 27, 1959. "I can say that because I wasn't one of the great Presidents; but," he added, "I had a good time trying to be one."[22] He would have been astonished by his sudden rise in popularity during the 1970s. Once called a liar, cheat, fool, coddler of subversives, and the worst President in history, he began to appear in retrospect refreshingly independent, straightforward, decisive, and courageous. Merle Miller's *Plain Speaking* (1974), a popular book presenting an attractive picture of the former President based on personal interviews, had something to do with it. So did the fact that in a period in which image and credibility were replacing character and principle as political preoccupations, there was something hearteningly authentic about a Chief Executive who frequently said and did exactly what he thought was right even though it wasn't always the politic thing to do.

★   ★   ★

Wonder

After his election to the U.S. Senate in 1934, Truman was amused by the advice he received from an old judge he had worked with on the county court, who had once worked for a Senator in Washington. "Harry," he said, "don't you go to the Senate with an inferiority complex. You'll sit there about six months, and wonder how you got there. But after that you'll wonder how the rest of them got there."[23]

Piano Player

Truman was once asked by a friend about the famous photograph taken of him playing the piano with actress Lauren Bacall sitting on the piano top, "What did Bess say when she saw the picture?" "Well," answered Truman, "she said maybe it was time for me to quit playing the piano."[24]

Old-Fashioneds

At the end of the workday, the Trumans liked to have a cocktail before dinner. Shortly after they moved into the White House, Mrs. Truman rang for the butler, Alonzo Fields, one afternoon and ordered two old-fashioneds. Fields, who considered himself a good bartender, quickly prepared the drinks, in chilled glasses, with fruit slices and a dash of bitters. Mrs. Truman tasted hers, thanked him, and made no other comments. But the next evening when she rang for Fields, she asked "Can you make the old-fashioneds a little drier? We don't like them so sweet." Fields then tried a new recipe, and again she said nothing. But the next morning she told J. B. West, the chief usher, "They make the worst old-fashioneds here I've ever tasted! They're like fruit punch." The next evening, Fields, his pride hurt, dumped two big splashes of bourbon over the ice and served it to the Trumans. Mrs. Truman tasted the drink and then beamed: "Now that's the way we like our old-fashioneds!"[25]

Fifteen Minutes' Leave

Once, when President Truman was visiting Kansas City, he invited Eddie Meissberger, a retired post office employee and a veteran of Battery D (Truman's World War I unit), for lunch. When Eddie arrived he found several other veterans of Battery D present. The President opened the drawer of a desk, grinned, went over and locked the door, got some old tumblers from a cupboard, then took out a bottle and poured each of his friends a drink. "Where is your glass?"

they asked him. Truman told them he couldn't take a drink right then because in the next room was a delegation of Baptist ladies from Independence whom he had promised to see in a few minutes. "But," he said, "I have a bad cold coming on, and I'll just put this away and take it out at home tonight and use it." And he put the bottle back in the desk. Then Eddie said: "Well, I'm on a government payroll, you know, and I don't know whether I should take one right now." "Well," said Truman, "as President, I'll give you fifteen—fifteen minutes of annual leave right now, and you can join the others." So it was "down the hatch" for all of Truman's former buddies.[26]

The Two Marshals

When Truman went to the Potsdam Conference in July 1945, he took an old Missouri friend, Fred Canfil, with him. One day after a meeting, Truman called Canfil over and introduced him to Stalin. "Marshal Stalin," he said, "I want you to meet Marshal Canfil." Truman did not explain that he had recently made Canfil a federal marshal in Missouri. But after that Canfil was treated with great respect by all the members of the Russian delegation.[27]

Turning Pages

One evening at Potsdam, President Truman hosted a party for Churchill, Stalin, and the other dignitaries that featured music by the young American concert pianist Eugene List, then an army sergeant. First, Truman played some of Paderewski's Minuet in G (years before the composer had given him suggestions for playing it), and then List put on a performance that thrilled the President and left Churchill bored stiff. Afterwards Truman asked List to give another performance and requested Chopin's Waltz in A Major, one of his favorites, for the program. It turned out that the Waltz was not in List's repertoire, so Truman had the music sent from Paris, and List spent an entire day practicing. When the time came to play, however, he confessed that he had not had time "to memorize, so if someone in the party would be kind enough to turn the pages for me I would be grateful." A young officer offered to help, but admitted he couldn't read music. "Just at that point," List recalled, "the President rose, and with a marvelously sweeping gesture said, 'No, I'll turn the pages myself.' " And he did. "Just imagine!" List told his wife later. "Well, you could have knocked me over with a toothpick! Imagine having the President of the United States turn pages for you!" He added: "That's the kind of man the President is."[28]

One-handed Economist

"Get me a one-handed economist!" Truman once demanded. "All my economists say, 'on the one hand, . . . but on the other.' "[29]

Toning It Down

Truman was forever slipping a "hell" or a "damn" into his public utterances, and Mrs. Truman was forever telling him, "You shouldn't have said that!" A lady prominent in the Democratic Party, according to an apocryphal story, once pled with Mrs. Truman to get her husband to clean up his language; she had just heard him refer to some politician's statement as "a bunch of horse manure." Said Mrs. Truman calmly: "You don't know how many years it took me to tone it down to that!"[30]

No Failure

About stories to the effect that his father had been a failure, Truman once remarked: "My father was not a failure. After all, he was the father of a President of the United States."[31]

Lawn-Mowing

In retirement in Independence Truman spent part of each day doing household chores. But there was one chore his wife Bess wanted him to do which he wanted to get out of doing: mowing the lawn. So Truman waited until Sunday morning, when the neighbors were beginning to pass the house on the way to church, got out the lawnmower, and started to cut the grass. Mrs. Truman, preparing to leave for church, was horrified. "What are you doing on Sunday?" she asked. "I'm doing what you asked me to do," he replied. She never again asked him to mow the lawn.[32]

Missouri Waltz

In March 1969, President Nixon (never a favorite with Truman) stopped off in Independence with Truman's old White House piano as a gift for the Truman Library. Truman, eighty-four years old and declining in health, met Nixon in the library, and the two shook hands. Then Nixon sat down at the piano and played "The Missouri Waltz," not realizing that Truman disliked the piece and had once called it "obnoxious as a state song." But the former President was extremely hard of hearing by now, and when Nixon finished his rendition, he turned to Bess and asked: "What was that?"[33]

Dwight D. Eisenhower
1953–61

When the slogan "I like Ike" was sweeping the country in the early 1950s, Dwight D. Eisenhower's mother sniffed, "Who's *that*?" To Mrs. Eisenhower he was always "Dwight"; she never called him "Ike."[1] But the rest of the country preferred the nickname. It seemed to go perfectly with the amiable, easygoing, and gregarious West Pointer who became President in 1952 and again in 1956. Even as a five-star general, Ike was anything but pompous. He was, in fact, exasperated by the army's "glory-hoppers." "I hope I never get pontifical or stuffed shirty with you fellows," he once told reporters.[2]

In the late 1930s, Eisenhower (1890–1969) served as aide to General Douglas MacArthur in the Philippines. He respected MacArthur's abilities, but was amused by his grandiloquence. "He's an aristocrat," he once said, "but as for me, I'm just folks. I come from the people, the ordinary people." When Philippine President Manuel Quezon offered to make MacArthur Grand Field Marshal of the Philippines, the latter was delighted and told Ike about it. "But do you think I really ought to accept that rank?" he asked, expecting a vigorous affirmative. "No, sir, I do not," said Ike frankly. "General, you're a hero in the American Army, and I think it would tarnish your image to accept a grandiose title like Grand Field Marshal." "The trouble with you, Eisenhower," said MacArthur coldly, "is that you're too *small-minded.*" A few days later, when Ike boarded a ship headed for the United States, his wife noticed a bottle under his arm. "Who gave you that?" she wanted to know. "The Grand Field Marshal of the Philippines," he told her. "Who?" she cried. "Mac," he grinned.[3]

"The reason I like you so much," Winston Churchill once told Ike, "is because you ain't no glory-hopper."[4] Ike of course enjoyed achieving the highest rank the U.S. Army had to give; and he was proud of being elevated to the Presidency. Still, he never became "stuffed shirty" either in the army or in the White House. Once, as commander of Allied forces in Europe during World War II, he visited an outfit near Aachen which was undergoing severe hardships. The GIs applauded warmly after he made a little speech, but when he stepped down from the platform and fell into the mud, they began laughing uproariously. But Ike laughed with them. "Something tells me," he said, "that my visit with you fellows has been a howling success."[5]

As President, Eisenhower used FDR's former retreat in the Maryland mountains for entertaining official guests, but he changed the name from Shangri-la to Camp David. Shangri-la, he said, was "just a little too fancy for a Kansas farm boy."[6] George Humphrey, his Secretary of the Treasury, never forgot the first time he met Eisenhower. "George," said Ike, as the balding Humphrey walked into the room, "I see you comb your hair the way I do."[7] To a pretentious gentleman who came by one day to explain in humorless detail why he couldn't attend a White House dinner, Ike said genially, "Ah, you'd be nuts to come."[8] Sometimes he referred to himself as an "old dodo" to his White House associates. But when his speech advisers tried to overdo his reputation for being down-to-earth, he was vastly amused. "Gosh," he cried, "someone around here is always feeding me all these 'folksy' phrases. Well, I'm folksy *enough* as it is, without their trying to make matters worse."[9]

There were numerous attempts to describe Ike's famous smile. It was, *inter alia,* boyish, glowing, vivid, warm, winning, leaping, charming, infectious, effortless, and hundred-watt. "Ike," Secretary of Defense James Forrestal told him right after World War II, "with your puss, you can't miss being President!"[10] But Ike resolutely eschewed presidential politics for a long time. When the possibility of running for President was first mentioned to him in 1943, he cried: "Baloney!" Told there was an Ike boom under way, he said firmly: "I am a soldier, and that's all I ever want to be. I'm no glory-hopper!"[11] In 1948, the pressure to run became serious, but he still held off. "Look, son," he told a reporter, "I cannot conceive of any circumstance that could drag out of me permission to consider me for any political post from dogcatcher to Grand High Supreme King of the Universe."[12] Not until 1952 did he finally agree to run on the Republican ticket, and in the fall of that year he won the election by a comfortable margin. At his inauguration a souvenir dealer in Washington, displaying buttons reading I LIKE EVERYBODY and I HATE EVERYBODY, said happily: "Most people like everybody today. We're not movin' the 'hate' ones except to kids."[13]

Despite his sunny, sky-blue temperament, Ike did not always preserve his equanimity. In the army he was known for his sulphurous temper when things went wrong; his knowledge of army expletives was always adequate to the occasion. As President, too, he had periodic outbursts of anger, touched off by what he thought was unfair criticism by political foes or by sloppy work on the part of his associates. Tom Stephens, his appointments secretary, thought Ike tended to wear brown whenever he was out of sorts. Stephens, in fact, got in the habit of keeping a watch out of the window for the President on his way to the office and flashing a warning to the secretaries if things looked threatening: "Brown suit today!" One morning, however, when Ike appeared in blue, he decided to tell him about his color theory; and after that the President wore brown less often.[14] Army-navy bickerings particularly infuriated Ike; one of his famous blowups came when a high-ranking general gloated over the failure of the navy's Vanguard rocket. "And what do you think this goddam three-star Army general said?" Ike cried angrily. "He said it was a great day for the Army, because the Navy had fallen flat on its face!"[15] "My God," exclaimed one of Ike's associates after one of his awesome explosions, "how could you compute the amount of adrenalin expended in those thirty seconds? I don't know why long since he hasn't had a killer of a heart attack."[16] Ike finally did have a heart attack in 1955; and after that he tried hard to keep his temper under control.

In public, Ike always tried to preserve his composure. He thought it was not only unseemly for the President of the United States to engage in personal attacks but also counterproductive. He had nothing but contempt for Republican Senator Joseph R. McCarthy of Wisconsin, who continued the witch-hunt he had begun under Truman into the Eisenhower years; but he refused to take him on personally. "I will not," he told his staff, pounding his desk, "I will not get in the gutter with *that* guy!"[17] When a Labor Department official briefed the Cabinet one day on a new kind of insurance for government employees called a "sudden death policy," Ike exclaimed: "I know one fellow I'd like to take that policy out for!"[18] But though he criticized "book-burners" in public and quietly encouraged Congressional leaders to keep the Wisconsin Senator under control, he refused to discuss him in public. He was delighted, however, when the Senate voted to censure McCarthy in 1954 and congratulated Senator Arthur Watkins of Utah for his "splendid" work as chairman of the committee that recommended censure. He had as little use for witch-hunting Senator William Jenner of Indiana as he had for McCarthy. "As for the Jenners and the McCarthys," he told Arthur Larson in August 1956, "I just don't want their support. McCarthy said he apologized to the American people for supporting me; that is just the way I want it and I wish he would say it again."[19]

Ike regarded himself as a conservative, "but an extremely liberal conservative"; while he was in the White House he talked much of "dynamic conservatism," the "middle way," "progressive moderates," and "modern Republicanism." He was distressed, though, by the opposition to his proposals for social-welfare legislation within his own party and by his dependence on Democrats to get programs he sponsored through Congress. For a while he even talked of starting a new party, but dropped the idea as impractical. Criticized for not exerting more vigorous leadership, he exclaimed, "Now look, this idea that all wisdom is in the President, in me, that's baloney. . . . I don't believe this government was set up to be operated by anyone acting alone; no one has a monopoly on the truth and on the facts that affect this country. . . . We must work together."[20] Leadership, he once said, involves "persuasion, and conciliation, and education, and patience. It's long, slow, tough work. That's the only kind of leadership I know or will believe in, or will practice."[21]

In foreign, as in domestic affairs, Ike strove to be a conciliator. He helped bring the Korean War to an end, insisted on working through the United Nations as much as possible, and sought friendlier relations with Russia. "The people who know war," he said, "those who have experienced it . . . I believe are the most earnest advocates of peace in the world."[22] To his bellicose Secretary of State, John Foster Dulles, he once said wryly: "You *are* a militant Presbyterian, aren't you?"[23] During his last months in office he traveled around the world trying to spread a message of good will. Though reporters accompanying him scoffed at his generalities—"Here we go again, around the world in eighty platitudes!"—most of them were impressed by the way he convinced millions of people in Europe, Asia, Africa, and South America that he was truly a man of peace.[24] To the end Eisenhower never wavered in his belief that the only way to win World War III was to prevent it.

★ ★ ★

No Leak

"Gentlemen," said General Eisenhower to a roomful of reporters during World War II, "I know you've all been guessing where we're going to attack next. Well, I'm going to let you in on the secret. Our next operation will be Italy, early in July. General Patton will attack the southern beaches, General Montgomery the eastern." "General," said one newsman, as the reporters gasped at the revelation, "if one of us leaked that plan, couldn't it be *disastrous*?" Ike nodded. "The slightest hint in your stories will tip it off to German intelligence," he said. "But I'm not going to censor you fellows. I'm just leaving it up to each man's sense of responsibility." "Wow," exclaimed one reporter, "what a dirty trick!" But not a word of the operation leaked out.[25]

Playing Games

George Allen, a Red Cross official, sent by President Roosevelt to England on an inspection trip, while in London got into the habit of playing bridge with General Eisenhower. One evening they started out with only a single deck of cards. In the first hand Allen, who was one of Ike's opponents, spoke up: "Wait a minute. I have the joker. I have to have another card." "Oh, no, you don't," said Ike. "That is the six of clubs. We lost the real six and you'll notice the markings in the corner." Allen laid down his hand, leaned back in his chair, and said: "Now, just a minute. If the Commander-in-Chief of all this armada, which is about to cross the Channel and lick Hitler, cannot afford one complete set of cards, then I have grave doubts that other and more necessary items of equipment with which we hope to win are adequate and ready." "George," said Ike solemnly, "let me tell you this. We are not going to be playing games with the Nazis."[26]

The Milky Way

One day, after the Allies had established themselves on the Continent, Ike went into a quartermaster store to get a new pair of shoes. His five stars were concealed by an old raincoat, so no one recognized him as he waited his turn in line. His aide fumed at the delay, but Ike silenced him. The store was hot, so Ike finally removed his coat about the time the sergeant in charge got around to waiting on him. Catching sight of the five stars, the sergeant cried, almost in disbelief: "Cripes! The whole Milky Way!"[27]

Solicitude

Ike enjoyed telling the story of the time he was strafed by German planes while visiting a British sector of the front. The British General in charge rushed over expressing great gratification that the Supreme Commander was unhurt. Touched by his solicitude, Ike thanked him warmly. "Oh," said the Britisher matter-of-factly, "my concern was that nothing should happen to you in *my* sector."[28]

A Job for Zhukov

After the war in Europe ended, Stalin invited Eisenhower to visit the Soviet Union. En route to Moscow by train, Ike was shocked by what he saw of Nazi destruction in Russia. In Moscow, he found Stalin humorless but Marshal Zhukov, the great Russian war hero, friendly and good-natured. During Ike's visit, Stalin gave him the honor of being the first foreigner ever to set foot on top of Lenin's tomb, where he stood five hours with Stalin reviewing a gymnastic spectacle in Red Square. "This develops the war spirit," Stalin told him. "Your country ought to do more of this. But not Germany!" That evening, Ike was shown films of Zhukov capturing Berlin. Afterward, Ike told the Russian commander teasingly, "If you ever lose your job in the Soviet Union, you can surely get one in Hollywood!" Zhukov laughed, but Stalin didn't. "Marshal Zhukov will never be without a job in the Soviet Union," he said solemnly.[29]

Popular Address

Eisenhower was President of Columbia University between 1948 and 1950 and had to attend a good many dinners and deliver many addresses. At one dinner he was to be the last of several speakers. Each of the others spoke at great length; and it was so late when Ike's turn came that he decided to discard his prepared text. After being introduced, he stood up and reminded his audience that every speech, written or otherwise, had to have punctuation. "Tonight," he said, "I am the punctuation—the period," and sat down. It was, he said later, one of his most popular addresses.[30]

Cross-Eyed Judge

When a group of Ike's advisers had wrestled with a problem until they were bleary-eyed and could scarcely communicate with each other, he told them he was reminded of a cross-eyed judge who went into court one day and found he had a cross-eyed jury. "What's your name?" he asked the first juror. The second juror replied, "John Jones." "I didn't speak to you," remonstrated the judge. The third juror chimed in: "I didn't say anything."[31]

Better You Than Me

James Hagerty, Ike's press secretary, once recalled: "President Eisenhower would say 'Do it this way.' I would say, 'If I go to that press conference and say what you want me to say, I would get hell.' With that, he would smile, get up and walk around the desk, pat me on the back and say, 'My boy, better you than me!' "[32]

Ike at Gettysburg

Eisenhower was an experienced writer. He once remarked to Arthur Larson: "You know that General MacArthur got quite a reputation as a silver-tongued speaker when he was in the Philippines. Who do you think wrote his speeches? I did." Both Larson and Emmet Hughes, who worked with President Eisenhower on speeches, attested to his skill with words. At his weekly presidential press conferences, however, Ike could be incomprehensible whenever he wanted to be. He was a masterly performer. He went to these conferences knowing exactly what he planned to say and what he intended to avoid saying by employing vague and evasive language.

In May 1954, when the Republic of China threatened to occupy some islands in the Formosa Straits, the State Department was worried about public reaction to anything the President might say about the crisis. "Mr. President," press secretary James Hagerty told Ike just before his weekly press conference, "some of the people in the State Department say that the Formosa Strait situation is so delicate that no matter what question you get on it, you shouldn't say anything at all." "Don't worry, Jim," said Ike. "If that question comes up, I'll just confuse them." And in 150 carefully chosen words he did just that.

But Ike's habit of rambling at press conferences whenever he wanted to "confuse them" was attributed to ineptitude rather than to shrewdness. One reporter, tired of Ike's periodic meanderings, rewrote Lincoln's Gettysburg Address as Ike might have delivered it. "I haven't checked these figures," the parody begins, "but 87 years ago, I think it was, a number of individuals organized a governmental setup here in this country, I believe it covered certain eastern areas, with this idea they were following up, based on a sort of national independence arrangement. . . ." And it concludes: "We have to make up our minds right here and now, as I see it, they didn't put out all that blood, perspiration and—well, that they didn't just make a dry run here, that all of us, under God, that is, the God of our choice, shall beef up this idea about freedom and liberty and those kind of arrangements, and that government of all individuals, by all individuals and for the individuals shall not pass out of the world picture."[33]

Option

At one Cabinet meeting during Ike's Presidency, Secretary of the Treasury George Humphrey told the President that the national debt might rise above the legal limit. "Who will have to go to jail if that happens?" asked Ike. "We will have to go to Congress," Humphrey reminded him. "Oh," cried Ike, "that's worse!"[34]

Golf

Eisenhower enjoyed playing golf when he was President, and his critics thought he spent too much time on the links. Auto stickers appeared, bearing the legend "Ben Hogan for President. If We're Going to Have a Golfer, Let's Have a Good One." Someone also made up a joke telling how Ike and his party asked permission to play through a foursome ahead of them on the golf course. "What's the hurry?" they were asked. "New York has just been bombed," was the answer. A Democratic Senator's reproof was gentler: he proposed a fund to protect squirrels from Ike's flying golf balls. When he heard this, Ike remarked, "I don't see any reason for producing another pressure group."

One day a White House visitor noticed that the President was wearing leather bandages on his left wrist. When Ike explained that he had a mild arthritic condition there, the visitor said he was glad it wasn't serious. "I should say it is serious!" exclaimed Ike indignantly. "It means that I can't play golf!"

One of Ike's favorite stories was about the golfer who tried to persuade a friend to join his foursome one afternoon. "I'd love to," said the friend, "but I promised my wife—" "Ah, come on, forget your wife," said the golfer. "Are you a man or a mouse?" "I'm a man," said the friend. "My wife's afraid of a mouse."[35]

THIRTY-FOUR

John F. Kennedy
1961–63

When John F. Kennedy (1917–63) took the oath of office on January 20, 1961, he was, at forty-three, the youngest man ever elected President. He was also one of the wittiest. To a friend he once gave a silver beer mug with the following inscription on it:

> There are three things which are real:
> God, human folly and laughter.
> The first two are beyond our comprehension
> So we must do what we can with the third.[1]

Kennedy's wit was not folksy like Lincoln's. It was plainer, directer, more urbane. But like Lincoln's it sometimes had ironic overtones and was wryly self-deprecating. And like Lincoln, JFK was bored by self-righteousness, false humility, and garrulousness. "It's a gift," said Arthur Krock. "He doesn't know how to be stuffy."[2]

Kennedy served in the navy during World War II. He was proud of his war record but never bragged about it. "Mr. President," a high school boy once asked him, "how did you become a war hero?" "It was absolutely involuntary," Kennedy responded. "They sank my boat."[3] Interviewed by Edward R. Murrow on television in the late 1950s, he called it "an interesting experience." "Interesting," murmured Murrow. "I should think that would be one of the great understatements."[4] There has been some disagreement as to how much of a war hero Kennedy was during World War II, but this much is clear: when the torpedo boat he commanded was wrecked by a Japanese destroyer in the South Pacific in August 1943, not only did he keep up the spirits of the survivors by his own playful exuberance but also saved the life of one man who was wounded by seizing the end of his life jacket in his teeth and towing him to an island three miles away. It was several days before Kennedy and his crew were rescued, and they suffered severely from lack of food and water during that period. But when young Kennedy finally heard the welcome voice of one of his rescuers crying, "Hey, Jack!" from a distance, he yelled back, "Where the hell have you been?" "We've got some food for you," came the reply. "No, thanks," said Kennedy. "I just had a coconut." A few days later he wrote a friend: "Thanks for your good wishes on our rescue. We were extremely lucky throughout. After today it won't happen again. . . . I went in to see the Doc about some coral infections I got. He asked me how I got them—I said, 'swimming.' He then burst out with, 'Kennedy, you know swimming is forbidden in this area, stay out of the goddamned water!' So now it's an official order. . . ."[5]

Kennedy always looked younger than his years and enjoyed telling friends how he was mistaken once for an elevator boy and several times for a page boy when he first entered the House of Representatives. Even after he became a Senator a guard intervened when he tried to use a special telephone in the Capitol. "Sorry, mister," he told Kennedy, "these are reserved for the Senators."[6] Kennedy's name skyrocketed onto the national scene when he received a surprising number of votes for the Vice-Presidential nomination in 1956; and his triumphant re-election as Senator from Massachusetts two years later led him to believe he had a chance at the Presidency in 1960. When a friend told him he would have no trouble getting the Vice-Presidential nomination in 1960, Kennedy smiled and said: "Let's not talk so much about vice. I'm against vice in any form."[7]

Catholicism was still an issue when Kennedy tried for the Presidency; so was the fact that his father, Joseph P. Kennedy, was enormously wealthy. "I'm not against the Pope," said Harry Truman, who at first opposed Kennedy's candidacy. "I'm against the Pop."[8] When reporters at a Gridiron Club dinner in Washington in 1958 teased Kennedy about his father by presenting a skit featuring the Massachusetts Senator singing "My Heart Belongs to Daddy" and "Just Send the Bill to Daddy," he took it in good humor. In the speech he gave afterward, he said: "I have just received the following wire from my generous Daddy: 'Dear Jack: Don't buy a single vote more than necessary. I'll be damned if I'm going to pay for a landslide.' "[9] In Wisconsin two years later, however, campaigning in the presidential primary, he was angered when a young smart aleck said to him, "Kennedy, I hear that your dad only offered two dollars a vote. With all your dough, can't you do better than that?" "You know that statement is false," Kennedy exclaimed. "It's sad that the only thing you have to offer is your vote, and you're willing to sell that."[10]

In November 1960, Kennedy won narrowly over Richard Nixon at the polls and became the first President who had been born in the twentieth century. As President, he sought a "New Frontier" in American politics, involving "invention, innovation, imagination, decision."[11] There were advances in civil rights under JFK, as well as the creation of a Peace Corps and the signing of a test ban treaty with Russia. But there was also an intensification of the Cold War: the Bay of Pigs fiasco, the Cuban missile crisis, and increasing involvement in Vietnam. "The chickens are coming home to roost," General MacArthur told the new President late in 1961, "and you live in the chicken house."[12]

Kennedy did not mind living in the chicken house; he enjoyed it enormously. "The job is interesting," he said at the end of his first year in office, "but the possibilities for trouble are unlimited. It's been a tough year, but then, they're all going to be tough."[13] Toughness did not faze him. "The only thing that really surprised us when we got into office," he said, "was that things were just as bad as we had been saying they were; otherwise we have been enjoying it very much."[14] "Let's see," he once said about some problems, "did we inherit these, or are they our own?" "Oh, well," he commented on another occasion, "just think of what we'll pass on to the poor fellow who comes after me."[15]

Kennedy's high spirits, even in times of trouble, brought a sense of hope and adventure to Washington and to the nation at large. His press conferences were sparkling; even his critics enjoyed them. And his playful remarks to friends and associates quickly became common currency in the nation's capital and elsewhere. When he decided to appoint his brother Robert Attorney General, his friend Ben Bradlee, knowing there would be an outcry, wondered how he would make the announcement. "Well," Kennedy told him, "I think I'll open the front door of the Georgetown house some morning about 2 A.M., look up and down the street, and, if there's no one there, I'll whisper, 'It's Bobby.' " "Don't smile too much," Kennedy told his brother when they went out to face the press, "or they'll think we are happy about the appointment." When critics said Bobby was too young and inexperienced to head the Justice Department and that he had never tried a case in court, Kennedy told them: "I can't see that it's wrong to give him a little legal experience before he goes out to practice law."[16]

When it came to public occasions, Fred Holborn, who was on the White House staff, thought the Presidency improved Kennedy's wit. "It used to be rehearsed," he said. "Now it's sharper, more spontaneous, less derivative. And ceremonies bring it out at its best, because he likes to poke fun at rituals."[17] When Kennedy attended a businessmen's luncheon shortly after his inauguration, he said: "It would be premature to ask your support in the next election, and it would be inaccurate to thank you for it in the past."[18] Receiving an honorary degree at Yale, he remarked: "It might be said now that I have the best of both worlds—a Harvard education and a Yale degree."[19] Reversing the cliché, he called Washington "a city of Southern efficiency and Northern charm."[20] When his youngest brother, Edward, was elected Senator from Massachusetts in 1962, he told a meeting of Democrats in Harrisburg, Pennsylvania: "I should introduce myself. I am Teddy Kennedy's brother."[21] *Time* once referred to Teddy as smiling "sardonically," and Kennedy had this to say: "Bobby and I smile sardonically. Teddy will learn to smile sardonically in two or three years, but he doesn't know how, yet."[22] When a lawyer who liked Robert Kennedy's racket-busting wrote to say that Bobby would make a better Chief Executive, Kennedy replied: "I have consulted Bobby about it, and, to my dismay, the idea appeals to him."[23] Unable to attend a testimonial luncheon for Postmaster General J. Edward Day, Kennedy sent his regrets and added: "I am sending this message by wire, since I want to be certain that this message reaches you in the right place at the right time."[24]

In June 1961, Kennedy met with Soviet leader Nikita Khrushchev in Vienna for foreign-policy talks. The encounter was by turns friendly and frosty. When they first met, Khrushchev tried to claim some credit for Kennedy's victory over Nixon. If he had released Gary Powers (the American U-2 pilot shot down over Russia in May 1960) just before the election, he said, Kennedy would have lost by at least 200,000 votes. "Don't spread the story around," Kennedy begged him. "If you tell everybody that you like me better than Nixon, I'll be ruined at home." Later on, Khrushchev asked Kennedy how he got along with Andrei Gromyko. "All right," said Kennedy. "My wife thinks he has a nice smile. Why do you ask?" "Well," said Khrushchev, while Gromyko squirmed, "a lot of people think Gromyko looks like Nixon." When the two men began a serious discussion of U.S.-Soviet relations, however, the bantering ceased, and the exchanges became heated. "Do you ever admit a mistake?" Kennedy finally exclaimed. "Certainly," said Khrushchev. "In a speech before the Twentieth Party Congress, I admitted all of Stalin's mistakes." "Those were Stalin's mistakes," Kennedy reminded him. "Not your mistakes." At lunch afterward, he noticed two medals on Khrushchev's chest and asked what they were. Lenin Peace Medals, Khrushchev told him. "I hope you keep them," said Kennedy thoughtfully.[25]

Kennedy left Vienna with increased concern about American-Russian tensions; but he never gave up his hope that with patience and determination he could make progress toward a better understanding between the two nations. As he told Khrushchev: "The journey of a thousand miles begins with one step."[26] While he was President he frequently said: "All I want them to say about me is what they said about John Adams, 'He kept the peace.' "[27] And in the speech he had intended to give in Dallas on November 22, 1963, the day of his assassination, he declared: "We ask . . . that we may be worthy of our power and responsibility, that we may exercise our strength with wisdom and restraint, and that we may achieve in our time and for all time the ancient vision of 'peace on earth, goodwill toward men.' "[28]

★   ★   ★

Breadwinner

One night at a Kennedy family gathering, Joseph Kennedy got to talking about family finances. "I don't know what is going to happen to this family when I die . . . ," he said. "No one appears to have the slightest concern for how much they spend. I don't know what is going to happen to you after I am gone." Then he turned to one of JFK's sisters and reprimanded her so severely that she left the room in tears. When she returned, JFK looked up and said,

"Well, kid, don't worry. We've come to the conclusion that the only solution is to have Dad work harder." Even Mr. Kennedy laughed at that.[29]

Smiles

JFK's father had a reputation of being a very competitive business-man, and he enjoyed the stories about how tough he was. When one of JFK's sisters was married, a newspaper reported that a member of Joseph Kennedy's staff had acknowledged, with a smile, that the cost of the wedding was in the six-figure category. "Now I know that story is a phony," commented JFK. "No one in my father's office smiles!"[30]

Hard Way

One night, when JFK was running for Congress, he appeared at a rally with dozens of other candidates who were running for the Massachusetts legislature. The chairman kept Kennedy waiting impatiently until a late hour while he introduced speaker after speaker as "a young fellow who came up the hard way." When JFK's turn finally came, he began his address by saying, "I seem to be the only person here tonight who didn't come up the hard way!"[31]

Insolence of Office

When he was a Congressman, JFK once parked his car in front of a "No Parking" sign in downtown Washington and told one of his friends, "This is what Hamlet means by 'the insolence of office.' "[32]

Necktie

Kennedy's clothes were expensive, according to Ted Sorensen, but always conservative and neat; he changed frequently and knew his large wardrobe intimately. Once, during a campaign, Sorensen needed a necktie, and Dave Powers handed him one he was sure that Senator Kennedy never wore. But Kennedy's first words upon entering the room were, "Is that my tie you're wearing?"[33]

Breakfast in Bed

One day when Kennedy was in South Boston, State Senator John E. Powers showed him the house where he was born. Kennedy looked at it with interest and said: "John, you're always talking about your humble origin. This house is a much nicer house than the one I was born in on Beals Street in Brookline. I came up the hard way." "Oh, sure," retorted Powers. "You came up the hard way. One morning they didn't bring you your breakfast in bed." Jack collapsed with laughter.[34]

Dream

In 1958, Kennedy, Lyndon Johnson, and Stuart Symington were all Democrat aspirants for the 1960 presidential nomination; JFK liked to tell the following story about the three of them. "Several nights ago," he said, "I dreamed that the good Lord touched me on the shoulder and said, 'Don't worry, you'll be the Democratic Presidential nominee in 1960. What's more, you'll be elected.' I told Stu Symington about my dream. 'Funny thing,' said Stu, 'I had exactly the same dream myself.' We both told our dreams to Lyndon Johnson, and Johnson said, 'That's funny. For the life of me, I can't remember tapping either of you two boys for the job.' "[35]

American Fah-mah

Speaking to a group of farmers in Sioux City, Iowa, in his clipped Cape Cod accent, Kennedy referred to the agricultural depression and cried: "What's wrong with the American fah-mah today?" As he paused dramatically for a moment, someone in the audience yelled: "He's stah-ving!" The audience roared with laughter, and so did JFK.[36]

High Regard

During the 1960 campaign, when JFK appeared on "Meet the Press," he told host Lawrence Spivak, "I suppose, Mr. Spivak, that you have a long list of challenging questions for me." Smiled Spivak: "Knowing my high regard for you, Mr. Senator, I don't think you'd want me to pull my punches." "No," murmured Kennedy, "but I wouldn't mind if you lowered your regard a bit."[37]

Indian

In Wisconsin, Kennedy was made honorary chieftain of an Indian tribe. Donning the headdress, he exclaimed: "Next time I go to the movies to see cowboys and Indians, I'll be us."[38]

Duck

A friend, comparing their common backgrounds, suggested that he and the President were pretty much alike. Kennedy peered at him. "You're not at all like me," he said. "You walk like a duck."[39]

Jackie's Husband

When the Kennedys visited France in 1962, Jackie, who spoke French fluently, charmed both the French people and General Charles de Gaulle himself. On his last day in Paris, Kennedy told reporters at a press conference in the Palais de Chaillot, "I do not think it altogether inappropriate to introduce myself to this audience. I am the man who accompanied Jacqueline Kennedy to Paris, and I have enjoyed it."[40]

Appreciation

In April 1961, President Kennedy decided to send Vice-President Johnson to visit a number of Asian countries, with Vietnam as a key stop. Johnson was unenthusiastic about going to Saigon, but JFK reassured him. "Don't worry, Lyndon," he said lightly, "if anything happens to you, Sam Rayburn and I will give you the biggest funeral Austin, Texas, ever saw."[41]

Small Type

Once, flying on Air Force One, JFK was asked by a reporter what would happen if the aircraft crashed. Kennedy smiled. "I'm sure of one thing," he said; "your name would be in the paper the next day, but in very small type."[42]

Lyndon B. Johnson
1963–69

Lyndon B. Johnson (1908–73) was the first Southerner since Wood-row Wilson to become President. He was also the first "real" Texan to occupy the White House. Texas is a great, big, huge state (as a native might put it), with an enormous range of weather, terrain, flora, fauna, people, customs, attitudes, and lifestyles. Still, to most outsiders, the word "Texas" conjures up images of cowpunchers, boots, ten-gallon hats, jeans, rodeos, Texas rangers, ranches, and Alamo *machismo*. From this point of view, LBJ seemed like the quintessential Texan to many Americans: big, loud, brash, friendly, informal, folksy, pushy, vulgar, and combative. He was all these things, and more. He had a remarkable memory, a razor-sharp mind, great comic gifts, and a Populist bent that made him eager as President to make life better for the masses of people. "He had the quickest, most analytical mind I've ever seen," said a New Deal official who observed him at work in Congress in the 1930s.[1] "Lyndon Johnson," said John Gardner, one of his Cabinet members, "was one of the most intelligent men I have ever known."[2] He was also one of the most energetic men on this planet.

Johnson's energy was enough to make even the somnolent Calvin Coolidge turn in his grave. "I don't want to be remembered as a can't-do man," LBJ once announced.[3] "Lyndon," said his friend Sam Rayburn, "behaves as if there were no tomorrow coming and he had to do everything today."[4] He was always on the go. He walked with what was known as "the LBJ trot."[5] He was a compulsive talker, continually on the telephone coaxing, haranguing, flattering, and mollifying people. He was bored by golf and fishing; his recreations—swimming, hunting, showing people around the LBJ ranch—tended to be fast-paced and at times frenetic. When one of his friends said of some public issue, "Lyndon will go the way the wind blows," another friend replied, "Maybe, but if he does, he'll probably beat the wind there."[6]

Johnson's vitality was spectacular. Once, during the 1964 campaign, he gave no fewer than twenty-two speeches in one day. In December 1967, he circled the globe, visiting one country after another, in four days, fifteen hours, and fifty-eight minutes. In July 1968, he visited five countries in Central America in one day. Just before leaving the White House in January 1969, he boasted that he had set a record as President by entertaining 201 foreign visitors there. "You've got to slow down," his brother told him shortly after he became President. "This pace will kill you, Lyndon." "Don't you go worrying about me," LBJ told him. "I'll pace myself. These first few weeks have been kinda hectic, but things will settle down pretty soon. Ain't near as bad as being Vice President. Not being able to do anything will wear you down sooner than hard work."[7] But he was never worn down by inaction. Bill Moyers, his press secretary for a time, once playfully told a group of editors: "I'm glad to be here today. At the last minute the President changed his schedule rather suddenly and I almost had to cancel. He has a way of doing that. Not too long ago, he telephoned me in my office and said, 'Bill, I'm going to Honolulu.' I said: 'Fine, Mr. President; I'll come over and talk to you about it. Where are you?' He said: 'Over Los Angeles.' "[8]

LBJ worked his subordinates as hard as he worked himself. He was impatient with slow work and intolerant of inefficiency. When he was director of the National Youth Administration in Texas in the 1930s he made people on his staff work evenings and weekends. One night as he was rushing around checking up on things, he came across a clerk sitting behind a high stack of letters looking miserable. Johnson asked what was wrong, and the man told him discouragedly that he was answering letters one at a time from the top of the stack and then finding later letters from the same people lower in the pile complaining that their earlier letters hadn't been answered. Outraged, Johnson grabbed the stack of mail and turned it upside down. "Start from the top now," he shouted, "and you'll get their latest letters first. That ought to cut your job about in half."[9] As Congressman and later as Senator he continued to be a slave-driver. "I don't have ulcers," he once laughed. "I give 'em!"[10] He used to boast that his aides had to keep milk handy in their desks to soothe their stomachs. Even his wife Lady Bird felt the pressure. "Lyndon was always prodding me to look better, learn more, work harder," she once said. "He always expects more of you than you think you are really mentally or physically capable of putting out. It is really very stimulating. It is also very tiring."[11]

LBJ was a hard taskmaster. He exploded in obscene wrath when people did not meet his standards of performance. Even when they did he couldn't resist teasing them, sometimes cruelly, on occasion. Said one of Johnson's friends: "Lyndon has a clock inside him with an alarm that tells him at least once an hour to chew somebody out. . . ."[12] Johnson admitted as much. "There are no favorites in my office," he once said. "I treat them all with the same general inconsideration."[13] Once he walked into the White House press office and, after glancing at the messy desk of Malcolm Kilduff, Assistant Press Secretary, said: "Kilduff, I hope your mind isn't as cluttered as your desk." Kilduff quickly cleaned up his desk; but a day or so later Johnson saw what he had done and said, "Kilduff, I hope your brain isn't as vacant as your desk."[14] At one conference he gave Secretary of Defense Robert McNamara and Undersecretary of State George Ball such a severe dressing-down that Dean Acheson interposed: "Mr. President, you don't pay these men enough to talk to them that way—even with the federal pay raise."[15] But LBJ's brother insisted, "If he doesn't bawl you out now and then, you ain't part of the family."[16]

Johnson never apologized for his outbursts of temper, but he usually tried to make amends afterward. One day when things went wrong, he blasted his aide Jack Valenti, who returned to his office in low spirits and continued his work. That evening his buzzer rang; it was Johnson calling. "Why don't you call Mary Margaret and see if she can come down to the White House. We can all have supper together. Would you like that?" "Fine, Mr. President," said Valenti. "I'll call her now."[17] On another occasion a visitor was astonished to hear Johnson, on the telephone, let lose a flood of profanity on George Reedy, his press secretary. But he was even more astonished when Johnson hung up and said, "Well, let's give

George his Christmas present now." When the guest expressed surprise, Johnson explained: "You never want to give a man a present when he's up—you want to do it when he's down."[18] But LBJ was kind and generous as well as callous and cruel. He always remembered the birthdays and anniversaries of his staff members, sent flowers and notes to people in the hospital, and even offered to help newsmen (with whom he often feuded) financially if they were in trouble.

Johnson's White House manners tended to be imperious. He liked to talk about "my Supreme Court." Once he even referred to the "State of *My* Union address" in a speech.[19] On one occasion, after reviewing some Vietnam-bound marines he started toward a helicopter, when an officer stopped him, pointed to another location, and said, "That's your helicopter over there, sir." "Son," said LBJ, "they are all my helicopters."[20] In January 1964, hearing of an upheaval in Panama, he told one of his assistants, "Hey, get me the President of Panama—what's his name, anyway? I want to talk to him." "Mr. President," said the aide diffidently, "that isn't protocol. You just can't do things that way." "Who the hell said I can't?" roared Johnson. "Now you just get him on the phone fast." When the connection was made and Roberto Chiari was on the line, Johnson cried: "This is President Johnson. Now, I know you have your own troubles because you've got an election in May. But I want this violence to stop right now."[21] At lunch once, Bill Moyers was saying grace, when Johnson bellowed: "Speak up, Bill! I can't hear a damn thing." Moyers looked up and said quietly, "I wasn't addressing you, Mr. President."[22]

Johnson loved praise and was upset by even the gentlest criticism. After delivering his first State of the Union address to Congress, he was surrounded by his former colleagues and showered with compliments. "Yeah," he whispered to one Senator, "I was interrupted by applause eighty times!"[23] After his speech proposing "Great Society" programs at the University of Michigan in May 1964, a *Newsweek* writer told him, "You had the crowd with you all the way, Mr. President," and noted that the speech had been interrupted by applause twelve times. "There were more than that," said Johnson impatiently and asked Jack Valenti, "How many applauses were there?" "Fourteen," Valenti told him; he included the cheers when the President was introduced and when he sat down at the end.[24] When plans were made to establish a Lyndon Johnson library, an order went out to the White House staff to save every bit of Johnsoniana—including memos, chits, and scribbled notes—for posterity. Bill Moyers, however, continued to use his wastebasket freely and was finally reprimanded by Johnson's personal secretary. A day or so later he went around to her office and dropped a pile of chicken bones on her desk. "Here's something else for the library," he said solemnly. "These are the leftovers from the President's lunch today."[25] Johnson's ego was the inspiration for many jokes in Washington. According to one tale, the Johnsons were visiting the LBJ Ranch and strolling along the Pedernales River one day when Lyndon said, "Bird, are there any reporters or Secret Service men around?" "No, honey." "Then let's try that walking on top the water again."[26] Another tale had it that on a visit to the LBJ ranch, Germany's Ludwig Erhard told Johnson, "I understand you were born in a log cabin, Mr. President." "No, Mr. Chancellor, I was born in a manger."[27]

For all of Johnson's highhandedness, his Presidency was not exactly imperial. Johnson thought of himself mainly as a kind of Big Daddy of the American people. He was folksy as well as domineering, always recalling (and exaggerating) his humble birth and reminding people of what "my Daddy told me." His Daddy, inter multa alia, told him: "that you ain't learnin' nothin' when you're talkin' "; "that you shouldn't rock the boat just for the fun of it"; "that it's better to win a convert than a fight"; "that the time to kill a snake is when you've got the hoe in your hands."[28] In addition to quoting his Daddy, Johnson liked to "press the flesh," that is, shake hands with as many people in a crowd as he could; at the end of a day of campaigning his hands were usually sore and blistered, and sometimes bleeding. With Senators, according to Barry Goldwater, he had two techniques: the Half-Johnson ("when he just put a hand on your shoulder") and the Full-Johnson ("when he put his arm clear around you and thrust his face close to yours").[29]

Johnson was a gifted storyteller. He liked to weave homespun anecdotes and amusing recollections into his speeches and conversations in order to underline the points he was making. He was forever improvising, embroidering, and exaggerating when spinning yarns, so his best stories had numerous versions. One of his favorites explained how he came to adopt the passage "Come, let us reason together," from Isaiah as his guideline. It was a former U.S. Senator,

according to one version of this story, who first called his attention
to the quote. In his early days as a politician, said Johnson, he got
into a fight with the head of a power company who wouldn't let
him build a little Rural Electrification Administration line in his
country district in Texas. LBJ finally blew up and told the man to
go to hell. But an ex-Senator who overheard the exchange reminded
Johnson that "telling a man to go to hell and then making him go
is two different propositions." Explaining, the ex-Senator said: "First
of all, it is hot down there and the average fellow doesn't want to
go. And when you tell him he has to go, he just bristles up and
he is a lot less likely to go than if you hadn't told him anything.
What you better do is get out the Good Book that your mama
used to read to you, and go back to the Prophet Isaiah and read
what he said. He said, 'Come now, let us reason together.' "[30] In
another version, it was Johnson's Daddy, of course, who steered
him to Isaiah.

Not everyone appreciated Johnson's folksiness. Some people, especially in the Northeast, were repelled by his Texas accent, his country-
boy manner, and his rambunctious style. When he playfully picked
up one of his dogs by the ears, he offended dog-lovers everywhere.
He upset the fastidious by swimming nude in the White House pool
and pulling up his shirt to show newsmen the scar from his gall
bladder operation. And he made horrified headlines when he raced
along a country road near his ranch at ninety miles an hour, sipping
beer from a can and scaring reporters in the back seat half to death.
Johnson possessed the social graces and could be courteous and
courtly when he wanted to. But he was also earthy to the core,
and at times he went out of his way to shock people. He scratched
himself and belched loudly whenever he felt like it, used four-letter
words freely at times, helped himself to food on other people's plates
at banquets, and if, in the midst of a conference, he had to go to
the bathroom, he sometimes made his conferees join him there. He
was both in awe of and resentful of the highly educated Ivy Leaguers
on JFK's White House staff. "Sam," he said to Rayburn shortly
after JFK became President, "you should see all the brains the President has rounded up in his cabinet and White House Staff. Why,
those that haven't graduated from Harvard are Ph.D.s—and some
are both." "Yes, Lyndon," said Rayburn, "but I wish just one of
them had run for sheriff in his home county."[31] After Johnson became
President himself, he began thinking as Rayburn did. He could not

escape a feeling that Ivy League Easterners looked down on him as an ignoramus and a boor. "I do not think that I will ever get credit for anything I do . . . ," he said early in his Presidency, "because I did not go to Harvard."[32]

It was the Vietnam War, not the Ivy League, that did LBJ in. If it had not been for Vietnam, said Averill Harriman, "he'd have been the greatest President ever. Even so he'll still be remembered as great."[33] Harriman was thinking of Johnson's domestic policies. "I do not want to be the President who built empires, or sought grandeur, or extended dominions," he once said. "I want to be the President who educated young children . . . who helped to feed the hungry . . . who helped the poor to find their own way and who protected the right of every citizen to vote in every election. . . ."[34] Johnson did all these things and more. His program for the "Great Society" embraced civil-rights legislation, federal aid to education, the expansion of Social Security, Medicare, a war on poverty, and measures to reduce pollution. It also included federal aid to the arts.

In June 1965, President and Mrs. Johnson held a Festival of the Arts at the White House (the first ever sponsored by a President) to which leading lights of literature, art, and music were invited. Poet Robert Lowell declined the invitation because he opposed the President's policy in Vietnam; and several of those attending expressed sympathy with Lowell's views. LBJ was upset by the criticism, but he concealed his irritation and was on hand with Lady Bird to welcome the guests. The festival lasted thirteen hours and included exhibitions of current American painting, sculpture, and photography, programs of American plays, movies, ballet, and music, and readings by well-known American novelists and poets. One participant was Sarah Vaughan, the great jazz singer; for thirty minutes she held her distinguished audience spellbound. Afterward, when the party was breaking up, a White House staffer found Miss Vaughan sobbing in her dressing room. "What's the matter?" she asked. "Nothing is the matter," said the singer. "It's just that twenty years ago when I came to Washington I couldn't even get a hotel room, and tonight I sang for the President of the United States in the White House—and then, he asked me to dance with him. It is more than I can stand!"[35]

★　★　★

Talking to District Engineer

When Johnson was about fifteen years old, he helped his father on a contract to build a small turn in one of the country roads. The work went slowly, and Mr. Johnson hoped his boss, the district engineer in Austin, would not find out that he was behind schedule. One day he sent young Lyndon to Austin to buy some equipment. While the boy was there he ran into the district engineer coming out of a building. "Howdy, Lyndon," said the engineer, "how's the work going with your father?" "Oh," said Lyndon, "we are not having such a good time of it. We're way behind schedule." And he gave details. The next day the engineer showed up at the work site and sharply rebuked Lyndon's father. "Lyndon," said Mr. Johnson after he left, "how do you suppose the district engineer found out about this?" The boy shuffled uneasily for a moment or two, then told his father what he had said in Austin. Looking intently at his son, Mr. Johnson said softly, "Lyndon, now remember this carefully. You just ain't smart enough yet to talk to a district engineer." After Johnson became President and someone on his staff leaked a story to the press without his authorization, he would hold up the press report and say: "I see you've been talking to the district engineer again."[36]

Birthplace

Johnson liked to claim a background similar to Lincoln's. Once, when he was showing some friends around his Texas ranch, he pointed out a ramshackle cabin as his birthplace. "Why, Lyndon," his mother said afterward, "you know you were born in a much better house closer to town which has been torn down." "I know, Mama," said Lyndon, "but everybody has to have a birthplace."[37]

Confusion

While he was a student at Southwest Texas State Teachers College in San Marcos, young Johnson became an assistant to Cecil Evans, the president. He threw himself into his work with such enthusiasm that Evans finally exclaimed: "Lyndon, I declare you hadn't been in my office a month before I could hardly tell who was president of the school—you or me."[38]

Objectivity

One of LBJ's favorite Depression stories had to do with a young man, desperate for a job, who appeared before a school board in the Texas Hill Country as an applicant for a teaching position. The board was impressed; the man was eloquent, well-informed, and conscientious. When the interview ended, one of the board members said, "Well, we think we would like to have you teach and we would like to retain your services. But tell us, there is some difference of opinion in our community about geography. And we want to know which side you are on. Do you teach that the world is round, or do you teach that the world is flat?" Said the young man at once: "I can teach it either way."[39]

Affirmative Results

One time when Johnson was in Congress, he told a new employee of his to call a government agency about a request from one of his constituents. The employee made the call; a few hours later LBJ came to his desk and asked for the result. "The thing is settled," the man told him, "because they insisted they couldn't do what you wanted." Johnson was furious. "I didn't ask you to get me a negative answer!" he stormed. "Say that I want this done for certain and get an affirmative answer!" The man promptly called again and this time used Johnson's peremptory tone: "Congressman Johnson will be satisfied with nothing less than affirmative action on his request." The official at once agreed to it. "From then on," said Johnson's employee afterward, "I concentrated on getting affirmative results, not negative."[40]

Foreman

"What's the hurry?" one Senator complained to another when the hard-driving Majority Leader, Lyndon Johnson, kept the Senate working late. "After all, Rome wasn't built in a day." "No," sighed the other Senator, "but Lyndon Johnson wasn't foreman on that job."[41]

The Johnson Treatment

When Johnson was Senate Majority Leader, he employed the "Johnson method" in seeking support for his strategy. He never just

shook hands with his colleagues; he poked them in the chest while
he cajoled them, stuck his head under their faces, put his arm around
them, and pawed them all over. Sometimes he even kicked their
shins as he was giving his pep talk. He was especially importunate
with Senator Hubert Humphrey of Minnesota. "Look," said Humphrey to some friends after an encounter with LBJ; pulling up his
trouser leg, he displayed a couple of cuts on his shins where Johnson
had kicked him and cried, "Get going now!"[42]

Information

Just before the 1956 Democratic convention, Senator Johnson called
Newsweek's Sam Shaffer to his office and dressed him down for quoting a Democratic politician on LBJ's plans at the convention. "If
you want to know what Lyndon Baines Johnson is going to do at
the convention," he scolded, "why didn't you come to Lyndon Baines
Johnson and ask him what Lyndon Baines Johnson was going to
do?" "All right," said Shaffer, "what is Lyndon Baines Johnson
going to do at the convention?" "I don't know," said Johnson.[43]

Learner

When Vice-President Johnson, in Paris on a mission for President
Kennedy, met General Charles de Gaulle for the first time, the latter
looked imperiously at Johnson and said loftily: "Now, Mr. Johnson,
what have you come to learn from us?" Johnson beamed and replied,
"Why, General, simply everything you can possibly teach me."[44]

Amarillo

On a visit to American troops stationed in Iceland and Greenland,
Vice-President Johnson was asked by reporters if he was uncomfort-
ably cold. "Golly, no!" replied Johnson. "We've got some of this
back home in Texas. You take the Panhandle, for instance. We get
hail there the size of a basketball, and the snow piles up so deep
the people have to follow the jackrabbit tunnels out when the spring
comes. Why, one of our boys who was up here in Greenland said
that life could be a heck of a lot worse. When a gloomy roommate
asked him how any place could be any worse, he answered, 'Well,
we could be back in Amarillo.' "[45]

LBJ and Russell Baker

Early in 1961, Russell Baker, then covering Capitol Hill for the *New York Times*, was coming out of the Senate when he ran into Vice-President Johnson. Johnson grabbed him, cried, "*You*, I've been looking for *you*,"pulled him into his office, and began a long harangue about how important he was to the Kennedy administration and what an insider he really was. While he was talking, he scribbled something on a piece of paper and rang the buzzer. His secretary came in, took the paper, and left the room; she returned a few minutes later and handed the paper back to him Still talking, LBJ glanced at the paper, crumpled it up, threw it away, and finally finished his monologue. Later Baker learned that Johnson had written on the paper: "Who is this I'm talking to?"[46]

Refinement

An American diplomat once met Vice-President Johnson at the Rome airport and on the way into the city instructed him methodically, as if he were an ignorant backwoodsman, on how to behave when he met the local dignitaries. Johnson listened patiently throughout. When they arrived at the hotel, the diplomat said, "Mr. Vice President, is there anything else I can do for you?" "Yes," said Johnson sharply, "just one thing. Button up your shirt."[47]

Desegregation

Shortly after he became President, LBJ integrated the Forty Acres Club, faculty club for the University of Texas, in Austin. He simply walked into the club's dining room with a handsome black woman on his staff. "Mr. President," said the woman rather nervously beforehand, "do you know what you are doing?" "I sure do," LBJ assured her. "Half of them are going to think you're my wife and that's just fine with me." After LBJ's appearance the club abandoned its age-old segregationist policy.[48]

Dialogue of Brothers

At the time of the 1964 convention, LBJ called his brother Sam to get suggestions for choosing his running mate that year. Sam was convinced his brother had already decided on Hubert Humphrey, but in order to smoke him out, he proceeded to use the "reverse-elimination gambit." "I kinda like Senator Pastore myself," he told LBJ. "Goddammit, Sam Houston," snorted LBJ, "what in hell's gone wrong with you? How could an Italian from a dinky state like Rhode Island possibly help me?" "There's Adlai," said Sam. "He's got the egghead vote good and solid." "Don't need him," said LBJ shortly. "With Barry Goldwater running, I look like a Harvard professor to the eggheads." "Maybe you oughta get a Catholic like Gene McCarthy," said Sam. "He's awfully strong in the Midwest." "He's not exactly what I'm looking for," said LBJ. "There's something sort of stuck-up about Gene. You get the impression that he's got a special pipeline to God and that they talk only Latin to each other." "How about Mayor Wagner or Daley?" "With Goldwater running, I don't have to worry about the big-city vote." "Well, hell, Lyndon," said Sam, "that leaves only Hubert, and you sure ain't picking him, are you?" "Now what the damn hell have you got against Hubert?" cried LBJ. "Plenty, Lyndon," said Sam. "For God's sake, he's been fighting you for years. No one's bugged you more on civil rights; and look at the way he's always harping about the oil people. He's a damned maverick, Lyndon." "Dammit, Sam Houston," cried LBJ in great exasperation, "you've got him all wrong. Hubert's a good man. I've made a goddamned Christian out of him. He's gone along with me on a lot of things. He also happens to be a helluva good campaigner." "He talks too much," interposed Sam. "Don't worry about that," said LBJ. "I'll get Muriel to keep him short." "So you've already made up your mind," said Sam, smiling to himself. "Not yet," insisted LBJ. "I'm keeping it open awhile. I want to talk with some more people."[49]

Deduction

Once Johnson played a game of dominoes with Arthur Krim, head of United Artists Corporation, who was spending a weekend at the Johnson ranch, and won two hundred dollars from him before the night was over. Next morning he took Krim to church with him. When the collection plate came around LBJ pulled out two hundred-dollar bills. "Here's the money I won from you, Arthur," he said, "It's going to a good cause." Then, as he dropped the bills into the plate, Krim smiled broadly and said, "That's fine, Mr. President. Now I can declare it as a deduction from my income tax."[50]

No Sermon

LBJ had a vast store of preacher stories. One of his favorites was about the clergyman who dropped his sermon notes while heading for church and couldn't retrieve them before the dog chewed them up. "When the preacher went into the pulpit," said LBJ, "he apologized to his congregation and said, 'I am very sorry, today I have no sermon. I will just have to speak as the Lord directs. But I will try to do better next Sunday.' "[51]

Crow and Owl

At a National Security Council meeting, LBJ looked ahead at the agenda, saw some knotty problems coming up, and paused to tell a joke to relieve the tension. "That reminds me of two Indians," he said. "The first invited the second home to dinner. 'What are you having?' asked the second. 'Crow,' said the first. 'Crow—that's not fit to eat, is it?' complained the second. 'Better'n owl,' replied the first."[52]

Salt of the Earth

LBJ was probably the earthiest man ever to occupy the White House. Asked, while he was Senate Majority Leader, why he didn't take one of Vice-President Nixon's speeches more seriously, he exclaimed, "Boys, I may not know much, but I know the difference between chicken shit and chicken salad." Of a Kennedy aide he once said: "He doesn't have sense enough to pour piss out of a boot with the instructions written on the heel." After becoming President he comtemplated getting rid of FBI Chief J. Edgar Hoover and then decided it would be too difficult to bring off. "Well," he said philosophically, "it's probably better to have him inside the tent pissing out, than outside pissing in." And once, driving around his ranch with a CBS television team, he stopped to urinate in the underbrush. "Aren't you afraid a rattlesnake might bite it?" asked a CBS cameraman. "Hell," snorted Johnson, "it *is* part rattlesnake."[53]

Fun

One day, shortly after he became President, while driving some reporters around his ranch outside Johnson City LBJ came across a big sow surrounded by a half dozen tiny piglets. Stopping his car abruptly, Johnson announced that he would pose for pictures if anyone in the party could catch one of the little pigs. At once a couple of the photographers hopped out of the car and started chasing the piglets. But, as Johnson had foreseen, the angry sow began charging furiously after them. As the reporters fell all over themselves trying to get out of the way, Johnson hooted with glee, honked the cow horn on his car and started yelling: "Whooee! Whooee!" Finally one of the reporters succeeded in running a piglet to the ground, and Johnson obligingly posed for a picture. "Mr. President," exclaimed the reporter afterward, "you're fun!"[54]

Special Delivery

LBJ insisted that Lawrence F. O'Brien take his oath of office as Postmaster General in a little post office in Hye, Texas, where he recalled mailing his first letter at the age of four. "It was about fifty-three years ago," said LBJ at the ceremony, "that I mailed my first letter from this post office. And Larry O'Brien told me a few moments ago that he is going out to find that letter and deliver it."[55]

Country Boy

When a railroad executive turned to Johnson and said, "I'm just a country boy—," Johnson interrupted: "Hold on, there. Wait a minute. When anyone approaches me that way I know I'm going to lose my wallet."[56]

Quit Listening

LBJ was a compulsive talker; he turned the guided tours of his ranch into long monologues. But when he took *Dallas News* columnist

Allen Duckworth on a ride around the ranch with Ed Clark, million-aire banker and lumberman, things didn't go as LBJ had expected. As soon as Johnson turned on the motor of his car, Clark started talking. Johnson sped over a few hills and then, becoming impatient, ordered Clark to stop talking. But Clark went on and on. "Clark, please shut up! " LBJ finally exploded. "I want to tell Duckworth something! " But Clark paid no attention to him. Finally Johnson gripped Duckworth's thigh. "If Clark won't stop talking," he cried, "you quit listening to him! "[57]

Higher Learning

At a small dinner party honoring Canadian Prime Minister Lester Pearson, Johnson lifted his glass to toast the assembly (which in-cluded Dean Rusk, Robert McNamara, Nicholas Katzenbach, and McGeorge Bundy) and cried: "It is gratifying to see at this table tonight the most superbly educated men in the world, for in this room there are three Rhodes scholars, four graduates of Harvard, three of Yale, and one from Southwest State Teachers College."[58]

Passing Lubbock

To make the point that you can push things too far, LBJ once recalled what had happened to Senator Tom Connally, an enthusiastic orator, when he got too wound up. "The Senator was speaking down home," said Johnson, "about the beautiful piney woods of east Texas. Then he moved on through the bluebonnets and out to the plains and down through the hill country to the Gulf Coast, and then he got back to the piney woods and started all over again. After he got all around the state that time and started in again about those beauti-ful piney woods and bluebonnets, a little old fellow rose up in the back of the room and yelled out 'The next time you pass Lubbock, how about letting me off?' "[59]

Redemption or Conversion

Johnson liked to tell the story of the woman who phoned her bank to arrange for the disposition of a thousand-dollar bond. The clerk asked her, "Madam, is the bond for redemption or conversion?" There was a long pause; then the woman said, "Well, am I talking to the First National Bank or the First Baptist Church?"[60]

Voting Rights

LBJ enjoyed the story of the two fellows who went to a graveyard just before a Texas election and began copying down the names on the tombstones. Up and down the rows they went getting names until they came to a tombstone so old and worn that it was hard to decipher the name on it. One of them wanted to skip it, but the other tried hard to read the inscription. "What's the matter with you?" cried the impatient one. "Why are you staying here?" "Well, Ah care," said the second fellow. "This man's got every bit as much right to vote as all the rest of these fellows here."[61]

Segregation

In a 1964 speech aimed at persuading businessmen to give American blacks greater opportunities, LBJ described the problems faced by Zephyr Wright, the family's housekeeper and cook, because of her color. "She has been with us twenty years," said Johnson, "she is a college graduate, but when she comes from Texas to Washington she never knows where she can get a cup of coffee. She never knows when she can go to the bathroom. She has to take three or four hours out of her time to go across to the other side of the tracks to locate a place where she can sit down and buy a meal. You wouldn't want that to happen to your wife or your mother or your sister, but somehow or other you take it for granted when it happens to someone way off there."[62]

Education and the Constitution

"I remember," LBJ once said, "when I was at San Marcos and was given a test by this history professor or political science professor, I forget which. The question he put on the blackboard was this, 'Discuss fully what the federal Constitution has to say about education.' So I did, and, hell, it must have gone on for ten pages or so. Well, I got that paper back with a big red F across it. And the professor wrote on the paper, 'The Constitution doesn't mention education.' Well, I decided right then and there that if there wasn't anything in the Constitution on the subject of education, there ought to have been. And I decided I was going to do something about it,

and if you look back on the bills that were passed during my administration, I think you might say that I have."[63]

Arrogance of Power

President Johnson was upset by his old friend Senator J. William
Fulbright's criticism of his Vietnam policy and by his warning against
the "arrogance of power" in high office. One evening in May 1966,
encountering Fulbright in the receiving line at a diplomatic reception,
he reached into his pocket, pulled out a penciled note from his housekeeper Zephyr Wright, and held Fulbright there. "A man can hardly
have an arrogance of power," he cried, "when he gets a note from
his cook talking up to him like this." Lady Bird tried to pull him
away, but he said, "Bird, I'll be ready in a minute," and started
reading the note aloud: "Mr. President, you have been my boss
for a number of years and you always tell me you want to lose
weight, and yet you never do very much to help yourself. Now
I'm going to be your boss for a change. Eat what I put in front of
you and don't ask for any more and don't complain." When LBJ
finished reading, Fulbright gave him a quizzical smile and moved
on.[64]

Geography

In addressing Democratic gatherings, LBJ frequently warned against
regional prejudices and called for "a truly national party which is
stranger to no region, an open party which is closed to none, which
knows no color, knows no creed, knows no North, no South, no
East, no West." But occasionally he poked fun at these points-of-
the-compass references. "Of course," he said in one speech, "I do
not want to go as far as the Georgia politician who shouted from
the stump in the heat of debate, 'My fellow citizens, I know no
North, I know no South, I know no East, I know no West.' A
barefooted, freckle-faced boy shouted out from the audience, 'Well,
you better go back and study some geography!' "[65]

Rebekah Baines Johnson Home

Before he left the White House, LBJ sponsored the construction of
a model nursing home in Austin. "We treat old people like we treat

animals," he told his special counsel Larry Temple. "Just put them
in a cage somewhere until they die." He said he planned to get
some money for the project from the Department of Health, Education, and Welfare, and he asked Temple to get additional funds
from the University of Texas. Temple persuaded Frank Erwin, Chairman of the University Board of Regents, to support the project,
and Erwin suggested naming it the Rebekah Baines Johnson Home
after the President's mother. When Temple told him this, LBJ blew
up. "Why should you tie my poor mother into that and tie me
into that?" he cried. "Somebody will catch this. The *New York Times*
will write it up that I was spending a bunch of federal money for
a memorial to my mother." He insisted that Erwin "forget that he
ever mentioned my mother in connection with it." After Johnson
left the White House the nursing home was finally completed with
the help of the Catholic diocese, and plans were made to name it
after a Catholic bishop. Hearing this, LBJ again exploded. "Larry,"
he told Temple, "what are they doing to me? You and Frank Erwin
promised me that they would name it after my mother. All these
years I have relied upon that, that it would be named for my mother."
"Mr. President," said Temple, "I thought you didn't want it named
after your mother." "Where did you get a silly idea like that?" cried
LBJ. "Why sure, I want it named after my mother. It would be a
great honor to have it named after her. You promised me it would
be named after my mother, and I counted on it, and now they aren't
going to." Shortly afterward, the Rebekah Baines Johnson Nursing
Home opened its doors.[66]

Bitch of a War

In his last years LBJ is supposed to have said of the Vietnam War
which destroyed his Presidency: "The kids were right. I blew it."
To Doris Kearns, Harvard professor who worked with him on his
autobiography, he confessed: "I knew from the start that if I left
the woman I really loved—the Great Society—in order to fight that
bitch of a war . . . then I would lose everything at home. All my
hopes . . . my dreams. . . ."[67]

Richard M. Nixon
1969–74

Richard M. Nixon (b. 1913), the first President ever to resign, was the most controversial of all our chief Executives. He was also one of the most elusive. H. R. Haldeman, his chief of staff, called him "inexplicable, strange, hard to understand," while special assistant Raymond Price said he was like Churchill's Russia: a mystery wrapped in an enigma enclosed in a paradox.[1] To Harry Truman, however, there was no mystery. "Nixon," he once exclaimed, "is a shifty-eyed, goddam liar, and people know it."[2] Truman's vehemence was understandable. Nixon launched his career in the late 1940s charging that the Truman administration was riddled with subversives and traitors; and in the fall of 1952, campaigning as Dwight Eisenhower's running mate, he said the Truman administration had "covered up this Communist conspiracy and attempted to halt its exposure."[3]

Then Nixon—who had acquired the nickname "Tricky Dick"— ran into trouble. In the midst of the 1952 campaign came the sudden revelation that some wealthy California businessmen were secretly supplementing Nixon's senatorial income with contributions of their own. Nixon insisted that the fund went to defray political expenses and was not spent for his personal use. He also insisted that the Communists were using the fund issue to smear him. But Eisenhower, who insisted that his running mate be as "clean as a hound's tooth," was inclined to drop Nixon from the ticket.[4] On September 23, therefore, Nixon appeared on television to explain the fund and defend his integrity.

The telecast attracted wide attention. In his speech, the embattled Senator made much of his humble beginnings and his rise in life by grit, determination, self-denial, and hard work. He also talked about his dog. "One other thing I probably should tell you," he said, "because if I don't they will probably be saying this about me, too. We did get something, a gift, after the nomination. A man down in Texas heard Pat on the radio mention the fact that our two youngsters would like to have a dog and, believe it or not, the day before we left on this campaign trip we got a message from Union Station in Baltimore, saying they had a package for us. We went down to get it. You know what it was? It was a little cocker spaniel dog, in a crate that had been sent all the way from Texas—black and white, spotted, and our little girl Tricia, the six-year-old, named it Checkers. And you know, the kids, like all kids, loved the dog, and I just want to say this, right now, that regardless of what they say about it, we are going to keep it."[5] *Variety,* the show-business journal, ridiculed the "Checkers speech" as "a slick production," but Hollywood producer Darryl Zanuck telephoned to say: "The most tremendous performance I've ever seen!"[6]

Nixon himself thought the speech had failed, and he wept. "I loused it up, and I am sorry . . .," he told friends. "It was a flop."[7] Outside the television studio, as his car pulled away, he slumped into the seat beside his wife and stared despondently out the window. Suddenly he spied a huge Irish setter bounding gaily alongside the car, barking noisily. "Well," he sighed, "we made a hit in the dog world, anyway." But actually he did better than that.[8] Thousands of telegrams poured into Republican national headquarters praising him, and in the end he remained on the ticket. Three years later, when he spoke at a luncheon given by the Radio and Television Executives Society, he could not resist a facetious reference to the famous telecast. At one point he leaned across the lectern, grinned, and asked: "You all remember the 'Checkers' speech, I suppose?" Then, as his audience chuckled, he said: "Well, I want you to be the first to know," and he paused dramatically, "I staged it."[9]

In 1960, When Nixon ran for President against Kennedy, there was considerable talk about a "new Nixon." He continued to be a hard-liner in foreign affairs, but he no longer went in for domestic witch-hunting. The 1960 election turned out to be extremely close, and there were voting frauds in several states. For a time Nixon considered the possibility of demanding a recount, but finally decided against it. "If I were to demand a recount," he explained, "the organization of the new administration and the orderly transfer of responsibility from the old to the new might be delayed for months. The situation within the entire federal government would be chaotic." Despite his decision, newsman Earl Mazo launched an investigation of the voting frauds and began running a series of articles about them in the *New York Herald Tribune*. Early in December 1960, after the first four articles had appeared, Nixon invited Mazo to his home for a chat. "Earl," he said, as they shook hands, "those are interesting articles you are writing—but no one steals the presidency of the United States." He went on to say that the country would be torn by partisan bitterness if there was an official challenge of the election result and that the damage to America's foreign relations might be irreparable. "Our country," he told Mazo, "can't afford the agony of a constitutional crisis—and I damn well will not be a party to creating one just to become President or anything else." Mazo agreed to drop the series.[10]

In 1968, when Nixon entered the presidential race again, the "new Nixon" once more became the talk of the town. "I believe there really is a 'new Nixon,' " wrote Walter Lippmann, "a maturer and mellower man who is no longer clawing his way to the top."[11] Nixon agreed. "There certainly is a new Nixon," he averred. "I realize, too, that as a man gets older he learns something. If I haven't learned something I am not worth anything."[12] What had he learned? Chiefly, that the Communist countries of the world did not form a monolithic bloc and that it might be possible to develop better relations with them. When he became President, he made a surprise visit to China to confer with Communist leaders there; he also attended a "summit" meeting in Moscow to reach an agreement on a strategic arms limitations treaty (SALT) for moderating the arms race. His great aim as President was to "create a new structure of peace in the world," and his achievements in that direction were considerable.[13] One night, discussing former Presidents with senior speech writer William Safire, he mused: "You think of Truman—a fighter. Eisenhower—a good man. Kennedy—charisma. Johnson—work. Me—what?" "Competence," exclaimed Safire; then, seeing Nixon's disappointment, he quickly added, "Sorry about that." "Hell," said Nixon, "if all we do is manage things 10 per cent better, we'll never be remembered for anything."[14]

Nixon wanted to be remembered for the things Woodrow Wilson

was remembered for: his efforts to establish a just and lasting peace in the world. Wilson was his favorite President; his picture was on Nixon's office wall. Nixon admired him so much, in fact, that shortly after his inauguration he had the huge desk Wilson had supposedly used moved into the Oval Office for his own use. He liked to sit with his feet on the Wilson desk while working, and after a while his heels began leaving scars on the top of it. Once, when he was on a trip abroad, someone noticed the damage to the mahogany surface and sent the desk out to be refinished. When Nixon returned and saw that his heel marks had been removed, he cried: "Dammit. I didn't order that. I want to leave *my* mark on this place just like other Presidents!"[15]

Nixon left his mark on the Presidency, but it was not precisely the mark he had hoped to leave. First came the fall of his Vice-President, Spiro Agnew. Caught in bribery and tax-evasion schemes, Agnew was forced to resign in October 1973. Nixon chose Republican Congressman Gerald R. Ford of Michigan to replace him. Then came Nixon's own downfall. In June 1972, during the presidential campaign, five men were arrested for burglarizing the Democratic headquarters at the Watergate apartments in Washington, D.C. It turned out that they were working for the Republican Committee to Re-elect the President. When he heard about it, Nixon authorized a cover-up. But the crime could not be concealed. Before long it came out that Nixon's inner-circle staff had planned the Watergate burglary and, when it fizzled, had tried, with the President's help, to keep their involvement a secret. All sorts of other revelations began surfacing during 1973 and 1974: the use of campaign contributions to win government favors; illegal use of such funds on behalf of the Watergate defendants; devious ways, including tax evasion, of making Nixon a millionaire; a campaign of political "dirty tricks" to ensure Nixon's victory in 1972; and plans to use government agencies to intimidate Nixon's political foes. In the end, twenty men who had been acting on the President's behalf were convicted of various crimes relating to Watergate. And despite Nixon's repeated protestations of innocence, it became abundantly clear that the President had been involved in the cover-up and obstruction of justice from the beginning.

By the summer of 1974, as the House of Representatives prepared to vote articles of impeachment against Nixon, even his staunchest friends and allies were urging him to resign. "There are only so many lies you can take and now there has been one too many," Senator Barry Goldwater exclaimed. "Nixon should get his ass out of the White House—today!" When Republican leaders, headed by Goldwater, met with the President to discuss the situation, Nixon reminisced about the Eisenhower years for a while and confessed that he had cried when Ike died. "If I were to become an ex-President," he went on to say, with a weak smile, "I'd have no ex-Presidents to pal around with." Then he got to the matter at hand. "I have a decision to make," he said gravely. "What I need to do is get your appraisal of the floor." "Mr. President," said Goldwater, "if it comes to a trial in the Senate, I don't think you can count on more than fifteen votes." "And no more than ten in the House, John?" Nixon asked House Minority Leader John J. Rhodes of Arizona. "Maybe more, Mr. President," said Rhodes, "but not much more." "And I really campaigned for a lot of them," said Nixon ruefully. "But that's all right. That's politics. Hugh, what's your assessment of the Senate?" "I'd say twelve or fifteen, Mr. President," Senator Hugh Scott of Pennsylvania replied; and he added: "Gloomy." "Damned gloomy," repeated Nixon. "These are sad times, Mr. President," said Scott as the meeting broke up. "Don't you bother about that, Hugh," said Nixon. "Do your duty and God bless you."[16]

On August 8, 1974, Nixon appeared on television to announce his resignation. "I would say only," he declared, "that if some of my judgments were wrong—and some were wrong—they were made in what I believed at the time to be in the best interest of the nation. . . ." A month later, in accepting a pardon by his successor, Jerry Ford, he said: "No words can describe the depth of my regret and pain at the anguish my mistakes over Watergate have caused this nation. . . ."[17] He did not seem to realize that Watergate was more than a blunder.

★ ★ ★

Last Press Conference

On November 5, 1962, Nixon lost his bid for the Governorship of California to Edmund G. ("Pat") Brown after a heated campaign. His disappointment was so tremendous that he was reluctant to appear before newsmen the next morning to concede defeat. "They're all waiting," press secretary Herbert Klein told him. "You've got to go down." "Screw them," cried Nixon; he thought the press had treated him unfairly during the campaign. "I told them you'd make a statement," insisted Klein. Nixon finally yielded.

"Good morning, gentlemen," said the defeated candidate grimly as he walked into the Cadoro Room of Los Angeles's Beverly Hilton, where more than a hundred newspapermen awaited him. "Now that Mr. Klein has made his statement, and now that all the members of the press are so delighted that I have lost, I'd like to make a statement of my own." As the newsmen gaped, Nixon went on to vent his deep-seated bitterness over the outcome of the election. "I congratulate Governor Brown . . . for his victory . . .," he said. "I believe Governor Brown has a heart, even though he believes I do not. I believe he is a good American, even though he feels I am not." Then he began to scold the press. "I am proud of the fact that I defended my opponent's patriotism," he exclaimed. "You gentlemen didn't report it, but I am proud I did that." Glaring at the reporters, he continued, "I am proud also that I defended the fact that he was a man of good motives, a man that I disagreed with very strongly, but a man of good motives. I want that—for once, gentlemen—I would appreciate if you would write what I say, in that respect. I think it's very important that you write it. *In the lead. In the lead.*"

Nixon rambled on for a few more minutes and then seemed about to end the conference. "As I leave the press," he said bitterly, "all I can say is this: for 16 years . . . you've had a lot of fun—that you've had an opportunity to attack me and that I think I've given as much as I've taken. It was carried right up to the last day." He recalled that during the campaign he had made a slip of the tongue which the *Los Angeles Times* dutifully reported; but that when Brown had also made a tongue-slip the *Times* overlooked it. "I think," he said angrily, "it's time that our great newspapers have at least the same objectivity, the same fullness of coverage, that television has. And I can only say thank God for television and radio for keeping the newspapers a little more honest." After a few more remarks along these lines, he finally exclaimed: "But as I leave you I want you to know—just think how much you're going to be missing. You won't have Nixon to kick around anymore, because, gentlemen, this is my last press conference. . . ." After it was all over, Nixon turned to Klein, who was obviously upset, and said: "I know you don't agree. I gave it to them right in the behind. It had to be said, goddammit. It had to be said."[18]

Stand Pat

Vice-President Nixon and his wife, Pat, one story goes, attended a Republican fund-raising dinner in Chicago where in his address Nixon warned Republicans against "the temptation to stand pat on what we have done." One reporter who covered the dinner was aghast when he saw page proof for his paper's first edition. There was an eight-column headline: "Can't Stand Pat, Says Nixon." The next time he delivered his address, according to the story (unfortunately apocryphal), Nixon said "stand still" instead of stand "pat."[19]

Seventh Crisis

In 1962, when Nixon was autographing his book, Six Crises, in a California bookstore, he asked one purchaser to whom he should address his greeting. "You've just met your seventh crisis," said the customer. "My name is Stanislaus Wojechzleschki!"[20]

Dropout

After losing the election to Kennedy in 1960, Nixon, who had not done well in TV debates with JFK, called himself a "dropout from the Electoral College because I flunked debating."[21]

Envy

After hearing Kennedy's inaugural address, Nixon happened to encounter Ted Sorensen, one of Kennedy's aides; they began discussing it. "I wish I had said some of those things," said Nixon. "What part?" Sorensen wanted to know. "That part about 'Ask not what your country can do for you . . .'?" "No," said Nixon. "The part that starts, 'I do solemnly swear.' "[22]

Stoned

Speaking to the U.S. Junior Chamber of Commerce in Detroit in June 1966, Nixon discussed his travels in South America, where stones had been thrown at him, and remarked: "I got stoned in Caracas. I'll tell you one thing; it's a lot different from getting stoned at a Jaycee convention."[23]

Enemies List

As President, Nixon put journalist Daniel Schorr, one of his critics, on his "Enemies List" and instructed the FBI to look into his background. When the story leaked out, Press Secretary Ron Ziegler was instructed to say that Schorr was under consideration for a White House appointment that someone had neglected to tell him about. Years later, to Schorr's surprise, he was invited to a dinner at which the former President gave an off-the-record briefing about his recent trip to Eastern Europe. When Schorr rose to identify himself and ask a question, Nixon gave no indication that he recognized Schorr's name. But at the end of the evening, unable to resist the temptation, Schorr went over to Nixon and said, "I'm not sure you will remember me, but. . . ." Nixon interrupted him with a hearty handshake and exclaimed: "Dan Schorr, of course I remember you. Damn near hired you once."[24]

Salary Boost

In an elaborately staged, televised ceremony in the White House East Room on the night of October 12, 1973, Nixon nominated Congressman Gerald Ford as Spiro Agnew's replacement as Vice-President. At the champagne reception after the announcement, Nixon put his arm around Ford's wife, Betty, and said, "It's all yours!" "Mr. President," said she, "I don't know whether you're offering congratulations or condolences." "Oh, well," returned Nixon, "the pay is better."[25]

Watergate

When Nixon appeared on "Larry King Live" in January 1992, two years before his death, King asked him: "Is it hard to drive by the Watergate?" "Well," said Nixon, "I've never been in the Watergate." "Never been in?" cried King, somewhat surprised. "No," said Nixon. Then he added: "Other people were in there, though— unfortunately."[26]

Gerald R. Ford
1974–77

Gerald R. ("Jerry") Ford (b. 1913) was the first man to become
President by appointment rather than by election. Appointed Vice-
President by President Nixon when Spiro Agnew resigned in disgrace,
he became the thirty-seventh President of the United States when
Nixon himself resigned under threat of impeachment. "He was,"
as his wife Betty put it, "an accidental Vice President, and an accidental President, and in both jobs he replaced disgraced leaders."[1] Not
long after he became President, Ford took a vacation in Vail, Colorado, to do some skiing. One night when he was eating dinner with
his family, one of the dogs had an accident, and a red-jacketed
White House steward rushed over to wipe up the mess. But Ford
got up from the table at once, took the rag away from the steward,
and cleaned the floor himself. "No man," he said, "should have to
clean up after another man's dog." Ford's gesture was typical. Good-
natured, unpretentious, and easygoing, he was anxious to show that
there was nothing "imperial" about his Presidency.[2]

Ford was "Mr. Nice Guy." He was, someone said, a "Boy Scout
in the White House." By his own admission, he was "disgustingly
sane."[3] "The nicest thing about Jerry Ford," said Michigan Senator
Robert P. Griffin, "is that he just doesn't have enemies."[4] Even
Congressman Paul ("Pete") McCloskey of California, who opposed
Ford on vital issues, thought well of him. "I can get tears in my
eyes," he said, "when I think about Jerry Ford. We love him."[5]

But Ford's critics questioned his capacity for leadership. In fact there was a tendency at first for some reporters to consider it newsworthy whenever Ford took any action at all in his capacity as President. To Ford's irritation, news stories in the early months of his Presidency reported that he was "acting presidential," "assuming a presidential posture," "going to play president," or "trying to look presidential." But Ford insisted he was not "acting presidential"; he *was* President.[6] One of his first presidential acts—pardoning Richard Nixon for "any and all crimes"—stirred up a storm. Ford hoped to "heal the nation's wounds" by his act, but many people thought it unfair to pardon Nixon while men who acted on his behalf were punished.[7]

Sixty-two when he entered the White House, Ford, a former college football player, was in splendid physical shape; he was without question the most athletic Chief Executive since Theodore Roosevelt. He continued to ski, swim, and play golf and tennis as President, and he was good at all these sports. Still, in May 1975, when he was coming down the ramp of his plane in Salzburg, Austria, his shoe got caught on a protuberance, and he tumbled to the tarmac below. He jumped to his feet unhurt but, to his surprise, reporters considered the fall a newsworthy event. Later that day his foot slid twice on the long, rain-slicked staircase at the Residenz Palace, and a legend was born: Ford was awkward and ungainly.[8] After Salzburg, every time Ford stumbled, or bumped his head, or fell in the snow, reporters conscientiously told the world about it. It came to be news, in fact, when he didn't stumble. CBS once reported that a campaign trip he made was "remarkably free of gaffes." But an Oklahoma reporter confessed: "I kept wishing the president would bump his head or skin his shins or suffer some small mishap for me to peg a paragraph on."[9]

Ford's press secretary, Ron Nessen, vigorously protested the way reporters were giving the American people the impression that Ford was a clumsy oaf. "The president," he told them, "is healthy, graceful, and he is by far the most athletic president in memory."[10] But on television Johnny Carson poked fun at Ford, and comedian Chevy Chase did takeoffs on the President's slips and falls on the "Saturday Night Live" show. "I'm an activist," Ford complained. "Activists are more prone to stumble than anyone else."[11] But he took the ribbing in good humor. In March 1976, he agreed to be on the same program with Chevy Chase at the annual banquet of the Radio-

Television Correspondents Association in Washington. Chase came first. While the band played "Hail to the Chief," he stumbled and fell across the entire width of the hotel ballroom, bumped his head on the rostrum, and then said, "I have asked the Secret Service to remove the salad fork embedded in my left hand." Ford laughed with everyone else. When his turn came, he got up, pretended to get tangled in the tablecloth, dropped dishes and silverware on the floor, and then, making as if to put the text of his speech on the podium, scattered papers all over the place. "Mr. Chevy Chase," he said, as the audience roared, "you are a very, very funny suburb."[12]

Jokes about Ford's intelligence were harder to take. When Ford was Republican Minority Leader in Congress in the 1960s, President Johnson, irked by the conservative Michigander's opposition to his "Great Society" proposals, made several unkind remarks that quickly got around in Washington. Ford, Johnson said, had "played football too long without a helmet." He also said that Ford "is so dumb he can't walk and fart at the same time." When Ford opposed his Model Cities legislation, Johnson told one of his assistants, "Joe, you've got a little baby boy. Well, you take his little building blocks and go up and explain to Jerry Ford what we're trying to do."[13] Ford took the jokes about him in good humor and pretended he didn't mind them. But occasionally he would remind people that he had graduated in the top third of his class at both the University of Michigan and the Yale Law School. In March 1968, he decided to respond to LBJ's jibes. While preparing a speech for the annual dinner of the Gridiron Club, he dug up an old leather football helmet that he had worn at the All-Star game in Chicago in 1935. He took it to the dinner, and, called on to speak, he stood up and tried to put it on. When the flaps didn't fit easily over his ears, he grinned and said it was because "heads tend to swell in Washington." He brought the house down with his clowning.[14]

Ford had tongue-slips as well as tumbles. "Mr. Ford often fumbles his words," noted *New Republic* writer John Osborne. "He often says more or less than he meant to say. He often had to confess later that he didn't mean to say exactly what he'd actually said."[15] "If Lincoln were alive today," Ford once said, in a widely quoted remark, "he'd roll over in his grave."[16] In a speech at Iowa State, he referred to "Ohio State" and then quickly corrected himself.[17] Speaking at Mesa College in Grand Junction, Colorado, he called the school "Meesa" and then "Messa" before he finally got it right.

"Well," he told the amused crowd, "we have some community names out in Michigan all of you could not pronounce either. I love you anyway."[18] During a speech he made in November 1974, newsmen listened in fascinated disbelief as he intoned: "You know we have three great branches of this government of ours. . . . We have a strong President, supposedly in the White House. We have a strong Congress, supposedly in the legislative branch. We have a strong Supreme Court, supposedly heading the judiciary system."[19]

Ford's worst slip came when he was debating Jimmy Carter on television during the campaign of 1976. "There is no Soviet domination of Eastern Europe," he said firmly in answer to one question, "and there never will be under the Ford administration." Pressed by the *New York Times*'s Max Frankel (who could scarcely believe his ears), Ford persisted: "I don't believe, Mr. Frankel, that . . . the Rumanians consider themselves dominated by the Soviet Union. I don't believe that the Poles consider themselves dominated by the Soviet Union. Each of these countries is independent, autonomous. It has its own territorial integrity and the United States does not concede that those countries are under the domination of the Soviet Union." Urged by his advisers to make clarifying remarks a few days later, Ford said in a public statement that "we are going to make certain to the best of our ability that any allegation of domination is not a fact." But this in turn necessitated another clarifying statement; and in the end Ford publicly acknowledged that there were Soviet military forces in Eastern Europe and "that is not what President Ford wants and that is not what the American people want." He also invited the leaders of several Eastern European ethnic organizations to the White House and told them: "I did not express myself clearly—I admit."[20]

In the election of 1976 Ford lost to Jimmy Carter by only a small margin. He consoled himself by noting that he had lost "a close one," but he was tremendously disappointed all the same. He had enjoyed being President and thought he had done a good job of restoring the faith of the American people in their government after what he called the "long national nightmare" of Watergate.[21] A few months before leaving the White House, he got into a discussion with William Scranton, former Republican Governor of Pennsylvania, who was more liberal than the President. "Bill," said Ford, "you didn't favor military aid to South Vietnam." "No, I didn't," admitted Scranton. "You were opposed to the Nixon pardon," Ford went on. "That's right," said Scranton. "You weren't enthusiastic about my economic program," continued Ford. "That's right," Scranton nodded. "My food stamp decision drove you up the wall," Ford reminded him. "It sure did," smiled Scranton. Ford puffed his pipe thoughtfully for a moment, then asked: "Why are you for me at all?" "Because," said Scranton, "you're the first President I ever knew whom I could talk to like that."[22]

Both Jerry and Betty Ford were deeply moved by Jimmy Carter's opening remarks on inauguration day in January 1977. "For myself and for our nation," said Carter after taking his oath of office, "I want to thank my predecessor for all he has done to heal our land."[23] A few days later the Fords flew to Houston to attend a dinner in memory of Vince Lombardi, the great football coach. The dinner was a benefit to raise money for cancer research, and Ford had agreed to be guest of honor when he was still President. As the plane neared Houston, Ford began brooding about his recent defeat and wondering whether the Houston fund-raisers would be let down by having an ex-President rather than a President at their banquet. "They thought they'd be getting a sitting President," he told Betty ruefully. "Don't worry, darling," his vivacious wife said consolingly, "it's me they're coming to see."[24]

★ ★ ★

Unrecognizable

On a trip to Oregon, Vice-President Ford stopped at Utah State to see his son Jack. When he reached the campus a crowd of students gathered, and he started shaking hands. As he went down the line he took the hand of a bearded fellow who, as Ford continued shaking hands, began to smile. It was Jack. He had grown such a crop of whiskers that his father did not recognize him.[25]

Mexican Dish

One evening Vicki Carr, an attractive singer of Mexican ancestry, entertained at a White House dinner. At the end of the evening, when President Ford escorted her out to the front portico, she asked, "What's your favorite Mexican dish?" "You are," said Ford, smiling. "That woman will never get into the White House again!" cried the First Lady, who overheard the remark.[26]

Ford and Brezhnev

In November 1974 President Ford went to Vladivostok to discuss the strategic arms limitation treaty (SALT II) with Russian leader Leonid Brezhnev. One afternoon Brezhnev grabbed Ford's left hand and began telling him how much his people had suffered during World War II. "I do not want to inflict that upon my people again," he said. "Mr. General Secretary," responded Ford, "I believe we made very significant progress. I hope the momentum of our meeting will continue and that next year we can finalize what we have accomplished here." Brezhnev's grip on Ford's hand tightened, and he looked him in the eye. "We have accomplished something very significant," he said, "and it's our responsibility, yours and mine, on behalf of our countries, to achieve the finalization of the document." "I am optimistic that we can," said Ford. "We have made so much headway. This is a big step forward to prevent a nuclear holocaust." "I agree with you," said Brezhnev. "This is an opportunity to protect not only the people of our two countries but, really, all mankind. We have to do something." Later, on leaving Vladivostok, Ford noticed Brezhnev enviously eyeing his heavy Alaskan wolf coat (a gift from a furrier friend); just before boarding the plane he impulsively took it off and gave it to the Soviet leader.[27]

Lost in the White House

The Fords owned a golden retriever named Liberty which they usually kept in a kennel on the ground floor of the White House. Because she was about to give birth to a litter, however, they shifted her to a room on the third floor where her trainer could watch her. One evening the trainer had to go out, so President Ford offered to keep the dog in his bedroom. "Mr. President," said the trainer, "she's no trouble at all. If she wants to go to the bathroom, she'll just come and lick your face." About three o'clock the next morning, the President was awakened from a sound sleep by a very wet kiss. Groggily, he slipped on his robe and slippers, took the elevator to the ground floor, went outside with Liberty, and waited there until she was ready to return. Then he returned to the house and pressed the button for the elevator. Nothing happened; someone had cut off the power. "Liberty," said Ford, "let's walk." So he opened a door to his left and climbed the stairs to the second floor. At the top of the stairwell was a door that led to the family quarters, but when he turned the knob he found it was locked. The third-floor door was also locked. Ford took the dog down to the first floor and tried to open the door there. But it was locked too. After walking up and down the stairs several times looking in vain for an unlocked door, Ford finally started pounding on the walls. The place at once came alive. Lights went on; Secret Service agents appeared. When they found out what the problem was they were a bit chagrined. But Ford told them not to worry; all he had missed, he said, was a few minutes' sleep.[28]

Jimmy Carter
1977–81

When Jimmy Carter (b. 1924) told his mother in the summer of 1974 that he was going to run for President, she said, "President of what?" His brother Billy was more impressed. "I'll be damned!" he exclaimed. "Jimmy's sure bit off a hunk this time," he told his wife that evening, adding: "But he might just do it."[1] Carter made his candidacy official in December 1975, but the silence following his announcement was spectacular. "Carter?" snorted one editor to a reporter who suggested interviewing him. "Running for President? Nobody's every heard of him. It's a joke. Go ahead and do the interview, but keep it short." Before long, however, people who had been sneering, "Jimmy who?" found that they had to take him seriously.[2]

Carter presented himself as an outsider in 1976. The issue, he said, was the division between "insiders" and "outsiders." "I have been accused of being an outsider," he declared. "I plead guilty. Unfortunately, the vast majority of Americans . . . are also outsiders."[3] Carter was not as much of an outsider as he claimed, and his social views were fairly conventional. Still, he had what his campaign manager called a "weirdo factor."[4] He was from the Deep South: the first President (if we exclude Wilson, who had resettled in the North) from that region since Zachary Taylor. He was a graduate of the U.S. Naval Academy: the first Annapolis man in the White House. And he was devoutly religious: a born-again southern Baptist.

Carter's most vivid childhood memory was of listening on the radio to the Joe Louis–Max Schmeling fight in the summer of 1936 with his family and some black people who lived nearby. After Louis clobbered Schmeling in the first round, the black visitors politely thanked Jimmy's father for letting them listen, walked quietly across the dirt road and the railroad tracks and entered a house about a hundred yards away out in the field. "At this point," Carter recalled, "pandemonium broke loose inside that house, as our black neighbors shouted and yelled in celebration of the Louis victory." He could never forget the evening: "all the curious, accepted proprieties of a racially-segregated society had been carefully observed."[5] As Governor of Georgia, Carter represented the "New South," and his acceptance of racial equality appeared to be genuine. "Blacks have a kind of radar about white folks," Andrew Young once explained, "and, somewhere along the line, Jimmy passed the test."[6]

Carter's boyhood dream was to become a naval officer, and in 1943 he entered the U.S. Naval Academy. He did creditable work there, and after graduating in 1946 rose rapidly through the ranks. In 1948 he applied for admission to the nuclear submarine program headed by Admiral Hyman Rickover and underwent a grueling interview with that stern and formidable taskmaster. During the interview, which lasted two hours, Rickover let him choose the subjects he wished to discuss, and Carter carefully picked those he knew most about. But as he went along, Rickover posed one tough question after another; before long Carter began to realize that he knew far less than he had thought. "He always looked right into my eyes," Carter recalled, "and never smiled. I was saturated with cold sweat." Finally Rickover asked a question that seemed easy: "How did you stand in your class at the Naval Academy?" "Sir," said Carter, his confidence momentarily restored, "I stood fifty-ninth in a class of 820!" But instead of congratulating him, Rickover asked another question: "Did you do your best?" Carter started to say, "Yes, sir," but then, gulping, confessed, "No, sir, I didn't *always* do my best." Rickover stared at him for a moment; then, as he brought the interview to an end, asked, "Why not?" Carter was quite shaken by this encounter. And though he was admitted to the submarine program he never forgot that final question: "Why not the best?"[7]

Carter used this question as the title for his campaign book, *Why Not the Best?* (1974). He also made Rickover's query one of the main themes of his 1976 presidential race. But he had always been something of a "superachiever." Jimmy, said one of his friends, is "the most disciplined person I've ever seen."[8] "Jimmy's nature," according to presidential aide Hamilton Jordan, "is to run a total effort everywhere."[9] Dr. Peter Bourne, presidential assistant for health issues, called him "one of the most put-together people I know."[10] And all of his associates agreed: "He doesn't like to lose." Carter made no secret of it. "Show me a good loser," he once said, "and I'll show you a loser."[11] During the 1976 campaign he "outworked everyone" on his staff. "He's tireless," said a supporter.[12]

Like most highly disciplined people, Carter had little patience with people he thought were not doing their best. At seven one morning, while he was Governor, a Georgia commissioner came running late onto the runway at the Atlanta airport, where Carter was waiting for him on a plane. The plane had just begun to taxi down the runway, but when Carter saw the man he told the pilot to take off. "If he can't be here on time," he snapped, "it's too bad." He was similarly miffed during the 1976 campaign when his aide Tim Kraft arranged his schedule in such a way that he would be late for a press conference. En route to New Mexico in a private plane, Carter ordered the pilot to fly low and ignore the bumps. Glaring at Kraft, he said, "I'd rather be fifteen minutes early than fifteen minutes late."[13] Carter's smile was famous; he had the biggest grin of any President since TR. But people who worked with him quickly learned about his "good smiles" and his "bad smiles."[14]

Carter was one of the most religious of all our Presidents. He experienced conversion in 1966, did missionary work in the Northeast for a time, read the Bible and prayed daily, continued teaching Sunday School after becoming President, and, in August 1979, even tried to persuade the President of South Korea, a Buddhist, to accept Christianity. On occasion he did his "Jesus bit," according to Ethel Allen, a black Philadelphia surgeon. "He comes up to me," she said, "puts his hands on my shoulders like he's giving me his blessing or something. Another time he'd cup my face with his hand, ever so gently, like he was the Messiah. It drives me crazy. I got real itchy when he did that. The thing is, it works. Most black people think it's fantastic."[15]

In an interview with *Playboy* appearing in November 1976, Carter tried to dispel the notion that he was a narrow-minded and self-righteous fundamentalist. He tried hard not to sin, he told the interviewer, but he recognized that he was going to do so anyway because he was human and therefore tempted. "I've looked at a lot of women with lust," he confessed. "This is something that God recognizes I will do . . . and God forgives me for it." He went on to say that he did not consider himself any better than the man who "not only looks on a woman with lust but who leaves his wife and shacks up with someone out of wedlock."[16]

Carter's language during the *Playboy* interview shocked some people and amused others. But many Americans found his candor refreshing and even reassuring. His story, on another occasion, of his encounter with the beautiful film star Elizabeth Taylor also pleased people who had doubts about his humanness. At a dinner party, according to Carter, he was seated across the table from the famous actress and found that he simply couldn't keep his eyes off her. At one point she looked over at him and directed a question his way. But Carter didn't seem to hear her; he continued to stare. "Well, Mr. Carter?" she said finally. Carter suddenly came to life. "I'm sorry, Ms. Taylor," he said sheepishly. "I'm sure you were talking to me, but I didn't hear a word you said."[17]

Carter's critics regarded him as essentially humorless. "He never told a joke in his life," said a Congressional leader. But one of Carter's advisers insisted that the President did have a sense of humor. "It's good," he said, "but he doesn't display it publicly, and he's not much good at it when he does."[18] Occasionally Carter was able to get off a *bon mot*. When a reporter asked him in 1975 how he would feel if he was told that his daughter was having an affair, he said he would be "shocked and overwhelmed." His daughter, he added, "is only seven years old."[19] On election day in 1976 he also tried to be facetious. Walking out of the voting booth in his hometown, he told people: "I voted for Walter Mondale and his running mate."[20] He made another light remark on a March 1979 visit to Egypt. While he was touring the Great Pyramid at Giza, the guide told him that the structure took only twenty years to build. "I'm surprised," he responded, "that a government organization could do it that quickly."[21]

In an address to some retired people in Hartford, Connecticut, in September 1979, Carter quipped: "As much as I admire you retired persons, I must admit that I am not yet tempted to join your ranks any time soon."[22] He was to join them sooner than he had anticipated. When he ran for re-election the following year he was swamped at the polls by Republican candidate Ronald Reagan, taking only 49 electoral votes to Reagan's 489 and trailing Reagan by more than

eight million popular votes. Carter was the first President since Herbert Hoover to be denied a second term after having won a first
one. Hoover had been undone by the Great Depression; the Great
Inflation, which reached double-digit proportions during the late
seventies, overwhelmed the Georgian President. But Carter's seeming
lack of direction, inability to work with Congress ("Carter," said a
senior Congressman, "couldn't get the Pledge of Allegiance through
Congress"), and frequent changes of position to accommodate critics
also contributed to the voters' disaffection with his Presidency.[23]

Carter acknowledged his defeat while the returns were still coming
in. The polls, in fact, were still open in some parts of the country
when he made his graceful concession speech. "I promised you four
years ago that I would never lie to you," he said, "so I can't stand
here and say it doesn't hurt. I've wanted to serve as President because
I love this country and because I love the people of this nation.
Just one more word. Finally, let me say that I am disappointed
tonight but I have not lost either love."[24]

★ ★ ★

Marching Through Georgia

When Carter arrived at Annapolis it was clear from the moment
he opened his mouth that he was a southern boy, so he quickly
acquired the nickname "Johnny Reb." One evening some upperclass-
men demanded that he sing "Marching Through Georgia." Carter
absolutely refused; he simply would not sing a song about Yankees
ravaging their way from Atlanta to the ocean. "No sir," he said
firmly, "I won't sing that one." For the rest of his days as a plebe,
the hazing was unrelenting; but he never did sing that song. Years
later, when he was campaigning for the Presidency, a high school
band greeted him with "Marching Through Georgia" when he arrived in Phoenix, Arizona. "Doesn't anybody realize that's not a
Southern song?" he cried impatiently.[25]

Learn to Box

When Johnson was running for President in 1964, Carter's son Chip
wore an LBJ button to school one day and some classmates hostile
to Johnson ripped it off. The next day he pinned the button to his
shirt again and again it was torn off. This continued for several

days; finally a gang of bigger and older boys roughed him up so
badly that he went home in tears. "Put the button back on," his
father ordered. "What if they tear it off again?" asked Chip. "Put
it on again," said Carter. "Then," said Chip, "they'll just tear it
off again." "Then," said Carter, "you just put it back on again, if
you want to wear it. Do what you want to do—and learn to box."[26]

Sharing

Carter believed in sharing household chores with his wife. "He helps
me with everything," Mrs. Carter told reporters. "He doesn't wash
and iron shirts, but he takes Amy for walks, he goes to the grocery
store for me, he helps with the cooking, and opening the mail. We're
both gone all the time, so when we're home, we share." Once, during
the 1976 campaign, Carter's mother found him peeling peaches.
"Jimmy," she cried reprovingly, "why are you peeling all those
peaches?" "Mother," he replied, "somebody's got to peel them. If
they don't get peeled and put in the freezer they'll spoil." A few
days later a *Playboy* interviewer, surprised to see the Democratic
candidate sewing a rip in his jacket while answering questions, exclaimed, "Say, do you always do your own sewing?" "Uh-huh,"
mumbled Carter matter-of-factly, biting off the thread.[27]

Party

During the 1976 campaign Carter attended a party in Beverly Hills
thrown by screen star Warren Beatty and attended by leading lights
from the entertainment world. When Beatty remarked at one point
that coming to his party might help Carter, a Southern Baptist,
to blunt the religious issue, Carter laughed: "If I come to Warren
Beatty's party, it should wipe out the issue!" Just before leaving,
he announced: "It is a real thrill to meet the famous people here
tonight. I hope I don't get to know too much about you!"[28]

Mister Carter

"If your brother wins," someone asked Carter's brother Billy on
election eve, "how will this change you?" "There's one change I'd
make," replied Billy. "If Jimmy does become President tonight, I'm
gonna make everybody call me *Mister* Carter for the first twenty-

four hours. Then everything can be the same; I'll be Billy again after that." When the news came through that he had won, Jimmy went up to the podium. "*Mister* Carter," he said, turning to his brother, "I want to thank you for waiting up all night to greet me." At these words there were thunderous cheers from the crowd that had gathered to celebrate Carter's victory.[29]

Inauguration

"I hear it's gonna be 40 degrees here in Washington tomorrow for the inauguration," said Billy Carter the night before his brother took the oath of office. "Jimmy must've been talkin' to the Lord again."[30]

Apologies

By spring 1979, when Carter visited New Hampshire, his administration was beginning to come under heavy criticism. When a newswoman in Portsmouth asked him whether his daughter Army ever bragged about her father's being President, Carter said, "No, she probably apologizes."[31]

Carter's Rain

Just before President Carter's helicopter landed in Justin, Texas, about forty miles northeast of the drought-stricken Dallas–Fort Worth area in July 1980, there was a sudden rainfall lasting for about ten minutes. Carter stepped onto slippery clay soil that only an hour earlier had been hard and rough. "Well," he smiled at the farmers who had gathered to greet him, "you asked for either money or rain. I couldn't get the money so I brought the rain."[32]

Ex-President

Carter quickly overcame his disappointment at losing his bid for re-election in 1980 and plunged into a host of activities after leaving the White House and returning to Georgia. He wrote his memoirs, raised money to establish a presidential library and museum in Atlanta, and founded the Carter Center to sponsor projects on behalf of human rights and the peaceful settlement of conflicts

around the world. Time and again he boarded planes to mediate
conflicts and monitor elections in various parts of the world. He
also joined former President Ford (with whom he became friendly
in the 1980s) in preparing a report on U.S. domestic problems,
The American Agenda, to present to President Bush shortly after
his inauguration in 1989. *Time* declared him to be "a superb ex-
President."

For the rest, Carter taught adult Sunday School classes at his
Baptist church in Plains, Georgia, and took his turn each year
mowing the church lawn. With his wife Rosalynn he also became
a member of Habitat for Humanity, a Christian organization
founded in 1976 to build houses for the poor, and put in a week
each year working as a carpenter. He became interested in poetry,
too, and, like John Quincy Adams and Abraham Lincoln, tried his
hand at it, with creditable results. Early in 1995 came his book,
Always a Reckoning, containing 44 poems, some of them autobi-
ographical (recalling his boyhood black friends) and some sociopo-
litical (about homelessness). The reviews—like the appraisals of
his post-presidency—were mostly friendly.[33]

THIRTY-NINE

Ronald Reagan
1981–1989

Ronald Reagan (b. 1911) came to politics late. He was fifty-five when he was elected Governor of California in 1966 and sixty-nine (even older than William Henry Harrison) when he became President of the United States in 1981. Before that he had been a radio sportscaster, a Hollywood film star, and a television host and performer. But he liked politics best. "When I was announcing sports I was happy and thought that was all I wanted out of life," he once said. "Then came the chance at Hollywood and that was even better. Now I'm doing something that makes everything else I've done seem dull as dishwater when I look back."[1]

In the entertainment world Reagan was regarded as a competent performer. After graduating from Eureka College, near Peoria, Illinois, in 1932, he got a job as sports announcer for a radio station in Davenport, Iowa, and then moved to Des Moines, Iowa, where he covered track meets, prize fights, baseball, and Big Ten football for station WHO and became one of the best-known sportscasters in the Middle West. He usually broadcast live, but on occasion did simulated broadcasts of Chicago Cubs games based on Western Union reports of each play. One day the wire died when Augie Galan was at the bat in a tight spot. But Reagan kept Galan fouling off pitch after imaginary pitch for six frantic minutes until the ticker came alive again and rescued him.[2] In 1937, he accompanied the Cubs to California for spring training and took a screen test. "Max," his agent told the casting director at Warner Brothers, "I have another Robert Taylor sitting in my office." "OK, sign him," said Jack Warner after seeing the screen test.[3]

In films Reagan was "a very good, very professional, and very competent actor," according to one producer, "without any confusion about getting artistic."[4] Altogether he made fifty-four films, moving gradually up from low-budget "B" pictures to first-class "A's" and winning praise for his performances in *Brother Rat* (1938), *Knute Rockne—All-American* (1940), and *King's Row* (1941). Directors liked him. He always showed up on time, knew his lines, and took direction gracefully. Soon he became "the Errol Flynn of the B's" (to use his own words) whom Errol Flynn of the A's liked to tease.[5] Just before one scene in *Santa Fe Trail* (1940), Flynn loosened Reagan's saddle, and when, on cue, all the performers leaped onto their horses and galloped away, Reagan was left sitting dazed in the dust. When another movie, *Desperate Journey* (1942), was being filmed, Flynn resented having to work on Saturday and by way of protest plied everyone with bourbon in his dressing room until shooting time. But Reagan emptied his paper cup into a spittoon when no one was looking and was the only one who was sober when it came time to shoot. The first line was Reagan's and he spoke it without hesitation. The second line was Flynn's. Flynn stood wavering uncertainly for a moment or two; then he glared at Reagan and cried: "Why don't you go f—— yourself?"[6]

Reagan never achieved Errol Flynn's—or Robert Taylor's—popularity as a romantic lead. World War II interrupted—and probably wrecked—his film career. When he returned to pictures after four years with the Army Air Corps making training films, he was unable to regain the momentum he had achieved just before the war. In 1951 he found himself playing opposite a chimpanzee in *Bedtime for Bonzo*. "I'm the one with the watch," he said jovially years later when handed a picture from the film showing him in bed with Bonzo.[7]

As Reagan's film career waned he moved to television. For eight years, he acted as host and occasional star of *General Electric Theater*, a half-hour TV series, and after that appeared in *Death Valley Days*, a weekly TV drama about the frontier era. He also became a spokesman for GE's personnel-relations program and toured GE plants throughout the country making speeches (mainly about Hollywood) to the firm's employees and to various civic groups. GE's chairman liked what he was doing. "You'd better get yourself a philosophy," he told Reagan. "Something you can stand for and something you think this country stands for."[8] The philosophy Reagan developed was ultra-conservative. He had once been a New Deal Democrat ("a near-hopeless hemophiliac liberal," he liked to say), but during the 1950's he moved steadily to the right.[9] By the early 1960's he was an impassioned defender of private enterprise and an unsparing critic of government programs undertaken during the Great Depression to preserve and strengthen the American system. During the presidential campaign of 1964 he made a TV speech for Republican candidate Barry Goldwater that was so effective that California millionaires begged him to run for Governor. "No way," he said at first. "You find a candidate and I'll campaign for him."[10] But in the end he agreed to run. "All wrong," Jack Warner is supposed to have said when he heard the news. "Jimmy Stewart for governor, Reagan for best friend."[11]

Reagan campaigned in 1966 as a "citizen-politician," promising to cut taxes and spending, and overwhelmed his liberal Democratic opponent at the polls. He took his oath as Governor a few minutes past midnight on January 2, 1967. "Well, George," he said to his old Hollywood pal George Murphy (by then one of California's Senators), "here we are on the Late Show again!"[12] As Governor, despite his right-wing rhetoric, Reagan turned out to be what one friend called a "closet moderate" and another "a Fabian conservative."[13] He did succeed in slowing the rate of government growth; but he was also forced to increase both taxes and spending during his eight years in office. Toward the end he ruefully admitted as much as one of his speech cards: "ALL R RFRMS & PENNY PINCH'G HS AMOUNTED 2 ONLY A HOLD'G ACTN AGNST BIGGR & COSTLIER GOVT."[14] As Governor, Reagan acted like the chairman of the board in a large corporation. He outlined general directions and made major decisions himself but left the execution of his politics to his aides. He usually got to his office a little before nine in the morning and left about 5:30 P.M. Sometimes he would poke his head into the conference room on his way out and call to his staff: "Hey, you guys, get out! Go home to your wives!"[15]

Regan's supporters began pushing him for the Presidency as early as 1968, but he held back. "It would be presumptuous of me to say I should run after two years as Governor," he told them. "If you think you're not up to it," said one of them impatiently, "tell us." "No," returned Reagan, "I feel I'm better qualified to be President than Governor." But he did not announce his availability until a few hours before the first ballot, and Richard Nixon easily won the nomination that year. "Son," South Carolina's Senator Strom Thurmond told him, "you'll be President some day, but this isn't your year." [16] Nineteen seventy-six wasn't his year either; he did well in the primaries but lost to Gerald Ford at the Kansas convention. But in 1980 it was clear sailing from the outset. He did splendidly in the primaries, was nominated on the first ballot in July, and went on to conduct a successful campaign against Jimmy Carter, promising a big tax cut, a reduction in government spending, and an increase in defense appropriations. He was convinced that his policies would end "stagflation," that is, reduce unemployment and check inflation; but as third-party candidate John Anderson of Illinois exclaimed: "How do you balance the budget, cut taxes and increase defense spending at the same time? It's very simple. You do it with mirrors." [17]

"There *are* simple answers," Reagan liked to say. "There just aren't easy ones." [18] Reagan's simplicisms bothered some people. During the 1980 campaign he talked of re-establishing "official" relations with Taiwan; but when China (whose good will George Bush, his running mate, was trying to cultivate in Peking) protested, he said lamely: "I misstated." [19] He called the United States "energy rich" (though it was becoming increasingly dependent on foreign oil), declared there was nothing inflationary about tax cuts (though many economists disagreed), and said that trees produced most of the nitrogen haze in the atmosphere (which is true but has nothing to do with the chemistry of smog). One day his office issued a statement about pollution which concluded: "Air pollution has been substantially controlled." The next day a reporter asked him whether he really believed that the air was clearing up. "I don't think I've said anything of the kind," said Reagan defensively. When the reporter pointed out that the statement had been released the day before under his name, Reagan exclaimed: "Isn't it substantially under control? I think it is." But when he flew back to Los Angeles a few days later his plane had to be diverted because of one of the worst smog attacks in the city's history. [20]

Reagan's ideal was a government that was by turns weak (at

home) and strong (abroad), but he never explained how it could be both. Instead he resorted to generalities. "At the heart of our message," he announced, "should be five simple familiar words. No big economic theories. No sermons on political philosophy. Just five short words: family, work, neighborhood, freedom, peace."[21] In a debate with Carter in Cleveland toward the end of the campaign he came through on television as an easy-going, relaxed, likeable, straightforward, and self-confident Middle American full of good intentions and lacking guile. Asked afterward if he had been nervous about debating the President, he exclaimed: "No, not at all. I've been on the same stage with John Wayne."[22]

On election day, when Reagan and his wife Nancy arrived at the polling place in his fashionable Pacific Palisades neighborhood, he was asked how he felt. "I can't answer till I get my mark," he grinned, indicating the cross marked "R.R." in front of the cameras.[23] Asked whom his wife would vote for, he laughed: "She's going to vote for some former actor."[24] That night, attending a victory celebration in Los Angeles, he told supporters: "Do you know, Abe Lincoln, the day after his election to the Presidency, gathered in his office the newsmen who had been covering his campaign and he said to them: 'Well, boys, your troubles are over now; mine have just begun.' I think I know what he meant. Lincoln may have been concerned in the troubled times in which he became President. But I don't think he was afraid. And I am not frightened by what lies ahead and I don't believe the American people are frightened by what lies ahead. Together, we're going to do what has to be done."[25]

Reagan thoroughly enjoyed being President. He loved the pomp and circumstance that went with it: presiding at ceremonial functions; hosting, with his wife Nancy, elaborate receptions and dinners at the White House; and executing snappy salutes as Commander in Chief of the armed forces, even though he was a civilian and not in uniform. He took pleasure, too, in delivering with panache the carefully crafted speeches prepared by professional writers on his staff. He also delighted in being a vigorous, no-nonsense President, who, though not bothering himself with details, took bold action time and again to show that the U.S. government was not to be trifled with: firing air controllers illegally on strike; bombing Libya in retaliation for terrorist acts; invading the tiny Caribbean island of Grenada to oust Marxist leaders. And, like other activistic Presidents, he turned out to be a big spender after all, though remembered by some more for his tax breaks for upper-income groups.

The lavish Reagan-sponsored spending went largely to the Pentagon. During his first years in the White House he presided over the biggest peacetime expansion of spending for the military in American history. He did it, he insisted, to intimidate the Soviet Union, but he also did it because he was convinced that "throwing money," so to speak, at the Pentagon was good for the nation's economy. It was possible, he explained during the 1980 campaign, to lower taxes, increase military spending, and balance the budget all at the same time. (George Bush, who called it "voodoo economics," then changed his mind when he was tapped for Vice-President.)

At the meeting with House and Senate leaders of both parties in the Oval Office late in 1986, Reagan took the opportunity to announce that military procurement expenditures didn't add anything whatsoever to the national deficit. When Oregon Senator Mark Hatfield, a moderate Republican, disagreed, Reagan cried: "You have played havoc with the military defenses of our country and squandered it all on wastefulsocialprograms" (with Reagan, Texas Congressman Jim Wright observed, wasteful social programs came out as one word). When Hatfield reminded him that military spending had doubled (from $148 billion in 1980 to almost 300 billion in 1986), while discretionary spending had been cut by slightly more than 10 percent, Reagan responded: "Our problem is that you have spent less than I asked for military strength and more than I asked on wastefulsocialprograms!"

Government spending was government spending, Hatfield reminded Reagan. Wasn't the President concerned with the overall spending rate and its effect on the national debt? Wouldn't he agree "that a dollar spent on a bomb adds just as much to the deficit as the same dollar would if it were spent on a school book"? Reagan shook his head. "I do *not* agree with that," he exclaimed, "and I would like Cap Weinberger to address that subject." Secretary of Defense Weinberger then got up and explained that money spent on military procurement added nothing to the deficit, because it was spent with American manufacturers who employed laborers who bought consumer goods from merchants who paid taxes on their incomes. "And, therefore," concluded Weinberger, "you see, it all comes back to the treasury in taxes."

Reagan's Congressional visitors were astonished. They realized that Weinberger's reasoning could apply to almost any expenditures that added to the nation's wealth (highways and waterways, for example, rather than weapons) and that it could apply even more forcefully to programs that were more labor intensive and less capital intensive. "There were probably twenty or more of us in the room," Congressman Wright reported afterward. "Nineteen, including Weinberger himself, knew that his contention was sheer sophistry. But one man believed it, because he chose to believe it. The President of the United States actually believed that day that military expenditures did not add anything to the deficit."[26]

The deficit did of course increase during the Reagan presidency and the national debt itself skyrocketed. By the time Reagan left office, interest on the national debt (in effect, transfer payments) had come to form a major part of the federal budget. Soon Reagan himself was joking about it: the national debt, he quipped, was big enough to take care of itself! At the same time the federal government continued as big and costly as ever in the 1980s (as former *Wall Street Journal* editor David Frum noted disappointedly), though Reagan continued to take frequent potshots at it.[27] It was clear that things weren't quite working out the way the President had promised voters in 1980, though his popularity continued undiminished and he won re-election by a landslide in 1984. This was partly because of the grace, charm, and cheery optimism he displayed, even in adversity, and partly because he seemed to make the nation (after the travails of Vietnam and Watergate) "stand tall" again in the eyes of the world. Even his political foes acknowledged that he was one of the most likable Chief Executives in American history.

There were jokes, though, about the "Great Communicator," as he came to be called. He hadn't been President for long before funny stories about his easygoing work habits and laid-back personal style were making the rounds. There were quips about his "tough four-hour days" and his lengthy naps that made even Calvin Coolidge seem like an insomniac. Johnny Carson said Reagan liked to take a "working nap" in the White House, and *Newsweek*'s Tom DeFrank said that in times of crisis the President "might have to suffer a few sleepless afternoons." When a zealous aide pressed him to make a decision, according to one tale, Reagan said, "I want to sleep on it a while," and, with Reagan, the joke went, "you know he gets right to it." "Have you heard," asked humorist Art Buchwald, "that President Reagan has spent many sleepless days over the Middle East?" The Iran-contra scandal had gotten so bad, it was said, that President Reagan was losing sleep in the afternoon over it. "Did Reagan know," went Youth for Democratic Action buttons in 1986, "or was he napping?"[28]

Reagan took all the joshing in good humor and even added to the jokes himself. "It's true that hard work never killed anybody," he liked to say, "but I figure, why take the chance?" Speaking to the White House Correspondents Association, he said he had been working hard, "burning the midday oil." And toward the end of his second term he teased about his plans for retirement. "As soon as I get home to California, I plan to lean back, kick up my feet and take a long nap." Then he added: "Ah, come to think of it, things won't be all that different after all!"[29]

Reagan continued to enjoy joking about his age, too, after entering the White House. In February 1981, when he turned seventy, the oldest man to occupy the Presidency, he thanked people for celebrating the "31st anniversary of my 39th birthday." Three years later, when he turned seventy-three and was planning to run for a second term, he told a group of senior citizens that he was still so active that he planned to "campaign in all 13 states." Discussing the trade deficit in another speech a little later, he pointed out that the United States had had a trade deficit in almost all the years between 1790 and 1875, and then added with a deadpan expression: "I remember them well. Of course I was only a boy at the time." He teased himself similarly a couple of years later in a speech to a business group in which he stressed brevity. "You'll remember," he said, "that George Washington gave an inaugural address of just 135 words and became a great President. Of course, there was William Henry Harrison. He spoke at his inauguration for nearly two hours, caught pneumonia and died within a month." Then came the zinger: "I told him to keep it short."[30]

Reagan received many nicknames while he was President—the Great Communicator, the Teflon President, Dr. Feelgood—but he was also the Chief of the One-Liners during his eight years in Washington. "When you go to bed with the federal government," he cracked, "you get more than a good night's sleep." Criticizing the Strategic Arms Limitation Treaty (SALT) of 1979, known as SALT II, he remarked: "Too much salt isn't good for you." He commenced a speech in Moscow in the spring of 1986 with: "Well, as Henry VIII said to each of his six wives, 'I won't keep you long.' " He even came up with quips when he was in the hospital for colon surgery in July 1985. "I'll tell you what I think of the House budget proposal so far," he said in a radio broadcast taped in the hospital. "I hope that it gets well soon. In fact, I told one of the fine surgeons who operated on me that if Congress can't make the spending cuts we need, I'm going to send him up there to do some real cutting." And he went on: "Forgive me, I just don't have as much stomach for that kind of talk as I used to."[31]

Reagan was Chief Jokester as well as Chief Punster and Chief of the One-Liners during his eight years in the White House. He had a treasure trove of funny stories to use on appropriate occasions, and he welcomed—even solicited—new jokes to add to his collection. His Secretary of State, George Shultz, according to *New York* magazine, sometimes included a joke in cables to Reagan from abroad so he could check on whether the President had read the cables when he got back to Washington. If Reagan said, "That was a great joke, George, I've been telling it to everybody," then Shultz knew his message had gotten through to the President.[32]

Reagan liked to insert jokes into his speeches in order to hold the attention of his audiences; but he used funny stories in personal encounters, too, in order to put people at ease and work his charm on them. One of his tales had to do with an engineer, a lawyer, and an economist who were arguing about which of them practiced the oldest profession. The engineer said that God created the universe out of chaos and "that was an engineering job." "Wait a minute," interrupted the lawyer. "The Bible says that in the beginning, before chaos, was 'the Word' . . . 'the Law.' So lawyers clearly came first." By this time the economist was laughing. "Who," he cried, "do you think created the chaos?" Reagan told this story to all three of his top economic advisers when he added them to his staff.[33]

Reagan's favorite jokes had to do with the Soviet Union. For years he had collected amusing anti-Soviet stories; he especially prized the wry tales told by the Russians themselves about the shortcomings of their system. "What are four things wrong with Soviet agriculture?" went one of the jokes; answer: "Spring, summer, fall, winter." In another Reagan favorite, a party official asks a farmer how things are going and the farmer says the harvest is so bountiful that the potatoes would reach the "foot of God" if piled on top of one another. "But this is the Soviet Union," says the commissar sharply. "There is no God here." "That's all right," rejoins the farmer. "There are no potatoes either." During the 1984 campaign Reagan told this particular joke so often that reporters became heartily sick of it.[34]

But jokes like these, ironically enough, helped Reagan develop a good relationship with Soviet leader Mikhail Gorbachev during his second term in office. When he met Gorbachev for the first time in Geneva in November 1985 to discuss arms control, he discovered to his delight that the Soviet leader not only had a good sense of humor, but that he also responded amiably to the anti-Soviet jokes which Reagan insisted on telling him. One of them was the old chestnut about the American who tells a Russian that the United States is so free that he can stand in front of the White House and yell, "To hell with Ronald Reagan!" "That's nothing," cries the Russian. "I can stand in front of the Kremlin and yell, 'To hell with Ronald Reagan!' too!" And there were other jokes, centering on Communist inefficiency and bureaucratic controls, which seemed to tickle the Soviet leader. One Reagan official thought that humor was the key to the personal relationship that developed between Reagan and Gorbachev. Reagan, he pointed out, "appreciates anybody who appreciates the irony of a situation, and who laughs openly and well." After one session, while the two world leaders were waiting for their wives, Reagan persuaded Gorbachev to join him in a little prank. When Mrs. Reagan and Mrs. Gorbachev arrived, they found their husbands standing in the lobby and looking impatiently at their watches, as if the women had been unconscionably late.[35]

"Reagan in Moscow!" marveled one White House official. "That used to be an oxymoron." Radical Rightists wrote the President off as a "useful idiot for the Soviets," but Reagan, once a hard-liner, insisted that Gorbachev's espousal of *glasnost* (openness) and *perestroika* (reform) in the U.S.S.R. opened the way for rapprochement with America's old Cold War foe. In June 1988, when a reporter reminded Reagan that he had once called the So-

viet Union "an evil empire," and wondered if he still felt that way,
the President shook his head impatiently and said: "No, I was talking about another time, another era."[36]

* ★ ★

Promising Actor

During World War II Reagan took time out from narrating training
films for the Army Air Corps to play a lead in a Warner Brothers
movie called *This Is the Army*, which composer Irving Berlin wrote
and produced. During the first week of shooting he was introduced
to Berlin five times and each time, he recalled, Berlin said he was
glad to meet him. Then one day Berlin sought him out. "Young
fellow," he said, "I just saw some of your work. You've got a few
things to correct—for example, a huskiness of the voice—but you
really should give this business some serious consideration when
the war is over. It's very possible that you could have a career in
show business." Reagan thanked him. But he wondered whether
Berlin just hadn't seen any movies or whether the war had been
going on so long that all of his pre-war movies had been forgotten.[37]

Young and Virile

A California state senator who favored prescribing birth-control de-
vices for teen-age girls without parental consent charged that "illegitimate births to teen-aged mothers have increased alarmingly
while Reagan has been in office." When someone sent Reagan a
newspaper clipping quoting the remark, Reagan wrote back:
"Thanks very much for sending me the clipping. . . . I have
never felt so young and virile."[38]

Cement

When running for governor Reagan campaigned vigorously against
a state withholding tax. On this issue, he said, his feet were set in
cement. But in 1971 California's finances were in such trouble that
his advisers told him the only way to deal with the crisis was such
a tax. Reagan called an emergency session of the legislature and
proposed the tax. Afterward, at a press conference, a faulty heating

system made a big racket as he announced his turnabout. The noise, he quipped, was the sound of the cement breaking around his feet. The capital press corps eventually presented him with a pair of his own brown shoes (supplied by his wife) set in cement; for a long time he kept it in his office for everyone to see.[39]

Controlled Anger

Reagan was usually good-natured, but on occasion he lost his temper and threw a pencil or his reading glasses across the room. But he always recovered quickly. "Look," he once told an aide, "I learned a long time ago that if you're going to throw a club in anger, throw it in front of you so you won't have to go back and pick it up."[40]

Recovery

"One day," said Reagan during the 1980 campaign, "I publicly declared that this is a depression and the President before the day was out went to the press to say, 'That shows how little he knows. This is a recession.' " Added Reagan: "If the President wants a definition, I'll give him one. Recession is when your neighbor loses his job, depression is when you lose yours, and"—here he paused as the laughs began—"recovery will be when Jimmy Carter loses his."[41]

Holy Communion

During the 1984 campaign, when Reagan was asked why he and his wife did not attend church on Sunday, he cited "presidential security" as the reason. But the Reagans' unfamiliarity with church services produced at least one minor crisis in 1980, according to Michael Deaver, a Reagan aide, whose memoirs appeared in 1988. During the 1980 campaign, he recalled, he arranged for the Reagans to attend an Episcopal church service one Sunday morning when they were in Virginia. "We were not told," wrote Deaver, "and I did not anticipate, that the eleven o'clock service would also be holy communion," a ritual, he added, that was "very foreign to the Reagans." After the sermon, as the Reagans were starting toward the altar to receive communion, Mrs. Reagan suddenly clutched Deaver's arm, "Mike!" she hissed. "Are those people drinking out of the same cup?" "It's all right," whispered Deaver. "They'll come by with the wafers first. Then, when the chalice reaches you, dip the bread in the cup, and that is perfectly all right. You won't have to put your lips to the cup." "What, what?" asked Reagan, who was slightly hard of hearing. Mrs. Reagan quickly gave him instructions: "Ron," she said, "just do exactly as I do." When they reached the altar, according to Deaver, Mrs. Reagan picked up a square of bread, dipped it in the chalice of wine, and was about to ingest it, when suddenly it slipped out of her fingers and plunked into the wine. And then, as Deaver watched in horror, Reagan, who had been watching his wife, picked up a square of bread, dipped it in the chalice, and then tossed it into the wine, where it floated next to Mrs. Reagan's wafer. The minister stared at the pieces of bread in the wine, shook his head doubtfully, and moved on. "Nancy was relieved to leave the church," Deaver remembered, but her husband "was chipper as he stepped into the sunlight satisfied that the service had gone quite well."[42]

Jelly Beans

When Reagan gave up smoking he found it helpful to pop jelly beans into his mouth after meals. On his first day as Governor the candymaker Henry Rowland gave him a large jar of his favorite candy, which he put on the Cabinet Room table. After that he got into the habit of bringing jelly beans to Cabinet meetings and handing them out during sessions. "We can hardly start a meeting or make a decision without passing around the jar of jelly beans," he told Rowland. And he once mused: "You can tell a lot about a fella's character by whether he picks out all of one color or just grabs a handful." But he also reflected: "Some political figures have endured in history as lions or conquerors or something equally impressive. It's a little frightening to think California history might record us as jelly beans."

After Reagan's election Henry Rowland told reporters: "There will be jelly beans in the White House, that's all I can say." He was right. The number of jelly beans consumed at Reagan's inaugural parties (forty million) almost equaled the number of votes he received in the election. "Everywhere I go," sighed economist Milton Friedman, "I see jelly beans." Though dentists and nutritionists expressed some concern, jelly beans became the First Candy during Reagan's Presidency. "If we had a concession on all the jelly beans passed out," said one of his aides, "we could pay off the national debt." During conferences with mayors, Governors, Congressmen, businessmen, trade unionists, and minority-group leaders, Reagan made free use of his beloved candy. He also kept a crystal jar full of Jelly Bellys (his favorite brand) for Cabinet meetings and encouraged department chiefs to reach for them "when you need some energy." At one session discussing budget cuts he fingered one playfully, said, "They tell me the purple ones are poisonous," and then popped it into his mouth as if to say that he was going to slash government spending regardless of opposition.[43]

Happy Birthday

Reagan turned seventy in February 1981 and joked about his age in a speech at a Washington Press Club dinner. "I know your organization was founded by six Washington newspaperwomen in 1919," he remarked; then, after a slight pause, added: "It seems like only yesterday." Middle age, he went on to say, "is when you're faced with two temptations and you choose the one that will get you home at 9 o'clock." And, after quoting Thomas Jefferson's advice not to worry about one's age, he exclaimed: "And ever since he told me that, I stopped worrying."[44]

One-Liners

President Reagan was famous for his one-liners. Even in emergencies he preserved his good humor and tossed off quip after quip to reassure those around him. An attempt on his life early in his Presidency left him as calm and unruffled as Theodore Roosevelt had been after a similar attack many years before.

Early in the afternoon of March 30, 1981, a deranged young loner pumped a fusillade of explosive bullets into the President, his press secretary, and two law-enforcement officers as they were coming out of the Washington-Hilton Hotel. Reagan was rushed to the hospital with a serious chest wound, but when he was wheeled into the operating room he grinned and told the surgeons: "Please assure me that you are all Republicans!" "Today," responded one of the doctors, "we're all good Republicans, Mr. President." A

few hours after surgery the President wrote his doctors a note
which parodied comedian W. C. Fields: "All in all, I'd rather be
in Philadelphia." A little later he sent another note from the
intensive-care section to White House aides waiting outside: "Winston Churchill said: 'There's no more exhilarating feeling than being shot at without result.' " Two hours later came a third note: "If
I had had this much attention in Hollywood, I'd have stayed
there."

  When doctors praised Reagan for being a good patient, he told
them, "I have to be. My father-in-law is a doctor." To the nurse
removing a trachea tube he said confidently: "I always heal fast."
Said she: "Keep up the good work." "You mean this may happen
several times more?" he cried in mock dismay. Greeting White
House aides the morning after surgery, he exclaimed: "Hi, fellas.
I knew it would be too much to hope that we could skip a staff
meeting." Told that the Government was running smoothly while
he was in the hospital, he pretended indignation: "What makes you
think I'd be happy about that?" And when he heard about the progress being made by the other men who had been wounded in the
assassination attempt he exclaimed: "That's great news. We'll have
to get four bedpans and have a reunion." The following evening
master of ceremonies Johnny Carson told his audience at Hollywood's Academy Awards ceremony (to which the President had
sent a pre-taped message), "I was tempted to call him and ask if
he had any more of those one-liners *I* could use!"[45]

State of the Union

In January 1983, just before Reagan delivered his State of the
Union address, bootlegged copies of the text reached members of
Congress and they were surprised to find it contained the un-
Reaganite sentence, "We who are in government must take the lead
in restoring the economy." Some of the Democrats decided to have
a little fun with the President. A few days later, when he came to
that line while delivering his address to Congress, they all jumped
up, by pre-arrangement, and gave him a standing ovation. For a
moment Reagan was taken aback; then, recovering, he smiled and
said playfully: "And there all along I thought you were reading the
newspapers!"[46]

Camp Diana

Like most of his predecessors in the White House, Reagan committed a fair number of gaffes while he was President. He greeted prizefighter Sugar Ray Leonard and Mrs. Leonard as "Sugar Ray" and "Mrs. Ray"; called Liberia's President Samuel Doe "Chairman Moe"; addressed Oklahoma Senator Don Nickles as "Don Rickles"; called Paul H. Nitze, his arms-control negotiator, "Ed Nitze"; and welcomed HUD Secretary Samuel Pierce at one gathering as "Mr. Mayor." When the Prince of Wales and his wife Diana attended a White House dinner, Reagan introduced them as the Prince of Wales and "his lovely lady, Princess David." The ballerina sitting next to actor Peter Ustinov gasped. "What?" she whispered. "Did he *really* say Princess David?" "Don't worry," Ustinov whispered back. "He's just thinking of next weekend at Camp Diana."[47]

Crisis

In a speech at Georgetown University in April 1984, Reagan talked about the "intricacies of diplomacy" and told a story about how he had recently almost caused an international crisis. At a state dinner honoring French President François Mitterand, he said, the Mitterands and the Reagans finished the receiving line and then walked from the East Room into the state dining room where all the guests stood waiting, according to custom, until Mrs. Reagan led the French President to her table and President Reagan led Mrs. Mitterand to his table on the opposite side of the room. Mrs. Reagan and Mitterand headed at once for their table, but Mrs. Mitterand stood frozen at Reagan's side, even though the butler motioned for her to walk toward the President's table. "We're supposed to go over there," whispered Reagan, "to the other side." But Mrs. Mitterand stood motionless and then whispered something back in French which Reagan didn't understand. There was an awkward silence as everyone stood waiting. Suddenly an interpreter ran over to the President and exclaimed: "She's telling you that you're standing on her gown!" Reagan moved on at once, so did Mrs. Mitterand.[48]

Reagan's SOBs

In March 1986, at the end of a press conference at which reporters had given him a rough time, Reagan turned to an aide and muttered "Sons of bitches!" Asked about the President's expletive afterward, presidential spokesman Larry Speakes insisted that the President "doesn't recall saying it," and added: "If he said anything, he said, 'It's sunny, and you're rich.' " But videotapes confirmed the fact that the President had made the remark and reporters started showing up in their subterranean White House offices wearing SOB ("Sons of the Basement") T-shirts. A few days later President Reagan turned up for breakfast with the reporters carrying a yellow T-shirt with the big black letters SOB on the front. Then he flipped the shirt over to show the other side: Save Our Budget; the reporters applauded. Reagan, *Time*'s Hugh Sidey concluded, "had not only SOB-ed them, he had defeated them"[49]

A Pen in Time

Early in his Presidency, Reagan agreed that as part of a nationwide prime-time address on the economy, he would get up from his desk, walk over to an easel, and draw a red line on a chart in order to show dramatically what would happen if Congress failed to enact his program. David R. Gergen, communications director for Reagan at the time, asked Reagan to come a few minutes early for a rehearsal, and the warm-up went well. When Reagan was finally on the air, he read his lines flawlessly, as usual, and then walked over to the easel. But at that moment Gergen and his aides realized they had forgotten to put the cap back on Reagan's red felt-tip pen after the rehearsal and that under the hot glare of the television lights the pen had gone bone-dry. Fortunately, one of Reagan's advisers spotted a second pen, grabbed it, hit the floor and crawled across the Oval Room to Reagan's feet (thus putting the Secret Service men on the alert), and held the new pen up for the President. With a twinkle in his eye, Reagan scooped up the pen, and, without missing a beat, announced to the camera that he would try his pen again. Then he drew the red line on the chart. "Presto!" wrote Gergen afterward. "A beautiful line, and the night was saved."[50]

Full House

In the 1950s, Reagan did a brief stint in Las Vegas as master of ceremonies and comedian with a quartet called "The Continentals." In January 1986, he was back in Las Vegas again as the main attraction at a fund-raiser for Jim Santini, Republican candidate for the Senate. "It's difficult for me to visit this city," Reagan told the crowd, "without remembering what seems now like another lifetime, when my name was one of those listed on the neon signs outside a major hotel." He went on to recall playing the dinner show when people in the audience "waved with their fork" at a good line. He also remembered his critics. "For those of you who are too young to remember those days," he said, "let me explain that I didn't sing or dance, which prompted some to predict that I'd never play Las Vegas again. And what do you know?" he went on gleefully. "Here I am, and playing to a full house!"[51]

Hollywood

In his memoirs, published two years after leaving the White House, Reagan wrote that he frequently heard the question, "How could an actor be President?" His answer: "I've sometimes wondered how you could be President and not be an actor."

In many respects the former Hollywoodian remained an actor while he was in the White House. He read his carefully prepared speeches and cue cards with skill and conviction; and he made his public appearances important occasions for encouraging a mood of confidence and contentment throughout the land. "He was an actor in the White House and out of it," wrote biographer Lou Cannon. "Acting was what he did best."

Hollywood remained paramount in President Reagan's outlook on life. He saw hundreds of movies in the White House and at Camp David (on television as well as on the big screen) while he was President, and he liked to quote lines from his favorites, old and new. "Where do you find such men?" (*The Bridges at Toko-Ri*, 1955), he asked at the ceremony commemorating Americans who had died on D-Day in June 1944. "Make my day!" (Clint Eastwood's *Sudden Impact*, 1983), he cried during one of his confrontations with Congress. On occasion he told stories, in public and in private, that came from movies, but which he seemed to think were based on actual happenings: the black messman cradling a machine gun at Pearl Harbor and firing away at the Japanese (possibly *Air Force,* 1943); the B-17 bomber pilot who went down with a wounded gunner instead of using his parachute (*A Wing and a Prayer,* 1944). Once, when his aides were debating whether the use of charts during a televised address might distract him from the text, he said airily: "Listen, I once made a movie with Wallace Beery [a notorious scene stealer]. After that nothing could distract me!" Another time, when someone asked him whether he was upset by Soviet leader Mikhail Gorbachev's "rising popularity" around the world, he said confidently: "No, I don't resent his popularity or anything else. Good Lord, I co-starred with Errol Flynn once."

Reagan loved war movies. He had acted in several during World War II (*International Squadron,* 1941, *Rear Gunner,* 1942, *Desperate Journey,* 1943), had seen scores of others, and took some of his best anecdotes from them. His beloved strategic defense proposal ("Star Wars") derived in part from one of his own movies, *Murder in the Air* (1940), centering on an American ray gun that could shoot down distant enemy aircraft. One of his favorite actors, moreover, was John Wayne, the macho star of numerous war movies and Westerns. "When push comes to shove," said one of Reagan's aides, "when Reagan has to make a big decision—and he doesn't make any small ones—he asks himself one question and one question only. He asks himself, what would John Wayne have done."

But Reagan liked peace movies too. His desire to share strategic defense technology with the Soviets was inspired, according to Colin Powell, his last national security adviser, by *The Day the Earth Stood Still* (1951), a movie in which an envoy from an advanced civilization visits planet earth to warn earthlings to "join us and live in peace" or be wiped out. After one visit with Gorbachev, Reagan gave the Soviet leader a video copy of *Friendly Persuasion* (1956), a movie about Quakers, because, he said, it showed not only the tragedy of war, but also "the problems of pacifism, the nobility of patriotism, as well as the love of peace." At a top-level briefing on MX missiles, he interrupted at one point to recount the plot of *WarGames* (1983), a movie whose message was that the only way to win the "game" of thermonuclear war was not to play it. It was his only contribution to the discussion.

Reagan loved action movies, but he liked the old-time Hollywood musicals too. In 1983, the night before he had to preside over a world economic summit in Williamsburg, Virginia, White House chief of staff James Baker gave him a briefing book to study. The next morning, however, he noticed the President hadn't even glanced at the papers, and when he showed his disappointment, Reagan had a ready explanation. "Well, Jim," he said, *"The Sound of Music* [1965] was on last night."[52]

Cashing In

Not long after leaving the White House, Reagan visited his former agent, Lew Wasserman, now a Hollywood mogul, in the Universal Studios commissary, and Wasserman asked him whether there was any way he could lure him back to the movies. No, said Reagan, with a grin, for that would be cashing in on the Presidency. "Well, Mr. President," returned Wasserman, "we don't necessarily have to pay you."[53]

Don't Get Around Much Anymore

In November 1994, when the annual Ronald Reagan Freedom Award dinner was held in Beverly Hills, California, plans had been made for the former President to be present to confer the medal on Israel's Prime Minister Yitzhak Rabin. But Reagan was unable to be there. A few days before, he had announced that he was suffering from Alzheimer's disease and would thenceforth make no public appearances. "When the Lord calls me home," Reagan said in his letter to the American people, "whenever that may be, I will leave with the greatest love for this country of ours and eternal optimism for its future."

Nancy Reagan appeared in her husband's stead at the dinner. "I'm sorry Ronnie can't be here," she told the guests. "But he sends you all his best wishes, and thanks you for being here. . . ." She then presented Rabin with his award, and the Marine Band began a program of popular American dance music, with a Marine in uniform singing lead vocals. "Missed the Saturday dance, Heard they crowded the floor," went the first song, Duke Ellington's popular 1942 number. "Couldn't bear it without you, Don't get around much anymore."[54]

FORTY

George Bush
1989–1993

Who was George Bush? A Connecticut Yankee or a good ole boy from Texas? A New England patrician or a regular guy from the Southwest? A Kennebunkportian or a Houstonian? An aristocrat with a touch of hauteur or a down-to-earth guy with the common touch? People weren't quite sure—even those who voted for him in 1988—and at times Bush himself didn't seem to know for sure.

Bush's New England credentials were impeccable. Born George Herbert Walker Bush in Milton, Massachusetts, in 1924, he spent his childhood in Greenwich, Connecticut, where he was chauffeured to Country Day School, and then prepped at the elite Phillips Academy in Andover, Massachusetts. His father, Prescott S. Bush, an investment banker and moderate Republican who represented Connecticut in the Senate from 1953 to 1963, was an imposing figure who set high standards of behavior for his children; and his mother, Dorothy Walker, perhaps even more influential, instilled a love of sports in the children, saw to it that they attended church regularly, and cautioned them against becoming too self-important because they had been born to privilege. "They believed in an old-fashioned way of bringing up the family—generous measures of both love and discipline," Bush recalled. "Dad taught us about duty and service; Mother taught us about dealing with life on a personal basis, relating to other people." There was a great deal of *noblesse oblige* in Bush's upbringing.[1]

During World War II, Bush enlisted at eighteen, served as the youngest pilot in the Navy air service, flew fifty-eight combat missions, and won three air medals. He was also decorated with a Distinguished Flying Cross for his performance during a raid on Chichi Jima in the Bonin Islands, where, in September 1944, he completed a bombing attack after his plane was hit by flak, then went down, and floated "four terrifying hours in the water" before being rescued by a submarine.[2] In 1945, while still in the service, he married Barbara Pierce, a Smith College student, and after the war entered Yale College, where he majored in economics and took his B.A. in 1948. At Yale he received a Phi Beta Kappa key, was initiated into Skull and Bones, Yale's prestigious secret society, and served as captain and first baseman on the university's baseball team.

Despite his New England upbringing, President Bush had plenty of Texas in his background too. Upon graduating from Yale he could have joined his father's investment firm in New York, but instead, at twenty-four, he chose to go to Odessa, Texas, to make his way in the oil-development business there. "If I were a psychoanalyzer," he mused years later, "I might conclude that I was trying to, not compete with my father, but do something on my own. My stay in Texas was no Horatio Alger thing, but moving from New Haven to Odessa just about the day I graduated was quite a shift in lifestyle."[3] In Texas he quit jogging in Bermuda shorts; there were too many hoots and hollers from passing truck drivers. He also shucked his pin-stripe suits and "elitist shirts," as he called them, and started wearing khaki pants and open-collared shirts the way the natives did. His language changed a bit, too, and he talked about "bidness" (business), "ed-jew-cay-shun," and "fixin' " to do things. But the preppy expressions he had absorbed as a youngster ("nifty," "getting into deep doodoo," "zip-a-dee-doo-dah") died hard. In 1988, when he ran for President and was trying to counter charges that he was a bit of a wimp by presenting a macho image in public, preppyisms on occasion threatened to undermine his efforts. At one campaign stop, when some workingmen offered him coffee, he asked for "just a splash." Charged with running a negative campaign, he insisted he wasn't going to let the Democrats get away with it when they pulled "that naughty stuff" on him. He also expressed great glee over the way campaign aide Lee Atwater was "getting into their knickers," that is, angering the Democrats.

Along more positive lines, he promised to "hit a lick for peace" if he won the election. None of this was exactly Texas talk. Bush, decided *New York Times* columnist William Safire, was "patrician, not folksy, and he clanks falsely when he puts on Joe Six-pack nonairs."[4]

During his Texas years Bush did better as a businessman than as a politician. He gradually amassed a modest fortune in the oil business, but failed in two bids for the U.S. Senate. He did serve two terms in the House of Representatives, however, and became known for his conservative, but not extremist, position on most issues. In the spring of 1968 he voted for the open-housing provisions of the Civil Rights Act and incurred the wrath of his Houston constituents. "It's just the right thing to do," he told a friend. To an angry group of businessmen with whom he met when he returned to Houston, he declared: "I did what I thought was right. We agree on most issues. This one we don't agree on. I hope I still have your support. But if I don't have your support, I hope I still have your friendship. If I don't have your friendship, I'm sorry, but I have to vote my conscience."[5] He was re-elected to a second term that fall without opposition. When he left Congress two years later, Wilbur Mills, Arkansas Democrat who chaired the powerful Ways and Means Committee on which Bush served, declared: "I was sorry to see him go. Everyone seemed to like him. . . . He had the makings of a valuable member."[6]

In 1970 Bush ran for the Senate for the second time and, following his defeat, held a series of posts in the Nixon and Ford administrations—ambassador to the United Nations, chairman of the Republican National Committee, head of the U.S. liaison office (later embassy) in Peking, and director of the Central Intelligence Agency—in which he became known for his caution, loyalty, and low-keyed style. In 1980 he returned to politics, entering the primaries as a candidate for the Republican nomination for President. He lost out to Ronald Reagan, but ended up as Reagan's Vice-President and spent the next eight years making it clear that he followed the popular President "blindly," as he put it, and deserved to be his successor in the White House.[7] In 1980 he had run as a moderate and dismissed Reagan's economic views as "voodoo economics." In 1988, when he entered the presidential race for the second time, he identified himself wholeheartedly with what was called "Reaganomics." He also played down his New England background in 1988, extolled pork rinds and beer (though in private he preferred popcorn and vodka martinis), and made much of his experiences in the Lone Star State. He had kept his official residence in Houston—a suite in a downtown hotel—all these years. Kennebunkport, Maine, where the Bush summer home was located, was only for vacations.

Not all Texans were impressed. "I think created Texans are as good as birth Texans," wrote columnist Molly Ivins in the *Dallas Times-Herald*. "Most of those who died at the Alamo had come from somewhere else. But Bush has to know that there are three things a Texan does not do. We do not use 'summer' as a verb. We do not wear blue ties with little green whales on them. And we do not call trouble 'doodoo.' We're not setting the standards high. But there they are."[8] Like Ivins, *New York Times* columnist Russell Baker was also amused by Bush's efforts to present himself as "Old-Shoe George," especially when on the campaign trail. In a piece entitled "The Ivy Hayseed," Baker exclaimed: "Who is he really? He is George Bush, Yankee son of rich and elegant investment banker Prescott Bush who became a Senator from Connecticut. He is George Bush of Andover and Yale. He is George Bush, who knows what a debutante ball is and doesn't know that Iowa farmers don't. He is top drawer, upper crust, one of the snobs. He summers in Maine and knows about sailing. He says 'Golly' and 'Gee' and 'Gosh,' and maybe even 'Darn' and 'Heck!' and says them naturally because he was brought up to believe that gentlemen don't use vile language."[9]

Bush was indubitably a gentleman, and within his family and in the privileged circles to which he was accustomed, he behaved with grace, charm, generosity, and good humor. "It's easy to underestimate George Bush," said an old Yale friend, "because he's so damned genteel and nice."[10] In the rough-and-tumble game of party politics, however, he seemed never quite at ease. In his encounters with the public he tried too hard to be "one of the boys" to come off at his best. On occasion his discomfort led him to burble when speaking off the cuff and the result was a curious way of saying things that *New York Times* reporter Maureen Dowd called "Bush-Speak."

The Bush-Speak that grew out of the Texas Yankee's awkward efforts to play the populist in public had to be heard to be believed. It wasn't just a matter of preppyisms and tongue slips, though these

were a part of it. Its real trademark was its meandering unpredict-
ability: aimless clauses, awkward adverbs, dangling predicates,
jaunty jump-cuts. If William Henry Harrison is remembered chiefly
for his interminable inaugural address in 1841, Warren G.
Harding for stumbling onto the word "normalcy" in one of his speeches,
Calvin Coolidge for his thriftiness in utterance, and Gerald R. Ford
for his wonderful gaffes (saying "Hiawatha" when referring to California Senator Hayakawa), George Bush may well be remembered, not without affection, for his wondrous prose, when speaking off the record. Soon after he became President, a reporter
asked the transplanted Texan how he would do things differently
in the White House from the way Reagan had done them, and
he responded amiably: "Like the old advice from Jackman—you
remember, the guy that came out—character. He says, 'And then
I had some advice. Be yourself!' That proved to be the worst advice I could possibly have. And I'm going to be myself. Do it
that way." [11]

★ ★ ★

Greek Philosopher

Early in his Vice-Presidency, Bush gave a speech that included a
quotation from Thucydides, but he had trouble pronouncing the
name of the ancient Greek dramatist. It was "the longest five seconds of my life," sighed one of Bush's speechwriters after hearing
the speech. "He kept trying to get it right and he mangled it worse
each time." One of Bush's aides suggested a change and Bush
promptly accepted it. And when he delivered the same speech at
his next stop, with the same quotation, he put it this way: "As the
Greek philosopher Plato once said. . . ." [12]

Falling in Love

One evening, when Bush was Vice-President, he had dinner at the
Russian embassy in Washington and sat next to Mrs. Gorbachev.
After a long meal the Russians presented entertainment in the form
of a large opera singer. "She was enormous," Bush recalled, "not
a particularly attractive woman, but of course with a beautiful
voice. After a while, actually it was about midnight—we should

have been out of there an hour before—I turned to Mrs. Gorbachev and kiddingly said: 'Oh, this is such lovely music. I think I'm falling in love.' Mrs. Gorbachev looked over and very seriously she whispered: 'You better not. Remember Gary Hart?' " Was she being serious? The writer George Plimpton asked Bush about it later on. "Oh, absolutely," said Bush. "Not a smile on her face." Then, just in case Plimpton thought he was putting Gary Hart down (Hart dropped out of the 1988 presidential race because of philandering), Bush mentioned he knew Hart and liked him. "A very pleasant fellow." [13]

Very

Once, according to former President Gerald Ford, Bush was in the Middle East, and during a sight-seeing tour asked the guide: "How dead is the Dead Sea?" Lisped the guide: "Very!" [14]

Light 'em Up

Bush, observed *Time*, "resembled nothing so much as a medieval boy king who woke up one morning to find himself atop the throne and began tugging at the bell ropes for servants, ordering up royal carriages and scheduling banquets and tournaments." The President almost admitted as much. "In case you haven't noticed," he liked to say, "I really love the job."

Like the boy king, Bush had a prankish sense of humor. Sometimes he greeted visitors in the Oval Room by placing a windup mechanical bumblebee on the floor and letting it buzz around a bit. And sometimes he walked around the White House with a voice-activated stuffed monkey that knocked itself on the head whenever he started talking. One August day when he was in Aspen, Colorado, he spied actress Melanie Griffith and her baby girl by the roadside, activated the special speaker in the rear of the limousine, and yelled at the kid: "What's the matter, Dakota? Never seen a talking car before?"

Bush's favorite car game was called "Light 'em Up." Sometimes, as his limousine moved through the streets, he picked out someone in the crowd, usually a woman or child, pointed to the person, and then waited until, suddenly, there was eye contact and the passerby realized, in a flash, "The President is looking at me!"

At this point the target's face lit up and Bush had won the game. Bush liked to play the game when he had a guest with him, and he always asked the guest to report on the progress of the game. "Did I get her?" he would ask. "Did I light her up?" If the guest was a local Congressman or Republican official seeking favors from the President, Bush's game left them bewildered and frustrated. But that was the aim of the game.

Bush was amused, not offended, by Dana Carvey, the comedian on the TV show "Saturday Night Live," who did satirical imitations of him, and he invited him to the White House more than once. One day the two of them stood in front of the fireplace in the Oval Room and talked at the same time, with Carvey doing Bush and Bush doing himself. And Bush doubled over in laughter as Carvey suddenly began chopping the air with one hand and imitating the way the President defended Dan Quayle, his Vice-President, against criticism: "Daaaaan Quaaaale—getting stronger, learning ev-er-y daaay!"[15]

Geoffrey

During a meeting of world leaders in London in July 1991, President Bush tried hard not to let it bother him that Mikhail Gorbachev was getting the lion's share of the attention. One night, however, his ego took a real blow. At Queen Elizabeth's dinner for the world leaders at Buckingham Palace, the wife of one of the foreign ministers came up to the President at one point and greeted him warmly. "Oh, Geoffrey," she cooed. "It's so nice to see you." Responded Bush stiffly: "I'm George Bush, the President of the United States." Sniffed the woman, "Well, you look a lot like Geoffrey," and drifted away. Two of Bush's Cabinet members— Secretary of State James Baker and Treasury Secretary Nicholas Brady—overheard the exchange and they couldn't resist addressing the President as "Geoffrey" for the rest of the evening.[16]

Read My Lips

In his acceptance speech at the Republican convention in August 1988, Bush announced: "And the Congress will push me to raise taxes, and I'll say no, and they'll push, and I'll say no again, and they'll push again. And I'll say to them: 'Read my lips: No new taxes.' " Peggy Noonan wrote Bush's acceptance address, and in her memoirs, appearing in 1990, she revealed that Bush's aides kept trying to take the "Read my lips" line out of the speech. "I kept putting it back in," she wrote. "Why? Because it's definite. It's not subject to misinterpretation. It means, I mean this."

But the "Read my lips" pledge eventually got the new President into trouble. In June 1990 he found himself agreeing to a rise in taxes after all in order to keep the deficit from getting out of hand. In October, moreover, Congressional Democrats proposed another deal: if the President agreed to a rise in tax rates for the affluent, Congress would agree to a cut in taxes on capital gains (one of Bush's favorite proposals). For hours Bush wavered, first indicating he would go along with Congress on the deal, and then, when Republican opposition mounted, announcing that it was unacceptable. One day reporters pursued the President as he jogged laps in St. Petersburg, Florida, pressing him to clarify his stand. "Read my hips!" he smirked, and jogged on.

Bush's little quip didn't help any. His acceptance of tax hikes in June 1990 in violation of his pledge hurt him badly with the hard right in his party and put him on the defensive when he ran for re-election in 1992. Not long after Bill Clinton, a saxophone player, defeated Bush at the polls that year, Professor Peter Schickele, the industrious (and whimsical) discoverer of P.D.Q. Bach, presented the premiere of a composition in New York City called "Lip My Reeds," which required musicians to play their reeds without the rest of the instruments. But Bush had already faced the music.[17]

Ex, Ex, Ex, Ex!

A day or so before Bush left the White House, Senator Alan Simpson dropped by to say good-bye, and Bush's last words, he reported, were: "Over and out!" On inauguration day, when Bush rode to the Capitol with the President-elect, he was pleased when Clinton noticed a sign in the crowd, THANK YOU PRESIDENT BUSH, pointed it out, and joined him in waving to the lone Bushie. He was also deeply touched by Clinton's reference in his inaugural to Bush's "half century of service to America." After leaving Washington, he made it clear that as ex-President he was going to refrain from criticizing his successor for the time being, because "I recognize that he's got a very difficult job."

In retirement Bush settled down in a red-brick house in Houston, started working on a book on foreign policy, planned his presidential library at Texas A & M University, and gave lectures around the country. "No more politics," he declared. "I've had it up to here," he told an interviewer, putting his hand on his throat. "George," said his wife Barbara, "is the best little dishwasher in Texas." George begged to differ. "Barbara makes the bed," he announced. "I make the coffee. And Millie [the dog] does the dishes."

When Bush joined former President Jimmy Carter at the Clinton White House in 1994 to push for the North America Free Trade Agreement (NAFTA), he listened to his successor's pitch for the trade pact, and remarked afterward: "I thought that was a very eloquent statement by President Clinton, and now I understand why he's inside looking out and I'm outside looking in." Bush told people he wanted to "de-imperialize" the ex-Presidency. At a Mideast ceremony a few days after the NAFTA meeting, when a White House staffer referred to him as "the President," he exclaimed: "Ex, ex, ex, ex!"[18]

In May 1995, however, the ex-President made headlines when he resigned from the National Rifle Association, expressing outrage over an NRA fund-raising letter which compared federal law enforcement agents to Nazi stormtroopers. The "broadside against federal agents," he told the NRA, "deeply offends my own sense of decency and honor; and it offends my concept of service to country. It indirectly slanders a wide array of government law enforcement officials, who are out there, day and night, laying their lives on the line for all of us." The warm response to his action showed that, like Jimmy Carter, Bush continued to exercise considerable moral influence after leaving the White House.[19]

FORTY-ONE

William Jefferson Clinton
1993–

Bill Clinton came to politics early, but he was not exactly a "born politician." When he was a youngster, his main interests for a time were religion and music, and he toyed with the idea of making them his life work. He enjoyed going to church, sang in the choir, and liked reading the Bible; and some of his older friends thought he would make a good Baptist preacher. Others, though, were more impressed with his musical gifts and figured he was headed for a career in music. He played tenor sax for the high school band in Hot Springs, attended band camps in the summer, organized a jazz trio—the Kingsmen—to play at his school, received first-place ratings at state band festivals, and was offered at least one music scholarship to attend college. By his senior year, however, politics was replacing music as his abiding passion.

JFK seems to have played some part in Clinton's decision to seek fulfillment in the political world. In 1963, when he was sixteen, he attended Arkansas Boys State, a camp where young people learned about the practical workings of the American political system, and then became a delegate to Boys Nation (sponsored by the American Legion) to observe the federal government in Washington at firsthand. He toured the nation's capital, glorying in its historic sites, dined on Capitol Hill with Arkansas's celebrated Senator J. William Fulbright, and, in the most exciting happening of all, got to shake hands with President John F. Kennedy, his boyhood hero, at a White House reception in the Rose Garden. It was, he thought ever afterward, a major turning point in his life. "When he came back from Washington, holding this picture of himself with Jack Kennedy. . . ," his mother recalled, "I knew right then that politics was the answer for him"[1] Years later, when he became President himself, he insisted on showing his mother the exact spot in the Rose Garden where the epiphanous event had occurred.

Politics was very much on Clinton's mind when he went off to college in 1964. At Georgetown University, where he studied international relations, then Oxford University, where he spent two years as a Rhodes Scholar, and finally Yale Law School, where he took his LL.B. in 1973, Clinton impressed his classmates as a likable eager beaver destined for a successful political career and maybe, even, the Presidency. One of his Georgetown friends recalled years later that the young Arkansan "exhibited all the signs of someone who was on the way to somewhere else and in a hurry to get there. If he had not been so totally amiable, genuinely kind, open, and friendly, he would have been heartily disliked by one and all, but he had absolutely no pretense about him and that, of course, made him irresistible."[2]

From one of his Georgetown professors, Clinton learned how to sleep only four hours a night and then take twenty-minute naps during the day to get more rest. All great leaders, the professor told him, handled sleep this way, and Clinton quickly mastered the technique. This meant he was able to fill his waking hours with varied and almost ceaseless activity. He read voraciously, did superior work in his classes, worked part-time to help pay his way, engaged in student politics (he was elected class president at Georgetown during his freshman and sophomore years), joined campus social clubs, and did a lot of sight-seeing wherever he happened to be. He had time, too, to be a do-gooder as well as a gofer. When he was a sophomore, he spent hours helping a freshman who was blind learn to get around the Georgetown campus on his own; did volunteer relief work in Washington following the riots touched off by the assassination of Martin Luther King, Jr., the apostle of nonviolence, in April 1968; and worked as a counselor in a student-sponsored clinic at Georgetown to help alcoholics. (His stepfather was an alcoholic whom he restrained from abusing his mother when he was a boy.) Withal he found plenty of occasions to get involved in lively rap sessions with his classmates on the issues of the day, large and small.

Warren G. Harding liked to bloviate; Bill Clinton, to schmooze. Schmoozing was more purposeful; it aimed at winning friends and influencing people as well as engaging in amiable chitchat. Clinton had a good memory for faces and names which flattered people; he also had a way of looking people straight in the eye and listening carefully to what they said, as well as making remarks of his own, that gave them the feeling he took them seriously. His critics, to be sure, found his style shrewd and calculating. "He crawls into your soul for maybe a minute or two," growled Max Brantley, editor of the *Arkansas Times*, "and then he's looking over your shoulder for the next guy in the room that he's going to do the same thing to."[3] But Clinton's friends insisted that his interest in other people was genuine and heartfelt. "He is an empathetic person," declared Betsey Wright, friend and gubernatorial aide for many years, "whose first motivation was to help people, and then to set up systems where they could help themselves."[4] Sometimes, when people he met at receptions and rallies told him their troubles, he was moved to tears; and he might even give them a little hug after listening to their tales of woe. After he became President, *New York Times* columnist Anna Quindlen called him "the huggiest Commander in Chief in the history of the Republic."[5]

Many Americans responded enthusiastically, at least in the beginning, to the big-hearted side of President Clinton's personality. Soon after he entered the White House, he was receiving more mail than any other Chief Executive in American history. Some of the letters accompanied gifts: coupons for McDonald's Big Macs (he was a fast-food fan), jogging caps and shorts (he was a runner), home-made remedies to clear his sinuses (he had allergies), and prescriptions for losing weight (he was a big eater). Other letters contained doctor and hospital bills, complaints about their costliness, and pleas that he do something to bring medical expenses under control. Still others dealt with personal problems—sexual molestation, alcoholic parents—and asked for help. "The thing I notice most . . . is the tone," observed Lillie Bell, director of White House Mail Analysis. "In the old days, people who wrote the President wrote him as a figure way up above them. But most people write to this President the way you would write to a friend. He's not way up there. There is no awe in the letters."[6]

Inability to inspire awe may have worked against Clinton. Though Americans liked to grouse about an imperial Presidency, they actually loved the pomp and circumstance that went with the White House and had a great deal of grudging respect for a President who came across as "a figure way up above them," even if they did not like his policies. It was all right, to be sure, for a Chief Executive to be a bit folksy, but if he was to be truly "presidential" he had also to be somewhat aloof, inaccessible, even regal. Unfortunately for Clinton, it was simply not in his nature to hold back, keep his distance, and check his feelings in public. He had to be himself: sunny, outgoing, cheerful, gregarious, warmhearted, and eager to connect personally with the people he encountered. He made himself so available (on the jogging track as well as on TV talk shows) that his critics said he lacked *gravitas*. "Clinton's one-on-one, eyeball-to-eyeball style of leadership is not something we are accustomed to in this country," observed the *Fort Worth Star-Telegram*'s conservative columnist Bill Thompson. "We've gotten used to the imperial presidency, to leaders who hand down edicts from on high and then retreat to their elegant Oval Office while the citizens wrestle with the results. Clinton doesn't operate that way. His idea of governing is to knock on your door and get you involved in the process."[7]

Dialogue, Clinton liked to say, was essential to leadership. "People engaged by their leaders in conversation," he said, "feel better about the outcome even if they would prefer a different one, simply because they are given a chance to have their say. Dialogue is the way to teach."[8] It was the way to learn, too, for Clinton. He had a habit of soliciting a variety of opinions before making up his mind, and he liked to join his White House aides in lengthy bull sessions so he could swap ideas with them about urgent matters. John F. Kennedy, it was said, gave the person talking to him about seven seconds to make an impression; Clinton was more likely to give him seven hours.[9] His tendency to be late for scheduled events came from his reluctance to break off conversations or to leave a group before talking to every last person in it.

Clinton disliked confrontations. He preferred conciliation and consensus to contradiction and conflict, and he invariably sought areas of agreement with people whom he knew held views quite at variance with his own. Like all intelligent people, he recognized that there were two (or more) sides to most questions, but since he tended to shift back and forth in his opinions as he made the rounds, he gave the impression of being wishy-washy, indecisive, and lacking a solid center. "Mother," he used to say, "there are two sides to every story." "Yeah," she always shot back, "my side and the wrong side!"[10] A bit of his mother's cocksureness might have been a help. During his first months in the White House his tendency to backtrack in the face of adverse criticism, and, sometimes, of agonizing in public about difficult issues, made him a tempting target for his enemies. "He's very much a consensus builder," observed reporter Brenda Blagg. "That's what he likes to do. He doesn't like to make anyone mad and, of course, in the process of trying not to make anyone mad, he makes somebody mad every time."[11]

Sometimes Clinton got mad himself. He thought the opinion industries unduly censorious, resented the fact they hadn't given him the customary "honeymoon" during his early months in the White House, and from time to time blasted the media to his friends and aides. In public, though, he usually succeeded in preserving his equanimity, no matter how irked he was by some of the questions reporters tossed at him during interviews and press conferences. Once, however, he flared up at a reporter and almost at once regretted it. In June 1993, right after Ruth Bader Ginsburg, his choice to fill a Supreme Court vacancy, had spoken movingly about her nomination, ABC's Brit Hume asked about the "zigzag quality" of the way he chose Ginsburg, and Clinton lost his temper. "How you could ask a question like that," he said angrily, "after the statement she made, is beyond me." But he soon made amends. At an impromptu press conference a couple of days later, he suddenly turned to Hume, newly married, and said playfully: "You know what I'm really upset about? You got a honeymoon and I didn't!" Hume beamed. So did White House aide David Gergen, who was trying to help Clinton with the media. "That was perfect!" whispered Gergen to one of his colleagues. It was of course vintage Clinton.

In January 1995, at the dedication of the William Jefferson Clinton Elementary Magnet School in Little Rock, one of the students asked Clinton how he coped with criticism. He answered by quoting Benjamin Franklin: "Our critics are our friends, for they show us our faults." He went on to elaborate: ". . . it's important not to take criticism personally. That is, a lot of times people try to hurt you personally, and you can't let that happen. So if someone criticizes you, ask yourself, 'Is it true what they're saying?' And if it's true, then say, 'Well, I'm going to try to improve. I'm going to try to do better.' "[13]

★ ★ ★

Thanksgiving

One Thanksgiving Day, when Clinton was about eight, his mother sent him to the grocery store to get some extra food for dinner, but instead of bringing back food he returned with another little boy. "Bill," said his mother, "who's your new friend?" "Johnny," replied Clinton. "He was at the bus stop and I found out that he wasn't gonna have a real Thanksgiving dinner so I brought him home to have Thanksgiving dinner with us." Then he pointed to a bag of chips in Johnny's hand and said: "Whoever heard of anybody having a big bag of Fritos on Thanksgiving Day? Mother," he added, "we're not going to hold still for that." His mother nodded. "You're right, we're not." Young Clinton, his mother said years later, "was forever bringing people home to eat."[14]

Clinton's D

When Clinton was in grammar school he usually received A's in all his classes. One day, however, he came home with a D in conduct on his report card. When his mother called the school to find out what was wrong, the teacher told her: "There's no real problem. It's just that he is so sharp and he's so alert he knows the answer immediately and will not give the others a chance. I have to get his attention one way or another and this is the only way I know how to do it because he is so competitive he will not be able to stand this D." It was Clinton's last D.[15]

Notable Exception

When Clinton entered the Yale Law School, there was a "black table" in the cafeteria where students took their meals. "This self-segregation was readily acknowledged," recalled William T. Coleman, one of the blacks, "and accepted by the major student body, with one notable exception." The exception: Bill Clinton, "a tall, robust, friendly guy with a thick Southern accent and a cherubic face," who violated the unspoken taboo by plopping himself down at the table one night to eat and chat.

At first Clinton's presence at the table caused discomfort; the blacks stared at him as if to say, "Man, don't you know whose table this is?" But the "tall guy with the thick Southern accent," according to Coleman, seemed oblivious to the hostility and soon engaged the black students in conversation. "He was immensely curious about people," Coleman remembered. "He has an ability, in a non-obtrusive manner, to get people to talk about themselves. He was fun and funny; on occasion, even raucous. He had the gift of the true story teller, in which he could take the simplest event, and in retelling it, turn it into a saga, complete with a plot and a moral. At the same time he was serious, and would discuss social and moral issues with concern, depth of knowledge and insight. By simply being himself, the Southerner dissipated the unspoken taboo and became a regular and welcomed member of our table." Clinton and Coleman, who became roommates during their second year at Yale, continued their friendship after Clinton entered Arkansas politics upon graduation and Coleman became a lawyer in Detroit.[16]

Bill and Hillary's Excellent Adventure

One day, when Hillary Rodham was passing through the student lounge at the Yale Law School, she overheard someone declaiming: "And not only that, we have the largest watermelons in the world!" When she asked who it was, friends told her: "Oh, that's Bill Clinton, and all he ever talks about is Arkansas." She was intrigued.

A few days later Hillary met Bill. Bill was chatting with a classmate, Jeffrey Glekel, in the law library about trying out for the *Yale Law Journal,* and when he noticed Hillary working at a nearby desk, it was his turn to be intrigued. "Little by little . . . ," Glekel recalled, "I noticed Bill's concentration began to slacken and his interest to wane. It was becoming clear to me that Bill's focus was somewhere other than the *Law Journal.* As I continued to talk, Bill's eyes seemed to wander; he appeared to be glancing over my shoulder with increasing frequency, while we continued to discuss whether or not he should participate in *Jour-*

nal activities." Suddenly Hillary got up, walked over, smiled at Bill, and said: "Look, if you're going to keep staring at me and I'm going to keep staring back, we should at least introduce ourselves." For a moment Bill was uncharacteristically tongue-tied, but he was soon chatting animatedly with Hillary, and Glekel decided to bow out. "I realized that I was fighting a losing battle on behalf of the *Law Journal* and excused myself," he said later, "little suspecting that Bill had found an asset that evening far more valuable than the *Law Journal* membership."

Hillary Rodham was a Midwesterner, but she eventually became an Arkansan. In the fall of 1974, she drove to Fayetteville (where Clinton taught at the University of Arkansas Law School) with her friend Sarah Ehrman, and, en route, Sarah kept asking: "Hillary, are you crazy, are you sure you want to go to Fayetteville?" When they reached their destination, it was the day of the Texas-Arkansas football game, and the town was overflowing with college students yelling the cry of the Arkansas Razorbacks, "Soo-ee, soo-ee, pig, pig, *pig!*" Again Sarah asked: "For God's sake, Hillary, are you crazy? You're not going to stay in this town. *Why* are you doing this?" Explained Hillary: "I love him." She soon joined Bill on the faculty of the University of Arkansas Law School, and in October 1975 they were married.

Bill was proud of his roots. At Yale he didn't bother to interview for the major law firms in the East because he intended to return to Arkansas upon graduation and get into politics. "All I wanted to do was go home," he recalled. "I thought I would hang out my shingle in Hot Springs and see if I could run for office." In 1974 he entered the race for Congress from his district and lost, but in 1976 he was elected attorney-general, and in 1978 became governor and went on to win four more elections as governor before entering presidential politics. *Arkansas Times* editor John Brummett thought Bill was "more Yale and Oxford than Arkansas," but Bill continued to identify himself with his home state. He loved to show friends from the East the sights and treat them to Arkansas specialties like fried pie. He also continued to pepper his remarks with the homely expressions he had learned as a boy. Speaking in Tennessee during the 1992 presidential race, he said he would be brief: "I can give you just rickety-tick what's been happening." And when talking in Pennsylvania about ideas that didn't take a genius to understand, he declared: "You don't have to be all broken out with brilliance, as we say at home, or a tree full of owls."

Hillary, reared a Goldwater Republican, became a Clinton Democrat and was indispensable to her husband. The two saw eye to eye on most matters and worked together as close-knit partners. Still, there were jokes about the Bill-and-Hillary ("Billary") partnership. After Bill became President, a popular story had it that when he was criticized for trying to give his wife a government job, he said, "Heck, if I weren't married to Hillary, she'd be the first in line for any of the appointments," at which a friend exclaimed: "Heck, if you weren't married to Hillary, you wouldn't be *making* any of these appointments!" The Clintons enjoyed the joke.[17]

Having Fun

When Clinton became attorney-general of Arkansas in 1977, he threw himself into his work with energy and enthusiasm and expected everyone on his staff to do the same. One Friday afternoon, when Joseph Purvis, deputy attorney-general, was so swamped with work that he was ready to collapse, Clinton walked into his office, sat down, handed him a stick of gum, and asked with a grin: "Joe boy, are you having fun?" Exploded Purvis: "What in hell did you say?" Returned Clinton amiably: "I asked you if you were having fun, because if you are not having fun, you better put this down and move to something else. When this becomes work instead of fun, it is time to move on."[18]

Standing in the Rain

When Clinton was elected governor of Arkansas in 1978, he became the youngest governor in the United States. In 1980, however, he lost his bid for a second term, and in 1982, when he tried again, he practically campaigned around the clock to be sure of victory. One cold, rainy morning, he got up at 3:30 a.m. and hurried off to the Campbell Soup Plant to canvass the workers arriving for the four o'clock shift. The workers going in for the shift change were amazed to see the young candidate shivering in the rain as he shook hands, and after a while a woman came out of the building, went up to him, and announced severely: "Mr. Clinton, I was going to vote for you but I don't think I can vote for you now. Anybody who would stand out here in the freezing rain and in the dark when they don't have to, isn't smart enough to be governor!" As she sailed off, Clinton started laughing and whispered to an aide: "I bet you she votes for me!" He won the election.[19]

Change of Mind

When Clinton was governor, the Arkansas legislature passed a bill at his suggestion giving a 100 percent tax credit for donations to the colleges and universities of the state. The bill came to his desk at the end of the legislative session and at that point people in the Department of Finance warned that the measure would encourage taxpayers to give "tons of money" for higher education to escape paying the taxes the state badly needed for other purposes. After hearing them out, Clinton decided to veto the measure after all, so he stamped it "disapproved," signed his name, and instructed the state troopers to put it in the mail slot of the House door, just before the twenty-day deadline for acting on the legislation. He then called up Joe Bell, one of the legislators, to tell him what he had done. "Well, Bill, you can't do that," expostulated Bell. "Remember when four or five months ago, I brought some college presidents into your office? We talked about this thing and you said if we passed it you'd sign it." Cried Clinton: "I did?" "Yes, sir," said Bell, "you said you'd sign it if we passed it."

After hanging up the phone Clinton had second thoughts. "I told these college presidents," he reminded himself. "I've got to keep my word." So he arranged for the state troopers to return to the House and rake around under the door with a coat hanger until they succeeded in extricating the bill he had disapproved. When they retrieved the bill and delivered it back to the Governor's Mansion, Clinton took his pen, blacked out his stamp of disapproval, put his initials on the side, and returned it to the House. His turnabout raised a rumpus in the Department of Finance. "Governor, this is catastrophic," people there remonstrated. "In a few months people will start writing these checks to the colleges and universities and the tax revenues will plummet." They finally convinced Clinton a second time, and in due course he called for a special session of the legislature to repeal the act. Afterwards, a reporter who had covered Clinton for many years observed dryly that Clinton "will not make a decision until he's studied it from every angle known to man."[20]

Clinton Time

Clinton, his mother fretted, seemed to have no concept of time. He was always at least twenty minutes behind schedule because he couldn't resist talking to a few more people and shaking a few more hands. When he was governor, she reported, he "would delay and delay and delay," and when he finally got to his airplane, he became impatient when the pilot insisted on going through the customary preflight checklist before taking off. "Come on," Clinton would tell him, "come on, let's go." But the pilot always looked him in the eye "in that John Wayne way pilots have," according to his mother, and said sternly: "You should've left a little earlier, Governor." Clinton's mother heartily approved of the reprimand. Once, after her son became President-elect, she bawled him out in public for keeping some people waiting. She had no patience with what people on his staff called "Clinton time."[21]

Car License Fee

Clinton was deeply disappointed by his failure to win a second term as governor in 1980, and for a time he wondered whether he should try again. One day, soon after the 1980 defeat, when he was on his way to visit his mother, he stopped at a service station to fill his tank. "You're Bill Clinton, aren't you?" said the attendant when he saw him. "Yes, sir," said Clinton. "Well, said the man, "I cost you eleven votes, son. And I loved every minute of it." "You did?" exclaimed Clinton. "I did," nodded the man. "It was me and my two boys and their wives and six of my buddies. We just leveled you." Cried Clinton: "Why did you do it?" Answered the man: "I had to—you raised my car license." Clinton tried to explain. "Let me ask you something," he said. "Look out there across this road. Remember when that road right there was in the front page of the biggest newspaper in this state, because cars were buried in it and I had to send tractors down here to get the cars out?" The man shook his head. "I don't care, Bill," he said. "I still don't want to pay for it." Clinton persisted. "Let me ask you something else," he said. "Would you ever consider voting for me again?" The man looked down at his shoes and then looked up at Clinton and said mildly: "You know, I would. We're even now." Clinton rushed over to the pay phone, called his wife, and announced: "We're gonna run!"

Even after launching his campaign for re-election, however, Clinton still wasn't sure the voters would forgive him for raising car license fees. Then came another encounter that gave him hope. One day he walked into a little country store, and a man standing there exclaimed: "Aren't you Bill Clinton?" "Yes, sir," said Clinton, and the man went on: "Well, son, I voted against you last time. But I'm gonna vote for you this time." Clinton was delighted. "That's wonderful," he grinned. Then he asked: "Why did you vote against me last time?" Replied the man: "I had to. You raised my car license." Persisted Clinton: "Well, why are you gonna vote for me this time?" To his surprise, the man replied: "Because you raised my car license." Clinton was puzzled. "Look, mister," he said, "it's close to the end of the election. I'm desperate for every vote I can get. The last thing in the world I want to do is make you mad. But, if you'll forgive me, it don't make a lick of sense for you to vote for me this time for the same reason you voted against me last time." Explained the man: "Oh, Bill, it makes all the sense in the world. You may be a lot of things, but you ain't dumb. You're the least likely one ever to raise that car license again, and I'm for you!"

Clinton won the 1982 election with 54.7 percent of the votes and became the first Arkansas governor ever to be defeated for re-election and later returned to the statehouse.[22]

18th Hole

Late one afternoon in September 1991, Arkansas Senator David Pryor played golf with Governor Clinton, and although they talked as they played, Pryor was surprised that they went through 17 holes of play without Clinton's ever mentioning presidential politics. Then, on the 18th hole, Clinton sliced his drive into the rough behind a pine tree. As they walked over to survey the ball, Clinton looked up at Pryor and asked: "What should I do?" Suggested Pryor: "Use a 2 iron and hit the ball back in the fairway." "No," cried Clinton. "What I want to know is should I run for President?" Pryor thought he should, and he did.[23]

De-escalation

Amiable and even-tempered in public, Clinton blew his stack in private, his aides well knew, if things went wrong in his campaign for President in 1992. Time and again they steeled themselves for the SMO (Standard Morning Outburst), as they called it. But they also knew the Democratic candidate usually calmed down soon after a big blow-up.

On September 1, 1992, at a campaign stop in Macon, Georgia, Clinton spoke to a group of senior citizens in the town square, but was surprised to find thousands of townspeople who came to hear him roped off from the event. "Your people told us they didn't want any Macon people here," a local official explained. Furious, Clinton went over to the ropes and spent the next few hours shaking hands with people in the summer heat. Later on he angrily confronted his aides and demanded to know who had made the decision to exclude the Macon people from the senior-citizen event. When his aides professed ignorance, he ordered one senior staffer to return to campaign headquarters in Little Rock to track down the delinquent. "I want him dead, dead," raged Clinton. "I want him killed, I want him horse-whipped." His aides had never seen him so furious. When the senior aide returned from Little Rock, Clinton took him aside. "I want to know who did this. I want him fired," he cried, downgrading the punishment. It turned out to be an unimaginative plodder at the lower levels of the campaign organization who had made the mistake, but whom Clinton knew personally. "Damn it," said Clinton, quieting down. "I hope he gets a real talking to."[24]

Crown Jewel

By the time Clinton became President, America's chief executives had long since given up what Mrs. Clinton called "a zone of privacy" in their lives. The media covered their activities daily, almost hourly, and a strict schedule and tight security governed their comings and goings. The White House had come to seem like a "Great White Jail" to some of its occupants. Clinton loved being President, but like his predecessors, at times he couldn't help feeling confined by the exacting regimen that went with the exalted position.

Soon after the inauguration, Clinton invited political consultant
Paul Begala (his "favorite phrasemaker") to visit the White House,
gave him a lively historical tour of the place, and finally took him
to the Oval Office. Begala was overwhelmed by the grandeur of
the President's office and by the thought of the momentous decisions that had been made there, and his knees practically buckled
as he surveyed the room. "Don't let it get you," murmured Clinton, as he observed his friend's reaction. Then he added dryly:
"This is the crown jewel of the Federal penal system!"[25]

Testing

On September 22, 1993, when Clinton appeared before a joint session of Congress to talk about health reform, he took a look at
the TelePrompTer during the welcoming applause and found to his
dismay that the speech he was to give wasn't on the screen. "Al,"
he whispered to the Vice-President, "this is the wrong speech! It's
last February's." Gore leaned over to look, saw the blunder, and
immediately sent over George Stephanopolous, the White House
communications director, to download the correct speech. As Stephanopolous fast-forwarded the tape and the words whizzed by,
Clinton could wait no longer and decided to wing it. For seven
minutes, as Stephanopolous labored to correct the mistake, he
talked about the health problems facing the nation and he did so in
such a confident and effortless fashion that no one—except his wife
and daughter—realized that he was improvising. And then, when
Stephanopolous finally reached the correct place on the TelePromp-
Ter, Clinton simply segued into the text before him as though he
had been using it all along. Afterward, when one of his aides asked
him what was going on in his mind during the crisis, he smiled
and said: "Well, I just thought, 'God, you're testing me!' "[26]

Clinton, Dole, and Gramm

The rejection of Clinton's health-insurance proposals in 1994 was
a setback for the President, and the capture of both branches of
Congress by the Republicans in November 1994 was an even more
serious blow. Still, Clinton was determined to seek a second term
in 1996, even though Republican challengers launched vigorous
campaigns for their party's nomination soon after the Congres-

sional elections. Kansas Senator Bob Dole (the majority leader) and Texas Senator Phil Gramm, the main contestants for the nomination, were soon snapping at each other, with Gramm, 53, hinting that Dole, 72, was too old to be President. Dole then released the results of a physical examination to show that he was in excellent health.

In August 1995, when Clinton, 48, and Dole, 72, appeared before the National Governors Association meeting in Burlington, Vermont, to discuss welfare reform, they also got around to debating another topic: personal health. "My cholesterol is lower than Clinton's," announced Dole. "My blood pressure is lower than Clinton's. My weight is less than Clinton's." Then he added, with a swipe at Gramm: "But I am not going to make health an issue in 1996." When Clinton came to speak, he said that Senator Dole had hurt his feelings, but that in any case he knew that his resting pulse was "much lower than Senator Dole's." But "that's not really his fault," he went on. "I don't have to deal with Phil Gramm every day." Just about then, almost as if to corroborate Clinton, Gramm issued a blast at Dole's welfare plan as a "deeply flawed proposal."[27]

Notes

Preface

1. Claude Fuess, *Calvin Coolidge* (Boston, 1940), 479.
2. Joseph B. Bishop, *Notes and Anecdotes of Many Years* (New York, 1925), 5.
3. Arthur M. Schlesinger, "The U.S. Presidents," *Life*, XXV (November 1, 1948), 65–74.
4. Malcolm Cowley, *The Literary Situation* (New York, 1954), 124–31.

1. George Washington

1. W. S. Baker, *Character Portraits of Washington* (Philadelphia, 1887), 120.
2. Charles Francis Adams, ed., *Memoirs of John Quincy Adams,* 12 vols. (Philadelphia, 1874–77), VIII:479.
3. "Editor's Table," *Southern Literary Messenger,* XXVI (February 1858), 153.
4. Cornelius C. Felton in *North American Review,* XCI (October 1860), 580.
5. Nathalia Wright, *Horatio Greenough: The First American Sculptor* (Philadelphia, 1963), 143–57; Henry F. and Katharine Pringle, "Silliest Statues You Ever Saw!" *Saturday Evening Post,* CCXXV (December 6, 1952), 45; Mary Clemmer Ames, *Ten Years in Washington* (Hartford, Conn., 1880), 104–5.

6. Nathaniel Hawthorne, *Complete Writings,* 22 vols. (Boston and New York, 1903), XXII:43.

7. James Parton, *The Life of Thomas Jefferson* (Boston, 1874), 369.

8. John Adams to Thomas Jefferson, July 1813, in Albert Ellery Bergh, ed., *The Writings of Thomas Jefferson,* 20 vols. (Washington, D.C., 1904–5), XIII:301; Gertrude Stein, "George Washington," *Four in America* (New Haven, Conn., 1974), 163.

9. Stewart Mitchell, ed., *New Letters of Abigail Adams, 1788–1801* (Boston, 1947), 35.

10. James Thomas Flexner, *Gilbert Stuart: A Great Life in Brief* (New York, 1955), 124.

11. Mason L. Weems, *The Life of Washington,* 1809 ed., ed. Marcus Cunliffe (Cambridge, Mass., 1962), 8–10.

12. Ibid., 12.

13. *Washington Post,* February 23, 1926, cited in Rupert Hughes, *George Washington: The Human Being and the Hero, 1732–1762* (New York, 1926), 46.

14. William Gordon, *History of the Independence of the United States,* 4 vols. (London, 1788), II:203.

15. Freeman Hunt, *American Anecdotes,* 2 vols. (Boston, 1830), I:206–7; John Corbin, *The Unknown Washington* (New York, 1930), 43–46, points out that not all Washington biographers accept the story as authentic.

16. G. W. P. Custis, *Memoirs of Washington* (Chicago, 1859), 132–34.

17. Charles Francis Adams, ed., *Familiar Letters of John Adams and His Wife Abigail Adams* (Boston and New York, 1876), 65; L. H. Butterfield, ed., *Diary and Autobiography of John Adams,* 4 vols. (Cambridge, Mass., 1926), III:322–23; W. E. Woodward, *George Washington: The Image and the Man* (New York, 1926), 266.

18. John Bernard, *Retrospections of America, 1797–1811* (New York, 1887), 93.

19. Paul Wilstach, *Patriots Off Their Pedestals* (Indianapolis, 1927), 32–33.

20. Paul F. Boller, Jr., *George Washington and Religion* (Dallas, 1963), 8–9.

21. Custis, *Memoirs of Washington,* 218–19 n.

22. Alexander Hamilton to Philip Schuyler, February 18, 1781, in Harold C. Syrett, ed., *The Papers of Alexander Hamilton,* 26 vols. (New York, 1961–79), II:563–68.

23. Claude Blanchard, *Journal* (Albany, N.Y., 1867), 152; Mathieu Dumas, *Memoirs of His Own Time,* 2 vols. (Philadelphia, 1839), I:52–53; Marshal Count de Rochambeau, *Memoirs . . . Relative to the War of Independence* (Paris, 1838), 73.

24. Francis R. Bellamy, *The Private Life of George Washington* (New York, 1951), 324.

25. Arthur D. Graeff, "Anecdotes Related in Pennsylvanian-German Almanacs," Part II, *The American-German Review*, VI (June 1940), 9.
26. Paul F. Boller, Jr., "George Washington and Civilian Supremacy," *Southwest Review*, XXXIX (Winter 1954), 14–16.
27. Ibid., 16–21.
28. Ibid., 21–22.
29. Edward Everett Hale, *Memories of a Hundred Years*, 2 vols. (New York, 1902), I:174.
30. Parton, *Life of Jefferson*, 95–96.
31. John C. Fitzpatrick, ed., *The Writings of George Washington*, 39 vols. (Washington, D.C., 1931–44), XXVIII:409, 423, 426–27, 479.
32. Hunt, *American Anecdotes*, II:284.
33. Max Farrand, ed., *The Records of the Federal Convention of 1787*, 3 vols. (New Haven, Conn., 1937), III:359.
34. Clarence Winthrop Brown, ed., *The History of the Centennial Celebration of the Inauguration of George Washington as First President of the United States* (New York, 1892), 41–58.
35. Washington Irving, *Life of Washington*, 5 vols. (New York, 1856–59), V:12–13; *Writings of Jefferson*, I:333–34.
36. John S. C. Abbot and Russell H. Conwell, *Lives of the Presidents* (Portland, Me., 1882), 53.
37. James Hart, *The American Presidency in Action* (New York, 1948), 86–87.
38. Boller, *Washington and Religion*, 137.
39. Flexner, *Washington*, 31; Elkanah Watson, *Men and Times of the Revolution* (New York, 1957), 39.
40. Custis, *Memoirs of Washington*, 416–20.
41. Bellamy, *Private Life of Washington*, 53–54.
42. Paul Leicester Ford, *The True George Washington* (Philadelphia, 1896), 306.
43. Herbert Asbury, *Ye Olde Fire Laddies* (New York, 1930), 67–69.

2. John Adams

1. Frank Donovan, ed., *The John Adams Papers* (New York, 1965), 247–48.
2. Page Smith, *John Adams*, 2 vols. (Garden City, N. Y., 1962), I:268.
3. L. H. Butterfield, ed., *Diary and Autobiography of John Adams*, 4 vols. (Cambridge, Mass., 1962), II:156.
4. Ibid., II:286–87 n.; IV:11–12.
5. Ibid., III:176.
6. Albert Henry Smyth, ed., *The Writings of Benjamin Franklin*, 10 vols. (New York, 1907), IX:62.

7. *John Adams Papers,* 209.
8. Paul Wilstach, *Patriots Off Their Pedestals* (Indianapolis, 1927), 101; Lester J. Capon, ed., *The Adams-Jefferson Letters,* 2 vols. (Chapel Hill, N.C., 1959), II:542; Worthington C. Ford, ed., *Statesman and Friend: Correspondence of John Adams and Benjamin Waterhouse* (Boston, 1883), 77.
9. Josiah Quincy, *Figures of the Past* (Boston, 1883), 77.
10. *John Adams Papers,* 328–29.
11. Peter Harvey, *Reminiscences and Anecdotes of Daniel Webster* (Boston, 1878), 210.
12. Gilbert Chinard, *Honest John Adams* (Boston, 1933), 344–45.
13. *Columbian Centinel,* July 12, 1826, cited in John Murray Allison, *Adams and Jefferson: The Story of a Friendship* (Norman, Okla., 1966), 320–21.
14. Anne Royall, *The Black Book,* 3 vols. (Washington, D.C., 1828–29), II:125–29.
15. L. H. Butterfield, ed., *Adams Family Correspondence,* 4 vols. (Cambridge, Mass., 1963), I:44, 47.
16. Charles Francis Adams, ed., *Familiar Letters of John Adams and His Wife Abigail* (Boston and New York, 1876), xv.
17. Ibid., 18.
18. *Diary and Autobiography,* III:326.
19. *John Adams Papers,* 55–56.
20. L. H. Butterfield, ed., *The Book of Abigail and John: Selected Letters of the Adams Family, 1762–1784* (Cambridge, Mass., 1975), 142.
21. *Diary and Autobiography,* III:418.
22. Charles Francis Adams, ed., *The Works of John Adams,* 10 vols. (Boston, 1850–56), III:201.
23. *Diary and Autobiography,* IV:36–37.
24. Ibid., IV:80–81.
25. Smith, *Adams,* II:890.
26. Ibid., II:1034.

3. Thomas Jefferson

1. James Parton, *The Life of Thomas Jefferson* (Boston, 1874), 618–19.
2. Dixon Wecter, *The Hero in America* (New York, 1941), 163.
3. Parton, *Jefferson,* 572–73; David Cushman Coyle, *The Ordeal of the Presidency* (Washington, D.C., 1960), 75–77.
4. Ernest Sutherland Bates, *American Faith* (New York, 1940), 306.
5. Margaret Bayard Smith, *The First Forty Years in Washington Society* (New York, 1906), 398.
6. Harriet Taylor Upton, *Our Early Presidents* (Boston, 1890), 165–66.

7. Charles Francis Adams, ed., *The Works of John Adams,* 10 vols. (Boston, 1850–56), II:514.

8. L. H. Butterfield, ed., *Diary and Autobiography of John Adams,* 4 vols. (Cambridge, Mass., 1962), III:336; *Works of Adams,* II:512 n.

9. Henry S. Randall, *The Life of Thomas Jefferson,* 3 vols. (New York, 1858), I:178–79 n.

10. Ibid., III:345.

11. Edward Ellis, *Thomas Jefferson: A Character Sketch* (Milwaukee, 1903), 92.

12. Albert Ellery Bergh, ed., *The Writings of Thomas Jefferson,* 20 vols. (Washington, D.C. 1904–5), II:227.

13. Lester J. Capon, ed., *The Adams-Jefferson Letters,* 2 vols. (Chapel Hill, N.C., 1959), II:575.

14. Paul Leicester Ford, ed., *The Works of Thomas Jefferson,* 12 vols. (New York, 1905), XII:477.

15. Parton, *Jefferson,* 733–34.

16. Sarah N. Randolph, *The Domestic Life of Thomas Jefferson* (New York, 1871), 421 n.

17. Randall, *Jefferson,* I:58.

18. Ellis, *Character Sketch,* 12.

19. Randolph, *Domestic Life,* 49 n.

20. Randall, *Jefferson,* I:415.

21. Arthur D. Graeff, "Anecdotes Related in Pennsylvanian-German Almanacs," *The American-German Review,* VI (April 1940), 11–12.

22. Randolph, *Domestic Life,* 306–8.

23. Smith, *First Forty Years,* 396–97.

24. Mrs. E. F. Ellet, *The Court Circles of the Republic* (Hartford, Conn., 1869), 69–70.

25. Randolph, *Domestic Life,* 327–28.

26. Randall, *Jefferson,* III:232.

27. Smith, *First Forty Years,* 228–30; *Writings of Thomas Jefferson,* XVIII:342–7; Philip A. Bruce, *History of the University of Virginia, 1819–1919,* 5 vols. (New York, 1920), II:298–301.

4. James Madison

1. Gaillard Hunt, *The Life of James Madison* (New York, 1902), 244, 316.

2. Virginia Moore, *The Madisons* (New York, 1979), 233.

3. *Register of Debates in Congress,* 24th Congress, 2nd Session (Washington, D.C., 1837), 193.

4. Henry Adams, *History of the United States of America,* 9 vols. (New York, 1889–90), VI:229.

5. Ibid., VIII:231.

6. John Quincy Adams, *The Lives of James Madison and James Monroe* (Boston, 1850), 23; Margaret Bayard Smith, *The First Forty Years of Washington Society* (New York, 1906), 107.

7. Mrs. E. F. Ellet, *The Court Circles of the Republic* (Hartford, Conn., 1869), 72.

8. Hunt, *Madison,* 299–300.

9. Smith, *First Forty Years,* 63.

10. Hunt, *Madison,* 14.

11. Ibid., 165.

12. Smith, *First Forty Years,* 235.

13. Henry S. Randall, *The Life of Thomas Jefferson,* 3 vols. (New York, 1858), III:313.

14. Paul Wilstach, *Patriots Off Their Pedestals* (Indianapolis, 1927), 240.

15. Maude Gilder Goodwin, *Dolly Madison* (New York, 1896), 246.

16. Hunt, *Madison,* 385.

17. Moore, *Madisons,* 160. A similar story is told of Andrew Jackson in Francis J. Grund, *Aristocracy in America* (New York, 1839), 250–51.

18. Ralph Ketcham, *James Madison: A Biography* (New York, 1971), 606.

19. Moore, *Madisons,* 328.

20. Katharine Anthony, *Dolly Madison: Her Life and Times* (Garden City, N.Y., 1949), 225, 396; Gamaliel Bradford, *Wives* (New York, 1925), 157–58; Paul Jennings, *A Colored Man's Reminiscences of James Madison* (Brooklyn, N.Y., 1865), 13; Moore, *Madisons,* 314–22.

5. James Monroe

1. George Morgan, *The Life of James Monroe* (Boston, 1921), 286.

2. James Morgan, *Our Presidents* (New York, 1926), 45–46.

3. W. P. Cresson, *James Monroe* (Chapel Hill, N.C., 1946), 130–33; Daniel C. Gilman, *James Monroe* (Boston and New York, 1883), 49; John C. Fitzpatrick, ed., *The Writings of George Washington,* 39 vols. (Washington, D.C., 1931–44), XXXV:127.

4. Jessie Benton Fremont, *Souvenirs of My Times* (Boston, 1887), 8–10.

5. Morgan, *Monroe,* 286.

6. Edward E. Hale, "Memories of a Hundred Years," *Outlook,* LXX (March 1, 1902), 549–52.

7. Samuel T. Pickard, *Life and Letters of John G. Whittier,* 2 vols. (London, 1895), I:25.

8. Morgan, *Monroe,* 353.

9. Mrs. E. F. Ellet, *The Court Circles of the Republic* (Hartford, Conn., 1869), 167.

10. Ibid., 104.

11. Maxim E. Armbruster, *The Presidents of the United States* (New York, 1960), 96.

12. Cresson, *Monroe,* 345.
13. Gilman, *Monroe,* 240.
14. Charles Francis Adams, ed., *Memoirs of John Quincy Adams,* 12 vols. (Philadelphia, 1874–77), VI:196–97.
15. Morgan, *Monroe,* 114.
16. Freeman Hunt, *American Anecdotes,* 2 vols. (Boston, 1830), I:138.
17. Cresson, *Monroe,* 156–59; Henry Ammon, *James Monroe: The Quest for National Identity* (New York, 1971), 159; Broadus Mitchell, *Alexander Hamilton: The National Adventure, 1788–1804* (New York, 1962), 399–410.
18. S. M. Hamilton, ed., *The Writings of James Monroe,* 7 vols. (New York, 1898–1903), IV:15–16.
19. Mary Clemmer Ames, *Ten Years in Washington* (Hartford, Conn., 1880), 219.
20. Allan McLane Hamilton, *Intimate Life of Alexander Hamilton* (New York, 1910), 116–17.

6. John Quincy Adams

1. John C. Fitzpatrick, ed., *The Autobiography of Martin Van Buren,* Vol. II of American Historical Association, *Annual Report for the Year 1918* (Washington, D.C., 1920), 152.
2. David C. Whitney, *The American Presidents* (Garden City, N.Y., 1967), 62.
3. Ibid., 58.
4. Thomas Adolphus Trollope, *What I Remember* (New York, 1888), 503.
5. Edwin P. Hoyt, *John Quincy Adams* (Chicago, 1963), 17.
6. John T. Morse, *John Quincy Adams* (Boston and New York, 1882), 73.
7. Ibid., 24.
8. Bennett Champ Clark, *John Quincy Adams* (Boston, 1933), 74.
9. Ibid., 82.
10. Morse, *Adams,* 30.
11. Ibid., 137–47.
12. Mary Clemmer Ames, *Ten Years in Washington* (Hartford, Conn., 1880), 210.
13. Leonard Falkner, *The President Who Wouldn't Retire* (New York, 1967), 14.
14. Morse, *Adams,* 214.
15. James Morgan, *Our Presidents* (New York, 1958), 53.
16. Charles Francis Adams, ed., *Memoirs of John Quincy Adams,* 12 vols. (Philadelphia, 1874–77), VIII:239–40.
17. Whitney, *American Presidents,* 63.
18. Josiah Quincy, *Memoir of the Life of John Quincy Adams* (Boston, 1858), 183.

19. Clark, *Adams,* 360.
20. Quincy, *Memoir,* 251–56.
21. *Memoirs of John Quincy Adams,* XII:116.
22. Whitney, *American Presidents,* 63.
23. Clark, *Adams,* 58–60; Samuel Flagg Bemis, *John Quincy Adams and the Foundations of American Foreign Policy* (New York, 1949), 88–89.
24. Hoyt, *Adams,* 73.
25. *Autobiography of Thurlow Weed,* 2 vols. (Boston, 1883–84), I:179; *Memoirs of John Quincy Adams,* VII:27–29.
26. Edna M. Colman, *Seventy-Five Years of White House Gossip* (Garden City, N.Y., 1926), 440–41.
27. Falkner, *President Who Wouldn't Retire,* 288, 292.
28. Daniel C. Gilman, *James Monroe* (Boston and New York, 1883), 251.
29. Mrs. E. F. Ellet, *The Court Circles of the Republic* (Hartford, Conn., 1869), 129–30.

7. Andrew Jackson

1. James Parton, *Life of Andrew Jackson,* 3 vols. (New York, 1861), III:170.
2. Ibid., 169.
3. John Spencer Bassett, *The Life of Andrew Jackson* (New York, 1925), 424.
4. W. W. Story, *Life and Letters of Joseph Story,* 2 vols. (New York, 1851), I:563.
5. *Argus of Western America* (Frankfort, Ky.), March 18, 1829, cited in Arthur Schlesinger, Jr., *The Age of Jackson* (Boston, 1945), 6.
6. Frederick A. Ogg, *The Reign of Andrew Jackson* (New Haven, Conn., 1919), 121.
7. Carl Sandburg, *Abraham Lincoln: The Prairie Years,* 2 vols. (New York, 1926), I:95.
8. W. H. Sparks, *The Memories of Fifty Years* (Philadelphia, 1870), 148.
9. Sarah K. Bolton, *Famous American Statesmen* (New York, 1888), 145.
10. Parton, *Jackson,* I:163–64.
11. Ibid., I:268–69, 293–94, 297–301.
12. Ibid., 392–94; August C. Buell, *History of Andrew Jackson,* 2 vols. (New York, 1904), II:268; John F. Kennedy, *Profiles in Courage* (New York, 1955), 85.
13. Ogg, *Reign of Jackson,* 31.
14. Glyndon G. Van Deusen, *The Jacksonian Era, 1828–1848* (New York, 1959), 44.
15. Parton, *Jackson,* III:283.
16. In order not to antagonize the South and the West, Jackson left the Su-

preme Court's decision unenforced, but it is not likely he uttered these words. Horace Greeley was the source of the statement. See William Graham Sumner, *Andrew Jackson* (Boston and New York, 1882), 227 n.

17. Francis J. Grund, *Aristocracy in America* (New York, 1839), 294.
18. Edwin P. Hoyt, *John Quincy Adams* (Chicago, 1963), 135–36.
19. John T. Morse, *John Quincy Adams* (Boston and New York, 1882), 73.
20. Buell, *History of Jackson*, II:305.
21. [Charles Augustus Davis], *Letters of J. Downing, Major, Downingville Militia, Second Brigade, to His Old Friend, Mr. Dwight, of the New-York Daily Advertiser* (New York, 1834), 26.
22. Parton, *Jackson*, III:683.
23. Buell, *History of Jackson*, II:411.
24. Parton, Jackson, I:64.
25. Ibid., 62–63.
26. Ibid., 107–8.
27. Ibid., 104, 108–9.
28. Ibid., 340–41.
29. Ibid., 341–42.
30. Dr. Archibald Henderson, "Jackson's Loose Living Common Sin of the Period," *Raleigh* (North Carolina) *News and Observer*, October 17, 1926; John S. Bassett, ed., *Correspondence of Andrew Jackson*, 7 vols. (Washington, D.C., 1926–35), I:5.
31. Parton, *Jackson*, I:228–29; Bassett, *Jackson*, 24.
32. Bolton, *Famous American Statesmen*, 159–60.
33. Leland Baldwin, *The Stream of American History*, 2 vols. (New York, 1953), I:423.
34. William Stickney, ed., *Autobiography of Amos Kendall* (New York, 1872), 638; Marquis James, *The Life of Andrew Jackson* (Indianapolis, 1938), 262–64.
35. Parton, *Jackson*, II:339–41.
36. Ibid., II:655.
37. Ibid., III:492–93.
38. Buell, *History of Jackson*, II:213.
39. "Andrew Jackson," *Harper's Magazine*, X (January 1855), 171.
40. Parton, *Jackson*, III:244–45.
41. Mrs. E. F. Ellet, *The Court Circles of the Republic* (Hartford, Conn., 1869), 164–65.
42. Benjamin Perley Poore, *Perley's Reminiscences of Sixty Years*, 2 vols. (New York, 1886), I:120–25; Robert Remini, *Andrew Jackson* (New York, 1966), 112–16, 24; Parton, *Jackson*, III:184–205.
43. Buell, *Jackson*, II:302–3.
44. Poore, *Perley's Reminiscences*, I:102.
45. Parton, *Jackson*, III:489.
46. Ibid., 549–50; I:113.

47. James, *Jackson*, 662; Schlesinger, *Age of Jackson*, 108–9; John Bach McMaster, *A History of the People of the United States*, 6 vols. (New York, 1883–1913), VI:203.
48. Buell, *History of Jackson*, II:245.
49. Poore, *Perley's Reminiscences*, I:138–39; Parton, *Jackson*, III:669–70.
50. Harriet Martineau, *Society in America*, 3 vols. (London, 1837), III:166.

8. Martin Van Buren

1. Benjamin Perley Poore, *Perley's Reminiscences of Sixty Years*, 2 vols. (New York, 1886), I:198.
2. Thomas Hart Benton, *Thirty Years View*, 2 vols. (New York, 1866), I:735.
3. Denis Tilden Lynch, *An Epoch and a Man: Martin Van Buren and His Times* (New York, 1929), 299.
4. Jabez D. Hammond, *The History of Political Parties in the State of New York*, 2 vols. (Albany, N.Y., 1842), II:473.
5. Edward M. Shepard, *Martin Van Buren* (Boston and New York, 1888), 186.
6. Lynch, *Epoch and Man*, 299; Holmes Alexander, *The American Talleyrand: The Career and Contemporaries of Martin Van Buren* (New York, 1935), 9.
7. John C. Fitzpatrick, ed., *The Autobiography of Martin Van Buren*, Vol. II of American Historical Association, *Annual Report for the Year 1918* (Washington, D.C., 1920), 171.
8. Shepard, *Van Buren*, 252–53.
9. Ibid., 151.
10. Poore, *Perley's Reminiscences*, I:131.
11. David C. Whitney, *The American Presidents* (Garden City, N.Y., 1967), 85.
12. Charles R. King, ed., *The Life and Correspondence of Rufus King*, 6 vols. (New York, 1898), VI:478.
13. Alexander, *American Talleyrand*, 406.
14. Ibid., 11.
15. Mrs. E. F. Ellet, *The Court Circles of the Republic* (Hartford, Conn., 1869), 269.

9. William Henry Harrison

1. Dorothy Goebel, *William Henry Harrison* (Indianapolis, 1926), 346.
2. *Baltimore Republican*, December 11, 1839, cited in Robert Gray Gunderson, *The Log-Cabin Campaign* (Lexington, Ky., 1957), 74.

3. Nicholas Biddle, *The Correspondence of Nicholas Biddle Dealing with National Affairs, 1807–1844* (Boston and New York, 1919), 256.

4. Gunderson, *Log-Cabin Campaign*, 124–29, 156–57; Freeman Cleaves, *Old Tippecanoe* (New York, 1939), 320–26; Goebel, *Harrison*, 347–53; *Autobiography of Thurlow Weed*, 2 vols. (Boston, 1883–84), I:492–93.

5. *Cleveland Axe*, July 9, 1840, cited in Gunderson, *Log-Cabin Campaign*, 77.

6. *Washington Globe*, August 18, 1840, and *Albany Rough-Hewer*, April 30, 1840, cited in Gunderson, *Log-Cabin Campaign*, 235.

7. David Crockett, *The Life of Martin Van Buren* (Philadelphia, 1835), 80–81.

8. *Cleveland Axe*, May 28, 1840, cited in Gunderson, *Log-Cabin Campaign*, 126–27.

9. Edward M. Shepard, *Martin Van Buren* (Boston and New York, 1888), 388–89.

10. Allan Nevins, ed., *The Diary of Philip Hone, 1821–1851*, 2 vols. (New York, 1927), II:652.

11. Charles Francis Adams, ed., *Memoirs of John Quincy Adams*, 12 vols. (Philadelphia, 1874–77), X:366.

12. *Cincinnati Daily Gazette*, April 13, 1841, cited in Cleaves, *Old Tippecanoe*, 328.

13. Mrs. E. F. Ellet, *The Court Circles of the Republic* (Hartford, Conn., 1869), 286.

14. Peter Harvey, *Reminiscences and Anecdotes of Daniel Webster* (Boston, 1878), 160–63.

15. Charles S. Todd and Benjamin Drake, *Sketches of the Civil and Military Services of William Henry Harrison* (Cincinnati, 1847), 208.

16. Benjamin Drake, *Life of Tecumseh* (Cincinnati, 1841), 126.

17. Ellet, *Court Circles*, 289.

18. Ibid., 287.

10. John Tyler

1. John Wise, *Recollections of Thirteen Presidents* (New York, 1906), 13–14.

2. Frank G. Carpenter, "A Talk with a President's Son," *Lippincott's Monthly Magazine*, XLI (1888), 417–18.

3. Lyon G. Tyler, *The Letters and Times of the Tylers*, 2 vols. (Richmond, Va., 1885), II:122 n.

4. *Richmond Enquirer*, July 15, 1842; *Niles' Register*, LXVI (1843):441.

5. Tyler, *Letters and Times*, II:361.

6. Ibid., I:369; Benjamin Perley Poore, *Perley's Reminiscences of Sixty Years*, 2 vols. (New York, 1886), I:325.

7. Henry A. Wise, *Seven Decades of the Union* (Philadelphia, 1872), 232–33.

8. F. B. Carpenter, *The Inner Life of Abraham Lincoln: Six Months at the White House* (New York, 1868), 152.

11. James K. Polk

1. Edward Lind Morse, *Samuel F. B. Morse: His Letters and Journals*, 2 vols. (New York, 1914), II:226.

2. Eugene I. McCormac, *James K. Polk: A Political Biography* (Berkeley, Calif., 1922), 246.

3. Charles A. McCoy, *Polk and the Presidency* (Austin, 1960), 531.

4. Charles Sellers, *James K. Polk, Continentalist, 1843–1846* (Princeton, N.J., 1957), 101.

5. Ibid., 105.

6. James Morgan, *Our Presidents* (New York, 1958), 98.

7. McCormac, *Polk*, 278 n.

8. Sellers, *Polk*, 51.

9. Ona Griffin Jeffries, *In and Out of the White House* (New York, 1960), 124.

10. John Bassett Moore, ed., *The Works of James Buchanan*, 12 vols. (New York, 1908–11), VI:110.

11. *The Diary of James K. Polk*, 4 vols. (Chicago, 1910), III:97–99.

12. David C. Whitney, *The American Presidents* (Garden City, N.Y., 1967), 102.

13. Allan Nevins, ed., *Polk: The Diary of a President* (New York, 1929), xvii; *Diary of Polk*, IV:264.

14. Anson Nelson and Fanny Nelson, *Memorials of Sarah Childress Polk* (New York, 1892), 38–39.

12. Zachary Taylor

1. James Morgan, *Our Presidents* (New York, 1958), 105.

2. Brainerd Dyer, *Zachary Taylor* (Baton Rouge, 1946), 280.

3. Morgan, *Our Presidents*, 106.

4. Benjamin Perley Poore, *Perley's Reminiscences of Sixty Years*, 2 vols. (New York, 1886), I:345–46.

5. Maxim E. Armbruster, *The Presidents of the United States* (New York, 1960), 153; John G. Nicolay and John Hay, eds., *The Complete Works of Abraham Lincoln*, 12 vols. (Harrogate, Tenn., 1894), II:63.

6. Oran Perry, ed., *Indiana in the Mexican War* (n.p., 1908), 140; Otto B. Engelman, "The Second Illinois in the Mexican War," *Journal of the Illinois State Historical Society*, XXVI (1933–34), 438.

7. Holman Hamilton, *Zachary Taylor: Soldier of the Republic* (Indianapolis, 1941), 247.

8. H. Montgomery, *The Life of Major-General Zachary Taylor* (Auburn, Ala., 1849), 345–46.

9. Ibid., 161.

10. Ibid., 154.

11. Ulysses S. Grant, *Personal Memoirs*, ed. E. B. Long (Cleveland, 1952), 48.

12. Holman Hamilton, *Zachary Taylor: Soldier in the White House* (Indianapolis, 1951), 147.

13. Poore, *Perley's Reminiscences*, I:362.

14. Dyer, *Taylor*, 334; Hamilton, *Soldier in White House*, 341–42.

15. Charles E. Hamlin, *The Life and Times of Hannibal Hamlin* (Cambridge, Mass., 1899), 201.

16. Mary Mann, *Life of Horace Mann* (Boston, 1888), 292–93.

17. Montgomery, *Taylor*, 56–57.

18. Silas Bent McKinley and Silas Bent, *Old Rough and Ready* (New York, 1946), 91–92.

19. Montgomery, *Taylor*, 346–47.

20. Ibid., 348–49.

13. Millard Fillmore

1. James Morgan, *Our Presidents* (New York, 1958), 109.

2. *Albany Evening Journal*, January 26, 1843, cited in Robert J. Rayback, *Millard Fillmore* (Buffalo, 1959), 136.

3. Rayback, *Fillmore*, 177.

4. Frank H. Severance, ed., *Millard Fillmore Papers*, 2 vols. (Buffalo, 1959), II:173–74.

5. Benjamin Perley Poore, *Perley's Reminiscences of Sixty Years*, 2 vols. (New York, 1886), I:385–86.

6. *Fillmore Papers*, II:351–54.

7. Ibid., 354–57.

8. Ibid., 483.

9. Ibid., 503.

14. Franklin Pierce

1. Roy Nicholas, *Franklin Pierce* (Philadelphia, 1931), 205.

2. Horatio Bridge, *Personal Reminiscences of Hawthorne* (New York, 1893), 131.

3. John S. Wise, *Recollections of Thirteen Presidents* (New York, 1906), 47–48.

4. Paul F. Boller, Jr., "Old Fuss and Feathers and the Fainting General," *Southwest Review,* XXVII (Spring 1952), 141–50.

5. Ibid., 146–47.

6. Nichols, *Pierce,* 224–25, 234.

7. Ibid., 83–86.

8. Peter Harvey, *Reminiscences and Anecdotes of Daniel Webster* (Boston, 1878), 251–52.

9. Harry Barnard, *Rutherford B. Hayes and His America* (Indianapolis, 1954), 503.

10. Nichols, *Pierce,* 523.

11. Ibid., 526.

15. James Buchanan

1. James Ford Rhodes, *History of the United States,* 8 vols. (New York, 1920), I:511–12; George Ticknor Curtis, *Life of James Buchanan,* 2 vols. (New York, 1883), II:107–16.

2. Philip S. Klein, *President James Buchanan* (Philadelphia, 1962), 6.

3. *The Diary of James K. Polk,* 4 vols. (Chicago, 1910), IV:355.

4. Augustus C. Buell, *History of Andrew Jackson,* 2 vols. (New York, 1904), II:404.

5. John W. Forney, *Anecdotes of Public Men,* 2 vols. (New York, 1873–81), I:64–65.

6. Klein, *Buchanan,* 275.

7. *Philadelphia Press,* January 24, 1860, cited in Klein, *Buchanan,* 210.

8. James Morgan, *Our Presidents* (New York, 1958), 130–31.

9. Mrs. Roger A. Pryor, *Reminiscences of Peace and War* (New York, 1908), 111–12; W. E. Woodward, *Meet General Grant* (New York, 1928), 164–65.

10. Horace Greeley, *Recollections of a Busy Life* (New York, 1868), 359.

11. Asa E. Martin, *After the White House* (State College, Pa., 1951), 225.

12. *Lancaster Intelligencer,* June 3, 10, 1868, cited in Klein, *Buchanan,* 427.

13. Klein, *Buchanan,* 24.

14. Ibid., 34–35.

15. L. A. Gobright, *Recollections of Men and Things at Washington* (Philadelphia, 1869), 184.

16. Abraham Lincoln

1. Carl Sandburg, *Abraham Lincoln: The Prairie Years,* 2 vols. (New York, 1926), I:vii.

2. Albert J. Beveridge, *Abraham Lincoln, 1809–1858,* 2 vols. (Boston and New York, 1928), I:531.

3. A. K. McClure, ed., *Lincoln's Own Yarns and Stories* (Chicago and Philadelphia, n.d.), 261.

4. Carl Sandburg, *Abraham Lincoln: The War Years*, 4 vols. (New York, 1939), III:301.

5. Ibid., III:311.

6. Sandburg, *Prairie Years*, II:243.

7. F. B. Carpenter, *The Inner Life of Abraham Lincoln: Six Months at the White House* (New York, 1868), 152; McClure, *Lincoln's Yarns*, 97–98; Silas W. Burt, "Lincoln on His Own Story-Telling," *The Century Magazine*, LXXIII (February 1907), 502; Charles C. Coffin, *Abraham Lincoln* (New York, 1892), 367–68; Anthony Gross, *Lincoln's Own Stories* (Garden City, N.Y., 1912), 222.

8. Richard Hanser, "The Laughing Lincoln," *Saturday Review*, XLI (February 8, 1958), 12.

9. Brant House, *Lincoln's Wit* (New York: Ace Books, 1958), 113.

10. Sandburg, *War Years*, III:339.

11. House, *Lincoln's Wit*, 203.

12. Coffin, *Lincoln*, 341.

13. *The Reminiscences of Carl Schurz*, 3 vols. (New York, 1906–8), II:340.

14. McClure, *Lincoln's Yarns*, 175.

15. Paul Selby, ed., *Stories and Speeches of Abraham Lincoln* (Chicago, 1900), 211.

16. Ibid., 190.

17. House, *Lincoln's Wit*, 123; Keith W. Jennison, *The Humorous Mr. Lincoln* (New York, 1965), 95–96.

18. Hanser, "Laughing Lincoln," 37.

19. Sandburg, *Prairie Years*, I:402; Anthony Gross, *Lincoln's Own Stories* (Garden City, N.Y., 1912), 54.

20. Lecture on "Discoveries, Inventions, and Improvements," Springfield, Illinois, February 22, 1860, in John G. Nicolay and John Hay, eds., *Complete Works of Abraham Lincoln*, 13 vols. (Harrogate, Tenn., 1894), V:100–101.

21. Sandburg, *Prairie Years*, II:406.

22. Sandburg, *War Years*, III:317; Dixon Wecter, *The Hero in America* (New York, 1941), 255.

23. Noah Brooks, *Washington in Lincoln's Time* (New York, 1895), 47. See McClure, *Lincoln's Yarns*, 305, for a different version.

24. Richard Hanser, "The Lincoln Who Lives in Anecdote," *Reader's Digest*, LXXIV (February 1959), 253.

25. Paul M. Angle, ed., *Abraham Lincoln by Some Men Who Knew Him* (Freeport, N.Y., 1950), 51.

26. Gross, *Lincoln's Own Stories*, 69.

27. Coffin, *Lincoln*, 369.

28. Wecter, *Hero in America*, 243; David Donald, *Lincoln's Herndon* (New York, 1948), 158; Roy Basler, *The Lincoln Legend* (Boston and New

York, 1935), 53–55; Sandburg, *Prairie Years,* II:355, 381; Sandburg, *War Years,* I:119, 182, 556, 557, 614; McClure, *Lincoln's Yarns,* 176.

29. Paul F. Boller, Jr., *Quotemanship: The Use and Abuse of Quotations for Polemical and Other Purposes* (Dallas, 1967), 21.

30. House, *Lincoln's Wit,* 136.

31. Richard Hofstadter, *The American Political Tradition* (New York, 1948), 136.

32. Basler, *Lincoln Legend,* 60; John Hay, *Lincoln and the Civil War in the Diaries and Letters of John Hay* (New York, 1939), 119–21.

33. Selby, *Stories and Speeches,* 270.

34. Alistaire Cooke, ed., *The Vintage Mencken* (New York, 1955), 79.

35. Jacques Barzun, "Lincoln the Literary Genius," *Saturday Evening Post,* CCXXXII (February 14, 1959), 30–64.

36. John G. Nicolay and John Hay, *Abraham Lincoln: A History,* 10 vols. (New York, 1890), X:351.

37. Ibid.

38. Coffin, *Lincoln,* 385–86.

39. House, *Lincoln's Wit,* 9; Jennison, *Humorous Lincoln,* 4.

40. McClure, *Lincoln's Yarns,* 54.

41. House, *Lincoln's Wit,* 13; Jennison, *Humorous Lincoln,* 13.

42. Wayne Whipple, *The Story-Life of Abraham Lincoln* (Philadelphia, 1908), 173.

43. Henry C. Whitney, *Life on the Circuit with Lincoln* (Boston, 1892), 43.

44. McClure, *Lincoln's Yarns,* 301–2.

45. Ibid., 315–16.

46. Ida M. Tarbell, *The Life of Abraham Lincoln,* 2 vols. (New York, 1895), I:246.

47. Jennison, *Humorous Lincoln,* 41.

48. Roy Basler, ed., *The Collected Works of Abraham Lincoln,* 9 vols. (New Brunswick, N.J., 1953–55), II:323.

49. George S. Hilton, *The Funny Side of Politics* (New York, 1899), 236.

50. Benjamin Perley Poore, *Perley's Reminiscences of Sixty Years,* 2 vols. (New York, 1886), II:69–70.

51. House, *Lincoln's Wit,* 91.

52. Poore, *Perley's Reminiscences,* II:144–45.

53. Ibid., 136.

54. Selby, *Stories and Speeches,* 150.

55. Mrs. John A. Logan, *Thirty Years in Washington* (Hartford, Conn., 1901), 473–74.

56. Gross, *Lincoln's Stories,* 169.

57. Angle, *Lincoln,* 114–15.

58. Whipple, *Lincoln's Story-Life,* 623.

59. House, *Lincoln's Wit,* 212; Sandburg, *War Years,* IV:146.

60. *Reminiscences of Schurz,* II:340–41.

61. McClure, *Lincoln's Yarns*, 32.
62. Hilton, *Funny Side of Politics*, 236.
63. McClure, *Lincoln's Yarns*, 367.
64. Emanuel Hertz, *Abraham Lincoln: A New Portrait*, 2 vols. (New York, 1931), I:238–39.
65. Selby, *Stories and Speeches*, 148–49.
66. Gross, *Lincoln's Stories*, 190–91.
67. McClure, *Lincoln's Yarns*, 274–75.
68. "President Lincoln's Leg Cases," *Magazine of American History*, XX (July–December 1888), 419.
69. Gross, *Lincoln's Stories*, 82.
70. McClure, *Lincoln's Yarns*, 123–24.
71. Whipple, *Lincoln's Story-Life*, 442.
72. Tyler Dennett, ed., *Lincoln and the Civil War in the Diaries of John Hay* (New York, 1939), 208, 210; J. G. Randall and Richard N. Current, *Lincoln the President: Last Full Measure* (New York, 1955), 200; Bennett Cerf, *Try and Stop Me* (New York, 1944), 258.
73. McClure, *Lincoln's Yarns*, 366.
74. Ibid., 293; David Homer Bates, *Lincoln in the Telegraph Office* (New York, 1907), 197.
75. McClure, *Lincoln's Yarns*, 314–15.
76. Selby, *Stories and Speeches*, 188–89, 204, 212–13; Salmon P. Chase, *Chase Diary*, Annual Report, American Historical Association (Washington, D.C., 1902), II:87–89; Carpenter, *Inner Life of Lincoln*, 209; Coffin, *Lincoln*, 342–46.
77. McClure, *Lincoln's Yarns*, 333.
78. Hilton, *Funny Side of Politics*, 236.
79. McClure, *Lincoln's Yarns*, 84–85.
80. Coffin, *Lincoln*, 481.
81. Poore, *Perley's Reminiscences*, II:167–68.
82. McClure, *Lincoln's Yarns*, 207–8, 304–5; Carl Sandburg, *Abraham Lincoln* (New York: Harvest, 1954), 703; Selby, *Stories and Speeches*, 218; Whipple, *Lincoln's Story-Life*, 643.
83. Sandburg, *Lincoln* (Harvest), 701, 704, 706; McClure, *Lincoln's Yarns*, 402–3; Col. W. H. Crook, *Memories of the White House* (Boston, 1911), 40.

17. Andrew Johnson

1. Robert W. Winston, *Andrew Johnson: Plebeian and Patriot* (New York, 1928), 105.
2. James S. Jones, *The Life of Andrew Johnson* (Greenville, Tenn., 1911), 27–28.

3. Winston, *Johnson*, 50.
4. Ibid., 104.
5. Frank Moore, ed., *Speeches of Andrew Johnson, President of the United States* (Boston, 1865), 285–86.
6. Lloyd Paul Stryker, *Andrew Johnson: A Study in Courage* (New York, 1936), 319.
7. Winston, *Johnson*, 167.
8. Lately Thomas, *The First President Johnson* (New York, 1968), 190–91.
9. Moncure D. Conway, "The President's Defence," *Fortnightly Review*, V (1866), 99.
10. Winston, *Johnson*, 195–96.
11. Thomas, *First Johnson*, 195–96.
12. *New York World*, June 9, 1864, cited in Stryker, *Johnson*, 71.
13. Hugh McCulloch, *Men and Measures of Half a Century* (New York, 1889), 373; W. G. Brownlow, *Taylor-Trotwood Magazine*, September, 1908, cited in Winston, *Johnson*, 265–66.
14. George W. Julian, *Recollections, 1840 to 1872* (Chicago, 1884), 257.
15. Thomas, *First Johnson*, 580.
16. W. H. Crook, *Memories of the White House* (Boston, 1911), 67; Stryker, *Johnson*, 723–24.
17. Jones, *Johnson*, 353–54.
18. *New York Tribune*, March 8, 1875, cited in Stryker, *Johnson*, 811.
19. George S. Hilton, *The Funny Side of Politics* (New York, 1899), 265.

18. Ulysses S. Grant

1. J. T. Headley, *The Life and Travels of General Grant*, 2 vols. (Philadelphia, 1880), II:225.
2. Dixon Wecter, *The Hero in America* (New York, 1941), 320.
3. Charles King, *The True Ulysses S. Grant* (Philadelphia, 1914), 31.
4. Ulysses S. Grant, *Personal Memoirs*, ed. E. B. Long (Cleveland, 1952), 22–23.
5. William Conant Church, *Ulysses S. Grant* (New York, 1899), 72–73.
6. Hamlin Garland, *Ulysses S. Grant* (New York, 1898), 174–75.
7. *Personal Memoirs*, 126–27.
8. Harry T. Peck, *Twenty Years of the Republic, 1885–1905* (New York, 1907), 107.
9. *Personal Memoirs*, 159.
10. Bruce Catton, *U. S. Grant and the American Military Tradition* (Boston, 1954), 187.
11. James C. Humes, *Speaker's Treasury of Anecdotes about the Famous* (New York, 1978), 43.
12. Garland, *Grant*, 257.

13. King, *True Grant,* 313–14.
14. W. E. Woodward, *Meet General Grant* (New York, 1928), 14.
15. *New York Tribune,* February 23, 1866, cited in Wecter, *Hero in America,* 326.
16. Ibid., 324.
17. *The Reminiscences of Carl Schurz,* 3 vols. (New York, 1906–8), III:304.
18. Wecter, *Hero in America,* 329.
19. George F. Hoar, *Autobiography of Seventy Years,* 2 vols. (New York, 1906), I:211.
20. Wecter, *Hero in America,* 337.
21. Horace Green, *General Grant's Last Stand* (New York, 1936), 297.
22. *Personal Memoirs,* 9–10.
23. Melville DeLancey Landon, *Wit and Humor of the Age* (Chicago, 1883), 664.
24. *Personal Memoirs,* 17–18.
25. Garland, *Grant,* 63.
26. King, *True Grant,* 254–55.
27. Peck, *Twenty Years of Republic,* 105–6 n.
28. Horace Porter, *Campaigning with Grant* (New York, 1897), 164–65.
29. Boyce House, *Laugh Parade of States* (San Antonio, 1948), 74.
30. Adam Badeau, *Grant in Peace: From Appomattox to Mount McGregor* (Hartford, Conn., 1887), 27.
31. Louis Untermeyer, *A Treasury of Laughter* (New York, 1946), 88.
32. Badeau, *Grant in Peace,* 281–88.
33. Chauncey M. Depew, *My Memories of Eighty Years* (New York, 1924), 278–79.

19. Rutherford B. Hayes

1. H. J. Eckenrode, *Rutherford B. Hayes: Statesman of Reunion* (New York, 1930), 333.
2. Maxim E. Armbruster, *The Presidents of the United States: A New Appraisal* (New York, 1960), 209.
3. *Chicago Tribune,* March 2, 1877, cited in Harry Barnard, *Rutherford B. Hayes and His America* (Indianapolis, 1954), 402–3.
4. James Grant Wilson, ed., *The Presidents of the United States, 1789–1914,* 4 vols. (New York, 1914), III:128.
5. Barnard, *Hayes,* 436.
6. Charles Richard Williams, ed., *Diary and Letters of Rutherford B. Hayes,* 5 vols. (Columbus, Ohio, 1924), III:484.
7. Allan Nevins, ed., *Selected Writings of Abram S. Hewitt* (New York, 1937), 381.
8. Eckenrode, *Hayes,* 313.

9. Charles Richard Williams, *The Life of Rutherford B. Hayes,* 2 vols. (Columbus, Ohio, 1928), II:416.

10. *Diary and Letters of Hayes,* I:130.

11. Alfred R. Conkling, *The Life and Letters of Roscoe Conkling* (New York, 1889), 540–41.

12. *Diary and Letters of Hayes,* III:644–45.

13. George F. Hoar, *Autobiography of Seventy Years,* 2 vols. (New York, 1906), II:15.

14. Barnard, *Hayes,* 480.

15. Hoar, *Autobiography,* II:14–15; Benjamin Perley Poore, *Perley's Reminiscences of Sixty Years,* 2 vols. (New York, 1886), II:349–50; *Diary and Letters of Hayes,* IV:304.

16. *Diary and Letters of Hayes,* III:557.

17. Barnard, *Hayes,* 496.

18. *Diary and Letters of Hayes,* III:640.

19. Williams, *Hayes,* II:415; Chauncey M. Depew, *My Memories of Eighty Years* (New York, 1924), 102.

20. Barnard, *Hayes,* 481.

21. Eckenrode, *Hayes,* 331.

22. Russell H. Conwell, *Life and Services of Gov. Rutherford B. Hayes* (Boston, 1876), 133–36.

23. "The Age of Innocence in the White House," *Literary Digest,* XLII (February 5, 1927), 41–42.

20. James A. Garfield

1. Alfred R. Conkling, *The Life and Letters of Roscoe Conkling* (New York, 1889), 596.

2. James Morgan, *Our Presidents* (New York, 1958), 202–3.

3. William R. Balch, *The Life of James Abram Garfield* (Philadelphia, 1881), 270–73; John M. Taylor, *Garfield of Ohio* (New York, 1970), 103.

4. Margaret Leech and Harry J. Brown, *The Garfield Orbit* (New York, 1978), 218; T. C. Smith, *The Life and Letters of James A. Garfield,* 2 vols. (New Haven, Conn., 1925), II:1027.

5. Leech and Brown, *Garfield Orbit,* 223.

6. Taylor, *Garfield,* 237.

7. Ibid., 231.

8. Ibid., 258.

9. Smith, *Life and Letters of Garfield,* II:1152–53.

10. Taylor, *Garfield,* 268.

11. Leech and Brown, *Garfield Orbit,* 244–45.

12. *Washington Star,* August 23, 1881, cited in Taylor, *Garfield,* 274.

13. *New York Evening Telegraph,* July 2, 1881, cited in Smith, *Life and Letters of Garfield,* II:1185.
14. Taylor, *Garfield,* 286.
15. Leech and Brown, *Garfield Orbit,* 174.
16. Ona Griffin Jeffries, *In and Out of the White House* (New York, 1960), 225.

21. Chester A. Arthur

1. David C. Whitney, *The American Presidents* (Garden City, N.Y., 1967), 180.
2. Charles Richard Williams, ed., *Diary and Letters of Rutherford B. Hayes,* 5 vols. (Columbus, Ohio, 1924), IV:23.
3. "To Whom It May Concern," *New York Times,* July 3, 1881, cited in Thomas C. Reeves, *Gentleman Boss: The Life of Chester A. Arthur* (New York, 1975), 241.
4. Richard Hofstadter, *The American Political Tradition* (New York, 1948), 173.
5. *New York Tribune,* February 12, 1881; *New York Semi-Weekly Tribune,* February 15, 1881; George Frederick Howe, *Chester A. Arthur: A Quarter Century of Machine Politics* (New York, 1934), 129–30.
6. "Indiana October Vote," *New York Times,* February 12, 1881; *The Nation,* XXXII (February 24, 1881), 122.
7. "A Talk with Governor Foster," *New York Times,* July 3, 1881.
8. Howe, *Arthur,* 254.
9. W. C. Hudson, *Random Recollections of an Old Political Reporter* (New York, 1911), 126.
10. James Morgan, *Our Presidents* (New York, 1958), 210–11.
11. *Cincinnati Commercial Gazette,* March 27, 1883, cited in Howe, *Arthur,* 244.
12. Howe, *Arthur,* 176.
13. Reeves, *Gentleman Boss,* 272.
14. Ibid., 273.
15. Howe, *Arthur,* 173–74.
16. "Arthur's Tranquil End," *New York Herald,* November 19, 1896, cited in Reeves, *Gentleman Boss,* 412.
17. Asa E. Martin, *After the White House* (State College, Pa., 1951), 306.

22. Grover Cleveland

1. Horace S. Merrill, *Bourbon Leader: Grover Cleveland and the Democratic Party* (Boston, 1957), 53.

2. Robert McElroy, *Grover Cleveland: The Man and the Statesman*, 2 vols. (New York, 1923), I:49.

3. Allan Nevins, *Grover Cleveland: A Study in Courage* (New York, 1932), 125.

4. *Albany Evening Journal*, March 21, 1883, cited in Nevins, *Cleveland*, 128.

5. George Parker, *Recollections of Grover Cleveland* (New York, 1909), 341.

6. Nevins, *Cleveland*, 128.

7. George F. Parker, "Grover Cleveland's Career in Buffalo, 1855–1882," *Saturday Evening Post*, CXLIII (August 28, 1920), 193.

8. McElroy, *Cleveland*, I:84.

9. Ibid., 86–88; Richard Watson Gilder, *Grover Cleveland: A Record of Friendship* (New York, 1910), 38–39; William C. Hudson, *Random Recollections of an Old Political Reporter* (New York, 1911), 178–80.

10. *New York World*, September 22, 1884, cited in W. A. Swanberg, *Pulitzer* (New York, 1967), 82.

11. Nevins, *Cleveland*, 163.

12. Hudson, *Random Recollections*, 190.

13. Nevins, *Cleveland*, 177; M. A. DeWolfe Howe, *Portrait of an Independent: Moorfield Story, 1845–1929* (Boston and New York, 1932), 151.

14. James Morgan, *Our Presidents* (New York, 1958), 221; George S. Hilton, *The Funny Side of Politics* (New York, 1899), 191.

15. Henry L. Stoddard, *As I Knew Them: Presidents and Politics from Grant to Coolidge* (New York, 1927), 196.

16. Nevins, *Cleveland*, 530.

17. Bess Furman, *White House Profile* (Indianapolis, 1951), 239.

18. *New York Herald*, March 3, 1886, cited in Nevins, *Cleveland*, 301.

19. David C. Whitney, *The American Presidents* (Garden City, N.Y., 1967), 192.

20. W. H. Crook, *Memories of the White House* (Boston, 1911), 197–98.

21. Carl Sandburg, *Always the Young Strangers* (New York, 1952), 33.

22. McElroy, *Cleveland*, II:259.

23. John S. Wise, *Recollections of Thirteen Presidents* (New York, 1906), 188.

24. Maxim E. Armbruster, *The Presidents of the United States: A New Appraisal* (New York, 1960), 230.

25. John Clark Ridpath, *Life and Work of James G. Blaine* (Philadelphia, 1893), 150–51; *The Nation*, November 6, 1884.

26. James Schermerhorn, *Schermerhorn's Stories* (New York, 1928), 90.

27. Crook, *Memories of the White House*, 196–97.

23. Benjamin Harrison

1. 77th Congress, 1st Session, House Document no. 154, 127–28, cited in Harry J. Sievers, *Benjamin Harrison, Hoosier Warrior: 1833–1865* (Chicago, 1952), 11.
2. Frank Earnest Nicholson, *Favorite Jokes of Famous People* (New York, 1927), 59–60.
3. *Indianapolis Journal,* September 28, 1883, cited in Harry J. Sievers, *Benjamin Harrison, Hoosier Statesmen: 1865–1888* (New York, 1959), 230.
4. Julia Foraker, *I Would Live It Again* (New York, 1932), 133.
5. H. J. Eckenrode, *Rutherford B. Hayes* (New York, 1930), 335.
6. Harry J. Sievers, *Benjamin Harrison, Hoosier President: The White House and After* (Indianapolis, 1968), 215.
7. Sievers, *Hoosier Warrior,* 9.
8. Henry L. Stoddard, *As I Knew Them: Presidents and Politics from Grant to Coolidge* (New York, 1927), 165.
9. John S. Wise, *Recollections of Thirteen Presidents* (New York, 1906), 199.
10. Stoddard, *As I Knew Them,* 173.
11. Sievers, *Hoosier Statesman,* 426–27.
12. Richard Hofstadter, *The American Political Tradition* (New York, 1948), 170.
13. David C. Whitney, *The American Presidents* (Garden City, N.Y., 1967), 203.
14. Sievers, *Hoosier President,* 43.
15. *The Autobiography of Thomas Collier Platt* (New York, 1910), 215, 252.
16. Arthur Wallace Dunn, *From Harrison to McKinley,* 2 vols. (New York, 1922), I:86–87.
17. Nicholson, *Favorite Jokes,* 59–60.
18. Sievers, *Hoosier Warrior,* xx.
19. George S. Hilton, *The Funny Side of Politics* (New York, 1899), 192.
20. Ibid., 193.

24. William B. McKinley

1. H. Wayne Morgan, *William McKinley and His America* (Syracuse, N.Y., 1963), 61.
2. George F. Hoar, *Autobiography of Seventy Years,* 2 vols. (New York, 1906), II:315.
3. Charles S. Olcott, *The Life of William McKinley,* 2 vols. (Boston and New York, 1916), II:341; James Morgan, *Our Presidents* (New York, 1958), 247.

4. Thomas Beer, *Hanna* (New York, 1929), 110.
5. *Ohio State Journal,* January 3, 1893, cited in Morgan, *McKinley,* 162.
6. Thomas B. McClellan, Jr., *The Gentleman and the Tiger,* ed. Harold C. Syrett (Philadelphia and New York, 1956), 120.
7. H. H. Kohlsaat, *From McKinley to Harding* (New York, 1923), 5.
8. Margaret Leech, *In the Days of McKinley* (New York, 1959), 437–38.
9. Hugh Baillie, *High Tension: The Recollections of Hugh Baillie* (New York, 1959), 29.
10. Olcott, *McKinley,* II:361–63.
11. Edmund Morris, *The Rise of Theodore Roosevelt* (New York, 1979), 600; Morgan, *McKinley,* 301.
12. Claude M. Fuess, *Carl Schurz, Reformer, 1829–1906* (Philadelphia, 1933), 349.
13. Maxim E. Armbruster, *The Presidents of the United States: A New Appraisal* (New York, 1960), 237.
14. Mrs. Garret A. Hobart, *Memories* (Paterson, N.J., 1930), 61.
15. Leech, *Days of McKinley,* 49.
16. *New York Sun,* April 20, 1898, cited in Morgan, *McKinley,* 378.
17. Olcott, *McKinley,* II:314; Walter Lord, *The Good Years* (New York, 1960), 40.
18. James Ford Rhodes, *The McKinley and Roosevelt Administrations, 1897–1909* (New York, 1922), 171; Olcott, *McKinley,* II:316, 324–26.
19. Bascom N. Timmons, *Portrait of an American: Charles G. Daws* (New York, 1953), 80.
20. Kohlsaat, *From McKinley to Harding,* 63–64.
21. *Mark Hanna: His Book* (Boston, 1904), 66–67.

25. Theodore Roosevelt

1. *The Education of Henry Adams* (New York, 1918), 417.
2. J. B. Bishop, *Notes and Anecdotes of Many Years* (New York, 1925), 122–23.
3. Richard Hofstadter, *The American Political Tradition* (New York, 1948), 210–11.
4. Nicholas Roosevelt, *Theodore Roosevelt: The Man as I Knew Him* (New York, 1967), viii.
5. William Roscoe Thayer, *John Hay,* 2 vols. (Boston and New York, 1915), II:55.
6. Lewis Henry, *Humorous Anecdotes about Famous People* (Garden City, N.Y., 1948), 98.
7. Corrine Roosevelt Robinson, *My Brother Theodore Roosevelt* (New York, 1921), 50.
8. Theodore Roosevelt, *Autobiography* (New York, 1913), 27–28.

9. Herman Hagedorn, *Roosevelt in the Bad Lands* (Boston and New York, 1931), 101.

10. *Autobiography*, 122–23.

11. Hagedorn, *Roosevelt in Bad Lands*, 279.

12. Henry F. Pringle, *Theodore Roosevelt* (New York, 1931), 172.

13. Hofstadter, *American Political Tradition*, 209.

14. Edward Wagenknecht, *The Seven Worlds of Theodore Roosevelt* (New York, 1958), 249.

15. Elting E. Morison et al., eds., *The Letters of Theodore Roosevelt*, 8 vols. (Cambridge, Mass., 1951–54), II:803.

16. Henry Cabot Lodge, ed., *Selections from the Correspondence of Theodore Roosevelt and Henry Cabot Lodge*, 2 vols. (New York, 1925), I:45; Edmund Morris, *The Rise of Theodore Roosevelt* (New York, 1979), 444.

17. Stephen Gwynn, *The Letters and Friendships of Sir Cecil Spring Rice*, 2 vols. (Boston and New York, 1929), I:326.

18. *Letters of Roosevelt*, I:504.

19. Henry F. Pringle, *Theodore Roosevelt* (New York: Harvest, 1956), 299.

20. H. H. Kohlsaat, *From McKinley to Harding* (New York, 1923), 77–78.

21. Arthur Wallace Dunn, *Gridiron Nights* (New York, 1915), 71–72.

22. Morris, *Rise of Roosevelt*, 614.

23. *Autobiography*, 242; Pringle, *Roosevelt*, 194–96.

24. Pringle, *Roosevelt*, 181.

25. Dixon Wecter, *The Hero in America* (New York, 1941), 380; Pringle, *Roosevelt* (Harvest), 144–56.

26. Wagenknecht, *Seven Worlds of Roosevelt*, 261.

27. David C. Whitney, *The American Presidents* (Garden City, N.Y., 1967), 217.

28. Joseph L. Gardner, *Departing Glory: Theodore Roosevelt as Ex-President* (New York, 1973), 71.

29. Joseph B. Bishop, *Theodore Roosevelt and His Time*, 2 vols. (New York, 1920), I:183–85; Gardner, *Departing Glory*, 43–44.

30. Gardner, *Departing Glory*, 116.

31. Charles Willis Thompson, *Presidents I've Known* (Indianapolis, 1929), 147–49; James Morgan, *Our Presidents* (New York, 1958), 226; Whitney, *American Presidents*, 226.

32. Alice Roosevelt Longworth, *Crowded Hours* (New York, 1933), 246–47.

33. Morgan, *Our Presidents*, 269; Wagenknecht, *Seven Worlds of Roosevelt*, 142; William Allen White, *Masks in a Pageant* (New York, 1939), 369–70.

34. Gardner, *Departing Glory*, 373.

35. Noel Busch, *T. R.: The Story of Theodore Roosevelt and His Influence* (New York, 1963), 330.

36. Donald Wilhelm, *Theodore Roosevelt as an Undergraduate* (Boston, 1910), 35.

37. William Roscoe Thayer, *Theodore Roosevelt: An Intimate Biography* (Boston and New York, 1919), 22.
38. Owen Wister, *Roosevelt: The Story of a Friendship* (New York, 1930), 5.
39. Busch, *Roosevelt,* 86.
40. Hagedorn, *Roosevelt in Bad Lands,* 284–85.
41. Ibid., 256.
42. Busch, *Roosevelt,* 42–43.
43. Pringle, *Roosevelt,* 186–87.
44. Morris, *Rise of Roosevelt,* 658–59.
45. *Autobiography,* 125.
46. Ibid., 124.
47. Ibid., 127.
48. Kohlsaat, *McKinley to Roosevelt,* 90–92.
49. Wister, *Roosevelt,* 87.
50. Thayer, *Roosevelt,* 262–63; Pringle, *Roosevelt,* 4.
51. Philip Jessup, Elihu Root, 2 vols. (New York, 1938), I:404–5.
52. Earle Looker, *The White House Gang* (New York, 1929), 137–45.
53. Stoddard, *As I Knew Them,* 296.
54. Emily Bax, *Miss Bax of the Embassy* (Boston, 1939), 154.
55. Gardner, *Departing Glory,* 129.
56. *Letters of Theodore Roosevelt,* VII:412–13.
57. Arthur Krock, *Memoirs: Sixty Years on the Firing Line* (New York, 1968), 103.
58. William Beebe, *The Book of Naturalists* (New York, 1944), 234.
59. Edmund Fuller and David E. Green, *God in the White House* (New York, 1968), 163.
60. Robinson, *Brother Theodore,* 363.

26. William Howard Taft

1. H. H. Kohlsaat, *From McKinley to Harding* (New York, 1923), 161–62.
2. Francis Russell, *The Shadow of Blooming Grove* (New York, 1968), 441.
3. Charles Willis Thompson, *Presidents I've Known* (Indianapolis, 1929), 228–29.
4. *The Autobiography of John Hays Hammond,* 2 vols. (New York, 1935), I:581–82.
5. Thompson, *Presidents I've Known,* 225; Arthur Wallace Dunn, *From Harrison to Harding,* 2 vols. (New York, 1922), II:85–6.
6. Thompson, *Presidents I've Known,* 217.
7. Ibid., 245.
8. David McCullough, *The Path between the Seas: The Creation of the Panama Canal, 1870–1914* (New York, 1977), 446.
9. Lewis Henry, *Humorous Anecdotes about Famous People* (Garden City, N.Y., 1948), 158–59.

10. Thompson, *Presidents I've Known*, 247.
11. Archie Butt, *Taft and Roosevelt: The Intimate Letters of Archie Butt*, 2 vols. (New York, 1930), I:85; II:535, 617; Joseph L. Gardner, *Departing Glory: Theodore Roosevelt as Ex-President* (New York, 1973), 126.
12. Ibid., 249.
13. Boyce House, *Laugh Parade of States* (San Antonio, 1948), 114.
14. Archie Robertson, *Slow Train to Yesterday* (Boston, 1945), 105.
15. *Autobiography of Hammond*, II:546–47.
16. Cleveland Amory, *The Proper Bostonians* (New York, 1947), 27.

27. Woodrow Wilson

1. William F. McCombs, *Making Woodrow Wilson President* (New York, 1921), 180, 208.
2. Walter Lippmann, "Woodrow Wilson's Approach to Politics," *The New Republic*, CXXXIII (December 5, 1955), 15.
3. Edith Bolling Wilson, *My Memoir* (Indianapolis, 1938), 356.
4. Raymond Fosdick, "Woodrow Wilson among His Friends," *Harper's*, CCXIII (December 1956), 58.
5. *The Autobiography of William Allen White* (New York, 1946), 479.
6. Alexander George and Juliette George, *Woodrow Wilson and Colonel House* (New York, 1956), xvi.
7. Charles Willis Thompson, *Presidents I've Known* (Indianapolis, 1929), 288.
8. Walter Lord, *The Good Years* (New York, 1960), 292.
9. Harold C. Syrett, ed., *The Gentleman and the Tiger: The Autobiography of George B. McClellan, Jr.* (Philadelphia and New York, 1956), 314.
10. Thompson, *Presidents I've Known*, 253.
11. John L. Heaton, *Cobb of "The World"* (New York, 1924), 267–70.
12. Joseph P. Tumulty, *Woodrow Wilson as I Knew Him* (Garden City, N.Y., 1921), 256.
13. Thomas A. Bailey, *A Diplomatic History of the American People*, 7th ed. (New York, 1954), 608.
14. Lloyd George, *Memoirs of the Peace Conference*, 2 vols. (New Haven, Conn., 1939), I:140–42.
15. "The Welsh Wizard," *Time*, LXXVII (June 23, 1961), 74.
16. Richard Hofstadter, "The Strange Case of Freud, Bullitt, and Woodrow Wilson," *New York Review of Books*, VIII (February 9, 1967), 3; Bailey, *Diplomatic History*, 611.
17. Ray Stannard Baker and William E. Dodd, eds., *Public Papers of Woodrow Wilson*, 6 vols. (New York, 1927), V:551.
18. Thomas A. Bailey, *Woodrow Wilson and the Great Betrayal* (Chicago, 1945), 16.
19. Ibid., 13.

20. Stephen Bonsal, *Unfinished Business* (Garden City, N.Y., 1944), 275.
21. Bailey, *Great Betrayal*, 15.
22. Ibid., 178.
23. Edith Wilson, *Memoir*, 297.
24. Bailey, *Great Betrayal*, 271.
25. Henry Cabot Lodge, *The Senate and the League of Nations* (New York, 1925), 214.
26. Edith Wilson, *Memoir*, 299.
27. Ibid., 305–6; Francis Russell, *The Shadow of Blooming Grove* (New York, 1968), 404–5.
28. James Morgan, *Our Presidents* (New York, 1958), 285.
29. Edith Wilson, *Memoir*, 319; Tumulty, *Wilson*, 509–10.
30. Tumulty, *Wilson*, 463.
31. Fosdick, "Wilson," 59.
32. Arthur S. Link, *Woodrow Wilson: A Brief Biography* (Cleveland, 1963), 33.
33. Em Bowles Alsop, ed., *The Greatness of Woodrow Wilson* (New York, 1956), 22.
34. Bill Adler, ed., *Presidential Wit from Washington to Johnson* (New York, 1966), 103.
35. Thompson, *Presidents I've Known*, 291.
36. Alsop, *Greatness of Wilson*, 28.
37. Ibid., 26–27.
38. Josephus Daniels, *The Life of Woodrow Wilson, 1856–1924* (n.p., 1924), 238.
39. Josephus Daniels, *The Wilson Era: Years of War and After, 1917–1923* (Chapel Hill, N.C., 1946), 624.
40. Faye Copeland and Lewis Copeland, eds., *1000 Jokes, Toasts, and Stories* (Garden City, N.Y., 1940), 540.
41. Edith Wilson, *Memoir*, 315.
42. Ibid., 97; Edmund W. Starling, *Starling of the White House* (Chicago, 1946), 91–93.
43. *Starling of the White House*, 64.
44. Daniels, *Life of Wilson*, 238–39.
45. Alsop, *Greatness of Wilson*, 32.
46. Tumulty, *Wilson*, 321.
47. James Schermerhorn, *Schermerhorn's Stories* (New York, 1928), 367.

28. Warren G. Harding

1. Francis Russell, *The Shadow of Blooming Grove* (New York, 1968), 52.
2. Ibid., 230; Eric F. Goldman, "A Sort of Rehabilitation of Warren G. Harding," *New York Times Magazine*, March 26, 1972, 82.

3. H. L. Mencken, *On Politics: A Carnival of Buncombe,* ed. Malcolm Moos (New York, 1956), 22, 25–26, 42.
4. Russell, *Shadow of Blooming Grove,* 347.
5. Ibid., 452, 483, 383, 485.
6. *The Autobiography of William Allen White* (New York, 1946), 616.
7. Russell, *Shadow of Blooming Grove,* 452.
8. Ibid., 472.
9. Arthur Krock, *Memoirs: Sixty Years on the Firing Line* (New York, 1968), 118.
10. Alice Roosevelt Longworth, *Crowded Hours* (New York, 1933), 325.
11. Andrew Sinclair, *The Available Man: The Life Behind the Mask of Warren Gamaliel Harding* (New York, 1965), 286.
12. Robert K. Murray, *The 103rd Ballot: Democrats and Disaster in Madison Square Garden* (New York, 1976), 144.
13. Edmund W. Starling, *Starling of the White House* (Chicago, 1946), 174.
14. Russell, *Shadow of Blooming Grove,* 444.
15. *The Autobiography of Lincoln Steffens* (New York, 1931), 843–44.

29. Calvin Coolidge

1. Claude Fuess, *Calvin Coolidge* (New York, 1940), 307–10; John Hiram McKee, *Coolidge Wit and Wisdom* (New York, 1933), 10; Duff Gilfond, *The Rise of Saint Calvin* (New York, 1932), 160–61; Ishbel Ross, *Grace Coolidge and Her Era* (New York, 1962), 82.
2. Thomas A. Bailey, *Presidential Greatness* (New York, 1966), 97.
3. William Manchester, *Disturber of the Peace: The Life of H. L. Mencken* (New York, 1950), 217.
4. H. L. Mencken, *On Politics: A Carnival of Buncombe,* ed. Malcolm Moos (New York, 1960), 139.
5. Fuess, *Coolidge,* 300–301.
6. Edward C. Lathem, *Meet Calvin Coolidge* (Brattleboro, Vt., 1960), 7.
7. Fuess, *Coolidge,* 300.
8. Louis Untermeyer, *A Treasury of Laughter* (New York, 1946), 85; Boyce House, *Laugh Parade of States* (San Antonio, 1948), 138; *Parade* (New York), June 21, 1964, 9.
9. Mencken, *On Politics,* 139.
10. Henry L. Stoddard, *As I Knew Them: Presidents and Politics from Grant to Coolidge* (New York, 1927), 529.
11. "I don't know whether he said it," said Mrs. Coolidge after her husband's death, "but it is just what he might have said." Lathem, *Meet Calvin Coolidge,* 151.
12. *The Memoirs of Herbert Hoover: The Cabinet and the Presidency, 1920–1933* (New York, 1952), 55.

13. Arthur Zipser and George Novack, *Who's Hooey: Nitwitticisms of the Notable* (New York, 1932), 50, 54, 56, 60.

14. Bennett Cerf, *Try and Stop Me* (New York, 1944), 261; House, *Laugh Parade,* 137.

15. E. E. Whiting, *President Coolidge: A Contemporary Estimate* (Boston, 1923), 91; Fuess, *Coolidge,* 153.

16. Cameron Rogers, *The Legend of Calvin Coolidge* (Garden City, N.Y., 1928), 22–23; Fuess, Coolidge, 29; Leewin Williams, *Encyclopedia of Wit* (New York, 1949), 1073.

17. McKee, *Coolidge Wit and Wisdom,* 56; Whiting, President Coolidge, 11.

18. Whiting, *President Coolidge,* 48–49; McKee, *Coolidge Wit and Wisdom,* 32; Fuess, *Coolidge,* 46; Lathem, *Meet Calvin Coolidge,* 136–37; William Allen White, *A Puritan in Babylon: The Story of Calvin Coolidge* (New York, 1938), 42.

19. Lathem, *Meet Calvin Coolidge,* 148; McKee, *Coolidge Wit and Wisdom,* 102; White, *Puritan in Babylon,* 35; Whiting, *President Coolidge,* 41–42; Donald R. McCoy, *Calvin Coolidge: The Quiet President* (New York, 1967), 15.

20. Fuess, *Coolidge,* 88; Ross, *Grace Coolidge,* 16; McKee, *Coolidge Wit and Wisdom,* 71; McCoy, *Quiet President,* 31; Rogers, *Legend of Coolidge,* 93–94; Whiting, *President Coolidge,* 64.

21. Ross, *Grace Coolidge,* 24; Fuess, *Coolidge,* 89; Lathem, *Meet Calvin Coolidge,* 64; McCoy, *Quiet President,* 33–34.

22. White, *Puritan in Babylon,* 65; Fuess, *Coolidge,* 91; McKee, *Coolidge Wit and Wisdom,* 1; Lathem, *Meet Calvin Coolidge,* 156; Cerf, *Try and Stop Me,* 259–60.

23. Ross, *Grace Coolidge,* 32; McCoy, *Quiet President,* 40; Fuess, *Coolidge,* 91.

24. "Personal Glimpses," *Reader's Digest,* LXXII (March 1958), 9.

25. Ross, *Grace Coolidge,* 36; McCoy, *Quiet President,* 50; Fuess, *Coolidge,* 478.

26. Fuess, *Coolidge,* 102; Rogers, *Legend of Coolidge,* 129.

27. Lathem, *Meet Calvin Coolidge,* 149; McKee, *Coolidge Wit and Wisdom,* 96; McCoy, *Quiet President,* 59; Rogers, *Legend of Coolidge,* 130; Whiting, *President Coolidge,* 101; Gamaliel Bradford, *The Quick and the Dead* (New York, 1931), 246.

28. *The Autobiography of John Hays Hammond,* 2 vols. (New York, 1935), II:694–95; McKee, *Coolidge Wit and Wisdom,* 28–29; Fuess, *Coolidge,* 479 n.; McCoy, *Quiet President,* 71; White, *Puritan in Babylon,* 138; Cerf, *Try and Stop Me,* 261.

29. Fuess, *Coolidge,* 475–76.

30. Lathem, *Meet Calvin Coolidge,* 156; Fuess, *Coolidge,* 472; James C. Humes, *Speaker's Treasury of Anecdotes about the Famous* (New York, 1978), 131.

31. McKee, *Coolidge Wit and Wisdom*, 22.

32. Lathem, *Meet Calvin Coolidge*, 150.

33. George Wharton Pepper, *Philadelphia Lawyer: An Autobiography* (Philadelphia and New York, 1944), 202; McCoy, *Quiet President*, 146.

34. White, *Puritan in Babylon*, 238.

35. McKee, *Coolidge Wit and Wisdom*, 42; White, *Puritan in Babylon*, 365; Rogers, *Legend of Coolidge*, 169; B. A. Botkin, *A Treasury of American Anecdotes* (New York, 1957), 153.

36. Fuess, *Coolidge*, 300; McCoy, *Quiet President*, 139; Untermeyer, *Treasury of Laughter*, 86; Humes, *Speaker's Treasury*, 31.

37. Ross, *Grace Coolidge*, 67; McKee, *Coolidge Wit and Wisdom*, 43; Lathem, *Meet Calvin Coolidge*, 159; Fuess, *Coolidge*, 300; McCoy, *Quiet President*, 160–61; Rogers, *Legend of Coolidge*, 156; Untermeyer, *Treasury of Laughter*, 85.

38. McKee, *Coolidge Wit and Wisdom*, 112; Lathem, *Meet Calvin Coolidge*, 150.

39. Fuess, *Coolidge*, 311.

40. Charles Willis Thompson, *Presidents I've Known* (Indianapolis, 1929), 356.

41. George Allen, *Presidents Who Have Known Me* (New York, 1950), 58; Humes, *Speaker's Treasury*, 110.

42. Lathem, *Meet Calvin Coolidge*, 151; McKee, *Coolidge Wit and Wisdom*, 4; Fuess, *Coolidge*, 478; Untermeyer, *Treasury of Laughter*, 84.

43. Lathem, *Meet Calvin Coolidge*, 148.

44. *Autobiography of Hammond*, II:694.

45. Fuess, *Coolidge*, 5; Ross, *Grace Coolidge*, 108; McCoy, *Quiet President*, 159.

46. Lathem, *Meet Calvin Coolidge*, 152; McKee, *Coolidge Wit and Wisdom*, 38.

47. Ross, *Grace Coolidge*, 38; McCoy, *Quiet President*, 296; Ona Griffin Jeffries, *In and Out of the White House* (New York, 1960), 322–24; Humes, *Speaker's Treasury*, 161; Bennett Cerf, *Shake Well Before Using* (New York, 1951), 13.

48. Fuess, *Coolidge*, 483.

49. Lathem, *Meet Calvin Coolidge*, 153; Fuess, *Coolidge*, 477.

50. Irwin H. Hoover, *Forty-Two Years in the White House* (Boston, 1934), 268; Ross, *Grace Coolidge*, 65; McCoy, *Quiet President*, 159.

51. Jacob M. Braude, *Speaker's Encyclopedia of Humor* (Englewood Cliffs, N.J., 1961), 230.

52. House, *Laugh Parade*, 116.

53. "Personal Glimpses," *Reader's Digest*, LXXIV (April 1959), 27–28.

54. McKee, *Coolidge Wit and Wisdom*, 2; House, *Laugh Parade*, 137; Fuess, *Coolidge*, 478 n.

55. McKee, *Coolidge Wit and Wisdom*, 66; Fuess, *Coolidge*, 106.

56. House, *Laugh Parade*, 140.

57. Edmund W. Starling, *Starling of the White House* (New York, 1926), 235–36; McKee, *Coolidge Wit and Wisdom*, 35–36; Lathem, *Meet Calvin Coolidge*, 155.

58. Lathem, *Meet Calvin Coolidge*, 155–56; McCoy, *Quiet President*, 292; White, *Puritan in Babylon*, vi–vii.

59. Lathem, *Meet Calvin Coolidge*, 85.

60. *Starling of the White House*, 212; Lathem, *Meet Calvin Coolidge*, 80; Bennett Cerf, *Good for a Laugh* (New York, 1954), 168.

61. *Starling of the White House*, 267; Hoover, *Forty-Two Years*, 131; McKee, *Coolidge Wit and Wisdom*, 21; Fuess, *Coolidge*, 478; Lewis Henry, *Humorous Anecdotes about Famous People* (Garden City, N.Y., 1948), 100; McCoy, *Quiet President*, 299.

62. McKee, *Coolidge Wit and Wisdom*, 114.

63. Lathem, *Meet Calvin Coolidge*, 98; Fuess, *Coolidge*, 479.

64. *Starling of the White House*, 236.

65. "The Well Known Human Race," *Reader's Digest*, XXIII (June 1933), 56–57.

66. Ibid., XXI (July 1932), 46.

67. McKee, *Coolidge Wit and Wisdom*, 12; Humes, *Speaker's Treasury*, 26.

68. Ross, *Grace Coolidge*, 283–84; McKee, *Coolidge Wit and Wisdom*, 14; Lathem, *Meet Calvin Coolidge*, 160; McCoy, *Quiet President*, 295; White, *Puritan in Babylon*, 436; Vera Bloom, *There's No Place Like Washington* (New York, 1944), 21.

69. McKee, *Coolidge Wit and Wisdom*, 9.

70. Ibid., 13.

71. Ibid., 103

72. Ross, *Grace Coolidge*, 281.

30. Herbert Hoover

1. Louis W. Koenig, *The Chief Executive* (New York, 1964), 357.

2. David C. Whitney, *The American Presidents* (Garden City, N.Y., 1967), 272.

3. David Hinshaw, *Herbert Hoover: American Quaker* (New York, 1950), 201.

4. Edward Angly, *Oh Yeah?* (New York, 1931), passim.

5. W. E. Woodward, *A New American History* (New York, 1936), 860.

6. Arthur Krock, *Memoirs: Sixty Years on the Firing Line* (New York, 1968), 126.

7. Bennett Cerf, *Try and Stop Me* (New York, 1944), 262.

8. Hinshaw, *Hoover*, xvii.

9. Richard L. Strout, "Mr. Hoover as a Terrapin Progressive," *The New Republic,* CXL (March 16, 1959), 19.

10. Edmund W. Starling, *Starling of the White House* (Chicago, 1946), 301.

11. Eugene Lyons, *Herbert Hoover: A Biography* (Garden City, N.Y., 1964), 328.

12. Ibid., 189–90.

13. "The Well Known Human Race," *Reader's Digest,* XX (November 1931), 56.

14. Hinshaw, *Hoover,* 85.

15. Lyons, *Hoover,* 179–80.

16. Ibid., 167.

17. Theodore G. Joslin, *Hoover Off the Record* (New York, 1934, 1971), 9–11.

18. Irwin Hood Hoover, *Forty-Two Years in the White House* (Boston, 1934), 219.

19. Bennett Cerf, *Good for a Laugh* (New York, 1952), 198.

20. Lyons, *Hoover,* 210.

21. Ibid., 337.

31. Franklin D. Roosevelt

1. Earle Looker, *This Man Roosevelt* (New York, 1932), 4.

2. Ibid., 91.

3. William E. Leuchtenberg, *Franklin D. Roosevelt and the New Deal* (New York, 1963), 8.

4. Arthur M. Schlesinger, Jr., *The Politics of Upheaval* (Boston, 1960), 425.

5. Frances Perkins, *The Roosevelt I Knew* (New York, 1946), 215.

6. Charles Beard and Mary Beard, *America in Midpassage,* 2 vols. (New York, 1939), I:225.

7. Adolf A. Berle, "Dreams and the Possible," *The New Leader,* XLVIII (February 1, 1965), 24.

8. Perkins, *Roosevelt,* 124.

9. Ibid., 328.

10. Ibid., 330.

11. Looker, *Roosevelt,* 4.

12. Perkins, *Roosevelt,* 108.

13. Ibid., 76.

14. Ibid.

15. Ibid., 6.

16. Ibid., 83–85.

17. Robert E. Sherwood, *Roosevelt and Hopkins: An Intimate History* (New

York, 1948), 204; Samuel I. Rosenman, *Working with Roosevelt* (New York, 1952), 349–50.

18. George E. Allen, *Presidents Who Have Known Me* (New York, 1950), 238–39; Booth Moody, *LBJ: An Irreverent Chronicle* (New York, 1976), 227.

19. "Next Week," Colliers, LXXXIX (June 18, 1932), 4.

20. Looker, *Roosevelt*, 35–38.

21. Eleanor Roosevelt, This Is My Story New York, 1937), 84.

22. James Roosevelt, *My Parents* (Chicago, 1976), 43; *New York Times*, July 27, 1917; Joseph P. Lash, *Eleanor and Franklin* (New York, 1971), 210–11.

23. Looker, *Roosevelt*, 43–44.

24. Arthur Schlesinger, Jr., *The Crisis of the Old Order, 1919–1933* (Boston, 1957), 406; Rosenman, *Working with Roosevelt*, 37; Perkins, *Roosevelt*, 44–45.

25. Eleanor Roosevelt, *This I Remember* (New York, 1949), 57.

26. Rosenman, *Working with Roosevelt*, 150–51.

27. Lash, *Eleanor and Franklin*, 608.

28. Arthur Schlesinger, Jr., *The Coming of the New Deal* (Boston, 1959), 14.

29. James Roosevelt, *My Parents*, 180–81.

30. Lash, *Eleanor and Franklin*, 595.

31. Eleanor Roosevelt, *This I Remember*, 254–55.

32. Ibid., 17; Grace Tully, *F.D.R., My Boss* (New York, 1949), 324.

33. *The Secret Diary of Harold L. Ickes: The First Thousand Days* (New York, 1953), 588–89; Harold L. Ickes, "My Twelve Years with F.D.R.," *Saturday Evening Post*, CCXX (June 19, 1948), 99.

34. James Roosevelt, *My Parents*, 217.

35. Ibid., 47.

36. "Fanny Hurst," *New York Times*, February 24, 1968, 29.

37. Carl Bode, *Mencken* (Carbondale, Ill., 1969), 310–11; Edgar Kemler, *The Irreverent Mr. Mencken* (Boston, 1950), 269–72; James Roosevelt, *My Parents*, 188–89.

38. Allen, *Presidents Who Have Known Me*, 10.

39. James Roosevelt, *My Parents*, 209–10.

40. Tully, *F.D.R.*, 318–20.

41. Lewis Henry, *Humorous Anecdotes about Famous People* (Garden City, N.Y., 1948), 192.

42. Frank Cormier, *LBJ: The Way He Was* (Garden City, N.Y., 1977), 221.

43. William D. Hassett, *Off the Record with F.D.R.* (New Brunswick, N.J., 1958), 66–67.

44. Eleanor Roosevelt, *This I Remember*, 284; Tully, *F.D.R.*, 335.

45. Eleanor Roosevelt, *This I Remember*, 172.

46. Rosenman, *Working with Roosevelt*, 321.

47. Sydney J. Harris, *Chicago Daily News*, quoted in "A Revealing Situa-

tion," *Reader's Digest,* XLIV (April 1944), 82; Sherwood, *Roosevelt and Hopkins,* 442–43; Tully, *F.D.R.,* 305.
48. Tully, *F.D.R.,* 301.
49. James F. Byrnes, *Speaking Frankly* (New York, 1947), 59.
50. Tully, *F.D.R.,* 115; Lash, *Eleanor and Franklin,* 655.
51. Hassett, *Off the Record,* 175.
52. James Roosevelt, *My Parents,* 169–70.

32. Harry S. Truman

1. "The Long Day," *Time,* XLV (April 23, 1945), 19; Margaret Truman, *Harry S. Truman* (New York, 1973), 208–9.
2. "U.S. Closes Ranks under Truman," *Newsweek,* XXV (April 23, 1945), 27; Mark Goodman, ed., *Give 'Em Hell, Harry* (New York, 1975), 17.
3. "U.S. Closes Ranks," 31; David Whitney, *The American Presidents* (Garden City, N.Y., 1967), 300.
4. Jonathan Daniels, *The Man of Independence* (Philadelphia, 1950, 23, 22–33; Alfred Steinberg, *The Man from Missouri* (New York, 1962), 209.
5. Steinberg, *Man from Missouri,* 13.
6. Jonathan Daniels, "How Truman Writes Those Letters," *Collier's,* CXXVII (February 24, 1951), 15.
7. Merle Miller, *Plain Speaking* (New York, 1974), 88.
8. Steinberg, *Man from Missouri,* 291.
9. Miller, *Plain Speaking,* 19.
10. Steinberg, *Man from Missouri,* 262.
11. Daniels, *Man of Independence,* 27; Steinberg, *Man from Missouri,* 263, 288.
12. Steinberg, *Man from Missouri,* 314, 317, 319.
13. Ibid., 323.
14. Ibid., 324, 329, 330.
15. Ibid., 330, 331, 332.
16. Ibid., 332.
17. Ibid., 409.
18. Ibid., 418.
19. Miller, *Plain Speaking,* 17.
20. Harry Truman, *Mr. Citizen* (New York, 1960), 63.
21. Steinberg, *Man from Missouri,* 428–29.
22. Goodman, *Give 'Em Hell,* 108.
23. Margaret Truman, *Truman,* 90.
24. Goodman, *Give 'Em Hell,* 184.
25. J. B. West, *Upstairs at the White House* (New York, 1973), 75.
26. Miller, *Plain Speaking,* 393–94.
27. Margaret Truman, *Truman,* 280–81.

28. "Eugene List," *Keyboard Classics*, July/August 1981, pp. 2–3.
29. "Free To Choose," *The New Republic*, CLXXX (March 22, 1980), 25.
30. West, *Upstairs at White House*, 75.
31. Goodman, *Give 'Em Hell*, 177.
32. Harry Truman, *Mr. Citizen*, 86–87.
33. Miller, *Plain Speaking*, 358 and note.

33. Dwight D. Eisenhower

1. Jules Archer, *Battlefield President: Dwight D. Eisenhower* (New York, 1967), 11.
2. Marquis Childs, *Eisenhower: Captive Hero* (New York, 1958), 140.
3. Archer, *Battlefield President*, 32–33.
4. Ibid., 85–86.
5. Ibid., 98.
6. Elmo Richardson, *The Presidency of Dwight D. Eisenhower* (Lawrence, Kans. 1979), 38.
7. Childs, *Eisenhower*, 167.
8. Merlo J. Pusey, *Eisenhower, the President* (New York, 1956), 98–99.
9. Emmet John Hughes, *The Ordeal of Power: A Political Memoir of the Eisenhower Years* (New York, 1963), 182–83.
10. Arthur Krock, *Memoirs: Sixty Years on the Firing Line* (New York, 1968), 280.
11. Archer, *Battlefield President*, 85–86.
12. Pusey, *Eisenhower*, 3.
13. Robert J. Donovan, *Eisenhower: The Inside Story* (New York, 1956), 7.
14. Ibid., 206.
15. Arthur Larson, *Eisenhower: The President Nobody Knew* (New York, 1968), 30–31.
16. Hughes, *Ordeal of Power*, 149.
17. Donovan, *Eisenhower*, 249.
18. Larson, *Eisenhower*, 13.
19. Ibid., 35.
20. Richardson, *Presidency of Eisenhower*, 25.
21. Peter Lyon, *Eisenhower: Portrait of the Hero* (Boston, 1974), 500–501.
22. Pusey, *Eisenhower*, 114.
23. Archer, *Battlefield President*, 166.
24. Merriman Smith, *A President's Odyssey* (New York, 1961), 170; Pusey, *Eisenhower*, 179.
25. Archer, *Battlefield President*, 79.
26. Dwight D. Eisenhower, *At Ease: Stories I Tell to Friends* (Garden City, N.Y., 1967), 285.
27. Pusey, *Eisenhower*, 103.

28. Ibid.

29. Archer, *Battlefield President*, 115.

30. Eisenhower, *At Ease*, 357.

31. Pusey, *Eisenhower*, 102.

32. George F. Will, *Fort Worth Star-Telegram*, May 13, 1980, 6A.

33. Lyon, *Eisenhower*, 641; Hughes, *Ordeal of Power*, 24–25; Garry Wills, *Nixon Agonistes* (Boston, 1969), 121–23; Eric F. Goldman, *The Crucial Decade—and After: America, 1945–1960* (New York, 1956; rev. ed., 1960), 304–5.

34. Donovan, Eisenhower, 144.

35. Richardson, *Presidency of Eisenhower*, 39; John Gunther, *Eisenhower: The Man and the Symbol* (New York, 1952), 34; Childs, *Eisenhower*, 261; Pusey, *Eisenhower*, 102.

34. John F. Kennedy

1. Bill Adler, ed., *The Complete Kennedy Wit* (New York, 1967), 12.

2. William R. Manchester, *Portrait of a President: John F. Kennedy in Profile* (Boston, 1967), 26.

3. Theodore C. Sorensen, *Kennedy* (New York, 1965), 18.

4. Arthur M. Schlesinger, Jr., *A Thousand Days: John F. Kennedy in the White House* (Boston, 1965), 86.

5. Manchester, *Portrait of President*, 162; James McGregor Burns, *John F. Kennedy: A Political Profile* (New York, 1960), 50–52; Adler, *Kennedy Wit*, 24–25.

6. Manchester, *Portrait of President*, 159.

7. Adler, *Kennedy Wit*, 27–28.

8. Kenneth P. O'Donnell and David F. Powers, *"Johnny, We Hardly Knew Ye"* (New York, 1970), 173.

9. Sorensen, *Kennedy*, 119.

10. Paul F. Fay, *The Pleasure of His Company* (New York, 1966), 17.

11. Schlesinger, *Thousand Days*, 60–61.

12. Manchester, *Portrait of President*, 10.

13. William H. A. Carr, *JFK: The Life and Death of a President* (New York, 1964), 138.

14. Schlesinger, *Thousand Days*, 343.

15. Sorensen, *Kennedy*, 294.

16. Benjamin Bradlee, *Conversations with Kennedy* (New York, 1975), 38; Carr, *JFK*, 132; *Time*, LXXVII (February 3, 1961), 14.

17. Manchester, *Portrait of President*, 161.

18. Carr, *JFK*, 133.

19. Sorensen, *Kennedy*, 18.

20. Schlesinger, *Thousand Days*, 673.

21. Carr, *JFK*, 139–40.

22. Bradlee, *Conversations*, 113.

23. Manchester, *Portrait of President*, 160.

24. Ibid., 161.

25. O'Donnell and Powers, *Johnny*, 340–41; Schlesinger, *Thousand Days*, 361.

26. Adler, *Kennedy Wit*, 12.

27. O'Donnell and Powers, *Johnny*, 397.

28. John F. Kennedy, *The Burden and the Glory*, ed. Allan Nevins (New York, 1964), 277.

29. Fay, *Pleasure of His Company*, 10–11.

30. Sorensen, *Kennedy*, 32.

31. O'Donnell and Powers, *Johnny*, 66.

32. Sorensen, *Kennedy*, 25.

33. Ibid., 24.

34. O'Donnell and Power, *Johnny*, 164.

35. Alex J. Goldman, *The Quotable Kennedy* (New York, 1965), 140.

36. O'Donnell and Powers, *Johnny*, 470–71.

37. "Lawrence E. Spivak," *New York Times*, March 10, 1994, D21.

38. Ibid., 161–62.

39. Ibid., 160.

40. Hugh Sidey, *John F. Kennedy, President* (New York, 1963), 188.

41. David Halberstam, *The Best and the Brightest* (New York, 1969), 165.

42. Jack Valenti, *A Very Human President* (New York, 1975), 285.

35. Lyndon B. Johnson

1. Harry Provence, *Lyndon B. Johnson: A Biography* (New York, 1964), 58.

2. Jack Valenti, *A Very Human President* (New York, 1975), 157.

3. Frank Cormier, *LBJ: The Way He Was* (Garden City, N.Y., 1977), 34.

4. Alfred Steinberg, *Sam Johnson's Boy: A Close-up of the President from Texas* (New York, 1968), 134.

5. Sam Houston Johnson, *My Brother, Lyndon* (New York, 1970), 147.

6. Steinberg, *Sam Johnson's Boy*, 360.

7. Johnson, *Brother Lyndon*, 134.

8. Liz Carpenter, *Ruffles and Flourishes* (Garden City, N.Y., 1970), 32.

9. Steinberg, *Sam Johnson's Boy*, 97.

10. Cormier, *LBJ*, 138.

11. Steinberg, *Sam Johnson's Boy*, 128.

12. Ibid., 632.

13. Ibid., 277.

14. Booth Moody, *LBJ: An Irreverent Chronicle* (New York, 1976), 185.

15. Steinberg, *Sam Johnson's Boy*, 735.
16. Johnson, *Brother Lyndon*, 135.
17. Valenti, *Human President*, 97–98.
18. Steinberg, *Sam Johnson's Boy*, 633.
19. Cormier, *LBJ*, 137.
20. Hugh Sidey, *A Very Personal Presidency* (New York, 1968), 98.
21. Steinberg, *Sam Johnson's Boy*, 725–26.
22. Bill Adler, ed., *The Washington Wits* (New York, 1967), 197.
23. Cormier, *LBJ*, 45.
24. Ibid., 79.
25. Johnson, *Brother Lyndon*, 156–57.
26. Steinberg, *Sam Johnson's Boy*, 718.
27. Ibid.
28. Ibid., 177, 454.
29. Barry M. Goldwater, *With No Apologies* (New York: Berkley, 1980), 196.
30. Valenti, *Human President*, 106–7; Cormier, *LBJ*, 35–36; Provence, *Johnson*, 58.
31. James C. Humes, *Speaker's Treasury of Anecdotes about the Famous* (New York, 1978), 57.
32. Sidey, *Personal Presidency*, 86.
33. Doris Kearns, *Lyndon Johnson and the American Dream* (New York, 1976), 263.
34. Ibid., 240–41.
35. Carpenter, *Ruffles*, 209.
36. Valenti, *Human President*, 104–5.
37. Sidey, *Personal Presidency*, 167.
38. Provence, *Johnson*, 35.
39. Ibid., 54.
40. Steinberg, *Sam Johnson's Boy*, 125.
41. "Washington Wags," *Reader's Digest*, LXXV (October 1959), 108.
42. Merle Miller, *Lyndon: An Oral Biography* (New York, 1980), 175.
43. Steinberg, *Sam Johnson's Boy*, 436.
44. William S. White, *The Professional: Lyndon B. Johnson* (Boston, 1964), 236.
45. Bill Adler, ed., *The Johnson Humor* (New York, 1965), 46.
46. David Halberstam, *The Best and the Brightest* (New York, 1969), 165–66.
47. Moody, *LBJ*, 232.
48. Miller, *Lyndon*, 366.
49. Johnson, *Brother Lyndon*, 168–70.
50. Ibid., 2–3.
51. Cormier, *LBJ*, 76.
52. Sidey, *Personal Presidency*, 223.

53. Halberstam, *Best and Brightest*, 528–29.
54. "Mr. President, You're Fun," *Time*, LXXXIII (April 10, 1964), 23a.
55. Cormier, *LBJ*, 160.
56. Ibid., 44.
57. Steinberg, *Sam Johnson's Boy*, 491.
58. Valenti, *Human President*, 157.
59. Cormier, *LBJ*, 77.
60. Ibid.
61. William Miller, *Fishbait: The Memoirs of the Congressional Doorkeeper* (Englewood Cliffs, N.J., 1977), 37.
62. Johnson, *Brother Lyndon*, 144.
63. Miller, *Lyndon*, 35.
64. Paul F. Boller, Jr., *Quotesmanship: The Use and Abuse of Quotations for Polemical and Other Purposes* (Dallas, 1967), 412–13.
65. Cormier, *LBJ*, 78.
66. Miller, *Lyndon*, 547–48.
67. Herman Wouk, "A Choice for Freedom," *Parade* (New York), October 19, 1980, 6; Joseph Kraft, "The Post-Imperial Presidency," *New York Times Magazine*, November 2, 1980, 78.

36. Richard M. Nixon

1. David Abrahamsen, *Nixon vs. Nixon* (New York, 1977), 172; Raymond Price, *With Nixon* (New York, 1977), 172; Raymond Price, *With Nixon* (New York, 1977), 18.
2. Abrahamsen, *Nixon vs. Nixon*, 172.
3. Gary Allen, *Richard Nixon* (Boston, 1971), 161.
4. "The Remarkable Tornado," *Time*, LX (September 29, 1952), 12.
5. "The Trial," *Time*, LX (October 6, 1952), 20.
6. Earl Mazo and Stephen Hess, *President Nixon: A Political Portrait* (London, 1968), 124, 120.
7. Garry Wills, *Nixon Agonistes* (Boston, 1970), 110.
8. Emmet John Hughes, *The Ordeal of Power: A Political Memoir of the Eisenhower Years* (New York, 1963), 40.
9. Abrahamsen, *Nixon vs. Nixon*, 165.
10. Price, *With Nixon*, 40–41.
11. Abrahamsen, *Nixon vs. Nixon*, 177.
12. Ibid., 167.
13. James D. Barber, *The Presidential Character* (Englewood Cliffs, N.J., 1972), 441.
14. William Safire, *Before the Fall* (Garden City, N.Y., 1975), 690.
15. John W. Dean, *Blind Ambition* (New York, 1976), 18–19.
16. J. Anthony Lukas, *Nightmare: The Underside of the Nixon Years* (New York, 1976), 559, 563–64.

17. Theodore White, *Breach of Faith: The Fall of Richard Nixon* (New York, 1975), 343; Gerald R. Ford, *A Time To Heal* (New York, 1979), 37, 170.

18. "California: Career's End," *Time*, LXXX (November 16, 1962), 28; "You Won't Have Nixon to Kick Around," *Newsweek*, LX (November 19, 1962), 31–33.

19. Safire, *Before the Fall*, 530.

20. "Signing Off," *Reader's Digest*, LXXVII (November 1962), 330.

21. Bill Adler, ed., *The Washington Wits* (New York, 1967), 109.

22. Ibid.

23. Jules Witcover, *The Resurrection of Richard Nixon* (New York, 1970), 136–37.

24. "You Won't Have Nixon To Kick Around Anymore," *Funny Times*, June 1994, p. 15.

25. Ron Nessen, *It Sure Looks Different from the Inside* (New York, 1978), 4.

26. Larry King, *Tell It to the King* (New York, 1988), 163.

37. Gerald R. Ford

1. Betty Ford, *The Times of My Life* (New York, 1978), 158.

2. Ron Nessen, *It Sure Looks Different from the Inside* (New York, 1978), xiv.

3. Jerald F. terHorst, *Gerald Ford and the Future of the Presidency* (New York, 1974), 215.

4. Ibid.

5. Richard Reeves, *A Ford, Not a Lincoln* (New York, 1975), 28.

6. Nessen, *Sure Looks Different*, 171.

7. "Was Justice Done?" *Newsweek*, LXXXIV (September 16, 1974), 19–23.

8. Nessen, *Sure Looks Different*, 165; Jules Witcover, *Marathon: The Pursuit of the Presidency, 1972–1976* (New York, 1977), 89.

9. Nessen, *Sure Looks Different*, 167.

10. Ibid., 168.

11. Gerald R. Ford, *A Time To Heal* (New York, 1979), 289.

12. Nessen, *Sure Looks Different*, 173.

13. Reeves, *A Ford, Not a Lincoln*, 25.

14. Gerald Ford, *Time To Heal*, 84.

15. John Osborne, *White House Watch: Ford Years* (Washington, D.C., 1977), 414.

16. "Phrasemaker," *Time*, LXXXIX (February 17, 1967), 24.

17. Nessen, *Sure Looks Different*, 171.

18. Reeves, *A Ford, Not A Lincoln*, 179–80.

19. Ibid., 181.

20. Gerald Ford, *Time to Heal*, 422–25; Nessen, *Sure Looks Different*, 269–76.

21. Nessen, *Sure Looks Different,* 8.
22. Gerald Ford, *Time to Heal,* 262.
23. Betty Ford, *Times of My Life,* 278.
24. Ibid., 279.
25. Ibid., 159.
26. Gerald Ford, *Time to Heal,* 207.
27. Ibid., 218–19.
28. Ibid., 317.

38. Jimmy Carter

1. Ruth C. Stapleton, *Brother Billy* (New York, 1978), 103.
2. Kandy Stroud, *How Jimmy Won* (New York, 1977), 21.
3. Bill Adler, ed., *The Wit and Wisdom of Jimmy Carter* (Secaucus, N.J., 1977), 96.
4. Jules Witcover, *Marathon: The Pursuit of the Presidency, 1972–1976* (New York, 1977), 330.
5. James Earle Carter, *Why Not the Best?* (Nashville, 1975), 36–37.
6, Witcover, *Marathon,* 306.
7. Carter, *Why Not the Best?* 58–59.
8. Stroud, *How Jimmy Won,* 209.
9. Witcover, *Marathon,* 196.
10. Stroud, *How Jimmy Won,* 28.
11. Carter, *Why Not the Best?* 98.
12. Stroud, *How Jimmy Won,* 237.
13. Ibid., 137.
14. Lloyd deMause and Henry Ebel, *Jimmy Carter and American Fantasy* (New York, 1977), 55.
15. Stroud, *How Jimmy Won,* 133.
16. Adler, *Wit and Wisdom of Carter,* 59.
17. Stroud, *How Jimmy Won,* 355.
18. Ibid., 231.
19. Adler, *Wit and Wisdom of Carter,* 27.
20. Ibid., 21.
21. "The Final Extra Mile," *Time,* CXIII (March 19, 1979), 20.
22. "Kennedy: Ready, Set . . . ," *Time,* CXIV (September 24, 1979), 15.
23. *New York Times,* August 5, 1979.
24. "The Republican Landslide," *Newsweek,* XLIV (November 17, 1980), 27–29.
25. James Wooten, *Dasher: The Roots and Rising of Jimmy Carter* (New York, 1978), 158–60.
26. Ibid., 245.
27. Stroud, *How Jimmy Won,* 153–54; deMause and Ebel, *Carter,* 80.

28. Stroud, *How Jimmy Won,* 339.
29. Ruth Carter Stapleton, *Brother Billy* (New York, 1978), 123–25.
30. DeMause and Ebel, *Carter,* 137.
31. "He Can Catch Fire," *Time,* CXIII (May 7, 1979), 19.
32. "A Hot Time for Heat Theories," *Boston Globe,* July 23, 1980, 5.
33. *Time,* CXLIV (October 3, 1994), 36.

39. Ronald Reagan

1. Helene Von Damm, ed., *Sincerely, Ronald Reagan* (New York, 1980), 126.
2. "Ronald Reagan Up Close," *Newsweek,* XCV (July 21, 1980), 31; Joel Kotkin and Paul Grabowicz, "Dutch Reagan, All-American," *Esquire,* XCV (August 1980), 27.
3. "Ronald Reagan Up Close," 33.
4. Ibid.
5. "Out of the Past," *Time,* CXVII (January 5, 1981), 23.
6. "Ronald Reagan Up Close," 34.
7. Richard Harwood, ed., *The Pursuit of the Presidency* (New York, 1980), 269.
8. Edmund G. (Pat) Brown and Bill Brown, *Reagan: The Political Chameleon* (New York, 1976), 151.
9. James Conway, "Looking at Reagan," *Atlantic Monthly,* CCXLVI (October 1980), 39
10. "Ronald Reagan Up Close," 39.
11. Edmund and Bill Brown, *Reagan,* 17.
12. Edmund G. (Pat) Brown, *Reagan and Reality: The Two Californias* (New York, 1970), 3.
13. Harwood, *Pursuit of Presidency,* 161.
14. Ronald Reagan Up Close," 47.
15. "Meet the Real Ronald Reagan," *Time,* CXVI (October 20, 1980), 22.
16. "Ronald Reagan Up Close," 48.
17. "The Iowa Debate Still," *New York Times,* January 7, 1981, A18.
18. Robert Lindsey, "What the Record Says About Reagan," *New York Times Magazine,* June 29, 1980, p. 34.
19. "A Case Study in Confusion," *Time,* CXVI (September 20, 1980), 21.
20. "Meet the Real Ronald Reagan," 17.
21. Harwood, *Pursuit of Presidency,* 254–55.
22. "Now, a Few Words in Closing," *Time,* CXVI (November 10, 1980), 18.
23. "Reagan Isn't Only V.I.P. at California Polling Site," *New York Times,* November 5, 1980, A22.
24. "Ronald Reagan, President-Elect," *New York Times,* November 6, 1980, A25.

25. Harwood, *Pursuit of Presidency*, 148–49.

26. "Wright Reconciled," *Texas Observer*, August 20, 1993, pp. 8–9.

27. David Frum, *Dead Right* (New York, 1994).

28. Joseph R. Conlin, *The American Past* (New York, 1993), 832; Ronald Reagan, *An American Life* (New York, 1990), 312–13; "Washington Diarist," *New Republic*, CXCIV (March 17, 1986), 43; "New Citizens Given Advice by Art Buchwald," *New York Times*, December 14, 1986, p. 22; "Washington Talk," ibid., December 20, 1986, p. 9; Gerald R. Ford, *Humor and the Presidency* (New York, 1987), 131.

29. "Will Reagan's Outlook Outlast Reagan?," *New York Times*, January 1, 1989, p. 10; Michael Deaver, *Behind the Scenes* (New York, 1988), 13; Stephen V. Roberts, "Angered President Blames Others for Huge Deficit," *New York Times*, December 14, 1988, p. 14.

30. Bill Adler and Bill Adler, Jr., "He Keeps His Wit About Him," *Parade*, October 11, 1981, p. 23; James Reston, "The Reagan Joke Book," *New York Times*, March 31, 1984, p. 8; Reston, "An Appeal for Patience," ibid., March 11, 1984, E21; "Importance of Subtlety," ibid., July 21, 1986, p. 10.

31. Morris K. Udall, *Too Funny To Be President* (New York, 1988), 233; "Festive Crowd Greets Ronald Reagan," *Fort Worth Star-Telegram*, July 21, 1985, A11; "Moscow Summit," *New York Times*, June 1, 1988, p. 6; James Reston, "Now the Silly Season," ibid., July 6, 1986, p. 13.

32. "No Comment," *Progressive*, March 1987, p. 14.

33. "The Magic of Reaganomics," *Newsweek*, CXII (December 26, 1988), 40.

34. "Reagan Makes a Hobby of Collecting Soviet Jokes," *New York Times*, August 21, 1987, B6; "Washington Talk," ibid., June 29, 1985, p. 8.

35. Larry Speakes, *The Reagan Presidency from Inside the White House* (New York, 1988), 167–68; Reagan, *An American Life*, 700; David K. Shipler, "In the Private Talks, Humor and a Deep Discouragement," *New York Times*, December 12, 1987, p. 6.

36. "Life After the Red Menace," *U.S. News & World Report*, CIII (December 21, 1987), 41; ibid., May 30, 1988, 8; "Reagan's 'Moscow Spring,' " *Newsweek*, CXI (June 13, 1988), 17.

37. Ronald Reagan with Richard G. Hubler, "At War with the Menace on the Left," *New York Post*, January 1, 1981, p. 19.

38. Von Damm, *Sincerely, Ronald Reagan*, 91.

39. Hedrick Smith et al., *Reagan: The Man, the President* (New York, 1980), 162–63.

40. "Ronald Reagan Close Up," 27.

41. "Reagan in Speeches," *New York Times*, October 19, 1980, p. 38.

42. Deaver, *Behind the Scenes*, 82–83.

43. Von Damm, *Sincerely, Ronald Reagan*, 66; "Moving-Up Day for the

Reagans," *Time,* CXVII (January 26, 1981), 25; "Candyman-Designate
for President-Elect's Sweet Tooth," *New York Times,* January 3, 1981,
p. 43; "Kick Jelly Beans, Reagan Told," *Fort Worth Star-Telegram,* January 24, 1981, 9A; Robert Seltzer, "Reagan Spells Relief J-E-L-L-Y-
B-E-A-N-S," ibid., February 15, 1981, 1C, 7C; "Bracing for Reagan's
Cuts," *Newsweek,* XCVII (February 23, 1981), 20; "The Unkindest Cuts
of All," *Time* CXVII (February 23, 1981), 12.

44. "Reagan's One-Liners," *New York Times,* February 6, 1981, A13.

45. "Reagan Out of Surgery," *Fort Worth Star-Telegram,* March 31, 1981,
A2; "Cooler Reagan Visits with Agent," ibid., April 5, 1981, A1; "Seriously, Folks . . . ," *Time,* CXVII (April 13, 1981), 30.

46. Christopher Matthews, *Hardball: How Politics Is Played—Told by One
Who Knows the Game* (New York, 1985), 213.

47. "Will Reagan's Outlook Outlast Reagan?," *New York Times,* January 1,
1989, p. 10.

48. Reagan, *An American Life,* 390–91.

49. "An Expletive from Reagan," *New York Times,* March 1, 1986, p. 5;
Hugh Sidey, "The Presidency," *Time,* CXVII (March 7, 1986), 28.

50. David R. Gergen, "Reagan's Most Important Legacy," *U.S. News &
World Report,* CV (January 9, 1989), 28.

51. "Washington Talk," *New York Times,* June 28, 1986, p. 7.

52. Reagan, *An American Life,* 393; Lou Cannon, *President Reagan: The
Role of a Lifetime* (New York, 1991), 50–64; Hendrik Hertzberg, "The
Child Monarch," *New Republic,* CXCIX (September 9, 1991), 27–36;
"The Magic of Reaganomics," *Newsweek,* CXII (December 2, 1988), 44;
Elizabeth Drew, "Letter from Washington," *New Yorker,* LXIV (July 4,
1988), 80; *Time,* CXVIII (August 10, 1981), 13; Martin Tolchin, "How
Reagan Always Gets the Best Lines," *New York Times,* September 9,
1985, p. 10; Joel Brinkley, "Reagan Takes Poke at Gorbachev," ibid.,
December 2, 1987, p. 8.

53. "Keeping Up Appearances," *Newsweek,* CXV (May 7, 1990), 22.

54. Bob Greene, "Alzheimer's Is Cruel Fate, Hits Reagan Hard," Tribune
Media Service, *Skiff* (TCU paper), Fort Worth, Texas, November 30,
1994, p. 7.

40. George Bush

1. Margaret Garrard Warner, "Bush Battles the 'Wimp' Factor," *Newsweek,*
CXI (October 19, 1987), 32; Denise Lavone, "President Bush's Mother,
Dorothy Bush, Dies at 91," *Fort Worth Star-Telegram,* November 20,
1992, pp. 1, 24.

2. "Bush, George (Herbert Walker)," *Current Biography, 1972* (New York,
1972), 63.

3. Harry Hurt, "George Bush: Plucky Lad," *Texas Monthly*, XI (June 1983), 143.

4. "A Glossary of Bushspeak," *Newsweek*, CXII (May 23, 1988), 21; Gail Sheehy, "Is George Bush Too Nice To Be President?," *Vanity Fair*, L (February 1, 1987), 122; William Safire, "Bush's Gamble," *New York Times Magazine*, October 18, 1992, p. 60.

5. Hurt, "Bush," *Texas Monthly*, 198.

6. *President Bush: The Challenge Ahead* (Congressional Quarterly, Washington, D.C., 1989), 94.

7. "Warrior for Status Quo," *Time*, CXL (August 24, 1992), 44; Sheehy, *Vanity Fair*, 50.

8. Quoted by Garry Wills, "The Ultimate Loyalist," *Time*, CXXXII (August 22, 1988), 25.

9. Russell Baker, "The Ivy Hayseed," *New York Times*, June 15, 1988, A31.

10. "Warrior for Status Quo," 34.

11. Emily Yoffe, "Bushspeak: A Glossary," *Texas Monthly*, XVII (March 1989), 99.

12. Michael Kramer, "Dukakis Is Ready To Play . . . Is Bush?," *U.S. News & World Report*, CIV (July 4, 1988), 27.

13. George Plimpton, "George Bush," *New York Times Magazine*, April 24, 1994, p. 33.

14. Gerald R. Ford, *Humor and the Presidency* (New York, 1987), 132.

15. "Warrior for Status Quo," 41; Michael Duffy and Dan Goodgame, *Marching in Place: The Status Quo Presidency of George Bush* (New York, 1992), 41–42, 49–50.

16. Maureen Dowd, "Leader of the Free World," *New York Times*, July 18, 1991, A7.

17. Michael Duffy, "A Case of Doing Nothing," *Time*, CXXXVII (January 7, 1991), 28; Eleanor Blau, "Audiences Abandon Hope," *New York Times*, December 26, 1992, p. 10.

18. John Leo, "Say It Again, George," *Boston Globe*, July 3, 1994; Hugh Sidey, "Bush's Flight into the Sunset," *Time*, CXLI (February 1, 1993), 47; Robin Toner, "Bush Says He's Happy with Life after Politics," *New York Times*, October 4, 1994, A12; Robert S. Ehrlich, " '92 Campaign Coverage Was Ugly, Bush Says in Thailand," *Fort Worth Star-Telegram*, January 21, 1994, S17; Sam Howe Verhovek, "No More Mr. President, Just a Texas Nice Guy," *New York Times*, January 5, 1994, A6; "Clinton Recruits 3 Ex-Presidents To Promote Trade Pact," ibid., September 15, 1993, A12; "Perspective," *Newsweek*, CXXII (September 27, 1993), 19.

19. "Letter of Resignation Sent by Bush to Association," *New York Times*, May 11, 1995, p. A14.

41. William Jefferson Clinton

1. *Washington Post National Weekly Edition*, August 24–30, 1992, p. 36.
2. Robert E. Levin, *Bill Clinton: The Inside Story* (New York, 1992), 50.
3. David Gallen, *Bill Clinton as They Know Him: An Oral Biography* (New York, 1994), 136.
4. David Maraniss, "Bill Clinton: Born To Run," *Washington Post National Weekly Edition*, July 20–26, 1992, p. 6.
5. Anna Quindlen, "I'm O.K., You're Bill," *New York Times*, January 24, 1993, p. 17.
6. "Mail by the Millions," *New York Times*, June 21, 1993, pp. 1, 11.
7. Bill Thompson, "So He's Not Quite Presidential," *Fort Worth Star-Telegram*, February 28, 1993, p. 2.
8. Michael Kramer, "Moving In," *Time*, CXLI (January 4, 1993), 33.
9. Jonathan Alter, "Less Profile, More Courage," *Newsweek*, CXXII (November 1, 1993), 33.
10. Virginia Kelley, *Leading with My Heart* (New York, 1994), 234.
11. Gallen, *Bill Clinton*, 152–53.
12. Stanley W. Cloud, "Clinton vs. the Press," *Time*, CXLI (June 7, 1993), 241.
13. Todd S. Purdum, "Far from Capitol's Din, A Hero at Clinton School," *New York Times*, January 5, 1995, A13.
14. Gallen, *Bill Clinton*, 25.
15. Ibid., 29.
16. Levin, *Bill Clinton*, 88–90; David Marannis, *First in His Class: A Biography of Bill Clinton* (New York, 1995), 237–38.
17. Levin, *Bill Clinton*, 90–91, 115; Garry Wills, "Beginning of the Road," *Time*, CXL (July 20, 1992), 33, 57; "On the Campaign Trail," *Fort Worth Star-Telegram*, June 14, 1992, A23; Marannis, *First in His Class*, 246–64; "Walter Scott's Personality Parade," *Parade Magazine*, August 15, 1993, p. 2.
18. Ernest Dumas, ed., *The Clintons of Arkansas* (Fayetteville, Ark., 1993), 33.
19. Ibid., 76; Gallen, *Bill Clinton*, 111–12.
20. Gallen, *Bill Clinton*, 155–57; John Brummett, *Highwire: The Education of Bill Clinton* (New York, 1994), 15–16.
21. Kelley, *Leading with My Heart*, 219; Gallen, *Bill Clinton*, 137–38.
22. Levin, *Bill Clinton*, 149, 152–53.
23. Ibid., xix–xx.
24. Bob Woodward, *The Agenda* (New York, 1994), 54–55.
25. Paul Begala to author, August 3, 1995.
26. Ibid.; *Time*, October 4, 1993, p. 31.
27. "As Dole Counts Calories," *New York Times*, August 1, 1995, p. A8.

Index